The Rise and Fall of the Danish Empire

Michael Bregnsbo · Kurt Villads Jensen

The Rise and Fall of the Danish Empire

palgrave
macmillan

Michael Bregnsbo
Department of History
University of Southern Denmark
Odense, Denmark

Kurt Villads Jensen
Department of History
Stockholm University
Stockholm, Sweden

ISBN 978-3-030-91440-0   ISBN 978-3-030-91441-7 (eBook)
https://doi.org/10.1007/978-3-030-91441-7

© The Editor(s) (if applicable) and The Author(s), under exclusive license to Springer Nature Switzerland AG 2022

This work is subject to copyright. All rights are solely and exclusively licensed by the Publisher, whether the whole or part of the material is concerned, specifically the rights of translation, reprinting, reuse of illustrations, recitation, broadcasting, reproduction on microfilms or in any other physical way, and transmission or information storage and retrieval, electronic adaptation, computer software, or by similar or dissimilar methodology now known or hereafter developed.
The use of general descriptive names, registered names, trademarks, service marks, etc. in this publication does not imply, even in the absence of a specific statement, that such names are exempt from the relevant protective laws and regulations and therefore free for general use.
The publisher, the authors and the editors are safe to assume that the advice and information in this book are believed to be true and accurate at the date of publication. Neither the publisher nor the authors or the editors give a warranty, expressed or implied, with respect to the material contained herein or for any errors or omissions that may have been made. The publisher remains neutral with regard to jurisdictional claims in published maps and institutional affiliations.

Cover illustration: The cover shows part of Carta Marina—Map of the Seas—with Scandinavia between the Atlantic and the Baltic Sea. It was composed by Olaus Magnus (1490–1557), the last Catholic archbishop of Sweden who went into exile in Italy because of the Lutheran Reformation. The map was printed in Venice 1539
Cover image: World History Archive/Alamy Stock Photo

This Palgrave Macmillan imprint is published by the registered company Springer Nature Switzerland AG
The registered company address is: Gewerbestrasse 11, 6330 Cham, Switzerland

Acknowledgments

The ideas in this book were developed during teaching at the Department of History at University of Southern Denmark. We owe a warm thanks to all the students and colleagues who have helped with discussions and suggestions.

When the book was accepted for publication in English we received very thoughtful and helpful comments from the anonymous peer reviewer for which we are also very grateful.

The book was translated by Susanne Boss who has done a magnificent job. Thank you so much!

We also would like to express our sincere gratitude to those who have generously supported the translation economically:

Magnus Bergvalls Stiftelse
Konsul George Jorck og hustru Emma Jorck's Fond
The Department of History, University of Southern Denmark
The Department of History, Stockholm University

Contents

1	**Introduction**	1
	An Empire is a World	3
	References	8
2	**The Empire in Himlingøje**	11
	References	23
3	**The Christian Empire of the North Sea**	25
	Emperor Gorm	34
	Canute the Great, the Emperor	41
	References	49
4	**Crusade Empires in the Baltic**	51
	The Conquest of Rügen	58
	From the Northalbing to the Lake Peipus	65
	Novgorod and Northern Germany	80
	References	88
5	**The Union Empire**	91
	The Kalmar Union's Early Period	93
	The Time of Discoveries	102
	Bloodbath and Reformation	109
	References	114
6	**The Princely State: The Decline of Baltic Power 1536–1720**	115
	State Type: Conglomerate State	115
	State Form: From Domain State to Tax State	121
	Active Commercial Policy	122
	Politics in the Vicinity of the Baltic Sea, the North Sea and Northern Germany; the Empire's International Position	125
	The Empire's Foreign Policy Until the Disaster of 1658	129

	Royal Absolutism	138
	The Gottorp Problem	139
	Revenge Attempts Against Sweden Within the Framework of Great Politics	140
	References	143
7	**From the Conglomerate State to the Unitary State 1720–1814**	145
	The Gottorp Problem	148
	Norway	150
	The North Atlantic	154
	Schleswig and Holstein	156
	The Colonies in the Tropics	159
	Danish, Nordic, or German Identity?	162
	The Empire and the Napoleonic Wars	163
	Conclusion	168
	References	169
8	**1814–1864: From United Monarchy to Nation-State**	171
	The German Confederation	173
	Advisory Provincial Estates	174
	"Denmark Will Not!"	176
	The Faroe Islands and Iceland	178
	India and Africa	179
	Dynastic Problems	180
	The Dissolution of Absolutism	181
	Civil War and Free Constitutions	182
	The London Protocol	185
	Two Conflicting and Incompatible Principles	185
	Popular Sovereignty in Other Parts of the Empire	187
	Constitutional Problems	189
	Ejder Politics	191
	The Catastrophe of 1864	193
	From United Monarchy to Nation-State	196
	References	196
9	**The Empire After 1864**	199
	Iceland, the Faroe Islands, and Greenland	201
	Southern Jutland/Northern Schleswig	208
	The Interwar Years and Mass Democracy	211
	The Empire and World War II	212
	References	217

10	**The Empire During the Cold War, International Integration, and the Welfare State**	219
	Southern Schleswig	220
	The Faroe Islands	222
	Greenland	223
	The Empire in the Twenty-First Century	228
	References	232
11	**The Danish Empire Through the Ages**	233
	Expansion of the Empire	233
	The Purpose of the Empire	235
	How Did the Empire Acquire Its Territories?	238
	How Did Territories Leave the Empire?	239
	The Danish Empire	240
12	**The Danish Legacy**	243
	Memory and Use of the Danish Past in Former Parts of the Empire	243
	Postcolonial Criticism on the Virgin Islands	244
	The Former Colonies in India and Africa	246
	Greenland	246
	Norway and Iceland	249
	The Faroe Islands	250
	Schleswig–Holstein	251
	Vikings	252
	The Danish Past—A Positive Memory	252
	References	255

General Literature in English   257

Index of Concept   265

Index of People   271

Index of Places   281

List of Figures

Fig. 1.1	Bust of Christian IV (1588–1648) in the Roman imperial tradition. https://de.wikipedia.org/wiki/Datei:Monument_Christian_IV._-_Gl%C3%BCckstadt_Germany.jpg (*Photo* Florian-Zet)	7
Fig. 3.1	Map: Scandinavian travel routes mid-eighth century until around the year 1000	28
Fig. 3.2	Trelleborg fortress. https://da.wikipedia.org/wiki/Vikingeborgen_Trelleborg#/media/Fil:Trelleborg_airphoto.JPG (*Photo* Thue C. Leibrandt)	37
Fig. 3.3	The Jelling Stone. https://commons.wikimedia.org/wiki/File:The_Jelling_Stone_-_VIKING_exhibition_at_the_National_Museum_of_Denmark_-_Photo_The_National_Museum_of_Denmark_(9084035770).jpg (*Photo* The National Museum of Denmark)	39
Fig. 3.4	Map: The North Sea empire	43
Fig. 3.5	Viking graffiti, Istanbul. https://commons.wikimedia.org/w/index.php?title=Special:Search&search=graffiti+hagia+sofia&fulltext=1&ns0=1&ns6=1&ns12=1&ns14=1&ns100=1&ns106=1#/media/File:Hagia-sofia-viking.jpg (*Photo* Not home)	46
Fig. 4.1	Map: The Baltic Sea empire	54
Fig. 4.2	"Battle at Tallinn", by C.A. Lorentzen 1809. https://da.wikipedia.org/wiki/Slaget_ved_Lyndanisse#/media/Fil:Danmarks_flag_1219_Lorentzen.jpg (Creative commons: Public Domain)	70
Fig. 5.1	Admiralty's banner of Eric of Pomerania. https://da.wikipedia.org/wiki/Danmarks_rigsvåben#/media/Fil:Skibsflaget_fra_Mariakirken_i_Lübeck.png (Creative commons: Public Domain)	96
Fig. 5.2	Map: The Kalmar Union	101
Fig. 5.3	The world map of Johann Ruysch from 1507–07. https://en.wikipedia.org/wiki/Johannes_Ruysch#/media/File:Ruysch_map.jpg (Creative commons: Public Domain)	106

Fig. 5.4	The Stockholm Bloodbath. Copy of illustration from the 1520s. http://www5.kb.dk/images/billed/2010/okt/billeder/object395449/da/ (Royal Library, Copenhagen: Public Domain)	113
Fig. 6.1	Map of the partition of the duchies in 1544	120
Fig. 6.2	The Icelandic bishop Guðbrandur Thorlaksson (1542–1627). (Wikicommons). https://commons.wikimedia.org/wiki/File:Portrait_of_Gu%C3%B0brandur_%C3%9Eorl%C3%A1ksson.jpg	121
Fig. 6.3	Map of the Baltic area during the seventeenth century	130
Fig. 7.1	Map: Tropical colonies of the Danish Empire	146
Fig. 8.1	Map: The united Danish monarchy (*helstaten*)	172
Fig. 9.1	Two black women in front of a hut at St. Croix. (The Royal Library, Copenhagen). https://commons.wikimedia.org/wiki/File:Two_women_in_front_of_a_house_at_St._Croix_(9468858855).jpg (National Museum of Denmark: Public Domain)	205
Fig. 9.2	Map: The plebiscite in 1920	210
Fig. 9.3	Norwegian activists occupying parts of Eastern Greenland in 1931. Yet, on April 5, 1933 the court upheld the Danish contention and the conflict then ebbed away (Ishavsmuseet, Aarvak, Norway)	212
Fig. 9.4	Soviet bombardments on Bornholm. (Bornholms Museum. *Photo* Svend Parksø)	216
Fig. 10.1	Danish police officers af Klaksvik 1955. https://commons.wikimedia.org/wiki/file:patruljerende_politi_i_klaksvig.jpg (Danish Police Museum: photo Svend Aage Larsen)	223
Fig. 10.2	Map: Greenland's central position during the Cold War	225
Fig. 12.1	Statue of the Dano-Norwegian missionary to Greenland, Hans Egede. https://commons.wikimedia.org/wiki/File:Egede_nuuk.JPG (*Photo* Svickova)	248
Fig. 12.2	Four Inuits having been abducted from Greenland, painted during a stay in Bergen in Norway in 1654. https://commons.wikimedia.org/wiki/File:Four_West_Greenlanders._Oil_painting_122_x_168_cm._Unknown_Artist._Bergen,_Norway,_1654.jpg (National Museum of Denmark: Public domain)	254

CHAPTER 1

Introduction

The Danish Empire: Rise and Fall. This sounds as a pretentious title for the small kingdom of Denmark, but it is inspired by English historian Edward Gibbon's grande opus, *Decline and Fall of the Roman Empire*. Released in 1776–88, it has since become a classic, not only serving as an unattainable standard for later historians due to its vivid narrative style, but also as a landmark work. It became an essential source for later generations in their understanding of the Middle Ages as a dark period and became a manifest for enlightened thought and rationality in the face of superstition and sensations.

We have chosen to title this book The Danish Empire: Rise and Fall—to stress the volatile and shifting nature of the political unit that throughout history has been called Denmark. Today, one rarely hears much about the topic of Denmark's having been a great and politically important power. Denmark is mostly understood as a small country content with its current modest political situation. It is certainly true that Denmark is a country that has become smaller over time. However, modern descriptions of Danish history have cultivated the idea that Denmark has *always* been a miniscule country and has always been threatened by its powerful southern neighbor, as evident in the traditional general histories of Denmark (Christensen 1977–92; Olsen 1988–91). Images of Denmark as a large country, a substantial political power, something that may even be called an empire, lie beyond the tradition of modern Danish history. This is what we would like to attempt to challenge, and therefore we have emphasized the phraseology of rise and fall in the title.

Gibbon posed the question of why the Ancient Roman Empire dissolved and collapsed. He had two main responses. The first described the alleged intolerance and fanaticism of the new Christian religion. Christians believed in life after death and as such, asserted Gibbon, would never make good citizens of society. Gibbon concluded that people who believed in a paradise or a hell simply couldn't be reasonable, rational, or trustworthy political actors. Gibbon's second response addressed the Germanic Barbarians who, fragmented by the swamps and forests in the north, had marched on Rome, warring and pillaging: terrible individualists who believed in personal freedom, they were not suited for living in a developed society, he claimed. Gibbon's interest in the fall of the Roman Empire reflected the concerns he had for his contemporary English Empire, whose power was also based upon its naval supremacy. The same year that Gibbon's opus was published, the individualistic Germanic Barbarians, as he saw them, tore themselves from England, when the American colonies declared independence. Within the borders of mainland England, religious Christian fanatics, according to Gibbon, in the form of extremist Methodists, pietists, and other various denominations threatened the rationality of English citizens of the 1700s.

Gibbon's book was clearly influenced by his own time, as this book is as well. One could argue that it is certainly a long time ago that Denmark has been even close to being anything resembling an empire. Instead, it has become a nation, which has otherwise served successfully as a sufficient framework for the writing of Danish history. However, the past few decades have posed important questions regarding how nation-states were founded, and whether the nation will continue unchanged. Before 2000, many believed that the nation would disappear and be replaced by a "European perspective," with regional variations that span across the older, constructed national borders (Mørch 1996; de Boer et al. 2020). In the grand scheme of historical perspective, the concept of a nation is relatively young. This may inspire consideration of within which categories one should examine the history of Denmark. This is precisely what numerous historians have contended in recent years, despite few truly putting it into practice and writing an alternative history of Denmark.

However, it seems certain now that considerations of the nation-state's impending dissolution were exaggerated: most states in Europe have consistently been functioning nations, while others have recently had a relatively strong resurgence. Only time will tell whether it is a true revival of lasting consequence, however, historiography in Europe has increasingly turned towards a nation-oriented context in recent years (Bakardjieva et al. 2020, Delanty 2021). To a certain extent, this applies to Denmark and other Western European states but is particularly applicable to many countries in Eastern Europe following the fall of the Berlin Wall in 1989. Countries that were part of the Soviet Empire and, later, part of the Eastern Block suddenly gained and capitalized on the opportunity to emphasize their own unique national characteristics. The Covid-19 pandemic came in 2020, when this introduction was written, and led to the closing of national borders and a very strong emphasis on the national instead of the common European (Woods et al. 2020).

How does one set aside the framework of a nation's history, whether it is already withering on its own or blooming with new potential? One possibility is to carefully select a new framework of historical understanding. That is precisely what this book will ultimately attempt: to understand the history of Denmark as the history of an empire's rise and fall.

Many Danish historians of the twentieth century tacitly assume that Denmark has always had the same size and political influence that it has today. If asked directly they would agree that it is an incorrect assumption. Yet history continues to be written accordingly: addressing how the territories that lie within the *current* borders of Denmark have changed over time. The border duchies of Schleswig and Holstein are mentioned due to the political problems they have always caused. Scania in southern Sweden is seldom referred to as a Danish territory as it was during the Middle Ages; other former Danish regions as Halland and Blekinge in Sweden are rarely addressed at all, not to mention the Baltic islands of Gotland, Øsel (Saaremaa), Rügen, and the country of Estonia. The Danish Empire actually stretched from the North Cape in northern Norway to Hamburg in Germany for over three hundred years, roughly equivalent to the distance between Hamburg and Sicily. This book hopes to recognize, include, and allocate these territories within their accurate place time and in history, such as England in the Viking Period, Norway from the time of the Kalmar Union between 1397–1814, Greenland, the Faroe Islands, the West Indies, and Colonies in Africa and India. While Denmark's history should be acknowledged in its collective entirety, it should also remain in its European context. Denmark was at times a relatively large power in Europe, and functioned as a direct threat, particularly to many of the smaller Germanic principalities of the south: it wasn't until later in history that these power dynamics became inverted.

How did the Danish Empire function in practice? What motivated or forced the territories to remain together, and what did each territory contribute? Was there an economic and cultural division of labor between various areas of the empire, or an exploitation and forced transfer of resources from peripheries to center? And, last but not least, is it possible to comment on how individual citizens within the empire perceived their own position? These are questions that, once answered, should collectively aid in formulating an understanding of what were important among numerous factors in keeping the Danish Empire together for hundreds of years in spite of the shifting extension of its territories.

An Empire is a World

The word "empire" derives from the Latin term "*imperare*," to reign, and for the Ancient Romans, meant the power of command (Fibiger Bang et al. 2020). The power to command could be enforced to various degrees. The highest power of command was a mortal dictator, who, in times of war, was given by the Romans unlimited power to lead the military. In principle, this unlimited power would then be relinquished at the end of the war. However, Julius Caesar proclaimed himself dictator for life in 44 B.C.E. It is from Caesar that the Germanic word *"kejser,"* emperor, was derived. The title of dictator became banned after Caesar, and his successors (including Augustus) utilized the title of imperator, among others. However, in practice, their power was equally unlimited to that of Caesar's. As a result of this Roman foundation, the words *empire* and *emperor* put an emphasis on the concentration of power in the person who ruled. This concept continued with the Byzantine Eastern Roman emperor who, ruling until 1453, operated with the title *"autokrator,"* as an autocrat who neither had anyone above or equal to himself.

However, the concept of "emperor" has another origin beyond that of the Roman Empire: a Semitic root of "king of the kings." This root entered European languages via the Old Testament, but is also apparent in a variety of cultures in the East and in many different languages, such as *shahin shah* in Persian, *khawan khan* in Mongolian, *amir malikun* in Arabic, etc. In that tradition, an emperor is a ruler presiding over several kings, and an empire includes several kingdoms. In other words: an empire is a large state with a diverse range of peoples. This notion defined by Gabriel Gérard in 1718 contrasts with the traditional description of a kingdom as a land based on a singular, more homogenous nation (Duverger 1980).

While the focal point for the above-mentioned definitions in the early 1700s centered around the concept of nation, it was not necessarily an eighteenth-century concept: it has a strong medieval background that is closely linked to monarchy. The medieval kings were rulers of a people or a nation; not a piece of land—the kings of the Danes, the Norwegians, the Wends, the Goths, and so on. The stretch of a territory could change, but the people remained loyal to the ruler. As a result, an emperor was the ruler who gained control over several nations and kings.

Despite numerous concrete differences, empires throughout history have consistently retained some commonalities and shared structures. First, is simply their size: empires have conquered more land and more people than anyone could comprehensively grasp. This is why internal communication, coordination, and control have been deciding factors in preventing the dissolution of empires. Money or other economic tools, including food products and individuals varying from diplomats to slaves to soldiers, had to be transported over far and arduous distances. Roads and bridges were built in order to cross nature's obstacles of mountains and rivers in the Roman Empire's Europe, while post offices and caravanserais with food and fresh animals were built in the flat steppes of Asia and the Middle East, where it was easier to traverse but difficult to find shelter.

The size of an empire also impacts the diversity of the population; something that the ruler must learn to embrace. Disparate characteristics of empires include local laws, different languages, and various religions, while unifying factors often include ideological components such as the emperor's personage, a common coinage, and a central administrative government and sometimes an educational system.

Empires arise in times of upheaval, where established structures and power dynamics collapse. This is often a phase that includes violence: empires are characteristically forged from war, rarely from a peaceful diplomatic agreement between actors. When empires fall, they often leave a power vacuum, leaving an opportunity for war and unrest to emerge once again. The interwar period, when the empire is powerful and well-functioning, is usually peaceful: at least within the domestic borders of the realm. This lack of disruption has often been imposed: enforced and maintained by a strong military presence and strategic policies, such as the forced migration of certain populations. Nonetheless, it was a form of peace (Fibiger Bang et al. 2020, 9–11).

Much discussion has centered on the question of whether empires in general can be defined as "an expansive state striving to extend its geographical territory by engulfing other states or non- state societies" (Hornborg 2020, 437) and always strive for world domination. Such ambition may certainly be found in many of the great empires, and it is evident that at the very least, empires possess an inherent desire to expand. There are two reasons for this. The first is simply security. With each expansion of an empire follows new borders to new neighbors, who may easily find themselves threatened, and must be held at bay, creating a security dilemma. The second explanation is finance and economy. Due to their size and degree of militarization, empires are extremely expensive to govern: new sources of tax revenues and other resources by way of conquest were a necessary measure in order for most empires to finance their military and administration.

When new territories become incorporated into an empire, new managerial structures within existing establishments are instituted. It has typically occurred in a manner where the empire would purge the top leadership of the local administration and replace it with its people, leaving lower leveled administrators who possessed valuable local knowledge to remain in power. This entails that true empires could only be established in areas where a form of administration had previously existed, with a form of social hierarchy. This preliminary phase of transition offers various opportunities for local power brokers and administrators who seek to support the new empire. In other words, newly conquered territories give rise to a new category of people who, with local culture and background, gain novel and alternative means of authority and legitimacy by supporting the empire.

One can in very general terms distinguish among the various ways in which empires are formed. While it can easily become very theoretical and oversimplified, it is still a beneficial way to see the diversified development of the Danish Empire in a new light.

Empires can be forged between two or more equal parties. Countries who are relatively evenly matched participate in lengthy competition over the same political and economic area, which results in one conquering the other, bringing the two states under one ruler. Alternatively, two or more countries may find it necessary to form a union in order to combat external stressors and a common, stronger enemy. Empires can also be formed between two or more unevenly matched parties. For example, when an existing empire expands, it integrates newly conquered land. This is also the case when two completely different civilizations unite into an empire, such as nomads and settled peoples, resulting in combined military strength and strong economic capacity. Examples of this can be traced in most of the new dynasties of China, which were founded by nomadic rulers from the steppes (Fig. 1.1).

But what does all this have to do with Denmark? Present-day Denmark is the successor of a much larger political entity which at shifting times has comprised England, the other Nordic countries, large parts of the Baltic Sea area, the duchies of Schleswig and Holstein, the Northern Atlantic isles of Greenland, Iceland and the Faroese Island in addition to the oversea colonies in India, Africa and the West indies. In periods, it was a regional and Northern European superpower. The defeat in 1864 against Prussia was, however, considered so traumatic among Danes in general, that this narrative about the past was forgotten in Danish history writing. Since 1864, Denmark became a small state, and after 1871 entirely negligible next to the new and powerful German empire. The Danish state now had to rely on non-military means to survive.

To secure social coherence and thereby the survival of the nation, a number of so-called typical Danish values were formulated in the decades after 1864 and till the beginning of the twentieth century. They included political democracy, equal access to education and culture independent of social status, equality and social security, consensus, and cooperation across classes. Peace and international legal order in foreign policy are important, as also cooperation with Nordic neighboring countries that allegedly share the same values with Denmark.

The past with a Denmark as a dominating power in the Baltic and the North Sea and with many hard and bitter wars with Sweden—not to talk about the role as a colonial power with oversea possessions—did not fit well into this understanding of what it is to be Danish that was created after 1864. The position as a weak, peaceful, and militarily inferior nation-state was projected back in history to earlier epochs. The History of Denmark was written as if "Denmark" had always been identical with the modern small state of Denmark. Danish historians, no matter their political or ideological conviction, have all written Danish history in a simplistic way with little reflection upon the content of their main study object. As the name of the state, Denmark, has been kept by the present-day state, they have written about the territory comprised by present-day Denmark without deliberating upon the fact that the state earlier in history was much larger, and what that could have of consequences for the functions of the state, internally as well as in relation to foreign powers. A title as "The history of the class struggle in Denmark" is a witness to this focus on present-day borders.

Fig. 1.1 The Danish emperor. During the reign of Christian IV (1588–1648), the Danish empire lost much of its power and influence. That made it even more imperative for the ruler to present himself internationally as powerful and important. Christian IV was well educated and interested in history. Nordic antiquity as well as Ancient Roman were elements in much of the art he patronized. He had himself depicted as a Roman imperator—a new Augustus, in a bronze bust that is still today a part of the Royal Danish collections of the Rosenborg Castle in Copenhagen. The original bust is c 1 meter tall and made by François Dieussart in Christian's later years, most probably 1644. At that time, several unfortunate wars had ruined the empire and severely weakened its political and military power. There were good reasons for Christian IV to bolster the prestige of himself as well as of the empire. He chose to do so by presenting himself as a warrior and heroic ruler, in the Roman imperial tradition. The bust illustrated here is a copy in Glückstadt in Holstein, revealed in 1992 to mark Christian IV's foundation of the city 375 years earlier, in 1617. In 1864, Glückstadt became part of Prussia, but the history as part of the Danish empire was still being commemorated more than 130 years later. https://de.wikipedia.org/wiki/Datei:Monument_Christian_IV._-_Gl%C3%BCckstadt_Germany.jpg (*Photo* Florian-Zet)

Yet, this multi-territoriality of state Danish state was of course always in the mind of the political decision-makers and their views and decisions were impacted by this. However, since Danish history has traditionally be written as if the Danish state of former ages was identical with the present-day small power named Denmark, many of the acts and decisions by former decision-makers have been misunderstood and underrated by later historians.

Increased internationalization, European integration, and globalization make it possible but also necessary to think about history in a new way to pose new questions to old sources and find new perspectives and interpretations. That was the background for writing this book in Danish in 2004. Much has changed now almost twenty years later when it comes in a revised, English translation. The value of European integration has been questioned and even lead to Great Britain breaking away from the European Union, and the Covid-19 pandemic has resulted in closed borders and poignant nationalistic rhetoric even among the Nordic countries. But that makes it even more important to point to historical alternatives to the nationalistic frame of interpretation. We have chosen to understand the multi-faceted and changing state construction, of which the kingdom of Denmark has been a part through history, as an empire. We are using the term "the Danish empire" to be aware of the multi-territoriality of former ages and what this meant. In other words, "empire" is being used as an analytical tool to break with the nationally self-centered historiographical tradition. We understand an empire as an area over which somebody has power to command, and which is composed of several different territories and peoples. Empire is a broad and inclusive concept and can be applied to societies and periods so different as the Viking age, the Kalmar Union, the regional Baltic power at the time of King Christian IV, the Union state or the present commonwealth (rigsfællesskab). Furthermore, it can be used about very different state types such as the premodern tribal societies, tribute state, the high medieval personal union, conglomerate state, the unitary state, the free constitutional state, and democracy.

References

Bakardjieva Engelbrekt, A., et al. (eds.). 2020. *The European Union and the Return of the Nation State. Interdisciplinary European Studies*. London: Palgrave Macmillan.

Christensen, Aksel E., et al. (Eds). 1977–92. *Danmarks historie*. Vol. 1–10. Copenhagen: Gyldendal.

de Boer, Dick E.H., et al. (eds.). 2020. *The Historical Evolution of Regionalizing Identities in Europe*. Bern: Peter Lang.

Delanty, G. 2021. Return of the Nation-State? De-Europeanisation and the Limits of Neo-Nationalism. *Journal of Contemporary European* Research 17: 102–115.

Duverger, Maurice. 1980. *Le concept d'empire*. Paris: Presses universitaires de France.

Fibiger Bang, Peter, et al. (Eds). 2020. *The Oxford Worlds History of Empire. Vol 1: The Imperial Experience*. Oxford: University Press.

Gibbon, Edward. 1776–88. *The History of the Decline and Fall of the Roman Empire*. London: W. Strahan, and T. Cadell.

Hornborg, Alf. (2020). Imperial Metabolism: Empire as a Process of Ecologically Unequal Exchange. In *The Oxford Worlds History of Empire. Vol 1: The Imperial Experience,* ed. Peter Fibiger Bang et al., 437–459. Oxford: University Press.

Mørch, Søren. 1996. *Den sidste Danmarkshistorie: 57 fortællinger af fædrelandets historie*. Copenhagen: Gyldendal.

Olsen, Olaf, et al. (Eds). 1988–91. *Politikens og Gyldendals Danmarkshistorie*. Vol 1–16. Copenhagen: Politiken and Gyldendal.

Woods, Eric Taylor, et al. 2020. COVID-19, nationalism, and the politics of crisis: A scholarly exchange. *Nation and Nationalism* 26: 807–825.

CHAPTER 2

The Empire in Himlingøje

"Denmark has been a country and a people since at least the beginning of the 700's." This nearly fanfare triumphant declaration was posited by a work about Danish foreign policy, which was published in 2000 (Albrectsen 2000). It was an elegant, but misleading statement. Denmark was neither a common people nor a unified kingdom with established borders until very late in history. Instead, Denmark was a geographic entity like that of Spain, England, or Germany, which had long consisted of several kingdoms or principalities that fought among themselves over the exact limitations of jurisdictions and political power. Denmark was an area, in which many petty kings fought each other, and sometimes one succeeded in subduing others under his rule and thus became a ruler of rulers. This was a much more labile and unstable situation than the formation of a country and a people the formation of a nation state. By using the concept "empire" for Denmark and "emperor" for these rulers, we want to stress the difference to traditional "state-formation" history writing, but also to point to the fact that these rulers often were inspired directly by the classical Roman empire or by contemporary European empires.

When understood as an empire, Denmark's history goes much further back than the year 700: to at least the beginning of the Common Era (for a splendid general introduction, Jensen 2001–2004. See also Myhre 2003, 67–81). The great Roman empire reached its most northern extent in the year 9 AD, when the famed commander Varus was ambushed in the Teutoburg Forest. All three legions fell to nearly 15,000 Germanic peoples, who were led by Herman, or in Latin Arminius. The Teutoburg Forest is not far from what is now called Osnabrück, and is the midpoint between the Rhine and the Elbe rivers. The Roman expedition had intended to push the Roman border northwards, to reach the Elbe River. When Emperor Augustus learned the news of his troops' surrender to the germanic people, he ripped his clothes and cried out in sorrow: "Varus, give me back my legions!" The Roman army proceeded to retreat, and gave up their endeavors to expand north. Thereafter, the border became established: starting from the Rhine's mouth in the North Sea, following the river to around Mainz, turning south-east until Regensburg, whereafter it followed the Danube, snaking downwards before terminating in the Black Sea. This border, the Roman *"limes,"* became heavily fortified with moats, palisades, watchtowers, and permanent barracks. Europe was split in two. Yet, this did not mean that there was no contact between the Roman south and Germanic north. The reality was quite the contrary: the south still relied on northern mercenaries for the Roman army, and the Romans leveraged their established divide-and-conquer strategy to correspond with their enemy's enemy. This meant establishing contact with the people living farther north of the *Limes*: the Scandinavians. Ultimately, the presence of the Roman Empire resulted in the establishment of other empires in the North: perhaps inspired by the Roman example, perhaps to defend and balance against its power (Jørgensen et al. 2003; Grane 2011; James et al. 2020).

The Romans retreated to safety behind the Rhine after their defeat in year 9. They did not simply seek safety behind palisades and trenches: in the next thirty years they made contact with an array of rulers who lived within the territory of Denmark. We know most about a great commander in Hoby on on the southern island of Lolland (Klingenberg et al. 2017). When discovered and excavated in 1920, his burial mound was brimming with beautiful Roman treasures, such as a complete Roman drinking set, including cups, pitchers, and bowls—the only complete set in the entire world found outside of the Roman empire itself. A small bronze vase with a clover-shaped neck to pour wine; a large, flat bowl for blending wine and water whose base of glittering bronze displays a long-legged figure of the foam-born goddess Venus, surrounded by pudgy cherubs with admiring expressions. Hoby's commander likely enjoyed the scene. Perhaps the most exquisite part of the collection was two silver pitchers with beautiful handles and motives from ancient Greek Homeric epic. One shows a scene of King Priamos of Troy, kneeling before the hero Achilles begging for the delivery of his son Hektor's body, who was murdered by Achilles the day before. The other pitcher displays Odysseus stealing the demigod Heracles' bow—the key to conquering Troy—from Filoktet, who is affected by a snake bite. Perhaps the commander knew these tales beforehand, or read them in Latin or Greek which, cannot be determined. However, these pitchers are evidence that the thought pattern of Antique heroism was known to those who lived on Lolland nearly two thousand years ago.

Within the same thirty years as the discovery of Hoby grave, nine other sites were found: seven in Jutland, one on Funen, and one in Falster. These gravesites also contained Roman luxury objects, weapons, and art. Several reasons for the existence of these sites have been proposed by modern scholars. Perhaps the Romans simply carried out recruitment campaigns in the Danish region and gave gifts to various commanders. Or the Danish rulers had moved south and joined forces with the Romans—either individually or as a group—to battle against any of the Roman Empire's many enemies. Perhaps the grave found in Hoby belonged to a powerful military leader in the Roman legion who after years of service returned home laden with gifts and accolades. He would then have been able to use these items to build his net of alliances with other rulers in Denmark, whose ties would be bound with Roman gifts. Or perhaps this is the first hint of empire-building in Danish territories, which took lessons from the Romans, including the exchange of Roman symbols of status and luxury. However, it is not for another hundred years before we clearly begin to see evidence of a full-fledged Danish empire, whose core was Himlingøje (Storgaard 2001).

Himlingøje is located in the western region of the Danish island Sealand, near the slope adjacent to Tryggevælde Å and the border to the peninsula of Stevns. Today, Himlingøje is a small and unassuming village, but its landscape is distinctly marked with grave mounds that serve as evidence of the central role that Himlingøje played for over one hundred years in an empire. The earliest grave mounds are from year 150, and the latest from a little after 300—but the most monumental part of the landscape dates much further back. Rane's banks lay only a kilometer north from Himlingøje: standing at 48 meters over sea level, it's the highest point in Sealand. It provides a view over Copenhagen, Roskilde, and even the farthest edges of Stevns. A grave mound from the Bronze age is located at its summit, whose colossal size testifies to a history of riches and great lineages up to a thousand years before the Himlingøje dynasty.

Some of the most beautiful and valuable Roman artifacts outside the bounds of the Roman Empire were found in the Himlingøje burial mounds (Price 2015). Today, the glass items are perhaps the most impressive, such as a fragile, light green drinking glass, and—particularly—a handsomely curved drinking horn made of glittering violet-red glass. Other than that, the sites brim with gold, bronze objects, vases, and pots. Silver plates and pitchers are gilded with golden reliefs of deer and warriors with swords featuring spherical pommels. Many of these items are Roman, but some are southern European or locally Danish. One may once again contemplate how these rich artifacts made their way to Himlingøje. Some were likely diplomatic gifts, sent by the Romans to distant northern allies. Many of these objects may also be war trophies, won by Himlingøje warriors in battle in the south, either with or against the Romans. The swords with a sphere on the pommel of the hilt—depicted on the artifacts—were originally a Roman design: they became widely popular among the Marcomanni, a Germanic tribal confederation who lived along the Donau border and fought for the Romans and against the Goths who slowly swept down through Western Europe. Warriors from Himlingøje likely participated in the Marcomannic wars at the end of the second century, earning Roman accolades which they brought back home, if they were lucky enough to return alive. One of the buried remains is that of a young man around 20 years of age: he was cut into small pieces before he was buried at the gravesite. This likely means that he met his end far away from Himlingøje and was returned home: transporting corpses long distances at this time was typically done by quartering the deceased and either cooking or salting them for transport.

The most interesting aspect of the Himlingøje burial mounds, however, are the imperial insignias. Three types of these insignias are present. The first is an arm ring made of a particular type of solid gold, which was specifically used as a sign of royalty for the most eminent princes of the Sarmatians. The Sarmatians were Indo-European nomadic, equestrian people from the South Russian steppes. They had for several hundred years served as mercenaries for the Romans, and settled just south of the Danube border in present-day Bulgaria. This area was becoming increasingly threatened by the Goths. A ruler in Himlingøje had such close relations with the Sarmatians, that he evidently received their most esteemed distinction. He not only received this insignia but also used it to reward his own allies and associates. Over the next hundred years, the sarmatic gold ring would become a common insignia for princes in Western Europe, used to build connections over long distances.

For shorter distances, the Himlingøje rulers used rosette fibulae as a reward for allies: the second type of insignia. A fibula is a form of pin or brooch worn on clothes which, up to approximately 400, was used by both genders, and thereafter only by women. The fibulae produced in Himllingøje were made of silver with large gold and silver rosettes, some with very early rune inscriptions and swastikas. Most of this particular type of fibula were found in Sealand and eastern Funen. Many were found in northern and western Jutland, but several have also been found in southern Norway, central Sweden, on Bornholm and Gotland, as well as in Poland and in present-day Lithuania. A picture begins to emerge of a well-established empire centered in Himlingøje with direct possessions or politically dependent territories that were linked together by the Sea of Kattegat and the Baltic Sea. The Empire began to develop new connections: several graves from the second half of the third century are known from the Gothic area just north of the Black Sea, containing the remains of female chieftains who have been adorned with precisely these fibulas from Himlingøje. This may be a flimsy base on which to build big conclusions, however, there was apparently a conscious policy of alliance between Himlingøje and the Gothic kingdom, which was sealed with a series of arranged marriages.

The third form of insignia was the snakehead rings. These rings are found in contemporary graves all over Denmark: again, mostly found on Sealand, East Funen, and Jutland, but also as far away as Thuringia in Central Germany. Snakehead rings are massive gold finger rings with one, two, or three snake heads. This clearly indicates a form of hierarchy or ranking system in which some rulers were considered higher placed than others. The uniform design of the rings, which differed from each other solely by the number of snake heads, is reminiscent of later formalized social systems with various classes of rank. In all cases, like the rosette fibula, snakehead rings were insignias and symbols that linked rulers from different parts of the empire, marking their loyalty to the dynasty in Himlingøje.

This first fairly well-known Danish empire lasted no more than a hundred years. From the mid-200s, the lavish burial mounds in Himlingøje ceased to be built and other centers of power began to develop. The power shifted to the west, and in the subsequent time it was especially in Funen that a new imperial nucleus developed. It lied in Gudme, where politics and religion clearly united to strengthen one another. The name Gudme itself means "home of the god or gods," and is surrounded by Gudbjerg, Albjerg and Galdbjerg—"the mountain of the gods", "the holy mountain," and "the sacrificial mountain," respectively (Nielsen et al. 1994; Randsborg 2007). In the mid-200s, Gudme grew into an enormous settlement. At its height, it included 50 large farms, each with houses up to 35 meters in length. In its center stood a huge hall of 47 meters in length, until 2009 the largest known structure from ancient Denmark, whose roof was supported by 16 wooden columns, each 80 cm in diameter. Roman gold and silver, as well as a larger hoard of Roman coins, were found inside the hall. However, it is far more interesting to consider the surrounding farms: it turns out that Gudme was a major location of the forging of precious metals. Gold, silver, and bronze were imported into Gudme, such as Roman statues that were cut into scrap pieces to be melted and reforged.

Between Gudme and the nearest beach lay one of the two burial sites containing thousands of tombs. Many have fine objects and even Roman goods, but the truly opulent tombs were not located there. This indicates that the placement of this particular burial ground was done with a conscious agenda. Outside visitors would have had to proceed through this city of death to reach the ruler of Gudme, thus receiving a visceral impression of the dynasty's age and lasting continuity. In fact, there are even graves from before the birth of Christ at the site, but the vast majority of the graves emerged once Gudme began to expand in the 200s. Visitors would have come down from the beach near Lundeborg, only approximately 4 km to the east, where a huge market with tents and stalls was hosted each summer, stretching along almost a kilometer of the beach. All sorts of metal work, bone and amber, and many other items were manufactured and traded here. For example, ships' nails were found in the thousands, suggesting that Lundeborg was likely also an important shipyard in its time.

Gudme was an impressive construction, and the ruler must have been located at the site near the main hall, but no dynastic tombs have yet been found, such as those in Himlingøje. This means that either the archeologists simply haven't found them yet, or they are buried elsewhere for unknown reasons. Regardless, there certainly isn't a lack of graves of rulers on Funen from this time period, which offers an impression of the empire's extent. For example, one may start by looking at Sanderumgård, near Odense, where two extremely rich tombs from around 250–300, each containing magnificent gold fibulae with twists and inlaid gems which have otherwise only been found from digs in Funen and Poland. At the same time, the tombs are filled with artifacts that show a close connection to rulers directly to the south, in Saxony and Thuringia all the way down by the Roman border near the source of the Danube in the west. Finally, there is also clear evidence of a more distant, eastern connection in the graves at Funen.

Shortly after the mid-300s, a high-ranking woman was buried in Årslev together with a person who had no grave gifts: perhaps her personal slave who followed her to death? Her numerous and expensive jewelry shows connections to many places, such as Poland, among others (Storgaard 1994). Her hoard includes seven identical golden pendants. Each pendant consisted of a gold disk with the face of a lion and two small chains that connect the disk to a strange, small seven-armed figure inlaid with three gems: perhaps a double eagle, or even a symbol of the tree of life. The three red gemstones could symbolize the Holy Trinity. The jewelry is characteristic of the wealthiest Gothic women just north and west of the Black Sea. However, the most exciting part of this find is a small sphere of rock crystal, which in ancient times was believed to be ice that was frozen so deeply that it would never thaw again. In this crystal ball are inscribed Greek letters, a palindrome word: ABLANATANALBA. A palindrome is a word that can be read both front and backwards. The inscription means something along the lines of "God with us." It is a mysterious chat for meditation or magic that was widespread among Gnostics and was ultimately also used by Aryan Christians. Many of the Goths had become Christians, specifically Aryans, during the 300s. If the woman in Årslev had come as a Gothic princess from the Black Sea to Funen to seal political connections over several thousand kilometers, she evidently seemed to also be a Christian. She would have known the content of the Good Gospel via the brand-new translation of the New Testament of the Bible into Gothic, which Bishop Ulfila had finished near the Black Sea around 370.

Himlingøje and Gudme were the hearts of empires with excellent connections to the Roman Empire, the Goths on the Black Sea, powers along the Baltic Sea, as well as to Germanic nations located between Denmark and the Danube border of the Roman Empire. There were likely other hubs within Denmark's geography, which had links far and wide, and perhaps even had an imperial structure: however, these are more difficult to prove with the available archeological material. Nevertheless, it is easy to show how these political entities were in many ways inspired by the Roman Empire in their design. One clear example is the establishment of several ramparts in South Jutland during the first millenium. The oldest is Olgerdiget, which probably dates back to the middle of the 100s, but it was maintained and expanded for the following three hundred years. The Olgerdiget rampart starts a couple of kilometers south of Åbenrå, and stretches southwest all the way to Tinglev: 12 km in total. The structure is impressive, consisting of a moat, a grave, an even larger moat, and three to five rows of solid oak palisade fortifications. 90,000 oak trees in total were felled over the years to be used for these palisades. A similar structure, named Æ Vold, was started a hundred years later, after the mid-200s. It extends east to west and lies just north of Åbenrå. Æ Vold is somewhat shorter than the Olgerdiget, but was constructed in the same format with moat, tomb, and palisade. In Æ Vold, though, only one row of oak trees is used for the palisades, and the distance between the two moat structures is only approximately 15 kilometers. The curious thing is that these two rampart sites face each other: the tombs in Olgerdiget are located to the north with the palisade rows to the south, and in Æ Vold it is reversed.

The two large ramparts in southern Jutland are replicas of the Roman border ramparts at limes: both those at the Rhine-Danube, and Hadrian's wall located between northern England and Scotland. These Roman sites are almost contemporary with the earliest stage of the Olgerdiget structure. In other words, two political powers seem to have maintained good relations with the Roman Empire as they expanded, and divided the country between themselves along Åbenrå. Mirroring the Roman example, they marked this border with moats and palisades. There was no concrete defense force, as it was nearly impossible to fully staff a 12-kilometer rampart. Rather, the structures marked a political boundary, rendering it only necessary to defend the border if the other Danish ruler threatened an invasion or escalation of conflict. It was likely that the ramparts were equipped with watchtowers and lookouts, which would have been able to call in reinforcements or quickly mobilize a greater force if there were signs of imminent trouble. The Roman limes also operated on such a system. This surely means that the area between the two ramparts was a kind of no man's land, a disputed zone in which it at times would have been extremely dangerous to live. This also indicates that the borders of these ramparts would have been populated by a large number of soldiers. Or perhaps, the local population in these areas participated in military service as well as tending the land. At very short notice, they would have had to drop everything related to agriculture, mobilize, and move out fully armored. Living in a border area of this kind meant spending much of their lives preparing for war.

While these remarks are certainly toeing speculation, the pure size of these ramparts and their Roman character highlight that incredibly well-organized political powers were involved in their establishment. While there were several rulers throughout the area of Denmark, there was enough manpower and financial resources to afford each leader the opportunity to militarize with pomp and circumstance. These elements are preconditions for the picture that we get of the influence of the Himlingøje and the Funen empires across Northern and Eastern Europe. The mass ritual offerings of weapons to the gods found in the surrounding marshes offer a very direct and detailed impression of the period's extensive militarization.

Offering weapons to the gods is an old tradition in Denmark. In earlier times, singular showpieces were typically sacrificed. However, at the start of the Common Era, something decidedly new began to happen. Weapons were literally thrown into the sacrificial marshes by the thousands: both magnificent weapons that would have been carried by commanders, and quite ordinary weapons belonging to the infantry. The entire army's equipment was clearly sacrificed at the same time: before meeting their end in the marshes, the weapons were rendered useless by being destroyed, broken, or shattered. The first known instance of these mass sacrifices was found in the Ejsbøl bog at Haderslev in Souther Jutland. It was abandoned in the earliest years following the birth of Christ, presumably around the time of Varus' great defeat in the Teutoburg Forest in year 9. However, Ejsbøl bog would continue to be repeatedly used for similarly large weapons sacrifices over the next 500 years. The equipment of four large armies was destroyed and sacrificed in the same marsh during that half-millennium: relatively typical for ritual Danish weapons offerings. These bogs clearly bear evidence of having a long history.

During the first few hundred years of the Common Era, weapons were sacrificed in large quantities in several places in both Jutland and Funen, and a single place on the island of Lolland. From around 200 and onwards, bogs throughout the rest of Denmark began bearing signs of weapons sacrifices in this style. The uneven geographic distribution may be in part due to chance as well as archeological uncertainty. Many bogs were excavated in the nineteenth and first half of the twentieth century: the excavation methods and documentation were more lax and much less documented than done today. All uncertainties aside, it is nevertheless clear that the phenomenon began around the birth of Christ, and that there were many centers throughout Denmark. There is also the advantage that the chemistry is different from bog to bog: in some sites, iron objects are preserved while all organic matter has decomposed, while in others, wood and leather are preserved and metal objects are lost. Taken together, this mosaic of information gives an excellent impression of the army's equipment.

The bog sites contain all kinds of weapons (Nørgård Jørgensen and Clausen 1997). Shortly after the year 200, we begin to find longbows of yew nearly two meters long. These bows could reach distances of up to 100–150 meters, and at shorter distances were incredibly impactful, even having the ability to pierce chainmail, also found in the bogs. However, the most common weapon was a spear, used by the infantry, spanning at least 2.5 meters. In some bogs, thousands of spearheads have been found, most of them bent or broken into halves, which are then thrown into the bog several hundred meters apart, before being put back together by the labors of archeologists. Thousands of shields have also sunk into the bogs: while some have preserved their wooden disk, most of them only retain the smashed metal framing, the shield boss, which would have been fastened in the center of the shield. These bosses are in turn found in numerous designs, ranging from simple and inexpensive sword-repellants to ornate and chiseled artifacts made of precious metals. A particularly special group of sacrificed weapons are the many swords. Most turn out to be Roman swords, which made their way north either as semi-finished or finished products that were subsequently altered. The blade is Roman, sometimes inlaid with the gunsmith's trademark, sometimes inlaid with an auspicious figure of the war god Mars, formed with thin copper wire into the steel of the sword.

This hilt, however, is quite often local Scandinavian or Germanic handiwork, made of various kinds of wood, silver, gold, or even ivory, but with designs and embellishments that are clearly not Roman in nature. Perhaps the owners of the swords respected the technological capability of Roman gunsmiths, but also wanted to assert their independence and emphasize their individuality by choosing the hilt and its decoration. What is most interesting, however, is that a close examination of these thousands of swords shows that they were all quickly replaced when a new Roman model arrived on the market. Swords were not something that was passed down through several generations, on the contrary: they were replaced as soon as a more effective or simply fashionable sword became available. And even more interesting is that these swords in Danish bogs were replaced and renewed as quickly as they were in the Roman Empire itself. This means, therefore, that there was no delay between the production of Roman goods and their arrival to Scandinavia. Instead, these shifts in popular style happened concurrently.

The culmination of these weapon finds give a good impression of how an army was organized in those early centuries. At the head of the army were generals, some donning silver or gold masks, all with magnificent swords and shields. They headed a small cavalry: the remains of horses, bridles, harnesses, and many tracks have been found in the bogs (Dobat et al. 2015). This indicates that being a rider bore a distinctive rank in Denmark even two thousand years ago, another trait shared with the Roman Empire. The majority of the army fought with spears and shields. A somewhat smaller group fought with swords and even a kind of chain mail or body armor. However, it is not easy to determine whether the swordsmen constituted a separate corps, or whether they were commanders of the infantry spear troops. The last group were the archers, who presumably would not have been the same as the spearmen. Several war dogs were also sacrificed. Judging from skeletal remains, these dogs were densely built with an enormous, strong jaw—much like modern rottweilers. Despite their resilient physique, these dogs nevertheless met their end and eventually sunk into the marsh.

What can be excavated from these bogs today, and why were these items initially placed there? Where do these artifacts originate from? The standardized nature of the weapons won't offer many hints on this front, and certainly not the Roman items. Instead, the personal equipment of the soldiers shows distinct geographical features. In particular, archeologists have been able to compare the styles of combs and firesteels to begin to trace where the soldiers originated from. These items in particular are designed slightly differently from place to place and suggest a fascinating pattern of dispersal. The weapons from the 100s suggest that the soldiers originated from the German area in southern Denmark. In the 200s, the weapons belonged to soldiers from Germany and Southern Norway. From the end of the 200s into the 300s, from central Norway and central Sweden. Some have sought to explain these origins: that Denmark was attacked by warriors from these areas from time to time. Modern archeologists have described in vivid images the warning pyres being lit one after the other down along the coast of Jutland to warn of the arrival of heavily armed Norwegians landing on the beaches, getting defeated, and ending in the depths of the bogs. However, there is a serious issue with this explanation. So far, no skeletons have been found. No foreign soldiers were sacrificed, and no mass graves near the weapons have been found (Ilkjær 2002).

There is a more natural explanation: that the battles actually happened abroad in Germany, Norway, and Sweden, and after the battles the Danish army commander ordered the weapons broken, stored into crates, and brought them home to show their triumph, as the commander knew that other, true empires, did. Such a decision initially sounds rather cumbersome and labor-intensive, simply expensive, but it could actually have been quite a rational investment from a commander's perspective. It created a form of political capital. First, one must consider that a few thousand years ago, stories and tales became credible when they were re-enacted and ritualized, preferably with original props. No matter how many witnesses were able to enthusiastically recount the battle, the victory would only be truly believed at home if the audience physically saw the bounty. This concept that victories won outside the border must inevitably be manifested as trophies and memories at home. Second, a truly triumphant parade would have shown to the Jutland and Funen neighbors that the commander was on par with the Roman champions. Leading a triumphal procession through the city of Rome was the greatest accolade that a military commander could achieve in the Roman Empire. The Roman procession would be led by the championing force, followed by the bounty, and finally the enemies' armor, weaponry, and equipment. If the enemy army commander was captured alive, he became an important part of the triumphal march and was spectacularly displayed. The procession would end in the Jupiter Temple at the Capitol, where the weapons were sacrificed to the gods and placed in the temple. Later, most weapons would be recycled and reused in the Roman army. In fact, the Danish weapons sacrificed in the bogs can very well be viewed as a close mirror of the Roman triumphal traditions, with one major difference: the sacrificial enemy weapons were completely destroyed, and could not be used later. Today, we don't know much detail about these Danish ceremonies. Perhaps the Danish army commander would have stood at the head of the procession bound for the sacrificial marshes, and—just like his Roman counterpart—was joined by a slave at his side who continuously whispered in his ear, "Remember, you are only a mere human being."

An empire must be connected and bound both physically and ideologically. It is no coincidence that it is precisely in the first few centuries following the birth of Christ that transportation and communication networks were systematically established, expanded, and strengthened in Denmark. There have of course always been roads, and the ancient road running along the Jutland ridge from north to south—the "Army road" or the "Oxen road"—must date back to the Stone Age, but the new roads were different. These differences have been closely studied at Tryggevælde Å, which splits Stevns from the rest of Sealand. One could cross this large stream near Spjellerup and Elverhøj via two roads that have been repaired and expanded over time, but archeologically can be dated back to the wattle and plank roads from the Stone Age. Two or three roads were enough for a couple of thousand years, but by the time of the Himlingøje Dynasty, another eight more roads were built to traverse Tryggevælde. These roads were deliberately planned, and of a completely different nature from that of the ancient, haphazardly developed roads. Now they were piled, drained, and supported with gravel and crushed rocks, retrieved from many kilometers away, before the actual road was paved using large, flat stones. These stones were carefully carved to fit together in order to form a smooth, uniform surface. This was a road meant to be used. It was a road created in the same system as the corresponding roads throughout the Roman empire, whose main task was to advance troops as quickly as possible. Of course, this does not rule out that the roads were used by others such as traders, but they would probably have had to wait patiently for the soldiers to pass. The eight roads built across Tryggevælde indicate that the rulers of Himlingøje must have kept a large portion of its populace battle-ready, and expected to receive more people from the east. People, namely troops, from Stevns, and others coming sailing from much farther away. The development of these road networks continues over the following centuries. One of the most prominent examples of this is the Ravning Meadows Bridge in Jutland from the second half of the 900s: it stretches over 700 meters, and consists of a solid wooden bridge built on top of large oak trunks, which are driven 3–4 meters into the muddy and soft subsoil.

Ravning is located just west of Vejle, and the bridge made it possible to cross the Vejle stream and large stretches of meadows, saving many kilometers of detour. The bridge is located a few kilometers south of the important royal center of Jelling, and was clearly a major military facility, potentially for a whole new dynasty, which would ultimately have a crucial bearing on the history of the future Danish empire. We'll return to that topic again soon.

Denmark is divided among several islands, and the early Danish empires spanned areas that could only be reached by sailing. We know very little about the early boats, but some specimens have been found in the sacrificial moors of the bogs. We know some details from ship tombs, where the ruler was put to rest in his ship which would be enclosed in a burial mound. However, these types of ship-based graves only emerged in Denmark starting in the seventh century. They were sleek, clinker-built rowing vessels that could carry 20–40 men on board. A ship found in the lavish burial of Sutton Ho in England dating back to 625 could carry 80 men: there must have been several of these types of ships that we simply don't know today—yet archeologists still do amazing finds. In the 400s and 500s, there was a shipyard located at Lundeborg near Gudme on Funen, whose many nails show that ships were significant and commonly used, but we know nothing about the organization of this possible fleet.

Common symbols were as important as transportation and military might for the cohesion of the empire. It was not only about rings and other magnificent jewelry, but also probably about the writing that came to Denmark in the second century. One may ponder the function writing actually had in an overwhelmingly oral society. Why use writing at all? An argument emerged, starting in the eleventh and twelfth centuries, that writing is meant to save records from disappearing due to the fragility of time and ephemeral memory, but this was likely a modern understanding in the Middle Ages. Most unwritten societies appear to have nurtured a healthy skepticism of the written word, and a reasonable suspicion that it could be cheated, manipulated, and rewritten. What cannot be altered, is what true and trustworthy men have experienced for themselves, or have been told by other, wise men. In the beginning, writing was hardly supposed to function as the collective memory of society, nor was it needed to address a sudden desire of individuals to have their own name in splendor. In contrast, writing has instead served an apparent function for the ruler who, finding himself removed from everyday society, was not known by his subjects in person. The written word was used to delineate the emperor, or whichever title he used in Denmark, as well as a particular honor bestowed to the loyal supporters of the ruler.

The earliest known inscription in Denmark merely consists of a name, *Harja*. It is etched into a bone comb, which was found among the weapons sacrificed in Viemose, dating back to about 120 CE (Stoklund 2003). The name is written in the old rune alphabet, the 24-character futhark, which during the 600s was replaced by the simpler, 16-character futhark. The word *furthark* itself is formed by the first six letters of the series, just as "alphabet" is simply the first two letters of the Greek alphabet, alpha and beta. The runes are a special alphabet, adapted from Latin, and used for centuries in the same way as the Roman imperial Latin letters—first and foremost for memorials, and for those who had a connection to the emperor (Imer 2010).

It is difficult to detail the Danish empires that emerged during the first five hundred years CE, but we do know that their reaches were vast. They were certainly not alone but were instead surrounded by comparably strong empires with vassals in various geographic areas. A dynasty of rulers was established in Old Uppsala of Sweden with just as much wealth as the Danes, artifacts with the same imperial insignias, and jewelry and weapons with shared symbols: these elements display a close connection to the south and to England. This Uppsalan Empire still marks its surrounding landscape with three monumental graves in an extensive gravesite, which were used from at least the 400s to the 600s. Other similar political structures emerged and expanded their existence in and around Denmark before they also were eventually succeeded by new powers. Written sources on the empire's history begin to emerge in the 700s and—particularly—in the 800s. Though these initial sources still pale in comparison to the available archeological material, they offer a unique opportunity to investigate the ideological state of the empire a little closer. They do reveal new facets and perspectives, but it is important to keep in mind that the empire, as a structure and political organization, was several hundred years old by that time.

REFERENCES

Albrectsen, Esben. 2000. Dannevirke. Det ældste monument over dansk sikkerhedspolitik. In *Danmark i syv sind. Tusind års dansk udenrigspolitik*, ed. Carsten Due-Nielsen et al., 9–17. Copenhagen: Gyldendal.
Dobat, Andres S., et al. 2015. The Four Horses of an Iron Age Apocalypse: War-Horses from the Third-Century Weapon Sacrifice at Illerup Aadal (Denmark). *Antiquity* 88 (339): 191–204.
Grane, Thomas. 2011. Zealand and the Roman Empire. In *The Iron Age on Zealand: Research Status and Perspectives*, ed. L. Boye, 101–111. Copenhagen: Det kgl. nordiske Oldskriftselskab.
Ilkjær, Jørgen. 2002. *Illerup Adal: Archaeology as a Magical Mirror*. Århus: Moesgaard Museum.
Imer, Lisbeth M. 2010. Runes and Romans in the North. *Futhark: International Journal of Runic Studies* 1: 41–64.
James, Simon, et al. (eds.). 2020. *The Oxford Handbook of the Archaeology of Roman Germany*. Oxford: Oxford University Press.
Jensen, Jørgen. 2001–2004. *Danmarks Oldtid*, vol. 1–4. Copenhagen: Gyldendal.
Jørgensen, Lars, et al. (eds.). 2003. *The Spoils of Victory—The North in the Shadow of the Roman Empire*. Copenhagen: The National Museum.
Klingenberg, Susanne, et al. 2017. Hoby: An Exceptional Early Roman Iron Age Site in the Western Baltic Region. *Acta Archaeologica* 88: 121–137.
Myhre, Bjørn. 2003. The Iron Age. In *The Cambridge History of Scandinavia*, vol. 1, ed. K. Helle, 60–93. Cambridge: Cambridge University Press.
Nielsen, P.O., et al. (eds.). 1994. *The Archaeology of Gudme and Lundeborg*. Copenhagen: Akademisk forlag.
Nørgård Jørgensen, A., and B.L. Clausen (eds.). 1997. *Military Aspects of Scandinavian Society in a European Perspective, ad 1–1300*. Copenhagen: Publications from The National Museum.
Price, T. Douglas. 2015. *Ancient Scandinavia: An Archaeological History from the First Humans to the Vikings*. Oxford: University Press.
Randsborg, Klavs. 2007. Beyond the Roman Empire: Archaeological Discoveries in Gudme on Funen, Denmark. *Oxford Journal of Archaeology* 9: 355–366.
Stoklund, Marie. 2003. The First Runes—The Literary Language of the Germani. In *The Spoils of Victory—The North in the Shadow of the Roman Empire*, ed. Lars Jørgensen et al. Copenhagen: The National Museum.
Storgaard, Birger. 1994. The Årslev Grave and the Relations Between Funen and the Continent at the End of the Late Roman Period. In *The Archaeology of Gudme and Lundeborg*, ed. P.O. Nielsen, et al., 160–168. Copenhagen: Akademisk forlag.
Storgaard, Birger. 2001. Himlingøje - barbarian empire or Roman implantation? In *Military Aspects of the Aristocracy in Barbaricum in the Roman and Early Migration Periods*, ed. Birger Storgaard, 95–111. Copenhagen: The National Museum.

CHAPTER 3

The Christian Empire of the North Sea

The period from around 700 until 1100 was marked by several events: the restoration of the Roman Empire under Frankish Charlemagne in 800, and the conversion to Christianity of several Danish kings, who with this new faith could establish an empire around the North Sea (in general, see Jensen 2001–2004; Myhre 2003, 81–93; Forte et al. 2005). The Danish empire again changed character around 1100, by shifting its attention from west to east.

The last Roman emperor was the child, Romulus Augustus, who after a year as emperor was forced by the Germanic commander Odoaker to willfully abdicate the imperial throne on the September 4, 476. The Merovingian King Klodevig was baptized a short while later as a Catholic, and thereafter entered into a close connection with the Bishop of Rome, the pope. Odoaker and Klodevig were both Germanic, and—as many others—had previously held important military posts in the Roman army, either in the Western Roman Empire in Italy, or the Eastern Roman Empire in Byzantium.

The role of emperor disappeared in Rome, but the idea of a Western emperor was kept alive, and his functions generally fulfilled by the pope in cooperation with the Merovingian commander, as well as distant Byzantine rulers. A new nation, the Lombards, spread down through Italy at the end of the 500s, leaving a legacy that lasted for centuries. Around the year 1200, the Danish Chronicler Saxo described the ability of these long-bearded Danes, the Lombards, to shake the very foundations of Rome and their consequent rise to fame throughout all of Europe, feared among all nations (Saxo 8.13.2). There is actually a faint kernel of truth to this description. Contemporary writers of the Lombards, Jordanes from the mid-500s and Paul the Deacon from the latter half of the 700s, collected the accounts about migratory people who had left the island of Scandza—Scandinavia, or probably rather Scania in present-day southern Sweden, during the middle ages part of Denmark. Scandza was the hive of peoples or the womb of nations, Jordanes explained, from where mighty warriors swarmed out and conquered the known world. Whom these migratory peoples were, how many, and why they left is unfortunately impossible to ascertain (Halsall 2007; Heather 2010). Nevertheless, it is quite clear that the 600s and 700s were a troubled period, which lay the foundation for new and powerful state institutions in Western Europe in general. The Byzantine Empire faced stress from major plague epidemics, internal strife, and attacks from steppe nomads who invaded the northern Byzantium and the Balkans in the 600s. Simultaneously, Islam emerged as a religion in 622, and during the first Caliphs quickly became a great power also politically. By the mid-700s, it stretched from France in the west to the Chinese border in Central Asia in the east. Though it was no longer a unified empire, these Muslim conquests in the west contributed to permanently changing the political landscape of Western Europe. The pope conclusively turned away from Byzantium, and the emergent kingdom of the Franks became a decisive factor in the future history of Europe. The Frankish Empire became the new Rome.

A Muslim army assailed Gibraltar in 711, initiating an effective and targeted conquest of the Iberian Peninsula, which was triumphant slightly more than ten years later. The Islamic army then continued across the Pyrenees, their raiding troops reaching far into France. They were stopped in 732 by Charles Martel in the battle of Poitiers, little more than 300 km southwest of Paris. In later history writing and still today, this battle has become iconic and depicted as an important turning point in the entire history of Europe which may be exaggerated (Fouracre 2000). Still, it was the beginning of a new Frankish dynasty, the Carolingians, whose first king was anointed and inaugurated by the pope in 754. On Christmas Day in the year 800, Charlemagne was crowned Roman emperor in St. Peter's Church in Rome. The Empire was restored.

Only five years after Charles Martel's victory over the Islamic armies, preparations for another series of fortifications and large ramparts in Denmark began, such as the famous Danevirke. 30,000 oak trees were felled in the year 737. Such precise dates can be determined based on tree rings. The trees were used to build a long rampart stretching roughly ten kilometers along Jutland's southern border from the Schlei Fjord in the east, all the way to the swampy areas near Hollingstedt to the west. From the Baltic to the North Sea. Danevirke remained in use and was expanded on several occasions until the 1100s. However, this first major phase of construction seems to have been conducted very quickly. Danevirke was the largest military installation in northern Europe of its time, and would remain so for a very long time. But the ramparts themselves were not the only comprehensive and effective fortifications of their time. For example, trees felled in 726 were used to line and reinforce the interior of the 11-meter wide and more than 500 meter-long Kanhave Canal, which cuts across Samsø. The purpose of this canal was clearly to pass ships across the island, rather than having to sail all the way around: thus controlling the waters between Funen, Jutland, and Sealand. A formidable power seemed to be emerging and quickly expanding in southern Jutland. As previously done, this expansion process included the construction of trading hubs and transfer points for goods, supplies, and soldiers. The oldest parts of Ribe on the west coast of Jurland and Hedeby on the eastern side date back to the first half of the 700s, and they continued to be protected and developed, but also regulated and controlled by the local ruler. In 808, King Godfred brutally demolished Reric, located at the bottom of the Mecklenburg Bay near modern-day German city Wismar, and transferred the city's population to Hedeby. The area of Hedeby was now marked by a new half-circular defense wall around it, protecting it from attacks from the land side (Fig. 3.1).

Danevirke may seem big, and this has been used by modern historians in arguments as evidence that Denmark must have been united as one empire under one king: only a centralized and powerful royal power could control such a large installation (Albrectsen 2000). This is hardly a convincing nor well-calculated argument. The patron of Danevirke was not necessarily insignificant, but it is extremely difficult to measure power (particularly power of an empire) based upon the size of buildings at a time when labor was based on a system of slavery, and thus very cheap. Danevirke is a large installation, but for example the site of Olgerdige from the 100s was actually bigger and included far more giant oak trees. No one has yet claimed that Denmark was a united kingdom under one ruler already around the year 100. If one looks closely at the archeological finds of recent years, there are also clear signs of other and equally large centers of power in Danish territory. In Sealand alone, several sites from this period have been found (Brink and Price 2008).

Denmark's fourth-largest lake is Tissø in West Sealand, which was the center for powerful rulers for at least four hundred years, from the beginning of the 600s to 1030–1040. Archeologists have since the late 1990s investigated an area that stretches nearly one and a half kilometers along the banks of the lake and has been expanded in several phases. This area spans a total of around 50 hectares and is thus the largest known site of Danish antiquity. Just as in Gudme, there was a large hall in the center of the location, which in its final form was 48 meters long and over 12 meters wide. Within the expansive palisade enclosure are a number of large buildings and workshops, and archeological excavations show signs of both lively production levels and distinct wealth. There are remnants of a major production of silver and bronze jewelry and other luxury goods, as well as production of iron weapons and riding equipment. One of the more splendid discoveries from this site is a twisted necklace of pure gold, weighing 1.82 kilos, making it Denmark's largest gold find from the period between 500 and 1000. But perhaps the most interesting discovery is a small seal made of lead with an inscription that is quite difficult to read. It turns out to have originated from the imperial Byzantine administration of the mid-800s and belonged to the imperial representative Theodosios (Bjerg et al. 2013, 149–150). We know from several sources that a diplomatic emissary was sent by the emperor in Constantinople to the emperor

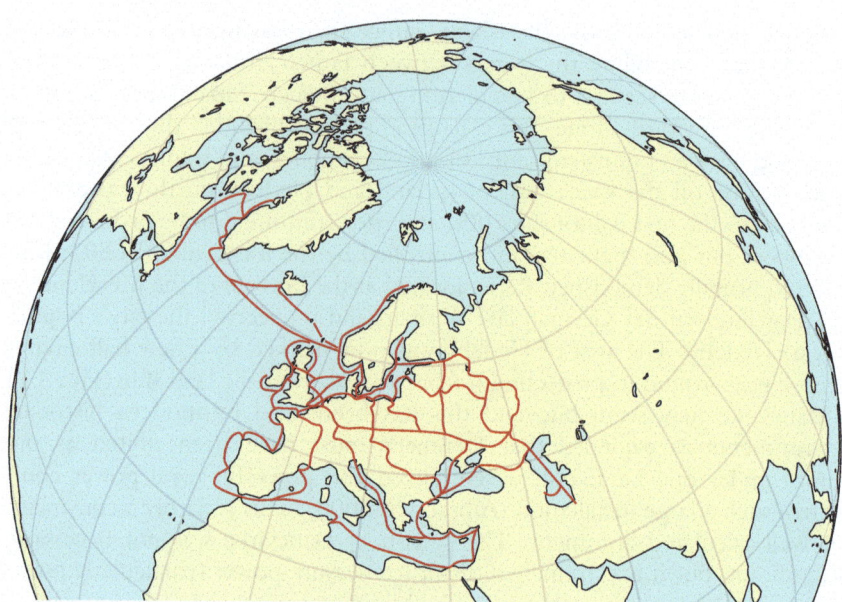

Fig. 3.1 From the mid-eighth century until around the year 1000, Europeans became much more mobile than earlier, and new contacts were established over long distances. It was a period with Muslims attacking in the entire Mediterranean and with peoples from the Eastern steppes advancing far into the centers of Western Europe. At the same time, large groups of Scandinavians traversed long distances while plundering or trading. Among the most precious commodities, they could offer were their military skills, in high esteem among rulers everywhere. Scandinavians served as abroad as elite soldiers for years or settled as colonists as far away as the fjords of Greenland or on the Ukrainian steppes. The upheld connections back to Scandinavia for generations, confirmed and strengthened by marriages. The Danish empire has comprised cultures as different as hunters and fishers along the Arctic Ocean and even on the Eastern coast of America; steppe nomads in Russia, sophisticated Christian and Islamic urban societies and the overwhelmingly agrarian areas in England and France, solid planted in local soil. Religiously and linguistically, the empire was a bowl of different impulses and trends that were introduced to or at least influenced Scandinavia. The map here illustrates but a few of the routes that were commonly used by Scandinavians in the period

of France in the early 840s, in an effort to—among other things—establish a military alliance between the two rulers. The delegation either continued to Denmark or sent a subsection thereto, where it sought out audiences with the most important of the Danish kings. The seal from the empirical war diplomate has been found also in Venice, Trier, and in Denmark in Tissø, Ribe, and Hedeby. Other findings also show that Tissø was in contact with many places elsewhere: from Ireland, across France to Finland and all the way to the Arab caliphate. It was possible to reach Tissø by sailing from the Great Belt between

Funen and Sealand: once ships reached the place, goods could be transported further by boat far into Sealand via several streams, while the headquarters of Tissø remained relatively protected and removed from the ambush attacks that settlements along the coast were otherwise exposed to. The sheer size of the site at Tissø has amazed, and is slowly being excavated and examined in the first years of the twenty-first century. It has been described as a rich man's estate, and perhaps even as the original headquarters of the powerful Sealand Hvide clan. In size and wealth, the Tissø site is reminiscent of Gudme, and there is no indication that the ruler of Tissø was subservient to those who in the 700s built Danevirke. Although we don't have any written evidence of a king in Tissø, it would be plausible to speak about such a ruler in Tissø, as we have a full testimony of kings at other contemporary centers of power, such as Lejre, near Roskilde.

Lejre was built during the same period as Tissø, from around 700 into the 1000s. The two sites are very similar. They share the same traces of handiwork, fine jewelry, and objects. The buildings in Lejre seem to have been constructed according to a fixed plan designed for the area. Lejre includes several country houses more than 40 meters in length, as well as a giant hall with curved walls: its length at 60 meters was significantly longer than the one at Tissø. Unlike Tissø, there are several large burial mounds located at Lejre: these have not yet been examined and studied, but may very well date from this period. One particularly magnificent memorial is an 86-meter ship-setting, rendering it the largest in the Nordic region, and there have likely been at least six ship-setting constructions at Lejre. These large oval formations of stones were the settings for funerals of the time, which were only available to and used by the top tiers of society. Lejre was monumental, and the place itself was commemorated and described in literature that, while recorded in writing in the 1000s, we know to be based on older accounts. The Old-English poem of Beowulf (Beowulf 1973), which linguists believe to have been composed perhaps as early as the 700s and transmitted orally, tells of King Hrotgar in the great hall: the gold-giver who was revered by his men and lived a harmonious life with his queen. However, one night the great hall was attacked by the monster Grendal, from the depths of the nearby lake. Each night the creature attacked and dragged one of Hrotgar's men down into its lair. The hero Beowulf arrives from Sweden offering his help: he lies in wait in the hall before killing the monster. The next night, Grendal's mother attacks in revenge, and Beowulf hunts her, following her all the way down to her cave to fight in its depths, before finally defeating and killing her.

The Beowulf poem opens with the dawn of history. At the beginning of time, a ship arrived in Denmark, with no crew and no one to steer: only an infant lying on a sheaf of corn was onboard. It was King Scyld Scefing (in Danish: *kong Skjold*), the first king in Denmark and the ancestor of all the Scyldings. This story is supported by Icelandic sagas and Danish historical works in the 1100s. Together, these works construct formidable pedigrees connecting many famous and fictitious figures, including both Roar and Rolf

Krake placed in the great hall of Lejre. The names are derived from many sources, and some of them are certainly fabricated. Overall, however, these stories rightfully grasp that Lejre was a seat of royal power for hundreds of years. In addition, Lejre was also apparently an important religious center. The bishop Thietmar of German Merseburg described the pagan sacrificial ceremonies at Lejre (Thietmar 1935, 22-24):

> The capital of this kingdom is Lejre in Sealand, where they meet every nine years in January and sacrifice to their gods, 99 people and just as many horses, dogs, and roosters - in the absence of hawks - and they fully and firmly believe that these sacrifices will serve the gods of the underworld, satisfy them, and make them forget their sins.

Thietmar wrote around 1018 and dates the cruel and bloody sacrificial ceremonies in Lejre to the first half of the 900s. Thietmar was well-informed both about Danevirke and about Danish tenth century kings in Jelling, rendering his statement on Lejre as the capital of the Danes a strong piece of evidence that there were more kings in Denmark right up to the year 1000. The various kings joined networks, where through alliances they would attempt to gain enough political support to assert themselves militarily. These networks, of course, extended beyond the present-day borders of Denmark and Scandinavia. Archeologically, early links can be detected between the Swedish graves of Uppsala and southern England, as demonstrated in the famous Sutton Hoo site dating back to the mid-600s. Excavations at other sites suggest a close connection between rulers in Norway and Scotland. Close links are also found between West Jutland and England since at least the 400s, perhaps even manifesting as an outright migration of peoples from Jutland and Angeln together with Saxons. These connections were old, established, and maintained for centuries.

The English missionary Willibrord traveled to Denmark in or a few years prior to 714; in actuality, he was sent by the Frankish ruler of the time. It was a peculiar era, where a Frankish mission to the territories of Denmark is nearly unthinkable without it being explicitly arranged with the connivance of a local ruler. Unfortunately, whoever this ruler may have been, was never detailed and is lost to history. When Willibrord arrived, however, he was received by King Angantyr, who was "crueler than a beast and harder than a stone," and Willibrord had to return to England nearly empty-handed (Alcuin 1873, 9). He only brought with him thirty boys who were then baptized and Willibrord began to educate them in the Christian faith. They were to be sent back to Denmark in the future, as missionaries who knew the local language. This was a fairly common practice in the Middle Ages: the royal missionaries would as a rule try to raise boys who were wealthy and had powerful family connections. In a time of war, these young men were often simply taken hostage. If there was peace, they were exchanged voluntarily as well as sent to seal alliances. Smaller rulers sent their sons to rulers with more power. Thus, since the beginning of the 700s, Danish magnates and kings tried to ally with the Frankish kings in order to strengthen their own position within Denmark. The possibility of converting to Christianity became a permanent feature of these negotiations in the future.

Around the year 812–813, the Danish king Harald Klak formed an alliance with Charlemagne: as part of the agreement he brought an archbishop Ebbo of Reims back to Denmark as a missionary. However, it was for naught, as Harald was deposed by other Danish kings. Ebbo quickly explained that it would surely benefit Harald's war—as well as increase the emperor's support—if he converted to Christianity. Harald, along with his wife and son, was therefore baptized in Mainz. It was a major political event. The new emperor Louis the Pious was Harald's godfather, and sent him magnificent baptism gifts, including a particularly exquisite horse and some spectacular weapons. Therefore, Harald returned with confidence to Denmark in 826, but was soon expelled, and spent the rest of his life serving as an intermediary, a buffer, between Carolingian France and Denmark. In his entourage, Harald had Ansgar, a missionary, who built a church in Hedeby. Later Ansgar returned on another mission to Sweden, earning him in modern times the title of "the Apostle of the North."

Harald Klak's alliance with the mighty Frankish ruler was a sensible policy of balance, particularly because other Danish kings had joined other alliances, choosing to fight against Charlemagne and Louis. King Godfred mobilized his army around Danevirke in 804 in order to halt an expedition of Charlemagne into the north. He also conquered the city of Reric from Charlemagne's allies, the Slavic Obotrites, and razed it to the ground. This earned Godfred an enduring legacy. The historian Saxo in around the year 1200 described Godfred as nearly that of an emperor in the north, capable of matching Charlemagne in the south as his equal. King Godfred subdued the Saxon dukes who as a tax, Saxo asserted, were to pay a hundred white horses each time a new Danish ruler came to the throne, as a sign that "they recognize our People's empire" (Saxo 8.16.3). Charlemagne was forced to retreat to the other side of the Rhine and did not want to risk combat, wrote Saxo. Godfred decided to go through Frisia into the German territories and from there initiate a true conquest: however, he was killed by his own men in an ambush. Via the history writing of Saxo, Godfred was able to effortlessly move into all subsequent Danish history as a hero who fought for Danish independence against the German emperor. It is uncertain how much of that statement is actually true.

Godfred certainly was not an insignificant ruler who could easily be passed over. An Osfred of Scania acted as guarantor on Godfred's behalf in a peace settlement in 811, so he must have been Godfred's ally. In 813, Frankish sources described that the southern part of Norway belonged to the most remote region of Godfred's kingdom: the local population there paid taxes to him, but eventually revolted and the unrest had to be quelled by force. Southern Norway, Scania, and southern Jutland have thus belonged to

Godfred's kingdom, but the areas between including the rich archeological sites in Tissø and Lejre could certainly have belonged to other Danish kings.

Contemporarily with Godfred's rule, the first reports on Viking attacks began to emerge: these attacks were subsequently called Viking raids, and have been understood as characteristically Scandinavia (Forte et al. 2005; Brink and Price 2008; Price 2015). However, the term "viking" was rarely used at that time. If the term was employed, it was to describe pirates or simply criminals, and did not refer specifically to Danes or Scandinavians. In the summer of 793, the Lindisfarne Monastery in Northumbria was attacked and looted following a spring season filled with tornadoes, lightning, and fire-breathing dragons in the sky. Consequently, England and other parts of Europe were subjected to one attack after another. All these occurrences were hardly anything qualitatively new. Attacks had happened in these areas before and probably been quite common, but now they began to be chronicled in the records of English and French monasteries. The important trading town of Dorestad on the Rhine was attacked and looted for several consecutive years starting in 834. In 840 and 842 London and Southampton were targeted, and in 841 the first viking armies began to sail up the Seine to threaten Paris, which was besieged and was ultimately forced to buy itself an expensive peace in 845.

Ireland had previously been the target of Norwegian warriors, and in 851 Danes also started raiding the island. In 853 Ivar became king of Dublin and later participated in the conquest of York in 866. In 844 and 846 some of the armies that had fought in France pressed onwards to Galicia in northern Spain, and even to Arabic Lisbon: according to some later Spanish sources, these troops were dispatched by the Danish king Horik. In 854, 70 ships, led by Björn Ironside and Hastings, sailed from England via Spain to Morocco, into the Mediterranea, ultimately reaching Italy. Although it is difficult to measure the scale of these battles compared to earlier periods with fewer sources, it seems clear that the battles from the mid-800s onwards were vaster in scope, earning attention from their contemporaries who became the victims. There are three main reasons for this intensification of warfare.

First, it is clear that the Nordic longship had developed into a maneuverable and efficient war machine: Danish and Scandinavian fleets were famous and desired by other rulers for centuries to come. It probably wasn't until around 1200 that other countries off the Atlantic coast built equally strong fleets; in the Mediterranean it probably happened in the early 1100s. Until then, the Scandinavians had a significant advantage at sea.

Secondly, the expansion in the 800s shows that Scandinavia was an extremely rich area. There is a very specific reason for that. With the rise of Islam in the 600s and the conquest of large parts of the Mediterranean world until the beginning of the 700s, Europe's economic center of gravity shifted to the east. The link between East and West in the Mediterranean was left un-interrupted, but the Arab gold mines and new efficient exploitation of the Silk Road and its access to the East's lucrative trade system provided an economic boost to the Byzantine Empire, particularly to the capital of

Constantinople. The Scandinavians had access to this via the Gulf of Finland, Lake Ladoga in northwest Russia, and along the great Russian rivers to the Black Sea (Bjerg et al. 2013). Islam actually brought Scandinavia closer to being Europe's economic center, becoming bridge and a transit area between the East and West. The vast quantities of gold coins found in Scandinavia clearly illustrate this. So far at least 200,000 Arabic gold coins have been excavated by archeologists, and with the spread of metal detectors more and more are discovered each year. Yet it is still only a small percentage of the many coins that were buried, and they represent only those treasures that were not dug up again by their owner or his heirs. Most of these immense riches were later invested towards war technology and political capital, in ships and men.

Third, most of these raiding expeditions were not random looting. Nor did they reflect a large-scale war between Denmark and other countries or between two cultures, one European and one Scandinavian, or between two religions, one Christian and one pagan. Rather, they were a natural element of an intricate political game between a variety of different rulers, with opponents and allied partners coming together across the political and religious spectrum.

The Danish wars in England were a continuation of old alliances across the North Sea. In northern England, Danish armies were apparently well received by the local population, whose elite probably had ancient Scandinavian roots. Several groups of warriors joined together to form the "great army" in 865, and in the coming years they conquered relatively easily East Anglia and Northumbria, which starting in around 870 came under Danish control. The Great Army threatened the kingdom of Mercia and Wessex in southern England, where it was stopped by King Alfred the Great. The warriors were soon followed by peasants who settled and cultivated the land. Danish had a lasting influence on the English language, and northern England became known as the Danelaw, the area under Danish law and control. We do know the names of several danish commanders and kings located in England from the 800 and 900s. However, we don't know if these kings also simultaneously ruled over anything back in Denmark. English sources say that they occasionally returned home to Denmark. This indicates that the relationship would have been close at the time, and the involvement in England clearly had a profound effect on the political hierarchy and power dynamics in Denmark.

The same certainly applies to the Frankish empire. One of the most important defensive strategies of the French king against the attack of the Scandinavian armies was to quickly ally himself with other Scandinavian rulers who were given land to which to defend. One of these rulers included the aforementioned Harald Klak, who had fought in England and with the help of Louis the Pious actually came to rule in Denmark as king, if only briefly. Although Harald Klak was driven out of Denmark just a year after becoming king, he consequently served as a Frankish border prince for several years. His son Godfred tried again in 855 to leverage his base in France to fight for a kingship in Denmark; yet just as his father, this endeavor was in vain. The most famous out of the posterity of Scandinavian princes in Frankish service was Rollo, who acquired Normandy in 911 and whose descendants would become great princes and kings throughout Western Europe and the Middle East in the 1000s and 1100s. A good many Danes settled along with Rollo in the area, especially around Rouen, as evidenced by Scandinavian and Danish influence on the local place names. However, the extent of Danish influence on the rest of the French language was far less than on English. It is impossible to determine whether Rollo was originally Danish or Swedish. We also don't know the exact connection between Rollo and Hardeknud, who likely came from Normandy, and who actually succeeded in returning to Denmark and becoming a king. He was the father of Gorm the Old, the first ruler of Denmark that we know from historical Danish sources who may have used the title emperor.

Harald Klak had converted to Christianity, as well as many—but not all—of the Scandinavian military commanders in England and France. It seems that conversion was part of contemporary political negotiations, but not always a necessity to form alliances. For example, after military defeat, the loser could be required to be baptized along with his army. This occurred in 934 when the Danish king Gnupa lost a battle to Henry I the Fowler in his kingdom surrounding Hedeby. Of course, it also meant that later rulers could apply religion for reverse purposes, and put themselves at the head of a rebellion and try to get crowned as king by seeking to re-establish paganism. One thing is clear, however: Christianity was well-established in Denmark and had been so for a long time even before what is traditionally referred to as the Danish conversion period.

Emperor Gorm

The oldest narrative source on Danish soil, the elder of the two Jelling Rune Stones, dates back to the mid-900s. Its brief inscription reads, "King Gorm made this monument for Thyra his wife, the 'Bod' of Denmark." *Tanmarkar but,* the "Bod of Denmark" was obviously a badge of honor and is often translated as the "Adornment of Denmark." It gave rise to many speculations about its precise meaning which ultimately lay behind the subsequent medieval tales of Queen Thyra's efforts to fortify Dannevirke against attackers from the German south. However, perhaps it wasn't Thyra after all who was Denmark's "Bod." In 1915, the otherwise hypercritical Scanian historian Lauritz Weibull suggested that the title should rather be understood as a term for Gorm and that it meant "emperor" (Weibull 1948–49). The interpretation was bold and the evidence quite thin: primarily due to the fact that a text, more than two hundred years younger, translated *"Bod"* into the Latin word *"decus,"* which in some cases could be interpreted as an imperial title. Weibull's thesis was silently neglected by later Danish historians. But could it hold some weight? Could Gorm have perceived himself as emperor and ruler of an empire? On closer inspection, this is not wholly unlikely, since during the mid-900s there was a vacuum of imperial power in the larger European theater.

The mighty empire of Charlemagne was plagued by internal strife following his death in 814. With the peace of Verdun in 843 the empire was divided into three parts, the western territory to France and the eastern to Germany. For over a hundred years, the two countries balanced each other so that neither of them became strong enough to claim imperial power. Therefore, around the middle of the ninth century, a number of emperors suddenly appeared elsewhere. Alfonso of León proclaimed himself emperor in the 960s, as he was well on his way to conquering the neighboring realms in Spain. He used the Latin *imperator* as a title. Concurrently, the English King Edgar also took the imperial title, as he was unifying the various English kingdoms under his authority and he also became ruler of the Danelaw. He used the Greek title *basileus*, which, according to the intricate Byzantine court ceremony, actually refers to a ruler who is subordinate to the true Eastern Roman emperor, the *autokrator*. However, in the Latin-speaking world, *basileus* was still clearly perceived as an elevated imperial title. In the 980s, the Bulgarian Khan felt powerful enough to start using the title of *tsar*, another imperial appellation. And at the same time, King Otto of Germany struggled to re-establish and restore the Roman Empire of Charlemagne. In 755 he won a decisive victory at Lechfeld over the Magyars, a fierce nomadic people from the eastern steppes, whose raids stretched as far into Europe as Marseilles. Otto enjoyed enormous prestige from this, and gained the opportunity to concentrate on expanding his empire elsewhere. In 962 he arrived in Rome, and was crowned by the pope as emperor. That year is often used to date Germany's genesis, but—perhaps more importantly—962 really marks the restoration of the Western European empire. Gorm was in good company if the word "but" on his rune stone is to be understood as an imperial title. If this is the case, he would be one of the first of the royal lineage to proclaim himself emperor, if the Jelling Stone indeed dates from around 950. Such a title would also have implied that Gorm ruled over several countries, although we cannot name with certainty which countries these were.

The evidence of Gorm's imperial role is slim, but several of his descendants were to express their role as imperators quite unequivocally. His two immediate successors may not have used the imperial title, but they still certainly felt and acted like rulers over several peoples. They gained such roles through successfully conquering wars, conflicts that were beginning to be understood as religious missionary wars. Harald Bluetooth officially converted to Christianity in 965. It was likely a part of an alliance with the new Emperor Otto I the Great, who had supported the missionary dioceses in Ribe, Aarhus, and Schleswig since 948. Harald's baptism showed a clear stance during an ambiguous period when Christianity and paganism long lived side by side and developed into a form of mixed religion, as can be witnessed in coins from the time of in the Danelaw (also known as the Danelaugh) with the name of pagan god Thor on one side and Saint Peter's name on the other. The German clergy Widukind described the conditions at Harald's court in the mid-960s: "The Danes have been Christians since time immemorial, but still they worship pagan idols. ... They affirmed that Jesus is indeed God, but there are other gods greater than Him, particularly those who give the mortal stronger signs and miracles" (Widukind 1882, 65). But now Harald became a Christian as part of a bargain and began a deliberate conquest of Denmark, which he summarized roughly twenty years later on the great Jelling Rune Stone: "Harald set this stone after Gorm his father ad Thyra his mother, the Harald who conquered all of Denmark and Norway and converted the Danes to Christianity." To enable this great conquest, it was necessary to be able to transport an army quickly and efficiently. Harald's longest structure was the bridge traversing the Ravninge meadows, 700 meters long and 5.5 meters wide, the bridge dates back to around 980. It was an awe-inspiring experience for a traveler from the south to cross the valleys of Vejle Ådal using this monumental bridge. Such an introduction to the power of the ruler of Jelling was certainly intentional. Beyond a display of power, the bridge was also used to quickly transport soldiers, saving many hours of detour, so that they could quickly reach southern Jutland, where Harald simultaneously fortified Dannevirke and protected Hedeby with fortification, just as it had been done for Aarhus and Ribe (Fig. 3.2).

The conquest of Denmark occurred through the construction of barracks fortresses, whose particular and precise geometric design reflects the discipline that must have prevailed among the soldiers. The forts are completely circular and intersected by two streets that go exactly north–south and east–west, and where the two streets traverse, stood a small but very tall building. Seen from above, these castles are a copy of Jerusalem's blueprint at the time. The building in the center can have been a miniature copy of the Church of the Holy Sepulchre in the Holy City, with Golgotha, the center of the world. The castles had a military significance, but they were also a strong ideological symbol of Harald's new religion, a mirror of coins with a large cross which Harald began to issue around the same time. These ring fortresses are called Trelleborgs named after the first one discovered near Slagelse on Sealand, which was surveyed in the 1930s. They date back to around 981, and those found so far are spread evenly across today's Denmark. Aggersborg in Vendsyssel is the largest at 240 meters in diameter. From it, Harald could control the Limfjord and the important northern coast of Jutland. It could serve as both a launch point for the conquest of Norway, of which Harald boasted about on his Jelling Stone, and it could help to master the important and tightly navigable waters between Norway, Denmark and England and Scotland. Fyrkat was centrally located in the west of Northern Jutland, Nonnebakken in Odense lay close to the old pagan cultural center, and Trelleborg by Slagelse was located near the Tissø site. Borgringen near the city of Køge was found and escavated as late as 2014 and have protected—or conquered—the important eastern part of Sealand with Stevns. Finally, it is also possible that there was a Trelleborg in Scania. Place names suggest it, but the ring fortress that the archeologists have found is estimated to be much older. These Trelleborgs only existed for about 30 years, then their function

Fig. 3.2 The perfectly circular Trelleborg fortress near Slagelse on Sealand has an inner diameter of 136 meters, 3 of the other known Trelleborgs measure 120, and one in Northern Jutland 240 meters. Villages were destroyed and locals slaughtered, children killed and dumped in old wells, all covered by these new fortifications when they were built in a very short period around 980 when King Harald Bluetooth won for himself all Denmark. Historians have discussed the inspiration for these constructions and pointed to various places in medieval Western Europe. They are actually geometrically perfect and totally symmetrical as the antique Roman military camps, but round instead of rectangular. It is not impossible that King Harald had some knowledge of Roman military architecture, for example from the fourth century Vegetius' book on *Military matters* (de re militari). Vegetius wrote "Nothing is more important to know in warfare than to fortify a camp." The basic measure for the trelleborgs is the Roman foot. The precision with which the Trelleborgs are built is exaggerated and has no practical purpose, but could be the result of King Harald's attempt to demonstrate himself as par with the emperor—the classical Roman emperor and maybe also the contemporary German one. https://da.wikipedia.org/wiki/Vikingeborgen_Trelleborg#/media/Fil:Trelleborg_airphoto.JPG (*Photo* Thue C. Leibrandt)

was obsolete. They were clearly Harald's starting point for controlling his newly conquered land, converting the territories to Christianity, and fighting the other local kings. While this must have required quite a large and well-commanded army, it remains uncertain how such a force was organized at the time. From the thirteenth century, we know of a naval "lething" system for the Danish territories, in which the whole country was divided into districts that were obliged to provide ships and men for the navy under royal control. We do not have sources to determine how far that system dates back, but it is plausible that it existed in Harald's time. The organizational and administrative capacity was clearly sufficient, and the use of force to persuade disobedient individuals to bear their share of the burdens would hardly have been a novel concept to Harald.

Jelling was the starting point for the new powerful ruler and was transformed by Harald into a monument, a historic memorial honoring the source of his power and an ideological proclamation no less clear than the Trelleborg's image of Jerusalem. The center of Jelling was surrounded by a palisade with hundreds of oak poles, delineating a rhombe-formed area of 360 × 360 meters, more than 12 hectares. Right in its center is the largest known burial mound from the Viking Age, encircled by a large stone ship-setting within the palisade. It was the burial place of Gorm. Harald constructed another burial mound centered at one point of the ship-setting's tip. He also erected a church on the center line between the two mounds, to which he may have transferred the remains of his father Gorm to an honorable burial at the high altar of the new church. If he did so—it is disputed—Harald must have persuaded himself and his priests that Gorm had been a Christian or almost a Christian. A post-mortem baptism of a pagan would have been totally against all church regulations.

Right in the middle between the two burial mounds, Harald raised the large Jelling Stone. On one side of the stone, there is a proud figure of the victorious Christ on the tree of life with intertwining patterns of leaves—the tree of life (Jensen 2017)? On the other side of the Jelling Stone, there is a scene of a ferocious lion battling a dragon. The only place in the Bible where Christ and the lion appear in the same verse is Genesis 49: 8–10, where it is prophesied to the dying patriarch Jacob that the scepter shall not depart from the lion of Judah until Messiah has come. In the medieval Bible interpretation, it was understood as a promise from God that the Jews should have kings until Christ's arrival, and thereafter the old dominion should give way to the new. But at the same time, the new king, Christ, was to receive his power from the old, from David, who became a role model for all the kings of the Middle Ages. Harald thus clearly stated that his conversion to Christianity bestowed upon him a new authority over that of the ancient pagan kings. Simultaneously, he stressed that he also continued the old pagan lineage by descending from Gorm. Modern historians sometimes got lost in speculations on whether anyone actually had specialized knowledge of the Bible and Christianity at the time of Harald's conversion. The Jelling Stone's symbolic scenes are actually extremely well-chosen and show great familiarity with the contemporary Christian world of thought. The stone is carved in such a style that is strikingly reminiscent of contemporary large illustrated and handwritten Bibles from Germany. The Jelling monument is a cult site to commemorate the Danish dynasty's founder, and is reminiscent of churches of Emperor Otto the Great's and other large impressing architectural monument of the time

3 THE CHRISTIAN EMPIRE OF THE NORTH SEA 39

◄**Fig. 3.3** The large Jelling Stone was raised by King Harald Bluetooth to commemorate his father, King Gorm, and his mother, Queen Thyra. It probably dates from the early 980ies. The Runic inscription has been interpreted differently by scholars. In the eighteenth century, it was believed to read "haraltr kessor uan tanmaurk" (Harald the Emperor conquered Denmark). It raised a problem as to how to interpret the title, and one historian suggested that it had been applied by an itinerant German Rune-writer, "perhaps out of ignorance, perhaps to flatter Harald." In 1820, Finn Magnusen read the inscription as "haraltr ies sor uan tanmaurk" (Harald who swore [to introduce Christianity] and won for himself Denmark), while runologists today simply understand the sentence to mean "Harald who won for himself Denmark." The large Jelling Stone and the small Jelling Stone (raised by King Gorm, c 950) contain the first mentioning within present Danish territory to use the designation "Denmark"; in England it is known from ninth-century sources. The name means "The march of the Danes." Danes are known from both Gothic, Frankish, and Greek sources from the sixth century. It may mean simply "people," or perhaps "people from the lowlands." Mark designates a border area, but it is a bit peculiar for people to call the area they inhabit a border area. Perhaps the name of Denmark is actually German meaning "The border area to Germans inhabited by the Danes." The illustration shows Christ the conqueror on one of the three sides of the big Jellin Sstone. The colors are reconstructed as they may have looked in the tenth century, for a Viking Age exhibition at the Danish National Museum, 2013. https://commons.wikimedia.org/wiki/File:The_Jelling_Stone_-_VIKING_exhibition_at_the_National_Museum_of_Denmark_-_Photo_The_National_Museum_of_Denmark_(9084035770).jpg (*Photo* The National Museum of Denmark)

(discussed in Randsborg 2008). Jelling was comparable to the largest European memorial sites, as fitting for one who wanted to present himself as a great European ruler (Fig. 3.3).

Harald was later overthrown by a revolt and died in exile in 987 in Jomsborg, in Wolin at the easternmost corner of present-day Poland. Harald had been married to Tove, the daughter of the Slavic Obotrite Prince Mistivoi, but we do not know if Jomsborg was part of Harald's kingdom. Perhaps it was even thought of as a bridgehead for further expansion along the coast of the Baltic Sea. Harald's remains were returned to Denmark, and now lie buried in the new church in Roskilde on Sealand, beginning this church's long history as a royal burial site which it is still today. Under Harald the center of the empire clearly shifted east, from Jutland to Sealand, although it would have taken a long time before such a shift was firmly established. The circumstances of the rebellion against Harald are unclear, but his son Sweyn Forkbeard seemed to have played a role as the head of a pagan revolt. Quickly after his father's death, he seemed to have returned to Christianity.

Between 991 and 994, Sweyn Forkbeard initiated the first of several wars to establish a dominion in the old Danish part of England, which since 954 had been under the rule of various English kings. It should still be kept in mind that Danish and English were not fixed labels that were mutually exclusive. The English king was married into former Danish royal families and vice versa:

this also means that Sweyn likely had a strong inheritance claim to certain areas in England.

Sweyn initially collaborated with the Norwegian king Olav Tryggvason, and together they extorted large amounts of protection money from English cities in the coming years. 10,000 English pounds in precious metals one year, 36,000 pounds the next year, and so on. The two rulers clashed with each other around the year 1000, and Olav perished soon after in a naval battle against Sweyn. The English King Aethelred attempted to solve the issue in 1002, by ordering the ethnic cleansing of all Danes in his territories, which offers an impression of how much (or little) support Sweyn must have received from the locals on his raids. Many Danes were indeed killed, though some sought refuge in the churches. Sweyn intensified the attacks, and returned year after year, and escalated his exertion of force. The decisive blow was to be deployed in 1013, through the assembly of a splendid fleet. Each ship bore its commander's emblem: "lions cast in gold, birds perched on top the masts turned towards the wind, roaring dragons spit fire from their nostrils, bulls with stretched necks and twisted legs... rendered as if they were alive" (Encomium Emmae 12–13). Sweyn set out to "avenge the ancient offenses" (Adam 1876, 2:49) and one of the stated goals was to punish Aethelred, who had killed Sweyn's brother, Edward (the Martyr), 35 years earlier, making him a martyr. It was important for Sweyn to approach the war in England as a religious and just war, even though the potential revenues from the rich country is not unlikely to have played an enticing role. Sweyn finally succeeded in conquering the entirety of England, and a Danish empire on both sides of the Northern Sea was finally created. However, Sweyn did not live to enjoy the fruits of his efforts but died already in 1014.

CANUTE THE GREAT, THE EMPEROR

For three or four years after Sweyn's death, Aethelred and his son sought to regain dominion over England, and Sweyn's sons Canute and Harald attempted to share power over the empire. But by the death of Harald in 1018, Canute was left to rule over a very large kingdom, which he succeeded in further expanding and organizing in the years to come, earning him a position as one of Northern Europe's strongest rulers (Bolton 2017). Canute was fully aware of this, and he reflected his power through his use of titles. For example, he used honorifics such as, "Canute, emperor, anointed by Christ, the King of Kings, to rule the English on the Island." The word for emperor here was *imperator*. In some letters he used the Byzantine-sounding title "*basileus* over the brilliant and precious people of the English", in other addresses, he is just king. The titles were slightly adjusted according to whom he wrote, but the most common and perhaps the one intended to impress by its simplicity was merely "Ruler over Englishmen, Danes, Norwegians and some Swedes." Scotland had also surrendered to Canute in 1027, but was given no separate place in his honorifics.

As one of his first deeds, Canute hired professional advisers who could construct and promulgate an image of him as imperial ruler. This approach included hiring skalds on both sides of the North Sea, who praised him in high style narratives in the sumptuous and elaborate Nordic style. First, they highlighted his noble burden. He was descended from the Jelling dynasty and therefore stood first in line of the Danes, but he was also a direct descendant of Ivar the Boneless, who—alledgedly, he may be a totally fictitious figure—in 866 had conquered York and created a Danish kingdom there. Thus, Canute's claim of inheritance to England was better than that of Aethelred and his family. Canute's skalds praised him not only for his fortunes in war, as was otherwise deeply embedded in the Nordic tradition, but especially for his protective power. He was named the "greatest lord under the sun." Canute protected the country, just as the all-seeing Lord protects the glorious hall of the mountains, that is Heaven. Canute was dear to the emperor, and near to Saint Peter. "Canute protects the land, just as Byzantium's guardian - God - protects the sky" (Frank 2018, 207). The last verse of the bard divides the earth and sky between Canute and God, and almost resembled an attempt to outweigh Emperor Conrad. At his ascension as German King in 1024, Conrad was proclaimed "Deputy of the King of Christ" with the explanation that as Christ reigned in heaven, the emperor was to rule the earth. Canute was set even higher than the German king, at least according to his own skalds.

Medieval kings were monogamous and married only one woman at a time, but they would quite often have one or more high-ranking official mistresses to seal political ties. When Canute became the sole ruler of England, he dissolved his former marriage to Ælfgifu of Northampton and married Aethelred's widow, Emma, the daughter of Duke Rickard of Normandy. Canute maintained a close relationship with Ælfgifu into their future, but the marriage to Emma was ideal. Not only did it secure a solid claim over those parts of England which had been mastered by Aethelred. It also strengthened the relations between Danish kings and Normandy, which—while we no longer can trace their details—certainly had been close and dated back to before the year 900 (Fig. 3.4).

To administer his kingdom, Canute followed the characteristic model of empires: to delegate the rule to viceroys who were given responsibility for each of their territories. In England he chose to direct Wessex himself, which he presumably considered to be the core of the empire. Northumbria, Mercia and East Anglia were each subject to their own earl, respectively: Erik Håkonsson from Norway, the Anglo-Saxon Eadric Streona and the Dane Thorkell the Tall. The day-to-day command of Denmark was left to the Anglo-Saxon Ulf, who was married to Canute's sister Estrid. Norway was contentious. While Canute was busy establishing himself in England, Olav, later known as Saint Olav, tried to rebel and proclaim himself King of Norway. This led to a series of skirmishes culminating in the battle of Helge River at Scania in 1026. It ended with Canute consolidating his power over Norway and he was soon recognized as king. In 1030, his ex-wife Ælfgifu was set to govern Norway

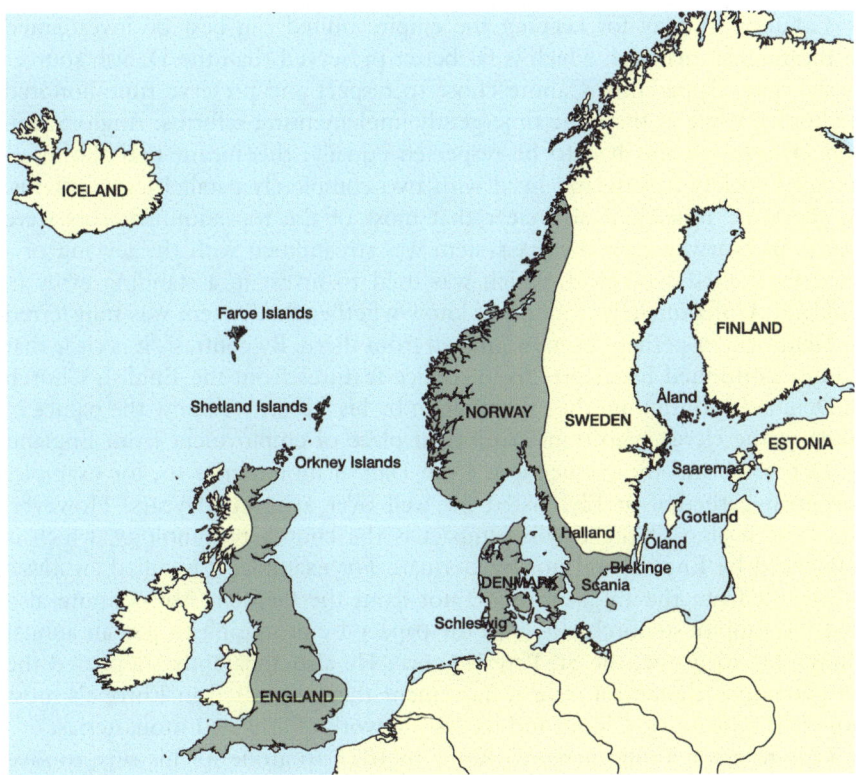

Fig. 3.4 During the first 1000 years CE, there were solid cultural and economic connections between Southern Scandinavia and both Eastern and Western Europe, as is evident from archeological findings. Political alliances were formed over very long distances, but because of the fragile source material it is impossible to determine the extent and the concrete content of them. Only around the year 1000 do we get sufficient written material to estimate more precisely the precise extent of the Danish empire. After the conquest in England by King Sveyn in 1013 and till the death of King Canute the Great in 1035, the Danish empire was oriented towards the west and bound together by the North Sea

with their son Sweyn, which they did with brutal efficiency, earning them a bad reputation in later history writing. Canute's deputy kings were hardly chosen because of their personal loyalty. Both Eadric and Thorkell already had a well-deserved reputation for the agility with which they changed from serving one ruler to the next. Such people are invaluable in an empire because they can negotiate on all sides and have networks on both sides of political boundaries, but of course, they must also be kept under close scrutiny. It is not uncharacteristic for an imperial ruler, that Canute almost immediately changed his mind and executed Easdric, and after five years deposed Thorkell and banished him, before eventually killing his own brother-in-law Ulf.

Canute's strategy for keeping the empire united can best be investigated in the English material, which is far better preserved than the Danish sources at the time. Apparently, Canute chose to respect and preserve time-honored traditions, while at the same time gently implementing reforms. Anglo-Saxon and Danish customs had to be respected equally: this meant that the intermingled society in England lived with two completely parallel legal systems. At the same time, it is also clear that most of the top administrators were Danes or Norwegians. The tax system was streamlined with the levying of a fixed fee, called a *heregeld*, which was used to invest in a standing army in England. Unfortunately, we do not know whether that system was transferred to Denmark, or perhaps even originated from there. By contrast, it is clear that Canute continued his efforts to introduce features from the English Church in Denmark, continuing the effort begun by his father. We know the names of some of the clergy who transferred their place of employment from England to Denmark, and the connections from Danish monasteries to, for example, the great cathedral in Ely, lasted for well over a hundred years. However, the clearest sign of the English impact is the church terminology, which is influenced by English and not by German. For example, it is called an *abbed* in Danish from the English abbot, not from the German Abt. Canute also tied the Empire's church closer to the papacy by promising to pay an annual church tax to Rome, the St. Peter's pence. He also apparently supported the burgeoning ecclesiastical reform movement that originated in Europe's most powerful monastery, Cluny, and its vast network of affiliated monasteries.

Canute made a pilgrimage to Rome in 1027 to atone for his sins, to save his kingdoms, and to seek the special protection of Saint Peter. This presumably means that he had taken a special oath to protect the pope. Canute was accompanied by King Conrad II of Germany, who was on his way to Rome to be crowned emperor, and Canute held a distinguished position in the ceremony. Eight years later, Canute's daughter Gunhild married Otto's son, the new emperor Henry III. Otto had first tried to get an agreement on a Byzantine princess for his son, but it fell through, and Canute's lineage was the most appropriate next choice. The political ties were sealed between two great rulers, and the marriage also meant that Otto recognized Canute's right to the area north of the Ejder river.

Canute died in 1035 and was buried in Winchester, after which the empire was restructured and in practice was divided among several family lines. Canute's son with Ælfgifu became king in England, his son with Emma became king in Denmark, and they fought against each other and against other half-brothers until both died in 1042, and no other descendants of Canute were left alive. In England, Edward (the Confessor) became king: he was the son of Emma and Æthelred and quickly married Edith, the daughter of Earl Godwin, who was part of the Danish royal family. In other words, this was a repetition of his father's policy when Canute married Edward's mother. In 1066, Edward died without heirs, and Edith's brother Harald Godwinson became king of England. However, in the same year, he fought a fierce battle at Stamford Bridge against the Norwegian Harald Hardrada, who had decided to conquer England. When the Norwegian King was defeated and killed, Harald Godwinson had to hastily retreat south to meet William the Bastard at Hastings, where Harald was killed. England was conquered by a duke from Normandy, who was related to Rollo and to the Danish kings, but whose political base was far from Denmark itself. In the future, England would become a part of another of the great empires of the Middle Ages, the Anglo-Aquitaine, which included land on both sides of the Channel as well as much of what is modern day southern France, which came to exist during almost the entire Middle Ages.

That did not mean that the inheritance claim on England was forgotten in Denmark. There were several direct attempts to conquer England in 1069, 1070, 1075 and 1085. This meant that later dynastic marriages were made with an eye for the ancient claim to England. There was a direct reference to this claim when other European rulers entered into alliances with Danish kings, even as late as the Hundred Years war in the mid-1300s. Still, it remains clear that a shift in the empire's focus began to take place from west to east in the latter half of the eleventh century.

Olav had returned to Norway from self-elected exile with his family in Novgorod to fight against Canute, but he died at the battle of Stiklestad in 1030 and was soon revered as a martyr. When Canute died, Norwegian chieftains displaced Ælfgifu and the son Sweyn Ælgifuson, and thereafter summoned Olav's son Magnus from Novgorod, whom they chose as king of Norway. In 1042 he also took power over Denmark, and for a short period, the two countries were once again under the same ruler. Magnus began an eager expansion into the Baltic Sea region towards the pagan Wends. He began by conquering Jomsborg and burning it down completely. In 1043 the famous battle of Lyrskov Hede occurred, which according to Adam of Bremen around 1070, was the greatest battle in Denmark up to that time, with 15,000 lying dead afterwards at the battle field. As the fighting began, the air was filled with the sound of the church bell from Trondheim, where Saint Olav is buried. Magnus cast off his chain mail, and, wearing only a red silk shirt he swung his father's double ax and fell many Wends. He was, as described by Adam, "dear to the Danes" (Adam 1876, 2:75) Magnus then began to mint coins with the Holy City of Jerusalem on one side, and the traditional Nordic long ax on the other. Additionally, several churches were founded and consecrated to Saint Olav. It was a war pleasing to God, and Olav clearly served both as a missionary saint and a common saint for both Norway and Denmark. There do not seem to have been any fundamental issues associated with having a ruler of Denmark who originated from Norway. Magnus had the right background, his grandfather being half-brother to Canute the Great (Fig. 3.5).

Magnus had to accept an offer of collaboration, extended to him by Harald Hardrada—his father's powerful half-brother—who returned laden with riches from years of service with the Byzantine emperor. Together they fought against Sweyn II Estridsson, who was determined to take over the legacy of

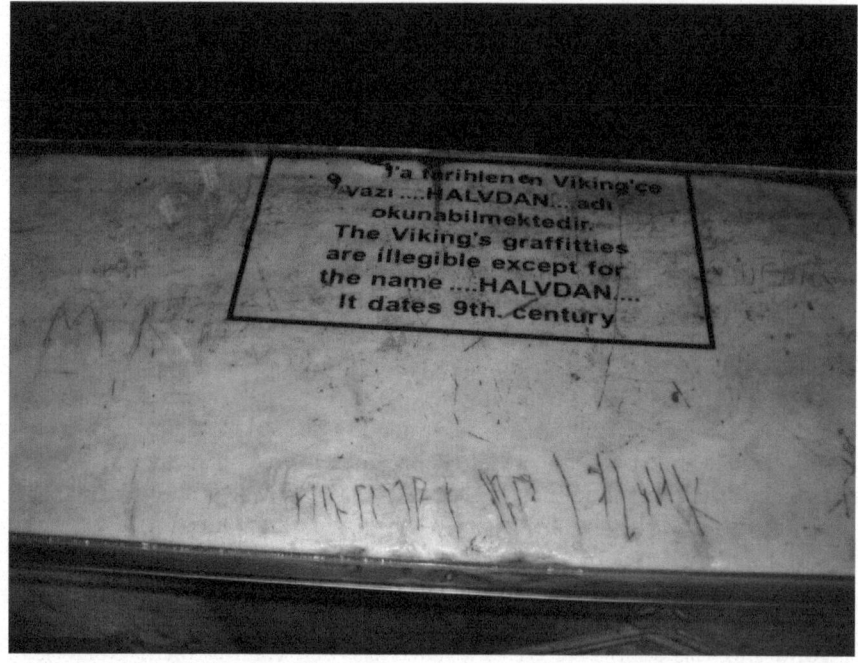

Fig. 3.5 "Halfdan was here." This is probably the message that the not very well preserved runes convey, carved in the marble on one of the upper galleries in the church of Hagia Sofia in Constantinople (present Istanbul). It is probably from the tenth or eleventh century and must have been written by a member of the Byzantine emperor's Scandinavian elite guard, the Varangians. One of their many duties was to follow the emperor from the palace to the church and guard and protect him during service. Modern historians have speculated that Halfdan has not understood any of what was going on during the prolonged Sunday service all in Greek, and has been bored and began carving his name in the letters of his homeland. That was a natural explanation still during most of the twentieth century, when historians understood Denmark as remote, isolated, and a bit pedestrian compared to the rest of Europe. In reality, Halfdan and other Scandinavians have served for years in Constantinople, many have learned Greek, and many have probably even been baptized. When eventually they returned home to Scandinavia, many brought with them new languages and Orthodox-Greek Christianity. Another short Runic inscription was found in Hagia Sofia in 2016, faint and difficult to read, but probably also containing a Nordic name. https://commons.wikimedia.org/w/index.php?title=Special:Search&search=graffiti+hagia+sofia&fulltext=1&ns0=1&ns6=1&ns12=1&ns14=1&ns100=1&ns106=1#/media/File:Hagia-sofia-viking.jpg (*Photo* Not home)

his maternal uncle, Canute the Great. When Magnus died in 1047, Harald had to return to Norway to secure his position there, and Sweyn Estridsson now became sole king in Denmark. After an additional conflict with Harald Hardrada, peace was made and sealed with marriage. After Harald's death in

1066 at Stamford Bridge in England, Harald's son Olaf Kyrre married Sweyn's daughter Ingrid, and Harald's daughter Ingegerd married Sweyn's son Oluf. Double marriages between siblings from two houses became a common system of alliance between Scandinavian royal dynasties throughout the rest of the Middle Ages. It gave the peace agreement greater security because it increased the chance that at least one of the marriages survived political upheavals and premature death. But in the longer term, it also provided new opportunities for conflict because the children from the two different marriages would have almost equally good inheritance claims to the same countries.

Under the rule of Sweyn Estridsson, the wars in the Wendish areas south of Denmark intensified. The relations between the two areas had been healthy, even at the dynastic level. Since Harald Blåtand, Danish kings had customarily arranged marriages for themselves or their children with Wendish rulers, and in line with this tradition Sweyn Estridsson's daughter, Sigrid, married Gotskalk. He had previously served Canute the Great in England and had tried to balance between Sweyn Estridsson and Magnus in their wars, but ultimately sided with the winner. In doing so, he gained a powerful ally in his attempts to recapture his father's old principality in the area surrounding the city of Lübeck. Many of the Slavic regions had become Christianized at around the same time as Denmark in the latter half of the tenth century. Christian dioceses were set up as far east as Brandenburg, but the Obotrites located along the Baltic coast renounced the faith and rebelled in 983, around 1000, 1018, and again in 1066. This continuous conflict split the Slavic ruling families. Some remained pagan and sought alliances in a pagan hinterland, while others converted to Christianity and sought alliances with neighboring Christian princes such as Sweyn Estridsson.

Around 1052–1053, the Archbishop of Hamburg-Bremen arranged a meeting with Sweyn Estridsson in Schleswig, and mediated an agreement with the German emperor on a joint missionary campaign against the pagans. The negotiations concluded with a great feast, after which the archbishop gave a sermon to Sweyn, promising him the benevolence of God if he fought against the pagans, and the crown of martyrdom if he died in battle. Then the Archbishop, according to Adam of Bremen, encouraged the king and the rest of the audience with a flaming speech including many powerful Biblical quotes, albeit not those warning against gluttony and women, for these sins are a part of the nature of the Danes. What followed was a series of wars, which at first appeared to bring success and lead to more permanent control of the pagan areas, but in 1066 the Danish and Wendish warriors were met with yet another violent pagan counter-attack. Gotskalk perished, and his wife Sigrid had to flee back to her father, Sweyn, with her young son Henry. It was evidently a defeat, but in the long run, the Danish kings eventually retained a claim on the territory of the Obotrites, which they then tried to assert when the opportunity arose.

Sweyn Estridsson was considered an important ally in Europe at the time, and had a close and personal relationship with the pope. After his appointment in 1073, the very first letter that the newly elected Pope Gregory VII wrote were delivered to Duchess Beatrice from Upper Lorraine, two bishops, Abbot Hugh of Cluny (Europe's most important monastic leader), and then to Sweyn Estridsson. Only then did the pope write to other rulers and inform them that he was now the head of the Christian Church. Sweyn had previously sent one of his sons to Rome to be crowned king, and now he offered Pope Gregory another of his sons to serve in the pope's palace in his personal guard. Instead, the pope suggested that Sweyn's son take control of an area, likely in Italy, to purge it of heretics. The proposal was ideal, and other members of the family from Normandy and Flanders had already begun to settle in southern Italy and were in the process of conquering Sicily from the Muslims. While we have no direct knowledge of whether Sweyn's son ultimately became a papal military commander, the pope's offer alone illuminates how central Sweyn was to the fabric of the European political scene in his time.

Therefore, it was also natural for Sweyn to become a vassal for Saint Peter, swear a special oath to support the pope, and as an extension also support the papal reform movements in the latter half of the 1000s. Some leaders actually donated their kingdoms to the pope, regaining it from him as a fief. Others merely agreed to support the pope financially and, if necessary, militarily (Riley-Smith 1997). Sweyn became part of a network that included kings and great princes throughout Western Europe, with most participants located in the periphery around the German empire. Sweyn's son Canute IV the Holy married Edel of Flanders, the daughter of Count Robert I of Flanders, another vassal of St. Peter. Thus, Sweyn Estridsson and Canute IV strengthened the Danish inheritance claim to England against William the Conqueror. More importantly, they built contacts with a very large variety of princes who wielded power in European politics: their contacts included for example all of the great leaders of the First Crusade.

The last half of the 1000s was characterized by the extension and consolidation of the Danish royal family's European network, which provided special opportunities and commitments in its aftermath. The period was also marked by the intensive expansion of a shared church structure and the spread of collective European ideas on religion, war, and martyrdom. In the long term, it was also crucial that there was a shift in orientation from west to east at this time: in the future, the Danish empire expanded along the Baltic Sea. At the end of the 1000s comes a a description of Denmark's division, summarizing it all in one simple sentence: "It is a great kingdom, that is very scattered" (Adam 1876, 4:1). At this point, the Danish empire consisted of Jutland with Schleswig as the southernmost diocese seat, Funen, Sealand, Scania and Halland. In addition, it included a number of islands: Samsø, Læsø, Lolland, Ærø, Møn and Falster. Bornholm, another island, is located far out in the Baltic Sea. It is summarized that the above-listed countries are under the Danish king and are both large and populous.

References

Adam. 1876. *Adami Gesta Hammaburgensis ecclesiae pontificum*, ed. J.M. Lappenberg. Hannover: Hahn.
Albrectsen, Esben. 2000. Dannevirke. Det ældste monument over dansk sikkerhedspolitik. In *Danmark i syv sind. Tusind års dansk udenrigspolitik*, ed. Carsten Due-Nielsen et al., 9–17. Copenhagen: Gyldendal.
Alcuin. 1873. Vita sancti Willibrordi. In *Monumenta Alcuiniana*, ed. Wilhelm Wattenbach and Ph. Jaffé, 39–61. Berlin: Weidemann. English translation by A. Grieve. 1923. Willibrord, Missionary in the Netherlands, 691–793. London: Society for the Propagation of the Gospel in Foreign Parts.
Beowulf: A Verse Translation. 1973. Trans. Michael J. Alexander. Harmondsworth: Penguin.
Bjerg, Line, et al. (eds.). 2013. *From Goths to Varangians: Communication and Cultural Exchange Between the Baltic and the Black Sea*. Aarhus: University Press.
Bolton, Timothy. 2017. *Cnut the Great*. New Haven: Yale University Press.
Brink, Stefan, and T. Douglas Price. 2008. *The Viking World*. London: Routledge.
Encomium Emmae Reginae. 1949. Ed. Alistair Campbell. London: Royal Historical Society.
Forte, Angelo, et al. 2005. *Viking Empires*. Cambridge: University Press.
Fouracre, Paul. 2000. *The Age of Charles Martel*. London: Routledge.
Frank, Roberta. 2018. A Taste for Knottiness: Skaldic Art at Cnut's Court. *Anglo-Saxon England* 47: 197–217.
Halsall, Guy. 2007. *Barbarian Migrations and the Roman West, 376–568*. Cambridge: University Press.
Heather, Peter. 2010. *Empires and Barbarians: The Fall of Rome and the Birth of Europe*. Oxford: University Press.
Jensen, Jørgen. 2001–2004. *Danmarks Oldtid*, vol. 1–4. Copenhagen: Gyldendal.
Jensen, Kurt Villads. 2017. *Crusading at the Edges of Europe: Denmark and Portugal c. 1000 – c. 1250*. London: Routledge.
Myhre, Bjørn. 2003. The Iron Age. In *The Cambridge History of Scandinavia*, vol. 1, ed. K. Helle, 60–93. Cambridge: Cambridge University Press.
Price, T. Douglas. 2015. *Ancient Scandinavia: An Archaeological History from the First Humans to the Vikings*. Oxford: University Press.
Randsborg, Klavs. 2008. King's Jelling. Gorm & Thyra's Palace, Harald's Monument & Grave – Svend's Cathedral. *Acta Archaeologica* 79: 1–23.
Riley-Smith, Jonathan. 1997. *The First Crusaders, 1095–1131*. Cambridge: Cambridge University Press.
Saxo Grammaticus. 2015. *Gesta Danorum: The History of the Danes*, vol. 1–2, ed. Karsten Friis-Jensen, trans. Peter Fisher. Oxford: Clarendon Press.
Thietmar of Merseburg. 1935. *Die Chronik des Bischofs Thietmar von Merseburg und ihre Korveier Überarbeitung. Thietmari Merseburgensis episcopi chronicon*, ed. Robert Holtzmann. Berlin: Weidmannsche Verlagsbuchhandlung.
Weibull, Lauritz. 1948–49. Tyre Danmarkr bot. In *Nordisk historia: forskningar och undersökningar*, vol. 1–3, vol. 1, 225–243. Stockholm. Natur och kultur [article first published in 1913].
Widukind. 1882. *Widukindi Rerum gestarum saxonicarum libri tres*, ed. Georg Waitz. Hannover: Hahn.

CHAPTER 4

Crusade Empires in the Baltic

With the conquest of Jerusalem on July 17, 1099, something qualitatively novel happened in world history (in general, see Bysted et al. 2012; Jensen 2017). The Crusaders had done what no one had ever done before; they had recaptured the Holy City from the pagans, as was formulated at the time. Knowledge of Islam was still scarce or non existent in Western Europe. The Crusade created a new perception of war, the goals of warfare, and it created a number of new institutions and political instruments that would have an impact on European history for the next several hundred years. The crusades were rapidly transplanted to areas beyond the Middle East, and alliances were established of whether they served the crusades.

The history leading up to the Crusades had a long record. Considerations of mission and just war were well-established. The novelty of these new developments was that war in itself could now be argued to serve a just purpose. In the past, there had always been misgivings on the part of the Church by sanctioning even the most just of wars, and the soldiers had to make penitence after the battle to atone for the sin that they had killed other humans. Now they could do so with clear conscience and even achieve spiritual benefactions and forgiveness of sins if they fought in the crusade. In short, European warlords could continue to do what they were best at—fight and kill—but they could now do so with good conscience in the eyes of the Church. The crusades strengthened the power of the popes, who were the ultimate authorization behind all crusades, but they also opened up opportunities for new conflicts between popes and emperors. Until the middle of the eleventh century, popes had been heavily dependent on lay rulers, especially the German-Roman emperor, who occasionally installed their own popes. After the mid-1000s, a movement of reform began within the church, which aimed, among other things, to make Saint Peter's successor independent of the emperor and preferably render him superior to the emperor. This was done in collaboration with the large monastic orders, particularly the order of Cluny, who built a large and wide-reaching network of papal vassals (Riley-Smith 1997). A decisive figure throughout this development was Gregor VII, Sweyn Estridsson's close contact. The time was ripe for reform when Pope Urban II in 1095 gave his famous sermon in Clermont in southern France, which received a passionate and perhaps unexpected response when the congregation shouted "God wills it. God commands it." Hundreds of thousands of Western Europeans went to Jerusalem the next spring, coming from all over the world. "They were like a swarm of locusts, warmed by the rays of faith, and their footsteps caused the earth to shake," a contemporary observer wrote (Guibert 1996, 2:10).

By this time Sweyn Estridsson had long passed, but one of his sons, also called Sweyn, participated in the crusades with an army of allegedly 1500 knights. They all perished at the Turks' arrows on the Anatolian High Plains in the summer of 1097. The young Sweyn's fiancé, Florina, also perished. She was the daughter of the Duke of Burgundy, who was also a Saint Peter's vassal. Rumors of young Sweyn's death spread throughout all of Europe and became a part of the extensive literature on the Crusades that emerged during the twelfth century.

The narrative was later expanded, and it was said that the sword of Sweyn was picked up and wielded by another crusader, and that it was him who became the first crusader to set foot on the wall of Jerusalem two years later. The worship of the heroic Sweyn reached new heights when he became the hero of the Italian poet Torquato Tasso's great poem "Jerusalem Delivered," dated 1581. Later Danish kings, such as Christian IV in the seventeenth century, charged historians to gather information about the crusader, and his heroic death was depicted on magnificent paintings. In the nineteenth century, with the development of modern source critique, the narrative was rejected as fiction. However, there are actually sound sources which prove not only that young Sweyn actually participated in the First Crusade, but that he did so as part of an agreement negotiated by Gottfried von Bouillon, one of the great leaders of the crusade and later the first regent of the Kingdom of Jerusalem. With Sweyn Estridsson's membership in the network of papal vassals, it would have been peculiar if there had not been Danish participation in the crusade. It was immediately followed up. The Kingdom of Jerusalem suffered from permanent shortages of men, as most of the Crusaders simply returned home once the city was conquered. Therefore, the efforts to persuade fighters take up arms to carry the cross and leave home to protect Jerusalem against Muslim counterattacks continued. The first king who accepted this invitation was Erik I the Good of Denmark, who traveled to Jerusalem with a fleet and with his queen, Bodil. Erik himself died en route on Cyprus in 1103, but Bodil and the remaining army arrived. Bodil also died on the Mount of Olives, but the many warriors must have been a welcome reinforcement for King Baldwin of Jerusalem, who was in dire need of backup at the time.

Thereafter a steady stream of Danish crusaders flowed to the Middle East, as far as we can judge from sparse sources. That these crusaders actually were many in number, is suddenly confirmed in one single event. When the Church of the Nativity in Bethlehem was renovated by the crusaders, probably in the 1120s, the previous saints' icons on the 44 pillars were restored, and only a couple of new saints were added: Saint Olaf of Norway and Saint Canute IV of Denmark. The two gained a prominent position and were the first saint images seen when entering Christianity's second holiest church (Ekroll 2021). The links to the Jerusalem Crusade became an important landmark for later Danish politics. Beyond this, the concept of crusades also had a direct influence on the design of the Danish empire by shifting attention to the Baltic Sea region (Fig. 4.1).

In 1108, the Archbishop of Magdeburg sent a letter to princes in Northern Germany and Flanders, urging them to fight against the pagan Slavic peoples who threatened Magdeburg (Constable 1999). He hellishly portrayed the pagan atrocities and their abhorrent rituals of slaughtering Christians and collecting their blood in large vessels on the pagan altars, mirroring the descriptions from Pope Urban II in Clermont. He then promised the participants in this war that they would receive the same remission of sins as those who went to Jerusalem, for their effort to fight for "our Jerusalem" in the north. Moreover, they could gain new lands and become rich. The Bishop's letter ended by saying that the Danish King Niels had already promised a mighty army of Danish fighters towards this effort. We do not know whether Niels actually participated in this war, but the letter clearly shows that the crusades had already become the backdrop for wars in the Baltic Sea, and that it offered a framework for an alliance among Christian princes. The letter also highlighted that Danish kings were core participants from the start.

Already before he went on crusade to the Holy Land, King Erik I the Good had fought bravely against the Wends on the other side of the Baltic Sea to convert them to Christianity, if we are to believe the contemporary bardic poems about him: "Beautiful ship on the early spring / The Wends' Destroyer armed / East from Garda, on the hollow / Wave, he spurred the mount of the sea" (quoted in Bysted et al. 2012). It was on his way home from the Garda kingdom, from Byzantium specifically, where Erik had served the emperor and became famous for his strength and height, his memory, and for the many languages he had learned in his youth. It was on his way home from the Garda kingdom, from Byzantium, where Erik had served with the emperor and was famous for his height and strength, for his memory and for the many languages he had learned in his youth. Three times Erik waged war against the Wends and he ultimately conquered Rügen, making the island pay tribute. When Erik led a crusade to the Holy Land, the ruling of the whole of Sealand and Rügen was left to Skjalm Hvide, who had a special interest in the area. A few years earlier, Skjalm's brother Aute had been killed by the Wends when he

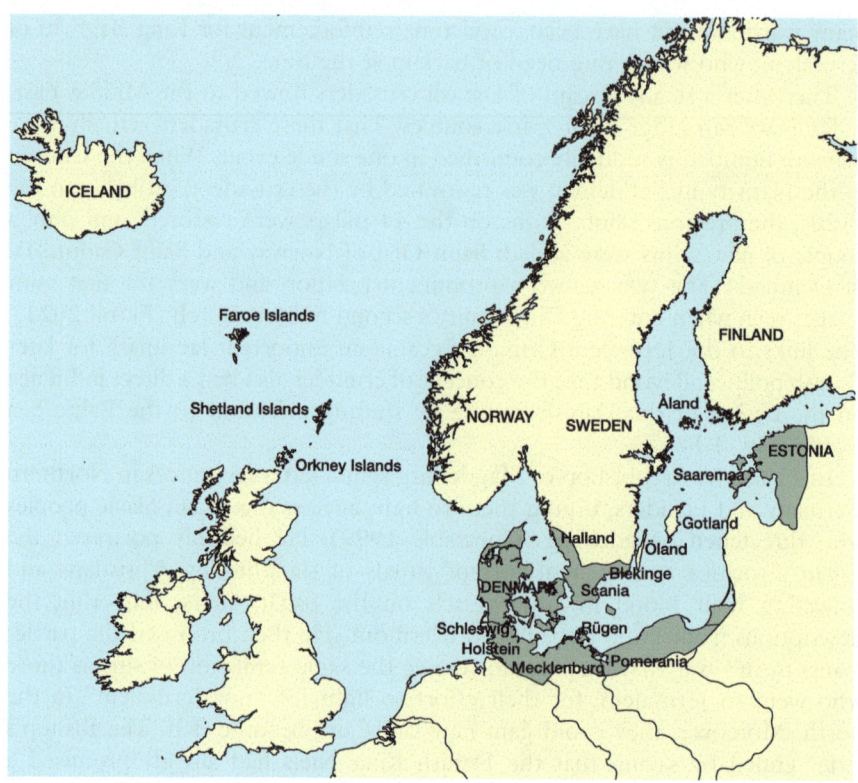

Fig. 4.1 From around 1100, the Danish empire changed its main orientation from west to east. It was still centered around an ocean, but now the Baltic Sea instead of the North Sea. The change may perhaps have been ideological. With the beginning of the crusading movement and the conquest of Jerusalem in 1099, it was increasingly felt more justifiable to fight pagans in the Baltic than Christians in England. The expansion in the Baltic was directed against important pagan cult sites as Arkona which was conquered and destroyed in 1168. In the 1180s, Danish rulers completed the conquest in Mecklenburg and ruled now an area stretching from Holstein in the west to Pomerania in east. With the great technological developments around 1200 and new, larger ships it became possible to extend the range of military expeditions as far as to Estonia which was conquered in 1219. Five years earlier, the German-Roman emperor had acknowledged Danish claim to all land north of the River Elbe. Large parts of the Northern German possessions were lost when King Valdemar II was imprisoned by one of his vassals in 1223, but enough was left to secure Danish control and connections throughout the Baltic all the way to Estonia

moved from Sealand to the island of Falster, and Skjalm had—together with Erik—planned a revenge expedition to Julin. The city was forced to deliver the perpetrators, who were tied to poles and had their bowels cut out, with the intestines pulled out and wound up on sticks until they expired in great torment. "It was a sad sight, but useful to the people," Saxo commented (Saxo 2015, 12.4.2), thus expressing one of the general concepts of the Middle Ages: that harsh mutilation punishments were necessary as general deterrent measures, to scare others from committing similar crimes. The strong castle of Julin was thus defeated, and Rügen had been conquered. But the island's Wendish population soon became independent again and became the subject of later Danish crusades in the twelfth century.

Around the same time as Erik the Good's conquest of Rügen, the Wendish population was also attacked from the west by Henry. As a baby, his mother had fled with him back to his father, Sweyn Estridsen, when her husband, Gotskalk, perished during the great Wendish rebellion of 1066. Now Henry Gotskalksen was grown, and in the first half of the 1090s he was supported by a Danish navy for a successful reclaiming of his father's land around the river Trave, where he began to build a strong castle at Old Lübeck. There he served as ruler for over thirty years, formally as a vassal of the Danish king, effectively with a very high degree of independence to wage wars and expand his territory to the east into the area of the Wendish Obotrites. When he died in 1127, his influence reached all the way to the mainland near Rügen. Henry was one of the first great frontier lords in the Danish empire, and the territory he conquered would remain a part of the empire for a very long time, only surviving due to a delicate balance between neighboring powers.

One of Henry's first major opponents was his cousin Canute Lavard, the son of Erik I the Good. When news of Erik's death in Cyprus reached Denmark, his brother Niels was elected king, while his son Canute became Duke of Schleswig. It is the first indication that Schleswig and Southern Jutland had a special status within the empire, but the concept of delegating choice areas to be ruled by members of the royal family was quite traditional. Erik the Good had been earl of Sealand before he became king, and his grandfather, Ulf, had ruled the whole of Denmark for Canute the Great while he was in England. Canute Lavard's position in Schleswig as vassal of the Danish king was thus not in itself unusual, but it is unique because he was also simultaneously the vassal of Duke Lothair of Supplinburg, the later German king with whom Canute had stayed. He was thus a subject of both the Danish and German rulers. Another complicating factor was that Canute Lavard also concurrently formed an alliance between equals, a union of friendship, with Duke Vartislav of Pomerania, who ruled on the other side of Henry's country. Vartislav thus gained support against his master, King Boleslaw III Wrymouth of Poland. But on the other side of Poland, Canute Lavard made yet another alliance by marrying Ingeborg of Kiev.

Considered together, these alliances show how immensely complicated and ambiguous it was to operate politically within an empire, where a dominion could be put together from vastly different territories, and where rulers effortlessly shifted from one empire to another. Canute Lavard was deployed by Lothair as king of the Wendish Obotrites when Henry died in 1127. Canute and his lineage could have continued as dukes and kings in the area and have had a career similar to that of the Earl of Brandenburg or the later Duke Henry The Lion of Saxony. Canute Lavard could also have claimed the power in Kiev for himself or for his son, Vladimir, who was raised by his grandfather Mistislav Vladimirovich of Kiev and Novgorod. Incidentally, Mistislav's mother was Gyda, daughter of Harald Hardrada, who died at Stamford Bridge in 1066. With a little good will, Canute Lavard also had some sort of inheritance claim to England through his wife. Ultimately, Canute's son instead became king of Denmark—later considered one of the greatest Danish kings at that—and changed his name from Vladimir to Valdemar. But this fate was certainly not guaranteed at birth, and it was a long and winding road for Valdemar.

From Schleswig, Canute Lavard began a series of looting and targeted crusades to the east, which were followed by church building and fortifications. At one point he blocked the entire Slien Fjord with two fortresses on each side, using wooden barrels and iron chains that could be stretched out across the fjord and prevent any ship from reaching Schleswig. In Oldenburg and Jurisburg, Canute built strong fortresses with central towers in stone, a modern design in comparison to the former palisade castles without a tower. Around 1130, the island of Fehmarn was conquered. The land was distributed among the king's noblemen, and eventually the island was colonized by Danish peasants who settled in new villages, which followed a very uniform pattern. Later Fehmarn became a disputed island between Danish and German powers, but it retained its integrated Danish-Slavic character for a long time.

At the same time as Canute Lavard's expansion along the Slavic Baltic cost, King Niels and his son Magnus tried to build an alliance network that could compete with that of Canute's. A marriage was made between Magnus and Richiza, the daughter of King Boleslaw of Poland, a joint crusade was also agreed among Niels, Boleslaw and the Norwegian King Sigurd Jorsalfar, who had undertaken a famous expedition to the Holy Land around 1110. In 1123 a joint crusade commenced against the apostates of Småland, who had taken up again sacrificing to the pagan gods. However, the crusade crumbled when the Danes grew tired of waiting for the Norwegians to arrive, and returned home. By the time Sigurd finally arrived, he was furious from being snubbed by the Danes, and as revenge plundered Scania, around Lund, and all the way to the city of Kalmar. He seized 1500 cattle and baptized many young children. Meanwhile, Magnus responded by stealing the large Thor's hammer in copper that the pagans housed in their temple on an island. He was later remembered in the region as "the robber of the heavenly spoils" (Saxo 2015, 13:5:5). Perhaps Magnus had plans to expand the Danish kingdom further into Sweden. He inherited the royal title over West Gothland (Västergötland) through his mother, Queen Margrethe Fredkulla, after his grandfather in the mid-1120s.

However, these plans were halted on January 7, 1131, when Magnus killed Canute Lavard in Haraldsted Forest, just north of Ringsted on Zealand. Medieval sources indicate different motives for the murder—fear that Canute would try to become King Niels' successor instead of Magnus, or that he was too closely associated with Emperor Lothair and had failed in upholding his duties as a Danish duke. Regardless, the consequences are clear enough. Lothair demanded revenge for the killing of his vassal and attacked Denmark, and in 1134 Magnus had to pay tribute to Lothair and accept to keep Denmark as fief for the German emperor. At the same time, Canute Lavard's brother Erik II Emune revolted and was elected king, first in Scania and then in Jutland, which is a clear demonstration of the unique structure of the Danish medieval empire. It consisted of a number of countries that had previously been independent and could still operate self-sufficiently, for example by choosing their own king. In 1134, these two parties collided at the Battle of Fotevik in Scania. Erik II's nephew David participated with a contingent of 300 German knights, which was likely crucial to the outcome of the extremely bloody battle. Four bishops and 60 other clergy were killed and Magnus himself perished. King Niels fled to Jutland and ended up seeking refuge in Schleswig. Oddly enough—for Schleswig had been Canute Lavard's headquarters—and the townspeople of Schleswig ultimately killed Niels on June 25, opening the city gates to Erik II.

In a system where the succession to the throne admittedly runs in certain family lines, but where the individual's position depends so much on personal political luck and power, a new ruler needs to pay close attention to any possible rivals. One of Erik II's first acts was to kill his brother Harald and then eight of his eleven sons, who were buried in unconsecrated ground. Two other sons were already dead, and only one escaped in disguise to Sweden. Erik's solution was not typical among Danish rulers of the Middle Ages, but neither was it an unfamiliar concept. A remarkably large number of members of the family were killed, blinded, castrated, or otherwise removed from the making plays for the king's throne. Erik II attempted in vain to conquer the southern part of Norway. However, he succeeded in conquering Rügen in 1135 and persuaded the pagans, by demonstrating his military power, to convert to Christianity. Later they again renounced the faith, but for the future Danish crusaders it was of immense importance that they had actually been baptized. It placed them in a whole new category, as apostates and not merely as pagans. The difference was, according to the medieval theories of war, that as a Christian one must defend himself against the assaults of the pagans, but not attack them or force them to become Christians. Apostates, on the other hand, must immediately face the choice between baptism and death and crusaders are allowed by any means to force the apostates "to return to the truth" they consciously and willingly had rejected. Erik's conquest was thus important, and it was marked by the rich endowment of a large monastery in Ringsted, which was to form the framework for the saintly cult that rapidly emerged near the place where his "beloved brother Canute had been so cruelly murdered."

In his first *vita*, his saintly biography, Canute was portrayed as an avid crusader who had spread the faith among pagan worshipers. In the same year it was written, in 1135, the magnate Peder Bodilsen and his powerful family, together with Archbishop Eskild, founded a monastery in the city of Naestved, only some 25 kilometers south of Ringsted. This monastery was consecrated to his namesake St. Peder and endowed with unusual large gifts in landed property, also all the way down to the southern tip of Falster, which must still have been a mission area at the time. Peder Bodilsen had previously noted himself as an ardent and stern reformer of church life, and he may well have been a vassal of Saint Peter and swore allegiance to the pope. This is pure guesswork, but it is ultimately certain that Peder and his family were actively involved in the crusades on the other side of the Baltic.

Erik II's legacy was mixed. The English monk, whom he had charged with writing his brother's biography, began the narrative by praising him: "Hail to you king, and grant that your imperial dignity, your kingdom, your imperial power, your scepter, your crown and your power be endless" (Vitae sanctorum danorum 1908–12, 189). The contemporary Roskilde Chronicle writes boldly that "in all things he was like Caesar, he overcame every difficulty, he would have no one beside him and no one above him, he was overpowering, bloated and mighty with malice" (Chronicon roskildense 1970, 31). Perhaps the most interesting element of this assessment, is simply that of the general impression: that the Danish king was, quite naturally, compared to an emperor.

The Conquest of Rügen

On Christmas Day 1144, the Christian Principality of Edessa was lost to Sultan Zenghi of Mosul. It was the first major defeat in the Latin Middle East, and when the news reached Western Europe, it was met with despair and determination. Something had to be done, and preparations were underway for a new crusade just as large as the first (in general, see Phillips 2007). An absolutely crucial force in this effort was Bernard of Clairvaux, abbot of the wide-reaching Cistercian order. Bernhard was a gifted speaker and traveled throughout northern Europe on a preaching mission, and it was also he who initially allowed Northern German princes to fight the pagan Slavic peoples instead of traveling to Edessa. He rationalized this on the theological grounds that the devil attacked Christianity on all fronts simultaneously, and that it was just as important to defend themselves in the north as it was in the south. This cumulatively led to the so-called Second Crusade in 1147, which was one crusade but executed on many fronts, as it was described by contemporaries. Crusades were led against Damascus, against several places in the Iberian Peninsula, and in the Baltic Sea.

In 1146, Cardinal Ubaldus hosted a church meeting in Odense to preach crusade and drum up support (Bysted et al. 2012; Jensen 2017). The reaction must have amazed him, because King Erik III Lamb of Denmark immediately abdicated and entered a monastery, thus becoming the first and so far the only Danish king to voluntarily surrender the throne. He also died shortly afterwards and presumably resigned due to illness. He was followed by Sweyn III, who was later nicknamed Sweyn Grathe. Grathe was chosen by the Sealanders, but the people of Jutland concurrently chose Canute, the son of Magnus (Nilsson) (who had killed Canute Lavard). The third individual to partake in the battle for the throne was Canute Lavard's son, Valdemar, who was now about 15 years old. The struggle developed into an eleven year war between Sweyn III, Canute, and Valdemar, and is often portrayed as a civil war. It is probably more accurate to see the conflict as formerly independent countries who now seized the opportunity to choose their own king. Conversely, these kings sought to expand their own power and unite the kingdoms over which their predecessors had ruled. During this same time period, several kings fought for power in Norway and Sweden as well.

The bloody wars in Denmark give a rare insight to the rulers' paths, both physically and mentally, to power within the empire. Sweyn III began his king's reign by working with Valdemar to declare Canute Lavard a saint and place his bones as relics upon the high altar in Ringsted. It was not recognized by Archbishop Eskild because it was a private canonization without the pope's acceptance, but it does show that Valdemar would henceforth use his father's miracles as an argument to support his own position as king. After that, Keld of Viborg, who had previously sought the pope for permission to mission and become a martyr among the pagan Wends, mediated between Sweyn and Canute by having them participate in a joint crusade against the Wendish Dobin, near present-day Rostock. They participated because the pope promised that if they fell, their souls would be in heaven before their blood cooled on the earth (Knytlingesaga 1919–25, 108). At Dobin, they met with a Saxon cavalry, and succeeded in occupying the city, baptizing the inhabitants and forcing them to free their Christian slaves. Then, according to Saxo, the Danish army withdrew because Sweyn and Canute did not trust each other. According to his contemporary, German historian Helmold of Bosau, retreat was because "the Danes are mighty warriors at home, but completely useless in real battle" (Helmold 1868, 65).

Once returned home, the wars continued, and around 1150 both Sweyn III and Canute sought help from King Conrad III of Germany, whom they respectfully referred to as emperor, even though he was not. In return for his support, they offered to participate in his crusade against the pagans. Although these efforts were for naught, when Conrad died two years later both the two kings met up with his successor, Fredrick I Barbarossa. Fredrick deposed Sweyn as king and granted Canute some lands and Valdemar with others, including the duchy of Schleswig, which had belonged to Valdemar's father. Everyone swore allegiance to Barbarossa.

The Danish Empire was both de facto and de jure subject to the German emperor. However, this system did not bring peace, and for the next five years the fortunes of war shifted back and forth, and all the peripheral areas of the Danish empire were utilized. Sweyn had to flee first to Sweden and then to Russia, allegedly Kiev, from which he returned with a mercenary army, which also included Saxons. Later on, Canute had to flee to Frisia, and Sweyn sailed an entire fleet to Schleswig and pulled the ships more than 10 kilometers over land to Hollingstedt, and then he ravaged Frisia with fire. At one point, Sweyn allied himself with the pagan Wendish king Niklot, and together they conquered Fünen. Valdemar would eventually ally himself with Niklot's son Pribislav and offered his daughter as a covenant to their alliance and Lolland as fief. Pribislav was Christian and present in Valdemar's camp when Danish fighters triumphantly returned with his father's head on a javelin.

After a few years, Valdemar switched sides and decided to support Canute. To seal the alliance he married Canute's half-sister Sophia of Kiev. It's important to remember that Canute was also the son of the same Magnus who had killed Valdemar's father Canute Lavard, and his change in alliance was hard to swallow for writers of his time. It was explained by her outstanding beauty which had totally betaken Valdemar. Hardly convincing, Sophia was a young girl only at that time. But Valdemar's change of ally highlights that moral actions were little conducive to a political career at the time, and flexibility was necessary if one were to survive the changeable political system of the Danish Empire in the eleventh century. In 1157, the three parties agreed to divide Denmark among themselves. Valdemar received Jutland, Canute Sealand, and Sweyn III Scania. The agreement was celebrated with a big party in Roskilde, which Canute hosted. In the darkness of the evening events took a dramatic turn, earning it the name of "The Blood Feast in Roskilde." Many perished, and Canute lay dead with his head split in two, while Valdemar fled with a severely wounded thigh. We only know the details of that night from Valdemar's devoted history writer Saxo, and according to him, the blame lay with Sweyn III. But the killing of Canute was clearly in Valdemar's favor. Later that year Sweyn was defeated by Valdemar in the Battle of Grathe Heath in Jutland and killed by local peasants. Valdemar was now sole ruler.

Until his death 25 years later, Valdemar led crusades on the other side of the Baltic Sea. The war fleets likely sailed every summer, with a frequency which continued under subsequent kings. Only in 1213 was it written in the annals: "In this year there was no crusade in Denmark" (DMA 1980, 78). This was so unusual that it was mentioned as a separate event. Valdemar's initial goal was the island of Rügen, and in 1168 all efforts were concentrated on this difficult task. Trebuchets were installed to fire upon the strong fortress of Arkona on the northern coast of Rügen, a close ring of besiegers cut off the inhabitants from outside reinforcements, and finally the city of Arkona fell. The pagan temple was demolished and the four-headed wooden statue of the idol Svantevit was chopped into firewood and used to boil soup for the army. These events were carried out on June 15, the day of Saint Vitus, in order for the saint to take revenge on the people of Rügen who had distorted his name into that of Svantevit and begun venerating him and had, as Saxo expressed it, "abandoned the true faith." In Slavic languages, Saint Vitus actually becomes "Svantevit."

The Danish expansion had along the way been supported by Duke Henry the Lion of Saxony. It was mostly a coincidence that he did not participate in the final conquest and thus did not get a share in the political power over the island of Rügen, to his great regret. On the other hand, Valdemar's Danish army had been supplemented by troops from the Pomeranian princes, Kazimir and Bugislav, whom if choosing between Henry the Lion and Valdemar usually had preferred the Danish king as lord.

Immediately following the conquest, the new land needed to be ensured a firmer and more permanent attachment to the empire, both politically and ideologically. Rügen was purged of pagan idols and twelve new churches were built and supplied with priests and income. The large lands that had previously belonged to pagan temples were now to be used to provide for Christian churches. In Arkona, the church was built using timber from the wartime trebuchets or catapults, meaning that the wood that had previously killed the bodies of Rügen's people, could now save their souls. This symbology was perhaps also intended to remind the new churchgoers of who held the true power. New Cistercian monasteries were founded on the mainland in the still pagan Western Pomerania and Pomerania, to provide missionaries and priests to new Christians and to future crusaders. Furthermore, their mere presence was supposed to render the area Christian. Sometimes it was perceived very literally: the Cistercian monks actually went around and cut large crosses into the ancient sacred oak trees (Jensen 2009). A type of symbolic baptism of the trees. Gradually the Cistercian monasteries in the rich West Pomerania developed into important stud farms which were highly sought after for breeding expensive war horses that were highly in demand. However, before this point, the monasteries were counter attacked by pagans and burned down, resulting in repeatedly relocation of the monasteries and an exposed life until complete Christian control of the area was re-established.

Direct political control over Rügen was almost immediately passed to a local member of one of the established princely houses, Jarimar I, who converted to Christianity. Danish colonies were apparently never established in the area, at least not to any large degree, and only a few place names are in the Danish language. King Valdemar conquered the city of Wolgast in 1164 and tried to transform it into a strong military border town to be ruled by Bishop Absalon of Roskilde and Bishop Sweyn of Aarhus, along with the King's cousin Buris Henriksen and populated by heavily armed Danish colonists. It was not a success. Only the Sealanders dared move into the newly conquered territory—those from Jutland refused—and the plan was abandoned.

There were major economic benefits associated with the conquest, but apparently the ultimate goal was not to acquire new land for Danish colonies, as opposed to the simultaneous German expansion into the same region with a massive breaking of new land with the help of German-speaking immigrants, sometimes from as far away as Flanders. Without a direct colonization, whatever the reason for its absence be, the most effective way for Valdemar to bring an area under control was to ally himself with local princes such as Jarimar I on Rügen. Jarimar knew the area, but a further advantage was that Valdemar gained access to his network. Later, Jarimar's daughter married the great Polish prince Wladyslaw III Spindleshanks (Laskonogi), who in the first decade of the thirteenth century was to work with Valdemar's son Valdemar II the Victorious on the further expansion along the coast of the Baltic Sea. An important element of the new arrangement of Rügen was, of course, that the new members of the Danish empire would also need to provide forces towards the pursuit of the ongoing crusades.

The Danish Empire was emerging as an important power. Arkona, Northern Europe's strongest pagan fortress, was finally conquered and a delegation was sent to the pope with the good news. At the same time, the Holy Land also sent a message to the pope regarding the severe pressure that Jerusalem was facing. This diplomatic delegation continued to France and England, where it succeeded in mediating peace between the two powers, and a large joint crusade was agreed upon for the summer of 1171. Its intent was probably to repeat the 1147 maneuver of waging holy war on many fronts, and Valdemar must have been involved in the preparations of it. The majority of these plans, however, had to be abandoned when King Henry II of England in Christmas 1170 ordered some of his trusted men to kill the Archbishop of Canterbury, Thomas Beckett. Henry was banned from participating in a crusade, and so the French king pulled out of the agreement as well. But Henry the Lion of Saxony traveled all the way to the Middle East, and Valdemar launched an attack on Pomerania. In September of that year, Pope Alexander III sent letters to rulers and personalities throughout Scandinavia, approving the crusade into the eastern Baltic, all the way to Finland.

The close link between the conquest of Rügen and the crusade efforts is shown by two things. First, the pope now acknowledged Valdemar's father, Canute Lavard, as a true saint. He had demonstrated his sacred power by the fact that his son had succeeded in defeating paganism. In a grand ceremony in Ringsted, Canute Lavard was solemnly canonized on June 25, 1170, and in the long liturgy written for the occasion, he is portrayed as a true and avid crusader (The Offices 2010). The liturgy is preserved to this day in a manuscript with notes so that one can even reconstruct the music with great precision. Secondly, Valdemar crowned his son, the young Canute VI, on the same occasion. In doing so, he sought to secure the inheritance of his lineage by having the chiefs swear allegiance to Canute VI: this may have been especially necessary if Valdemar were on his way to a large, far-reaching crusade. Several other kings in Western Europe let their sons be declared king and had them also crowned that same summer. Henry II of England had crowned the Young Henry of England, Afonso of Portugal his son Sancho, and Frederik Barbarossa had his son Henry (VI) crowned the year before. This political maneuver was clearly quite common at the time, and was directly connected to the continuing crusades.

During the latter half of the twelfth century, there appeared to be rapid technological developments which enabled and intensified further expansion. The longships became bigger, and more broad-bowed vessels with a greater load capacity were developed. In southern Jutland, the shipyards cleared large areas of forest, and the timber now had to be imported from the northern German and Wendish regions. The king made money on the ships as an investor and had both commercial and military interests in shipping ventures. At the larger European level, there was also a significant change from small to larger ships, which enabled the crusaders to sail to the Holy Land instead of traveling on foot all the way through Europe. Special carriers were developed for horses so that they could hang and sway to the movement of the waves and survive the long voyage instead of standing in narrow boxes in the bottom of the ships and kicking, each other or the wooden boxes. Aqueducts and wells were built on the piers in the main ports along the coast all the way through the Mediterranean, so that the crucial water replenishment activities now took only a fraction of the time it had done in the past. Similar types of developments took place in the Danish Empire and were an important prerequisite for continuing the crusades into more remote areas in the Baltic Sea area. At the same time, the management of the Danish fleet was reorganized, and now required that a quarter of the fleet be permanently mobilized throughout the sailing season.

When Valdemar died in 1182, he was succeeded by his son Canute VI, who was no less active as a crusader than his father. The expansion was focused along two vectors, east from Rügen and east from Schleswig, where Canute's brother Valdemar the Conqueror ruled as Duke. Around 1187, the Danish dominion in the area between Schleswig and Rügen was so strong that Canute adopted the title of "the king of the Wends," which later Danish kings maintained until 1972. The Danish empire grew year by year for almost half a century, from Rügen's conquest in 1168–1223. The inhabitants of the conquered territories had belonged to different rulers of different families, they spoke different dialects and even languages from completely different language families with little or nothing in common regarding structure, grammar, and vocabulary: Germanic, Slavic, and Finnish-Ugrian languages. In addition to practical organizations to keep the great kingdom together, a new and grand imperial ideology was crucial to address the state of new things.

This new ideological framework was provided by two historians, Sven Aggesen, who wrote ca. 1185, and Saxo, who may have written a bit later. First, the emphasis was on the awe-inspiring age of the empire. Sven Aggesen detailed the "Court Law," which regulated the relationship among the king's special elite warriors, and which Sven estimated dated back to Canute the Great in the first half of the 1000s (Sven Aggesen 1992). Back then, the Danish kingdom stretched from Thule in the north to the Greek empire in the east, and Canute ruled over many different peoples, Sweyn explained, all of whom would send their young sons to the king to serve in his curia, his court. They each brought their own customs, and therefore strict laws were needed to ensure that they did not disagree and began fighting among each other. They should work together, as members of one body, governed by the ruler, exactly as the body is governed by the head. Sven attributes this phenomenon to Canute the Great's time, but in reality, it fits brilliantly in his own time under Canute VI. He exaggerated the scale of the empire, but he accurately described the core problem of an empire: that it consists of many different peoples.

Saxo traces the history of the empire much further back in time, accentuating that it had always been Danish. Saxo emphatically emphasized that the first kings, Dan and Angel, had not immigrated from outside of Denmark, which was unique. Many other great works of history in the high middle ages began their narrative by telling how a people or ruler immigrated to and created a new land. Even the city of Rome was founded by Aeneas when he traveled around after the conquest of Troy with the Greek house gods, according to Vergil's great epos written in the first decades BCE. Saxo's work was clearly an attempt to trump Vergil and make the Danish empire older and better than the Roman one. The comparison continues throughout Saxo's work: in the time of Emperor Augustus when Christ was born, King Frodi ruled Denmark, and at that time a gold ring could safely be left on the road, no one would think of stealing it. There was peace in Denmark, just as there was peace in the Roman Empire under the rule of Augustus, and Frodi was nicknamed Fredegod, which probably means "the giver of peace." Peace and justice are the pervasive themes described by Saxo, and it gives his presentation a completely different sense of coherence than if he had chosen Christianity as the main unifying theme of the empire. Now he could present the enterprise or the obligation of the Danish empire as something much more fundamental, stretching back through the countless generations before the conversion to Christianity. It has always been the job of the Danes to teach their neighbors peace and justice, and the neighbors had always been troubled and aggressive, initiating war against the Danish empire. The whole line of thinking is Augustan and Roman, but it could also be easily transferred to Saxo's contemporary Christian theories of just war. One of the criteria for a just war was that it should always be defensive in nature. That is why it was so important for Saxo to emphasize that the Danes, all the way back in the distant past, had always been victims of attack and had justly acted in defensive response. This is also why it was important for Saxo to highlight the Wendish attacks on the Danish coasts in his contemporary time, which had left a very large part of Jutland deserted. Once the Wends had initiated violence, the wars of the Danish kings were merely just defensive wars. Archeological finds and Slavic place names in southern Denmark demonstrate that there was a mix of Danish-Slavic settlements in many places and a lively cultural exchange. However, this narrative was suppressed by Saxo in favor of a picture of old feuds and wars. Cohabitation was described as inevitably leading to confrontation. The

Empire's expansion was described as a simple defense. The Danish Empire was in every way compared to the Roman Empire, first the ancient and later the restored German-Roman Empire up to Saxo's contemporary, Emperor Fredrick I Barbarossa. The Danish empire was older than the ancient Roman empire, according to Saxo, and it ruled Northern Europe, a larger territory actually than that of the Romans. Even Emperor Charlemagne had been afraid of the Danish king Godfried, who would have conquered the Frankish Empire had he not been captured in a domestic plot against himself. For Saxo, the king was logically an important role as the unifying figure of the empire, while the people remained fragmented. These groups included the people of Sealand, Funen, Rügen, Jutland, Pomerania, Scania, and several others; all of which were united only by having a common king. In Saxo's narrative, the fatherland became metaphysical: it was synonymous with all that obeyed the orders of the king, and almost with the king himself.

With the writings of Saxo and Sven Aggesen, Danish kings gained an imperial history that could be accepted by all the inhabitants of the empire, old and new, and which was held together by the person of the king. The empire got a purpose, namely to fight against evil and to create justice. A similar ideology was evident among the kings of the time. Valdemar the Great issued charters in which, with the words of the English political thinker John of Salisbury, he compared the king to the head and the people—not only the soldiers as Sven Aggesen had written—to the many different limbs, each having their own function and being governed by the head. Canute VI leveraged words that would lead the thought of Bible quotes concerning the world-ruler sitting on his throne and judging all the different peoples of the earth. The cross was constantly an important unifying symbol. Valdemar issued coins with the crucifix on one side and the king with the olive branch—a symbol of the pilgrim or crusader—on the other. Canute portrayed himself on his great royal seal as a crusader in a long, wide robe with many embroidered crosses.

From the Northalbing to the Lake Peipus

King Valdemar II the Conqueror died in 1241 and was described by the English monk and chronicler Matthew Paris: "He had spent almost all his time spearheading crusades, from as soon as he was able to carry a weapon, and he had fought both in Frisia and Russia." Denmark during the first half of the thirteenth century was a crusader nation, and under the rule of Valdemar the Conqueror, who was king 1202–1241, a series of conquests created a unified kingdom which included the Baltic Sea Region from Holstein in the west to Estonia in the east, interrupted only by the possessions of the Teutonic Order in Pomerania and Livonia (Bysted et al. 2012; Jensen 2017). In this position, Denmark became an important element of European politics, particularly in relations between the German-Roman emperor and to the two main dynastic lines who fought for the imperial throne, the Welf and the Hohenstaufen. Alliances with the emperor interchanged with attempts to rebel against him.

Indeed, in 1240 there were even plans to elect the Danish king's son Erik IV Ploughpenny as the new German king to succeed Emperor Fredrick II.

In 1192, the king's cousin Bishop Valdemar of Schleswig rebelled and attempted—with aid from the Hohenstaufens and a fleet with Norwegian supporters—to launch an armed conquest of Denmark and proclaim himself king. However, he suffered defeat and was imprisoned in the Danish castle of Søborg for fourteen years. It was somehow a shame, as the combination of the royal and ecclesiastical offices in one person would have been novelty during the Middle Ages, and it is interesting to wonder what this cousin Valdemar would have actually done in practice, had he become a Bishop-King. Bishop Valdemar was actually son of that Canute, who was son of Magnus, who had killed King Valdemar I the Great's father, Canute Lavard. As a result, he had as good an inheritance claim on the Danish throne as Valdemar II the Victorious. It is quite understandable that King Valdemar II preferred to keep him soundly behind bars. However, by imprisoning him, a consecrated bishop within the church, it was also a profound violation of the church's freedoms and independent juridical status. Popes had to intervene. Especially Pope Innocent III did so when he ascended the papal throne in 1198, but he also stressed how unwillingly he did so. "If only he had never existed, this man, Bishop Valdemar of Schleswig, who violated the dignity of the episcopal office by attempting to unite royal power to priesthood. ... If only he had been turned into a pillar of salt once he took his hand away from the Lord's plow and looked back. Then he alone could have been washed away by the waters when he alone lamented his unfortunate fate, for on the cheeks of the church there would not be a single tear. It would have been better if he had died of his own sword, before he drew the secular sword" (Jensen and Nielsen 2003). Innocent emphasized that he only required Bishop Valdemar released for the sake of dignity of the episcopal office. After thirteen years, Bishop Valdemar was finally released in 1206 at the intervention of Queen Dagmar's intercession. He was then taken to Rome, but fled to Hamburg-Bremen, where, despite being excommunicated, he was elected archbishop with the support of the two competing candidates for the German imperial throne. They clearly used the opportunity to weaken the Danish ruler.

Valdemar the Victorious immediately aligned himself with Pope Innocent III, when in 1212 Fredrick II was appointed as German King. The alliance was sealed with the issue of the Golden Bull in 1214, in which Frederick acknowledged the Danish king's possessions north of the rivers Elde and Elben and the Wendish territories further east all the way to Pomerania, and in exchange King Valdemar and his descendants should maintain peace in the area and fight Fredrick's enemies. The Golden Bull is a clear sign of the German emperor's recognition of Valdemar's widespread power. It was coerced at a time when Frederick's resources were under pressure, but it was an important document that would ultimately be referred to many times later on. In the same year, 1214, Pope Innocent enabled the Frisians to crusade against Bishop Valdemar Knudsen, thus again lending important papal support to King Valdemar's policy. In 1215, the other candidate for German emperor, Otto IV of Braunschweig, attacked Denmark again with the help of Bishop Valdemar and with great force, but lost. The bishop ultimately had to renounce his diocese and enter a monastery where he lived until his death in 1236.

In 1193, the French king Philip II August proposed a marriage with the Danish king's sister Ingeborg, but already during the wedding ceremony his whole body began to shake, and the morning after the wedding he rejected and shunned her, and held her prisoner at remote castles for nearly twenty years. At first Phillip August claimed that the couple were too closely related according to ecclesiastical regulations, and later he alleged that Ingeborg had bewitched him on the wedding night making him impotent. The case not only attracted attention across Europe, but was also of great ecclesiastical and juridical importance: during this time, the Church was struggling to intently assert the concept of marriage as insoluble. Pope Innocent III was personally concerned with safeguarding marriage as a sacrament as well as a firm institution between not only families, but individuals. He got involved in the matter and threatened with excommunicating the king and announce interdict—the closure of churches all over France—unless Philip August took Ingeborg back and treated her with the honor that she as Queen was entitled to. It turns out that there was also a political element in this situation: whenever Valdemar promised his participation in a crusade, Pope Innocent III wrote to Philip August, imploring him to take Ingeborg back.

Pope Innocent's appeals were not successful until 1213, and perhaps only because Phillip wanted to assert Ingeborg's inheritance claim over England at that time. Philip also needed the pope's and thus Fredrick II's support prior to the Great Battle of Bouvines in 1214 against German King Otto IV and his English allied. Ingeborg survived her husband for several years and donated huge sums to pious foundations, which should, among other things, pray for Phillip August's soul. Historians have long theorized as to why Ingeborg was rejected by her husband. Most have tried to find a political explanation. The marriage was quite obviously an attempt to form a Franco-Danish alliance to balance against England, and part of the dowry apparently included Danish naval support during a French attack on England. Some have asserted that perhaps the French king changed political strategy and had less need for the support that came with Ingeborg. Still others have suggested with much creative imagination that Philip August was perhaps gay, an assumption for which we have no source whatsoever. These and other explanations do not account for the fact that Phillip August could very well have lived with Ingeborg as his official queen and pursued his other priorities in ways that would not have given him such fierce diplomatic problems as his decision to brutally banish her the day after their wedding. In fact, the only logical explanation is that Ingeborg, on the wedding night itself, frightened Phillip witless, so that he never dared to look at her again. What truly happened that night will forever remain unknown, but the most important lesson to learn in this context is the simple conclusion that in the formation of empires, large lands were linked together through personal alliances. This meant that there could be wide-ranging political ramifications in the few cases when two people turned out to dislike each other so much that they could not live together in the same place. Canute VI and Valdemar the Victorious would in the coming years continue to balance around the German empire. Had the union between Ingeborg and Philip August not soured, the Danish-French alliance would likely have created an unusually strong power in northwestern Europe, which would have been a potent counterweight to the German-Roman empire. In reality, quite the opposite happened.

King Valdemar the Victorious was first married to Dagmar, daughter of Ottokar of Bohemia (1206–1212). He later married Berengaria (1214–1221), who was the daughter of Sancho I of Portugal and the sister of Count Ferdinand of Flanders, who was one of Phillip Augusts' largest and most independent vassals and a sworn enemy of his liege lord. It was clear that Valdemar had now switched sides and was building an alliance against Philip August. From a larger European perspective, these marriages throughout the empire were intended to avoid committing too much to any one of the parties in line for the imperial throne, should one turn out to be the losing faction.

In 1219, Valdemar the Victorious vanquished with a fleet of 1500 ships the distant Estonian city of Tallinn, meaning in Estonian "Danish castle," thus overcoming the whole of Estonia (Selch Jensen et al. 2019). It was the denouement to a series of crusades since 1206, and had benefited from much financial and diplomatic planning. In 1217 the king had crowned his young son—also called Valdemar (the Young)—with his own hands and deployed him as co-ruler should he himself fall on the crusade expedition. The coronation was held in Schleswig, which had been Canute Lavard's main city and the starting point for his crusades against the Wends a hundred years earlier. The crowning happened on June 25 on Saint Canute Lavard's Feast day, just as the young Canute VI had been crowned during the canonization in 1170. In 1218, King Valdemar negotiated alliances with the other missionary powers in countries bordering Estonia, including Bishop Albert of Riga and his small but effective Livonian Brothers of the Sword Order. During the Battle of Tallinn, troops from Rügen, who had been conquered fifty years earlier, came to play a crucial role. Tallinn was conquered on Saint Vitus' Feast day of June 15, the same date as Arkona of Rügen had fallen. That similar events happened on the same dates with years apart was felt natural in the Middle Ages, if the day was dedicated to a saint with a special interest in these events. A modern and more skeptical age would argue that dates for big events and concerned efforts, for example in warfare, were coordinated and chosen by the participants with great care. According to a late medieval source, the Danish flag, a white cross on a red base, was hung in the sky during the battle at Tallinn and slowly fell down and secured the Danish victory. In the same year, a number of other crusades were pursued in Europe. Valdemar's brother-in-law Afonso II of Portugal conquered one of the most important Muslim strongholds in the Iberian Peninsula: Alcáser do Sal in 1217. In 1219, Valdemar's former in-laws' family, the Hungarian king András II, also fought at Acre in the Holy Land. In the same year, an important contingent of the so-called Fifth Crusade reached the Nile Delta and advanced towards Cairo, with participation from most European countries including some high-ranking Danish vassals. It is possible that all of these crusades were coordinated with Valdemar's efforts in Estonia in some way (Fig. 4.2).

The Danish Empire in the Baltic was now large and apparently well consolidated. However, it all collapsed in in the late hours in the morning 7 May of 1223 when King Valdemar and the young Prince Valdemar were taken hostage on the small island of Lyø near Funen, by one of the king's great vassals, Count Henry of Schwerin (Jensen 2021). King Valdemar had brought most of the kingdom's archive with him, so many of the crown's original charters of property and privileges are located in Schwerin today, but what the meeting was really about remains unknown. The king and his son were quickly brought through Schwerin to a secure castle in Germany, and lengthy negotiations began. Emperor Frederic II was strongly interested in gaining custody over King Valdemar as a prisoner and forcing him to accept a revocation of the Golden Bull, which the emperor claimed the king had violated. Count Henry offered Valdemar to Fredrick for 52,000 marks of silver. However, it came to nothing, mostly due to emphatic protests from Pope Honorius III. It turned out that Valdemar had secretly taken the cross and promised to lead a large crusade to Jerusalem, and therefore was now under the Pope's direct protection. The result was threat of immediate excommunication of Henry and interdict and closing of churches in his lands. After two and a half years of captivity, an agreement was finally reached: the king could be released in exchange for a sum of 44,000 marks of silver, 100 exquisite horses, and the transfer of several territories to the empire, including the area between Riber Elbe and River Ejder, as well as the important trading town of Lübeck. Throughout the negotiation process between Henry of Schwerin and the Danish representatives, the Grand Master of the Teutonic Order Hermann von Salza—Fredrick II's confidant—took a leading role. After his release, Valdemar was freed from his promises to pay ransom by the Pope on the grounds that he would not be able to lead a crusade to the Middle East if he were to spend the huge sum of money. Valdemar now sought a military resolution to the situation, but suffered defeat at the hands of Henry from Schwerin and his allied at Bornhøved on July 22, 1227. Thus, any further Danish military expansion in Northern Germany and the Baltic region was halted. Estonia was placed under the papal legate Wilhelm of Modena, before being passed on to the Order of the Sword Brethren in 1227. However, in 1238 the area was divided between Denmark and the Teutonic Order through a settlement between Valdemar and Hermann von Salza in the small village of Stensby on southern Sealand.

In the fifteen years following his release, King Valdemar sought to assert his interests by affording extra privileges to the trading towns along the Baltic Sea, which eventually received major concessions in the Scania market: Northern

Fig. 4.2 Before the decisive battle at the Milvian Bridge in Rome in 312, Constantine saw a cross in the sky and heard a voice saying *In hoc signo vinces*—"By this sign you shall gain victory." The miracle was repeated several times during history. Before the first crusade in 1096–1099, crosses were seen on the sky at several places in Southern France. In 1139, the Portuguese king experienced the same miracle before a decisive battle against the Muslims. Before the Children crusade in 1209, crosses were seen over the low horizon in Friesland. The same miracle happened to King Valdemar II during the conquest of Tallinn in Estonia in 1219. When the Danish crusaders were hardly pressed, heaven opened and the Danish flag with a white cross in red fell down and gave the Danes new strength to fight and gain victory. The miracle is known only from sources from the early sixteenth century, but they refer to earlier sources now lost. The painting by C.A. Lorentzen was made in 1809 when Denmark was in crisis both economically and politically. During the Napoleonic wars, England had attacked Denmark and simply confiscated the entire Danish fleet. A proud seafaring nation was left militarily crippled, and it was time to look back on former greatness and on Denmark as a country favored by God. https://da.wikipedia.org/wiki/Slaget_ved_Lyndanisse#/media/Fil:Danmarks_flag_1219_Lorentzen.jpg (Creative commons: Public Domain)

Europe's largest herring market and one of the king's core sources of income. In one instance Valdemar attempted to block the port of Lübeck in 1234, but thereby also prevented the transport of crusaders to Livonia and was forced by Pope Gregory IX to abolish the blockade.

Domestically, the political conditions in Denmark were characterized by harmony between the crown and the church to an extent that was unusual in Western Europe at that time. Valdemar the Victorious was wholeheartedly supported by Archbishop Anders Sunesen (1201–1222, resigned due to illness, died 1228). Anders was a personal study friend of Pope Innocent III and was appointed legate—with delegated papal authority—in charge of the mission throughout the territories in the entire Baltic Sea area. He was a tremendously well-educated scholar, as is evident in his Hexaëmeron, whose aim was to teach the youth impeccable and elegant Latin, with examples from a text which was theologically irreproachable and explained the dogmas of creation and redemption in 8040 hexameters. Anders Sunesen tried to reform the clergy by, among other things, encouraging celibacy, which had only limited success. He may have met the founder of the Dominican Order, Dominik of Osma, who was sent to Denmark in 1203 or 1204 to negotiate a marriage between a son of Alfonso VIII of Castile and a Danish princess. It ultimately didn't come to fruition, but Anders Sunesen showed great interest in the Dominicans in the future, who he invited to the Archdiocese of Lund in 1223; the following year the Franciscans arrived in Denmark via the port of Ribe on the westcoast of Jutland.

Both groups quickly became popular and soon received an important assignment in the mission areas along the Baltic, where during the thirteenth century they took over from the Cistercians the role of evangelizing and christening through preaching and pastoral care (Jakobsen 2021). The two mendicant orders were well-educated, poor, independent, pragmatic, and targeted. Both established a number of language schools in various places throughout Europe, and one can imagine that their monasteries in the Danish Empire must have included the study of Estonian and Slavic languages. They also directed large theatrical plays on Biblical history for new Christians and used a myriad of creative stage effects. One of the battle scenes in the Old Testament was played so vividly that the newly baptized Estonians ran away screaming because they thought they were truly being attacked again by crusaders. One of the great advantages of the mendicant orders was that they were mobile and did not have to follow the rule of the older order to stay in the same place forever. In the Baltic, they created a type of sailing monasteries that accompanied the fishermen around the summer to even the most remote fishing grounds.

The Danish Empire consisted of several diverse areas or provinces, each with their own legal system (Andersen 2011; The Danish Medieval Laws 2016). We know very little about how these systems were influenced by empire formations in the early Middle Ages and the High Middle Ages. However, it is evident that it became important to record the Medieval provincial code of laws in the late 1100s, a tradition that would be continued in the future. We do have preserved regional laws from Scania including Bornholm, and several for Sealand, but we unfortunately do not know of any Medieval laws pertaining to Rügen or Estonia. Finally, we have the Code of Jutland, which was issued in 1241 and would gain widespread use in Schleswig and Holstein. When comparing these laws, it is clear that they each have their own distinctive character, but that there were also attempts made to harmonize parts of the various statutes. It is an important discussion among legal historians whether the laws reflect the legal situation at a particular time or whether they contain both new statues and older ones, which were no longer applicable but were kept out of veneration for their tradition. Some historians have gone so far as to posit that they could find proto-Germanic rules in the Medieval Scandinavian regional lawcodes, which reproduced centuries-old rules that can be found in English and Frankish laws from as far back as the nineth century. The many similarities between the laws have been interpreted as indicative of something common, something proto-Germanic, while the differences have been more difficult to explain and have otherwise been rationalized as local customs. However, from an imperial perspective, it makes much more sense the other way around. The differences show that Sealand, Scania and Jutland have had different lawcodes, probably with long historical roots. The similarities show that, after the conquests of the various territories, the Danish king attempted to introduce a minimum of standardization among these various laws. Based upon the regional laws known today, they must have been subject to negotiations between the king and the local upper class and serves as a prime example of how empires have always had to balance between local custom and central government.

The traditional understanding of law of the Middle Ages was based on two concepts: the natural law that all people in all different societies must live by, and the revealed law that Christians knew through the Mosaic Law of the Old Testament and the commands of the New Testament. Both had the same divine origins and could therefore not be changed, so the task of rulers and jurists was to interpret the laws given and apply them within changing societies or to reintroduce laws that had been forgotten. Strictly speaking, one could not speak of a legislator at all, but only of an interpreter of law. In the first half of the thirteenth century, however, an alternative to the traditional view emerged: that legislation could in some cases now be viewed as an active and innovative process. This was the case with the collection of Church Laws issued by Pope Gregory IX in 1236, termed the Decretals, which supplemented the existing ecclesiastical law. However, contrary to previous collections of law and juridical decisions, the Decretals asserted that the pope could create new laws on the basis of the Natural Law. This occurred at a time when the papacy was nearing the peak of political and administrative centralization, which began with the reform movements in the late 1000s. This centralization collapsed just after the year 1300 with the transfer of the papacy to Avignon and the long-standing "Babylonian captivity," before the popes returned to Rome. Around 1260, Alfonso X the Wise of Aragon and Castile issued the legal code of Siete Partidas, which also included the concept of the emperor as an active legislator. Siete Partidas was conceived as a collective law for the many Spanish territories, now ruled by Alfonso, and which were to be united under one empire. A few years later, Alfonso's power was severely restricted by revolts among the nobility, and Siete Partidas would not become a common law for the Spanish territories until the late Middle Ages. In 1231 Emperor Fredrick II issued the Constitutions of Melfi, which were intended only to apply to part of the great German-Roman Empire, but also rendered the emperor as the authority who could create new laws and did not just simply pluck old laws out of thin air. Emperor Fredrick's laws survived, but his empire crumbled after his death in 1250. As one of his final deeds, Valdemar the Conqueror would issue the Code of Jutland in 1241, before he died a few weeks later.

The Code of Jutland differs from the laws of Sealand and Scania, because it clearly states that the king mandates the law, which must then be accepted by the people. The king seems to have had a different, and more active role in the Code of Jutland than in others: its purpose is clearly to create unity within an empire with so many divergent and local customs. It is highly disputed whether the Code of Jutland was intended to become a truly imperial law and apply beyond Jutland to all of the king's territories. Very many manuscripts containing the law has survived, and actually only two of 16 manuscripts dated before 1400 are directly designated as the Code of Jutland, while four are called the Law of the Danes. However, solid evidence is scarce, and it is not possible to reach any firm conclusion whether the law was intended to be applied for the entire kingdom. This would only happen much later during the Late Middle Ages, probably also because the King's stable empire experienced great crisis following his death. Nevertheless, these laws highlight that Danish legislation closely and immediately followed international developments. Archbishop Anders Sunesen was also fascinated by the legal realm, and authored an annotated translation of Scania Law into Latin. He and several others were also instrumental in introducing elements of ecclesial law, Canon law, into the Danish legal system, where it was advantageous. Decisions from the large church meetings quickly became applied also in Denmark. One example includes the ban against the use of ordeal by hot iron as evidence—that is, the accused to prove his innocence had to carry glowing iron and remain unharmed. This practice was banned at the Fourth Council in the Lateran in 1215 and very soon after also in Denmark.

Royal power strengthened its position vis-à-vis the magnates during the period from around 1170 to the 1240s. This was done by way of several strategies, including the expansion of a central administration with the creation of new offices, by not summoning the magnates to royal council meetings, and by increasing the crown's revenue through new forms of taxation. King Valdemar's Cadaster from around 1231 is an—incomplete—record of the king's income from the various parts of his kingdom. The records are often of a lapidaric nature, and include many different accounting principles, so a reconstruction of the King's administrative practice in any detail is not possible, but the source itself is evidence of a well-developed and centralized bureaucracy. It is possible to distinguish between two types of royal property, the territories which the king as an individual inherited from his ancestors (patrimonium), and the territories which he possessed as a result of his royal office, the so-called "kongelev" or crown land. This distinction is interesting. In Jutland and Funen, the king owned large family properties, while in Sealand and in Scania his possessions belonged to the office. The latter category would also include the lands that the king conquered, and so the distinction between the two types of property may date all the way back to before the year 1000. Similarly, Bornholm, Frisia, Rügen, and Fehmern were listed as royal offices. On the island of Falster the king owned over a quarter of the land, and on Lolland he owned under a tenth. All of the older cities were also listed as belonging to the royal office and provided large revenue in the form of customs and taxes. The land register also contained a shorter and a longer record of the possessions in Estonia, and also occasionally included a short list of geographic names from the Prussian, Lithuanian, and Latvian territories, though no income is listed from these areas. These lists show, however, that crusades were directed towards these areas and that they were within the Danish sphere of interest.

The Estonian lists show that the newly conquered country was ruled by powerful vassals, most of whom appear to have had more of a German background than Danish. Local Estonian noblemen were clearly only a small minority. In this case, the conquest was clearly followed by a purge of the local upper class. By 1218, King Valdemar received confirmation via papal privilege that all conquered land in Estonia should belong directly to the king. Combined, these revenues were enormous, and some historians have estimated that King Valdemar's income was more than five times that of Emperor Fredrick II's income from the German parts of his empire. It sounds tremendous, and all figures from the Middle Ages must be taken with a huge grain of salt due to the sparse source material. However, if the figures are true, it shows a crucial difference between the Danish and German empires. The Danish king stood much stronger in relation to his magnates and vassals than the German emperor, and the Danish king became the owner of newly conquered land, while the German emperor had to allocate such land to his vassals. The Danish Empire appeared to be more centralized and bureaucratized than the German one.

Militarily, the king's most important weapon was still the lething, the navy with its general conscription including each landowner with properties greater than a certain size. These landowners were mandated together, district for district, to build and maintain a warship, and personally drafted to participate as fighters on the ship, usually every three years. In this way, the king was in principle able to maintain an army of at least 1000 ships plus his own fleet as well as the private ships of the great magnates. However, full mobilization has been extremely rare. Starting around 1215 it became increasingly common for the lething soldiers to buy their freedom from this military service, after which the king could use the proceeds to pay mercenaries or other professionals. At the same time, the traditional Nordic longship was increasingly replaced by larger cog-type ships with a high fore and aft bow and wooden towers, which required a permanent and professional crew. The second core element of the king's armed forces consisted of the contribution of the vassals. It was essential that the royal power, at least until Valdemar the Victorious' death, had enough authority to assert the basically unlimited duty of the vassals, while the king's finances were good enough to reward the vassals with extensive and favorable benefices in form of land or income.

Following the banishment of Fredrick II by Pope Gregory IX in March 1239, it was a sign of the enormous international prestige which Valdemar had achieved when the pope sent the former abbot of Prémontré to Denmark to offer Valdemar's son Erik the crown as German king. However, Erik followed his father's guidance and declined. In March 1241 Valdemar died, and "the crown now really fell of the head of the Danes," as a contemporary annal noted (DMA 1980, 172). Erik was crowned king and tried to assert supremacy in the Baltic countries. Danish vassals fought with the Novgorod prince Aleksandr Nevsky against the Teutonic Order in the Battle of the Ice on Lake Peipus in 1242. As a result, Erik was granted part of the ecclesiastical taxes to carry out crusades in the eastern Baltic. However, it soon became clear that there were too many domestic issues to continue the expansion.

In 1245, a church meeting in Odense discussed measures against kings who exploited the church or bishops—the balance between king and church was broken and ushered in great strife with archbishops in exile and processes of the Roman Curia, which was soon to follow. At the same time, Erik's younger brother Abel was named Duke of Schleswig, a common position for sons of kings, and from there he rebelled openly and in 1250 ordered the assassination of his brother. The assassination caused consternation throughout all of Europe: Abel became a Cain. Nevertheless, Abel also became king after having cleared himself of any guilt by the oaths of 24 loyal men, most likely because Erik did not have any male heirs as king. Abel was crowned king, but only held the throne for two years, before he perished in battle against the Fresians, upon whom he had imposed additional taxes. While Abel's son Valdemar was traveling, he was jailed by the Archbishop of Cologne: the third son of Valdemar and Berengaria, Christopher, seized this as an opportunity. He quickly traveled around to all *things,* the general legal assemblies, and paid homage and was anointed and crowned in Lund, though not by the Archbishop, but instead by Schleswig Bishop who had the greatest seniority among the Danish bishops. This meant that Abel's own son had been passed over in line for the throne, leading to a nearly hundred year-long struggle between Abel and Christopher's descendants, which in the early 1300s threatened to annihilate Denmark as an independent kingdom.

Christopher tried in vain to prevent the election of Jacob Erlandsen as a new archbishop. Not only was he a highly educated clergyman and a wealthy nobleman, but also a close acquaintance of Pope Innocent IV. The relationship between the king and the archbishop quickly grew bad. In 1256 in the town of Vejle, a church meeting for the entire empire passed a resolution that directly and harshly began with the words: "As the Danish church is so much exposed to the grave persecution of tyrants ..." Its text asserted that if a bishop was imprisoned, all the churches of the country would immediately shut down and all divine acts cease, and the king—by the very act and without further trial—should be excommunicated if he was shown to have in any way been involved in the imprisoning, or knowingly failed to prevent the imprisonment. Such severe resolutions were not unknown in Europe at the time, just as the imprisonment of bishops was not uncommon, but the Vejle Constitution was particularly harsh in its formulations. Perhaps Jacob Erlandsen based his resolution upon writings of Innocent IV, who, following the news of Emperor Fredrick II's death in 1250, wrote a papal bull to the whole Christianity, whose enthusiastic first line was based on Isaiah's great prophecy: "Rejoice, heavens, rejoice, earth, for the tyrant is dead." Both documents deliberately use the word tyrant, which is the official term for a king who violates the church's rights, but also reminded the audience of contemporary discussions about when it may be just and necessary to kill a tyrant, whether or not he was king. Christopher surely had a bitter taste in his mouth when he became aware of the contents of the Vejle Resolution.

The decision of the church meeting was soon tested in practice. The bishop of Schleswig would already be imprisoned in 1256, but the mastermind of the plot was Duke Albrecht of Braunschweig. Although he was one of the Danish king's great vassals, it did not result in church closures and excommunication, probably because the true events of what had happened remained too unclear. However, on a February morning in 1259, Jacob Erlandsen was imprisoned by a Henry I of Mecklenburg, who scorned and humiliated the archbishop. Not only was Erlandsen tied, but he was also forced to wear a fool's hat attached with fox tails. The archbishop was taken to the castle Hagenskov in Funen, and now there was no doubt that the Vejle constitution could be applied. Excommunication and church closures were also immediately proclaimed, but certainly not implemented in all areas. Some continued to function as usual, either by conviction or pressure by the king. Others obeyed the Vejle Resolution. Bishop Peder of Roskilde fled to the farthest and safest part of his diocese, to the island of Rügen. There he called for a crusade against the heretical King Christopher. Prince Jarimar II and his son-in-law Erik, the son of the late King Abel, followed Bishop Peder first to Bornholm, where they conquered the royal castles and presumably received reinforcements from the archbishop's men at the strong castle of Hammershus. From there they moved on to Copenhagen, forced it to surrender and tore a hole in the city wall—near today's Jarmer's Plaza—to enter the city in a way befitting a conqueror. The army continued south across Sealand and reached the city of Næstved, where on June 14th it launched a major battle against royal forces. It is possible that Peder would have preferred to wait until the next day—the anniversary of Rügen's conquest in 1168 and Estonia's in 1219—to emphasize the nature of the war as a crusade against a ruler, who had attacked the church's men. The king's army likely hastened the battle precisely for the same reason. The result was an overwhelming victory for Bishop Peder and Jarimar: maybe around 1800 of the King's men fell, and as heretics, they were buried in a mass grave without any kind of ecclesiastical ceremonies. At the same time, Holsteinian forces had crossed the Ejder River and ravaged southern Jutland. Christopher fled and died quite suddenly in Ribe, two weeks before the big battle at Næstved. Soon it was rumored that he had been forgiven during communion, perhaps by Abbot Arnfast of Ryd Monastery in the Abel family's main territories. The situation could hardly have been worse for Christopher's widow, Margrethe Sambiria, and his young 11-year-old son, Erik Glipping, in the conflict. They also lost a battle at Lohede at Schleswig in 1261 and were held in captivity at Holstein. Aid came from Duke Albrecht of Braunschweig, who attacked Holstein, negotiated the release of Margrethe and Erik, and was rewarded with enormous fiefdoms on Als, South Funen and Langeland. At the same time, he was named as head of state for a few difficult years.

Until her death in 1282, Queen Margrethe Sambiria would play a crucial role in the empire, first as guardian of Erik Glipping and then as the defacto co-ruler. She settled in Nykøbing Falster with her own administration and was thus geographically well placed in relation to the territories she continuously communicated with. She maintained the connection back to her home of Pomerania, and ultimately chose to be buried there in the Cistercian monastery church in Doberan. She owned properties in southern Denmark, and from 1266 she was granted the title of Viceroy of Estonia. She managed this directly with a number of orders, which included the fortification of Tallinn, and together with Erik Glipping she ensured that Tallinn was granted the town privileges of Lübeck. The practical day-to-day administration of Estonia was in the hands of a royal governor, who was assisted by a council of 12–16 of the country's most powerful barons. Margrethe also sought to uphold the right to approve new vassals so that officers could not automatically inherit the position from their father. She negotiated with the Teutonic Order on alliances and waged war against Novgorod in eastern Estonia.

The battles between ecclesial and royal power did not end when Christopher died in 1259. Admittedly, Margrethe Sambiria released the archbishop, but there were no discussions about compensation, and the initial disagreements about areas of jurisdiction, the right to take men into service, and the bishop's duty to provide forces for the king's army remained unresolved. Jacob Erlandsen went into exile in Rome together with Bishop Peder of Roskilde, and proceedings continued at the papal curia until a settlement was finally reached in 1274. Peder returned home and served as bishop for just three years before his death; Jacob Erlandsen was barely within the boundaries of the archdiocese, when he died at Rügen. In the fifteen years from Erlandsen's incarceration to his death, Denmark was in principle under interdict, all churches were supposedly closed, and the punishment of excommunication of the king was passed down from Christopher to Erik Glipping. Several dioceses functioned smoothly, even in spite of papal envoys' restrictions; other dioceses were actually seriously affected and had trouble managing the sacraments properly. Although Margrethe was no less irreconcilable to Jacob Erlandsen than her deceased husband and her son, she nevertheless gained an important role as mediator for the pope, precisely because she did not officially sit on the throne. It was she who could approach the pope and suggest the sanctification of Erik Ploughpenning due to the many miracles that happened at his grave. It was also Margrethe who had the leverage to suggest that the pope introduce female succession in Denmark, in case Erik Glipping did not have sons. Both proposals could be used to meet the legacy requirements of the Abel family. King Erik Ploughpenning became a popular saint, but we do not know whether he ever received papal recognition, and direct female succession did not occur in the Danish royal house on that occasion. But these were very important issues, which the excommunicated Erik Glipping could not negotiate with the pope, in contrast to Margrethe.

Margrethe and the young Erik had been weakly positioned in 1259 and could easily have been deposed by Erik Abelsen of Southern Jutland, who had as much legal claim to the throne as Erik Glipping. This did not happen because of the support of Albrecht of Braunschweig and of nobles who likely saw personal advantage in supporting a weak royal power. In 1282, King Erik V. Glipping had to sign a charter of rights, later called Denmark's first constitution or the Danish Magna Carta. Among its most impactful laws were that the king's legal power must be defined and limited by the noblemen, and that the king was obligated to summon the noblemen every year to a parliament, to "Danehof" thus involving them directly in the government. It was hardly a document that Margrethe would have been happy about, but she died the same year it was signed. Four years later, the night of Saint Cecilia 1286, Erik Glipping was murdered in Finderup by a internal plot, "of his own men, with 56 stab wounds." The following summer, the royal Marshal Stig Andersen Hvide and a number of the empire's most powerful men were convicted of the murder and had wisely sought refuge with the king of Norway before the sentence. So far, there is nothing in the medieval sources which suggests that the convicted were innocent, even though the motive may remain obscure to us today. In the following years, the young king Erik VI Menved fought against the Norwegian king and the outlaws who targeted the coast of Sealand and attacked the strong castles of Sprogø and of Tårnborg by Korsør. Count Jacob, another of the very high-ranking outlaws, received support from Norway to maintain his position in the border region of Halland in the strong fortress of Hunehals, even though Erik Menved had repeatedly ordered it destroyed and torn down to the ground.

In Northern Jutland, the Norwegian king inherited great possessions through his marriage to one of King Erik IV Plowpenning's daughters, and offered Stig Andersen Hvide his support to settle on the island of Hjelm just outside Djursland in Jutland, where he built a castle and forced some of the king's coin masters, whom he had abducted, to mint fake coins. A central figure in these wars was Archbishop of Lund, Jens Grand who was of the king-killers' kin. He was imprisoned on April 9, 1294 and under mockery and insult led from Lund across the waters of Øresund and thrown into the stinking dungeons of Søborg on northern Sealand. He escaped with the help of a Morten the Cook and reached Rome, where a lengthy legal process began. Initially, Jens Grand won the case and was able to return in triumph, but the negotiations for compensation collapsed. Instead the king's high officials confiscated the church's estate in Scania and issued direct threats to anyone who dared assist the archbishop. Jens Grand fled to Rome again and a new process began. Eventually, Erik VI wrote a direct letter to Pope Boniface VIII threatening that he would never reconcile with Jens Grand whatever the pope did. The king's compensation was ultimately reduced to be purely symbolic, and in 1302 Jens Grand was relocated by the pope to the more distant Riga, which was far away from the Danish king, but still an important starting point for missions and crusades among the Lithuanians. It was also an important midway station on the road to Estonia and Novgorod. Jens Grand never took possession of his new diocese, but was, after much traveling, appointed archbishop to the see of Bremen in 1310, from which he was soon exiled due to difficulties in collaborating with locals. He was clearly not an easy personality. He spent the rest of his life at the pope's court in Avignon, where he made a living by, among other things, lending money until his death in 1327.

The many disputes in the latter half of the thirteenth century among royal contestants, dukes, and bishops can be understood as personal disagreements. In the full minutes from the pope's court one gains a clear impression that strong and stubborn personalities have clashed together without much interest in maintaining a positive climate for discussion and cooperation (Jensen et al. 1999). Jens Grand had publicly stated that "he did not care who was seated on the throne of Denmark, whether it was Duke Valdemar of Schleswig, a Jew, a Muslim or the devil himself": as long as was not one of King Christopher's descendents. He also stated that it was a pity that Erik Glipping had not been killed earlier, which would have prevented him from fathering a son. The conflicts can perhaps better be considered as a manifestation of other, more fundamental contradictions between two major institutions: the local king and the international church. There is a long tradition of this interpretation in Danish history writing, but perhaps it is simply too static a way of perceiving history. As if king and church carried the same meanings throughout the middle ages.

The ideological and physical combats should rather be viewed as something quite natural for an empire. Firstly, it was not certain which countries would be united under the same ruler—rulers did not consider the connections between country and people as much as they considered power. So it was a very natural thought for the Norwegian king to try to gain power over parts of Jutland by supporting the outlawed. Secondly, an empire consisted of a number of areas that were more or less closely attached to the empire, where it was typical for the peripheral territories to achieve greater independence and balance between other empires. The landscapes of Blekinge, Northern Halland and Southern Halland, Southern Jutland, the islands of Lolland, Falster, and Rügen, and to a certain extent the province of Estonia... All were ruled by a prince who was almost always a member of the Danish royal family. All these princes in principle obeyed the Danish king, but they also pursued an independent policy towards his neighbors. Scania was heavily dependent on the Archbishop of Lund and was governed in collaboration with the *gældker*, a special royal official whose title was only recorded in Scania. Northern Halland was a county between Danish and Norwegian possessions. Usually it was Danish, but if the Count had issues with the Danish king, for example by being accused of having killed him, he could immediately seek refuge with the Norwegian king. The alliance between the Abel family in southern Jutland and Jarimar's descendants on Rügen was an example of attempts to tie two outer territories together and gain strength in relation to the king in the center of the empire. Perhaps such an alliance—had it been upheld for some generations—could in the long run have led to the restoration of an entire mini-empire from Frisia to Rügen, as it had existed under Canute Lavard around 1130.

Finally, an empire is highly dependent on pursuing several political strategies concurrently. It is interesting that the Danish kings from Christopher I and even Erik VI Menved were the masterminds behind imprisoning archbishops and other clergy, yet they all ended up resolving the issues with changing popes and finding solutions, that were usually in the king's favor. Either the popes did not want to act too harshly, or the Danish empire has had other tasks that were just as important to the pope as it was to ensure the freedom of the archbishops. The empire stretched all the way along the Baltic Sea to Estonia and were adjacent to the territories of the pagan Lithuanians, the Orthodox Russian Church, and groups of shamanistic Mongols. A recurring consideration and complaint during these church disputes was that the people of the empire risked renouncing the faith if the churches were closed for too long due to the king's abuses. Here, popes and local ecclesiastical institutions clearly prioritized protecting and sustaining the newly-converted Christian areas. Perhaps the Danish kings were treated so lightly by the popes because they were indispensable for Christian crusades and missions in the Baltic Sea region.

Novgorod and Northern Germany

From about 1300, the Danish king stood at the helm of a vast empire and enjoyed so much international recognition that he in his conflict with the Danish archbishop could impose conditions on the pope. Twenty-five years later, the empire was divided among lien holders who installed puppet kings at their discretion and who for some years could even function completely without a king. However, starting in 1340 the empire began to rally, or rather reorganize, which lay a strong foundation for the enormous geographical expansion that would occur in the fourteenth century.

A moment of decisive expansion of the empire came by way of free will, when in 1298 the city of Riga completely surrendered to the Danish king on its own initiative and recognized Erik VI as lord over Riga, as well as three territories in the southern landscapes of Estonia which belonged to Riga. This unusual move was likely a reaction against the pressure that Riga had sustained at the hands of the Teutonic Order since 1268, when the Order had initiated numerous attempts to kidnap the Archbishop of Riga in the midst of a worship service. The fact that the city of Riga now turned to Erik VI was probably because he had publicly declared that he would strengthen and protect trade routes throughout the Baltic from Lübeck over Tallinn to Novgorod. Erik had already confirmed this by bestowing benefits on several cities on this route. King Erik's agreement with Riga contained a solemn condemnation of the Teutonic Order and its "outrageous and blasphemous imprisonment of an archbishop" (Bysted et al. 2012). Erik signed this only a few months after he himself received the pope's sharp condemnation of his imprisonment of Archbishop Jens Grand. Tallinn and Riga were two major support junctions along the sailing route to Russia, and both cities served as extremely important launch points for trade routes inland. It was therefore quite logical that in 1302 Erik VI succeeded the acquisition of Riga by entering into a peace and trade agreement with the economic superpower of the city of Novgorod. The empire was economically and politically strengthened, and was apparently perceived as an excessive threat by its neighbors. This resulted in a sudden shift in alliances among the other Nordic countries.

In 1296 a Danish-Swedish alliance was sealed with a double wedding: King Erik VI married Ingeborg, the sister of Swedish King Birger, and Birger married Erik's sister Margrethe in 1298. However, after the Danish agreement with Novgorod, Birger switched sides and formed an alliance directly opposed to Erik VI: Birger took those outlawed for killing King Erik V Glipping under his protection, and his Birger's brother Erik Magnusson became engaged to the Norwegian princess Ingeborg in 1302. At the time, she was then one year old. This became the chance for Erik Magnusson to take over as Duke of Northern Halland, which the Norwegian king had received in return for protecting the outlaws, and in the coming years he expanded his power considerably with parts of Western Sweden and with Båhuslen in Norway. Duke Erik Magnusson then captured his brother Birger in 1306 and, together with his brother Valdemar, assumed power over all of Sweden. Now Erik VI Menved came to the aid of Birger and went into Västergötland with a large army, but had to give up because of the unusually severe winter. The ice was several meters thick on the Sound between Denmark and Sweden, and one could even walk across the ice from Rostock in Northern Germany all the way to Denmark. The dukes Erik and Valdemar subsequently entered into an agreement with Erik VI's little brother Christopher (II); he shared their interest in taking over the throne of a brother. The agreement must have been kept a secret, because Erik VI rearmed in Scania and Småland by concentrating troops and supplies in the castle of Örkeljunga and then named Christopher commander. When Duke Erik Magnusson approached, Christopher surrendered the castle to him after a brief and halfhearted fight. After several battles the conflict reached a peace settlement in Helsingborg in 1310. Ingeborg of Norway had—at 7 years old—been engaged in 1308 with Magnus, the son of Swedish King Birger. The three Nordic kings now committed themselves to fight the dukes, their brothers, and agreed to stand together and support each other in all matters *perpetuis temporibus*—"in all eternity." It did not last long. Duke Erik Magnusson had gained a strong position in Sweden as nearly a co-regent to his brother, and in 1312 he was able to ensure that Princess Ingeborg of Norway ended up marrying him instead. At the same time, his brother Duke Valdemar married a daughter of the late King Erik II (Priest Hater) of Norway; her name was also Ingeborg. Duke Erik Magnusson was thus well on his way to creating a new empire consisting of Norway and Western Sweden. He would not get to enjoy it. In 1317, King Birger captured him and his second brother Valdemar, leaving them to quietly and slowly waste away to death in prison. However, this led to an uproar, and eventually Birger had to seek refuge in Denmark with Erik VI. The true victor was ultimately Duke Erik's son Magnus, who now inherited both Norway and Sweden. Magnus Eriksen was born in 1316 by Ingeborg of Norway, who had now turned 15 years old.

Eric VI Menved secured his position in the North German region in every conceivable way. The Duchy of Southern Jutland occupied a mixed position throughout the thirteenth century, with much of the authority belonging to the duke, but the king also retained a high income and control over the appointment of ecclesiastical offices. Many nobles in Schleswig and Holstein operated as vassals directly under the king, rather than under the Duke or Count. After Erik V. Glipping had to sign the charter of rights in 1282 and especially after the assassination of him in Finderup four years earlier, the Duke of Southern Jutland managed to weaken the royal power quite considerably. Revenue from coin minting and from the replacement of military service now went to the duke instead of the king, and more and more vassals began to choose the duke as their lord. The king had fewer nobles from southern Jutland to command when war erupted, and those left further succeeded in forcing the king to put limits to their service. Some rapprochement occurred after 1293, when Queen Agnes married Count Gerhard II of Holstein, who then supported Erik VI's policy. In the coming years, Erik embarked on expeditions against the rich cities of northern Germany, and in 1301 forced the city of Rostock to recognize himself as king. In 1304 the Golden Bull (that had first been issued in 1214) was reissued and reaffirmed that the German-Roman emperor recognized the right of the Danish king to all land north of the River

Elbe all the way to Pomerania. In 1307, Erik VI became lord of Lübeck and earned huge taxes from the rich city, while concurrently gaining control of the most important Western shipping ports for the Novgorod trade route. These gains were celebrated with a magnificent demonstration of power in Rostock in 1311, where King Erik knighted the Margrave of Brandenburg and 100 other noblemen, and gave each of them a scarlet cloak and a war horse. The party was magnificent and colorful, the tournament noble and heroic, and Erik himself was praised for his courtly virtues by one of the most popular minstrels of the time, Frauenlob. And the expansion continued. Despite counterattacks and military alliances among cities, North German princes and the Norwegian king, Erik succeeded in becoming the ruler over Wismar and Stralsund in 1318. This completed the string of cities from Lübeck to Novgorod: now only Greifswald remained outside his control.

The rampant expansion was financed with taxes and loans, which resulted in an extremely delicate financial balance. The Late Medieval agricultural crisis was perhaps already beginning to emerge, at least there were some catastrophic harvests in the first decade of the 1300s, and in 1312 and 1313 riots broke out among the peasants in Sealand and Jutland. They were brutally beaten and punished with mass executions, military control posts, increased corvée, and a new tax of a bushel of rye was levied on each marc gold in property valuation, the so-called "gold grain." A military expansion into the rich North German areas could have financed itself, but the warfare had become increasingly expensive. Under Erik VI, a naval reform occurred, so that the general provision of warships from all over the country was now finally replaced by a taxation in favor of large, permanently manned warships with professional soldiers, which were better but also more expensive. In addition, Erik began to more consistently use mercenary forces, which were paid with land, with income from property, or with loans taken out with mortgages on real estate. The largest lenders and mortgagees were the counts of Holstein. Again, it was a common method of financing at the time, and it had great advantages for a prince of war. Erik VI retained a legal claim to the large lands which he gradually mortgaged and lost their resulting revenue: just a single major military victory could have given him enough cash to redeem many of the mortgages. That did not happen, however, one reason is likely due to Erik's sad personal fate. Queen Ingeborg gave him fourteen children. Thirteen died as infants, and Ingeborg dropped the fourteenth out of a carriage, killing the child, after which she entered a monastery. When Erik died in 1319 a year and a half after Ingeborg, he had no direct heirs, and the Holstein mortgagees and Danish noblemen could place very high demands on his successor and play different candidates against each other, which would have been much more difficult if Erik had left behind a male heir to the throne.

After Erik's death, his brother Christopher became king after signing a hard-line charter with far-reaching concessions to the nobility that effectively limited his power. The Holstein count, Gerhard III, was one of the great lenders and in 1326 became the custodian of the young duke Valdemar

Eriksen of Southern Jutland. Gerhad III, together with dissatisfied bishops and nobility, united in appointing Valdemar (IV) Eriksen king that same year. During the negotiations about this matter, it was decided that in the future the Duchy of Southern Jutland should not be united with or linked to the Kingdom of Denmark, so that one person should reign over them both. This became a crucial point in all subsequent negotiations on the position of South Jutland. Consequently, this meant that the newly elected king resigned as duke, and was succeeded by Gerhard, who received Southern Jutland as hereditary fief.

Valdemar Eriksen had actually almost as strong as an inheritance claim to the throne as Christopher, and a civil war between the two kings ensued. Christopher was first supported by the North Jutland nobility and then by others in Southern Jutland, while Lübeck and other Hanseatic towns changed sides to align with whomever gave them the most privileges. Christopher had to go into exile in Rostock. He returned with better battle fortune and in 1329 he was strong enough to depose the young Valdemar and become reinstated as king. The new covenant was sealed with a marriage between his son Erik and a sister of Count Gerhard. However, it lasted briefly: in November 1331 the armies of the two rulers clashed, and after a long battle Christopher lost and fled. His son Erik soon died of battle injuries and Christopher spent his last short time in extreme poverty on the island of Lolland. When he died, the king's power was bankrupt and any revenue that was generated went directly to Gerhard III and his cousin, Johan the Gentle, who was half brother to Christopher. Together, the two had provided loans of 200,000 marks of silver, and Gerhard received Funen and Northern Jutland as collateral, while Johan received Sealand and Scania. Their administration of the mortgages took place according to local habits, but in contemporary and later propaganda of the time it was portrayed as a particularly harsh form of economic extortion. The minting stopped, every centralized royal army disbanded, and eight years followed without a king.

A song of lamentation of the time began with the words: "Sigh and twist your hands in anger, sorrowful, my fatherland." It continues to lament the lax morality of Danish noblemen and the urge to imitate everything German. It has been widely cited ever since and an important starting point to consider whether some form of Danish nationalism or patriotic sentiment existed in the Middle Ages (discussed in Jensen and Fantysová-Matejková 2020). There is no doubt that in the Middle Ages one could think of nations as attached to various stereotypical notions. For example, "from the Germans has never come anything but fraud and cunning," Rydårbogen wrote, or "from the German has never come anything but softness and sausages," written by Saxo. The Danes on the other hand were internationally known for being drunkards, perhaps even more than the English. Some, however, also emphasized Danish eloquence, and a single Paris professor at this time described that the Scandinavians were particularly good at necromancy. This kind of generalization existed at all levels: people from Scania were considered lazy and cowards, those from

Falster untrustworthy, while jutlanders always came to late. Of course, it is a form of nationalism, a sense of community between those who are of the same nation or people or lineage. It differs from modern forms of nationalism in several ways. It was less related to territory or land than nineteenth-century nationalism, and ones "fatherland" was a flexible concept. Usually, it described an area ruled by a king, and it could very well include newly conquered areas with a population that did not speak Danish. Medieval nationalism was also far less attached to language than the nineteenth century. The language was sometimes highlighted as a marker for distinguishing between Danish and German, but only in the Late Middle Ages, and perhaps surprisingly only a few times. This was likely due to the fact that there were very large dialectal differences, so it was difficult to speak about a particular form of common Danish language, and that German was becoming prevalent everywhere, geographically and socially. It left its mark. A very large percentage of modern Danish words and sentence structures are simply taken from German, especially during the 1400s. Linguists may debate whether it is a third or a half, but there is no doubt that there has been a massive linguistic influence from German in Danish. Not only did the German language have an influence, but many in the territories of Denmark were also able to express themselves in both Danish and German, and this apparently applies to all strata of the population. Thus, the various anti-German statements in several sources during the Middle Ages do not acknowledge the existence of a contradiction in practice. On the contrary, movement has been great across language boundaries, and large groups from German territories have slipped into the Danish-speaking community as noblemen and traders and craftsmen. Around 1400, every third fiefholder in Denmark had a German background.

Starting in 1332 there was no king in Denmark. Jutland and the islands were mortgaged, Scania was taken over by King Magnus Eriksen of Sweden. Estonia became an independent fief, as did Rügen, which did not belong under the Danish throne after 1325, although the island ecclesiastically continued to be part of the Roskilde diocese until 1660. In the same way the island of Fehmarn ceased to be part of the empire in 1326. Halland, Southern Jutland, and Holstein were ruled by dukes and counties without a king, and the northern German cities became independent or subject to local princes. In 1340 the Holsteins were on their way out of Northern Jutland, and Count Gerhard had decided to exchange territories, so that Duke Valdemar got Northern Jutland and Gerhard received Southern Jutland. But on April 1, 1340, Gerhard was assassinated in Randers in his room by an otherwise unknown Jutland petty nobleman, Niels Ebbesen. It has been interpreted by posterity as a national rebellion against German supremacy, but is rather an expression of the desire of the nobles of Northern Jutland for independence and rebellion, which was later directed with equal zeal towards Danish kings as to the Holstein count.

The empire would become restored by a determined and lucky effort by Valdemar IV, Christopher's younger son. He was raised by Holy Roman Emperor Louis IV and would continue to receive great support from the emperor and his family. Valdemar's first step was to marry Helvig, who was the sister of the Southern Jutland duke, therefore gaining access to the region of Northern Jutland areas that she held in mortgage. The schism between the two lines of the royal house, which dates back to 1252, was healed. Valdemar utilized his possessions financially to the limits and gained the reputation of getting money out of everything: it was said that he could not tolerate even the rivers running freely into the sea without installing watermills and earning revenue. The money was used for conquests, initially in the islands, and in 1343 he gained possession of Copenhagen and then several of the great castles in Sealand. In 1346, after lengthy negotiations, he sold Estonia to the Teutonic Order for the considerable sum of 19,000 marks of silver. It was a good deal, since Estonia was at that time in practice impossible for the Danish king to control. Large peasants revolts erupted against Danish suppression, and King Magnus Eriksen of Sweden lead a crusade against Novgorod in an attempt to extend the Swedish rule from Finland down the Baltic Sea to Estonia as well, and he was in the process of negotiating with the Teutonic Order. In those circumstances, Valdemar IV needed more money that could be used to redeem mortgages and buy military aid. This did not mean that later kings could not make a claim on Estonia, which also ecclesiastically remained under the archdiocese of Lund, but a de facto political supremacy was not since recreated. In 1360, Valdemar captured Scania, Southern Halland and Blekinge, thereby gaining access to the enormous revenue from the Scania market. At first, it was a short-lived pleasure. After a prolonged war with the Hanseatic cities, peace was forged in Stralsund in the year 1370, and the Hanseatic authorities gained control of Scania for fifteen years. But in 1361, Valdemar added a new territory to the empire when, in an enormously bloody battle, he conquered Visby and took possession of the rich island of Gotland, which with few interruptions remained a part of the empire until 1645. Danish monarchs continued to use the title "king of the Goths" until 1972, in respect for tradition much more than for political reality. The island of Øland also became part of the empire concurrently with Gotland.

Valdemar IV's policies were fierce and led to several revolts among the nobles of Jutland, supported by the Hanseatic cities. Valdemar's response was partly to fight power with power and partly to rely on foreign nobles who were not part of the local networks, but solely owed the king their position and loyalty. A large number of North German aristocrats were introduced in Denmark during the 1300s in this way. The most well-known individual was probably Henning Podebusk (also known as Putbus) from the town of Putbus on Rügen, who became a loyal supporter of Valdemar IV and earning the title of the seneschal of the realm as well as the king's deputy on several occasions. It provided opportunities in the diplomatic game when the seneschal sealed agreements on the king's behalf, which the king could later claim he was not bound by if his priorities shifted. These were opportunities that were exploited in numerous cases and which would have been more difficult to use in a modern nation-state system than in a medieval empire. Finally, Valdemar worked more consciously in a larger European context than most of his predecessors. In 1346–1347 he went to Jerusalem, where he was dubbed Knight of the Holy Sepulcher, although he had actually promised to go on a crusade against the pagan Lithuanians at the same time. The pilgrimage to the Holy City was an important step along the way that Valdemar, around 1351, could persuade the pope to levy a new crusade tax on all Danish churches, which Valdemar received half of in exchange for crusading in the Baltic Sea area. A large part of that tax helped finance the reconquering of Scania in 1360. In those same years, Valdemar began negotiations with the French king to support him in the Hundred Years' war and help him conquer England. Valdemar was both to deliver a Danish fleet and to legitimize the voyage with the Danish claim to England, which dated back to Canute the Great's time in the 1000s. And in 1364–1365, Valdemar traveled to the papacy in Avignon with King Peter of Cyprus, where he took the cross and promised to help Peter recapture Jerusalem, of which Peter was heir. Though nothing concrete came out of these plans, they were certainly not totally taken out of the blue, and Valdemar should be considered as one of many examples of the traveling warlords of the Renaissance, who, with their special abilities and good connections, could forge a career as ruler or prince in many different places. Ultimately, Valdemar's abilities were focused towards recreating the Danish empire, but his talents could easily have been applied to other territories. At the same time, European engagements provided both political and economic benefits, which were an important prerequisite for success at home. Valdemar's services to the emperor on these voyages was so excellent that Valdemar was rewarded in 1350 by receiving the city tax of Lübeck for a few years, a staggering sum.

Valdemar's politics created a new empire with important areas under the control of the Danish king as well as a strengthened royal power that outweighed that of the nobles. He also created important alliances with the rulers of the Baltic Sea through the marriages of his children. Valdemar's son Christopher died in 1363, and during one of his travels, Valdemar had agreed to pass his kingdom to his daughterson Albert VI of Mecklenburg. This would have meant that large northern German territories would again become part of the empire. However, this was prevented when Valdemar's second daughter, Margrethe, quickly ensured that her Oluf became Danish king after Valdemar's death in 1375. This succession signaled the beginning of the creation of an even greater empire.

References

Aggesen, Sven. 1992. *The Works of Sven Aggesen: Twelfth-Century Danish Historian*, Trans. Eric Christiansen. London: University College.
Andersen, Per. 2011. *Legal Procedure and Practise in Medieval Denmark*. Leiden: Brill.
Bysted, Ane, et al. 2012. *Jerusalem in the North. Denmark and the Baltic Crusades, 1100–1522*. Turnhout: Brepols.
Chronicon roskildense. 1970. In *Scriptores minores historiæ danicæ medii ævi* 1–2, ed. M. Cl. Gertz, 14–33. Copenhagen: Selskabet for udgivelse af kilder til dansk historie [1 ed. 1917–18. Copenhagen: G.E.C. Gad].
Constable, Giles. 1999. The Place of the Magdeburg Charter of 1107/08 in the History of Eastern Germany and of the Crusades. In *Vita religiosa im Mittelalter: Festschrift für Kaspar Elm zum 70. Geburtstag*, ed. Franz J. Felten and Nikolas Jaspert, 283–299. Berlin: Duncker & Humbolt.
DMA: *Danmarks middelalderlige annaler*. 1980. Ed. Erik Kroman. København: Selskabet for Udgivelse af Kilder til dansk Historie.
Ekroll, Øystein. 2021. Scandinavian Holy Kings in the Nativity Church of Bethlehem. In *Tracing the Jerusalem code*, vol. 1: *The Holy City Christian Cultures in Medieval Scandinavia (ca. 1100–1536)*, ed. Kristin B. Aavitsland and Line M. Bonde, 87–93. Berlin: De Gruyter.
Guibert af Nogent 1996. *Dei gesta per Francos* et cinq autres textes, ed. R.B.C. Huygens. Turnholt: Brepols. Translation: *The Deeds of God through the Franks*, a translation of Guibert de Nogent's Gesta Dei per Francos, by Robert Levine. Woodbridge, Suffolk: Boydell Press (1997).
Helmold of Bosau. 1868. *Helmoldi presbyteri Chronica Slavorum*, ed. G.H. Pertz. Hannover: Hahn. English Translation: *The Chronicle of the Slavs by Helmold, Priest of Bosau*. 1935, trans. Francis Joseph Tschan. New York: Columbia University Press.
Jakobsen, Johnny Grandjean, and Gögsig. 2021. Preachers of War: Dominican Friars as Promoters of the Crusades in the Baltic Region in the Thirteenth Century. In *Christianity and War in Medieval East Central Europe and Scandinavia*, ed. R. Kotecki, C.S. Jensen, and S. Bennett, 97–115. Leeds: Arc Humanities Press.
Jensen, Kurt Villads. 2009. Sacralization of the Landscape: Converting Trees and Measuring Land in the Danish Crusades Against the Wends. In *The Clash of Cultures on the Medieval Baltic Frontier*, ed. Alan V. Murray, 141–150. Farnham: Ashgate.
Jensen, Kurt Villads. 2017. *Crusading at the Edges of Europe. Denmark and Portugal c. 1000–c. 1250*. London: Routledge.
Jensen, Kurt Villads. 2021. Once and Future Crusades. Past and Projected Plans of Emperor Frederick II and King Valdemar II of Denmark, c. 1214–1227. In *The Crusades. History and Memory*, ed. Kurt Villads Jensen and Torben Kjersgaard Nielsen, 77–94. Turnhout: Brepols.
Jensen, Kurt Villads, et al. 1999. *Hellere fanden selv end Erik på tronen. Konflikten mellem Jens Grand og Erik Menved 1294–1302*. Odense: Universitetsforlag.
Jensen, Kurt Villads, and Jana Fantysová-Matejková. 2020. Creating Cohesion in Dynastic Conglomerates. Identities in Comparison: Medieval Bohemia and Denmark. In *The Historical Evolution of Regionalizing Identities in Europe*, ed. Dick E.H. de Boer, Nils Holger Petersen, Bas Spierings, and Martin van der Velde, 63–121. Berlin: Peter Lang.

Jensen, Kurt Villads, and Torben Kjersgaard Nielsen. 2003. Pope Innocent III and Denmark. In *Innocenzo III. Urbs et orbis*, ed Andrea Sommerlechner, 1133–1168. Rome: Società romana di storia patria.
Knytlingesagaen. 1919–25. In *Sogur Danakonunga*, ed. Carl Petersen og Emil Olson. Copenhagen. English translation: *Knytlinga Saga. The History of the Kings of Denmark.* 1986. Trans. Hermann Palsson and Paul Edwards. Odense: University Press.
Phillips, Jonathan. 2007. *The Second Crusade: Extending the Frontiers of Christendom.* New Haven: Yale University Press.
Riley-Smith, Jonathan. 1997. *The First Crusaders, 1095–1131.* Cambridge: Cambridge University Press.
Saxo Grammaticus. 2015. *Gesta Danorum: The History of the Danes*, vol 1–2. Ed. Karsten Friis-Jensen, trans. Peter Fisher. Oxford: Clarendon Press.
Selch Jensen, Carsten, et al. 2019. *Da danskerne fik Dannebrog.* Copenhagen: Det teologiske fakultet.
The Danish Medieval Laws. The laws of Scania, Zealand and Jutland. 2016. Ed. Ditlev Tamm and Helle Vogt. London: Brepols.
The Offices and Masses of St. Knud Lavard, vol. 1–2. 2010. Ed. John Bergsagel. Copenhagen: Royal Library.
Vitae sanctorum danorum. 1908–12. Ed. M.Cl. Gertz. Copenhagen: G.E.C. Gad.

CHAPTER 5

The Union Empire

With Valdemar's death, the Danish Council of the realm chose his grandson, Oluf, as king. However, Oluf's mother, Margrethe, acted as the king's guardian, and was the de facto ruler. 20 years later, Margrethe became a leading force behind the creation of the Kalmar Union, which eventually became one of Europe's most powerful and largest empires by geography. The Union's core countries—Norway, Denmark, and the Duchies—remained united as one empire for over four hundred years (In general, see Bysted et al. 2012; Helle 2003).

Margrethe married King Haakon of Norway in 1363 when she was ten years old, and moved to Norway in order to be raised as a queen by Merete Ulfstand, daughter of Saint Birgitta of Sweden (Etting 2004). That same year, the Norwegian-Swedish union dissolved, when the Swedish Council deposed Haakon's father as king, instead choosing Albert III of Mecklenburg as their ruler. While the political environment had certainly changed, a close relationship remained between Norway and Sweden, with many powerful noble lineages found in each kingdom. When Oluf, son of Margrethe, was elected by the council as king of Denmark in 1375, he was only five years old. Margrethe, as his guardian, gained strong and necessary support from Henning Podebusk, the powerful seneschal. When Haakon died in 1380, Oluf also inherited Norway, with the Norwegian Council's blessing. Consequently, a foundation was created for a dual orientation towards both the Baltic Sea and the Northern Atlantic in the following centuries. Norway encompassed the areas of Iceland and the Faroe Islands, as well as the Orkney and Shetland Islands. Beyond this, the distant territory of Greenland was also included, which still upheld consistent communications to the mainland and played a certain role in Norwegian literature, and even in the end of the 1400s began to be depicted on geographical maps. Most assumed that Greenland was attached to the northernmost area of Norway, and, together with the Sami lands, constituted an enormous unexplored field for mission, filled with pagans and mythical peoples. Others believed Greenland to be an island that held some connection to the lesser-known Vinland—America—where some missions and maybe even tentative colonization efforts were made in the 1100s. Whether attempts were still made to sail to Vinland in the late 1300s, and whether Vinland was considered to be an island or continental mainland remains unknown. However, by 1500, many believed that Greenland constituted the westernmost peninsula of the Asian continent. Norway received substantial revenues in the form of luxury goods such as walrus and narwhal ivory from its North Atlantic assets. However, its main source of revenue was fishing: herring and stock fish were crucial exports to the rest of Europe (Jensen 2007).

As the royal guardian, Margrethe led the struggle against the Hanseatic League, during which she succeeded in reconquering Scania and the Scania market in 1385. This was chiefly achieved through the extensive use of pirates, whom Margrethe secretly supported while she publicly made alliances with the Hanseatic League in order to combat the unchecked freebooting in the Baltic Sea. Due to her connections in the Swedish aristocracy, as well as her personal relationship with Saint Birgitta, Margrethe became entrusted with the estate of the Swedish seneschal Bo Grip after his death in 1383, thus gaining control of nearly half of the castles in Sweden and Finland. Danish expansion was well underway. However, Oluf died suddenly in 1387, just as he was of age to take control of the government. A rumor spread in the Hanseatic cities, that Margrethe had murdered her son in order to remain in power. There were even reports as late as 1402 that one could find a man in Prussia postulating that his name was Oluf and that he wanted to claim his royal birthright. This man was delivered to Margrethe and burned at the stake. Following Oluf's death, the question of who was the legitimate successor posed a direct threat to Margrethe's power. Ultimately this fear was resolved when the Councils of both Denmark and Norway named Margrethe as rightful heir to the throne, bestowing on her the title of "Supreme Lady Sovereign and Rightful Husband." This is an interesting and unique title, unknown from elsewhere, as it unites a female and male power-dynamic into an inclusive title, indicating that Margrethe now reigned in her own right: not as a wife or guardian to a male counterpart, despite her female gender. The fact that the Councils agreed to such an unusual title was not solely due to Margrethe's strength of character, but was also certainly influenced by their fear of Sweden's evolving political environment. Sweden was torn between two warring aristocratic parties: one of which vehemently rebelled against King Albert III of Mecklenburg. The Swedish Council chose Margrethe to rule in 1388, awarding her the same title as the Danish and Norwian Councils. The following year, Margrethe defeated Albert in the battle of Falköping, imprisoning him for the next six years. Stockholm was the last city still under control of the Mecklenburg family, and was finally occupied by Margrethe in 1308—again with the help of pirates, but also after tense negotiations with other political agents around the Baltic.

THE KALMAR UNION'S EARLY PERIOD

In 1388, Margrethe adopted her sister grandson, Bugislav of Pomerania, who now took the Nordic name Erik. He was recognized as heir of Norway and hailed as king of Denmark and Sweden in 1396. In 1397 a number of noblemen and clergy from all three kingdoms of Kalmar met, on the day of the Trinity, on July 13, which was hardly coincidental (Imsen 2007). Erik was now crowned king of all three countries by one ceremony, with the attendance of 67 noblemen and bishops, including one representative from the Orkney Islands. This assembly issued and sealed a Coronation whose main import was to acknowledge Erik's decision and right to rule the kingdoms virtually totally autonomous. A week later, a Union document was drafted, which apparently was never formally issued and published. It was written on paper and sealed by just ten nobles with imprinted seals—not the official and binding hanging seals—and what its official status was remains opaque. The Union document's content is fascinating in that it differs from the Coronation letter in several ways. It was an attempt to create a common basis for an empire of several countries, while also involving the noblemen, ensuring them some oversight over the king. It stated that there should be a common king among the three kingdoms in perpetuity. A common foreign policy must be pursued so that attack on one of the countries must be answered by all, and the document forbade the union countries from attacking one another. Feuds among the countries' nobles were forbidden. The king was obliged to respect each country's local laws and customs, and he could not place fiefholders from one country in castles of another country without the consent of the councilors of the realm. If war was waged outside the empire, it must be agreed by the king with the consent from the Councils of all three countries. The Coronation document and the Union document reflect two different perceptions of political power that were discussed in Europe at the times. According to one theory—the so-called *regimen regale*—power comes from above, and the ruler dictates over the people; that is reflected in the Coronation document. According to the other theory in the Union document—the *regimen politicum*—power comes from below, from the people who choose a king to exercise power on a daily basis, but ultimately must involve the people in important decisions. Throughout the Middle Ages, "the people" described in the union document refers, of course, to the top layer of the societal fabric: the aristocracy. The two divergent forms of state perception were contested throughout the fifteenth century and were of great importance to the rulers of the Kalmar Union, but in practice, *regime regale* was ultimately implemented.

The ensuing years were marked by numerous wars. Gotland was conquered by pirates and subsequently taken over by the Teutonic Order. An attempted conquest by Margrethe failed, but she was able to buy out the Order in 1407. During those same years, Margrethe served as guardian and protector of the widowed Duchess of Schleswig's young children, whom she cheated out of most of the duchy. This resulted in open war in 1409 between Margrethe and Erik on one side and an army from Schleswig and Holstein on the other. Magrethe was victorious, and as a result could enter into Flensburg as conqueror in 1412, but died four days later of the plague.

That the new empire held together was both the result of deliberate effort and lucky coincidences that had occurred during the 1300s. There apparently was an active interest in peace among the three Nordic countries after so many wars and feuds over the past generations. However, it is difficult to measure the durability of such rhetoric of peace. On the other hand, it is clear that the empire's territories had changed so many times that a common Nordic-North German aristocracy had emerged. It is doubtful whether it makes any sense at all to speak of a separate Danish or Norwegian or Swedish aristocracy around 1400: the noble houses were solidly interconnected through innumerable marriages. In the borderlands of the empires there are also unique lineages, who prospered by owning land on either sides of the borders and could establish contacts with both, such as the Thott's, always conscious of the strong family ties no matter where they had their individual basis at the time. Living on the frontier was an occupation that could very well be leveraged to feud against neighbors, but which nevertheless often carried the desire for peace. It was typical that the noble lineages along the border areas often got together to agree on a local separate peace, even as the kings continued to war against each other. It is also likely that the Union, with its centralization and distribution of centers of power, created better conditions for some nobles. Finland's magnates became less dependent on Sweden and a more equal part of the Union.

The three countries continued to act as independent entities in terms of legal status, although for some areas a standardization was slowly made. The Code of Jutland from 1241 developed into a form of Danish law for the whole realm and gradually replaced the various high-medieval regional laws (*The Danish Medieval Laws* 2016). The king became the supreme court in the three kingdoms, but enacted that function very differently. In Norway the law was delegated to government officials and handled nearly administratively, but in Denmark and Sweden there was actually a royal court, over which the ruler often presided personally. A particular problem was the boundaries between the different legal systems. After Margrethe's death, the question of Schleswig re-emerged. Erik of Pomerania demanded that the case be settled under Danish law, and in 1421 he got the Danish provincial councils to state that both Northern and Southern Jutland and even the areas further south belonged under Danish law.

During the same time, Erik of Pomerania gradually tried to introduce common institutions and symbols that consolidated the Union. Initially, it was an imperial seal with three crowns, with later attempts at a common weapon of the Union and a common flag that should be red with a yellow cross. When he buried his wife Philippa in 1430, Erik gave a great gift to Vadstena monastery by remunerating ten priests to read daily liturgies for her soul, requesting that they be dressed in red robes with yellow crosses, "named the realm's banner." Erik also built a principal administration, which presided over the entire Union, with one chief magistrate, one chamberlain, and one chancellor. This system was also facilitated by the fact that Erik, like Margrethe, consistently neglected to appoint new officials to the age-old administrative posts like *drost* (seneschal), *gældker* (the king's representative and economic responsible for Scania) and others. The Union developed a common chief herold in addition to the local heralds, who held titles for the given territories—the herald of Lolland and so on—and Erik instituted a knightly order, which of course belonged to the king personally and could be bestowed to anyone he found worthy. The knighthood came to act as a collective Union order. The three kingdoms each had their patron saint, Olav in Norway, Erik in Sweden, and Canute in Denmark (it did not matter much that there was an increasing confusion between Saint Canute King (who died 1086) and Saint Knut Duke Lavard (died 1131). The three royal saints were now depicted together as a special union trinity and a symbol of unity. At the same time, Bridget of Sweden became immensely popular following her canonization in 1393, and her worship was widespread in all the countries of the Union. In practice, she came to serve as a common saint and uniting symbol for the Union (Fig. 5.1).

Relations with the pope and Church were exceptionally fine. In a letter dated around 1400 to Pope Boniface IX, Margrethe described the vast realms of the new Kalmar Union, which were impossible to defend because they were surrounded by water on all sides (Boniface IX, letter 1401). Large swathes of pagan and even Christian neighbors had attacked the shores of the three kingdoms, and inspired by the devil plundered and burned and abducted men and women, killing them or persuading them to revolt. Therefore, Margrethe asked for the pope's assistance, and was quickly answered. In 1401, he wrote to the archbishops of the three Nordic kingdoms and commissioned them to preach crusades throughout the lands of the Kalmar Union and neighboring countries to gather crusaders to fight enemies of Queen Margrethe and the Roman Church. He intervened to reward Margrethe because of her and her ancestors' constant and devoted support for the Roman church. The participants in this crusade would receive the same rewards as those who went to Jerusalem and be cleansed from sin, and could gain the indulgence also by sending a deputy if they did not have the power to fight themselves, and one could even earn this spiritual reward by supporting the crusade through prayer. The only condition was simply to fight against Queen Margrethe's enemies, "whether they were pagan or Christian." These circumstances were completely unusual in a European context. It was clearly a real crusade, but its unique quality was the explicit permission to wage a crusade against Christians. In all other crusade privileges, it was conscientiously specified that crusades could

Fig. 5.1 Eric of Pomerania worked deliberately and targeted to create common symbols for the Kalmar Union he ruled, stretching from Greenland to Russia, from the uttermost northern point of Norway to Hamburg. It was created in 1397, and already the next year Eric had a seal made that combined the coat of arms of the four main countries: the three lions of Denmark, the lion with axe of Norway, the Swedish crowned lion on sinisterbend streams, and the griff of Pomerania. Throughout the fifteenth century, it became more and more elaborate and incorporated the two leopards of Schleswig, the nettle leaf of Holstein, the swan of Stormarn, etc. The coat of arms of the union are represented here on Admiralty's banner of Eric's fleet, but with the three Swedish golden crowns instead of the lion. The banner was taken as booty by a fleet from Lübeck during a naval battle in Øresund in 1427 and kept in the Hansa-city until it was lost during the Second Worldwar. It has been used as illustration in several Danish history books as "Danish naval banner," which is actually a bit surprising. It is obviously an imperial banner, not a national Danish one. https://da.wikipedia.org/wiki/Danmarks_rigsvåben#/media/Fil:Skibsflaget_fra_Mariakirken_i_Lübeck.png (Creative commons: Public Domain)

only be waged against pagans and nonbelievers, or against heretics and Christians who had deviated from the Church deliberately by disobeying the pope's commandments and thereby become heretics. Here he spoke without reservation of a crusade against Christians simply because they threatened the new Kalmar Union. The pope must have held Margrethe in high regard: at one point she even received a special papal seal to use when she wanted to send something directly and secretly to the pope—a kind of red phone. Unfortunately, we do not know how many secret letters Margrethe truly wrote to the pope.

One of the great political powers in the Baltic Sea was the Teutonic Order, which had created an independent state in Prussia which operated without a royal ruler and whose only authority was the pope (Christiansen 1997; Urban 2003; Kubon 2016). The Order was established in the Baltic Sea area around 1220 and moved its headquarters to Marienburg in Prussia (present Malbork in Poland) in 1309. Its task was to conduct continuous crusades against local pagans. This was termed the annual *Preussenreisen*, "Prussian voyage," which attracted large crowds of nobles from all over Northern Europe, who were registered with the Order and for a while would participate in battles and bloody raids against the pagans. The most popular were the summer trips, but they often had difficulty penetrating the swampy territories. The winter voyages reached farther when meadows and rivers were frozen. Once the hunts were complete, the most distinguished of the participants were celebrated by being seated at the high table along with the Order's High Master in Marienburg, and some were even allowed to hang their coat of arms in the large assembly hall. The main opponents of the German Order were the pagan Lithuanians, who not only managed to remain pagan but also created a well-organized kingdom that stretched from the Baltic to the Black Sea. In 1386, the Lithuanian grand duke married the Polish princess and converted to Christianity. In principle, the goal of the German Order ought thus to have been achieved, but nevertheless the order continued its crusade till the end of the Middle Ages. In 1410, the Teutonic Knights suffered a severe defeat at Tannenberg against a Polish-Lithuanian army, and at a large church meeting in Konstanz in 1414–1418, the order was severely criticized for abuse of power, brutality, and for effectively frightening people away from the path of Christianity instead of converting them. Erik of Pomerania took advantage of this. Immediately after the church meeting, where the bishops of the Danish empire were well represented, he contacted the Polish-Lithuanian ruler. The goal was to create an alliance between the two giant unions in Northern Europe, to counterbalance the Teutonic Order. In 1419, it was agreed that, the two parties should attack Prussia from both fronts, and when the Order was defeated, its possessions were to be distributed among the victors. It was then decided that Erik should gain Estonia. This war was ironically termed a crusade because the Teutonic Order was accused of having turned heretical by working with the Orthodox Russians. At the last moment, Erik backed out of the alliance, with seemingly no clear reason, and by 1423 he had now forged an "unbreakable peace" with the Teutonic Order. An important reason for this reversal became clear: he wanted the Order to support his battle against the counts of Holstein over Southern Jutland.

Eric of Pomerania launched an immense voyage around Europe in 1423–25, just as Valdemar IV had done. We can follow his trip in some details through the receipts for the enormous loans he raised on the way to finance the expedition, and which he never paid back. Erik also reached Jerusalem and was knighted at the Holy Sepulcher. An important goal of the trip was to secure the position of Southern Jutland as part of the Union. The counts of Holstein had been dukes of Southern Jutland since 1326 and kept the territory as hereditary fief. Now King Erik began a lengthy process to change that (Hedemann 2018). First, it was decided by Danish courts that the Holsteins had violated any right to property by waging war against the Danish king, as they had done in the years leading up to the death of Queen Margrethe. Then, as mentioned, the Danish provincial councils resolved that Southern Jutland was Danish because the Danish language was spoken in the area. This enabled Erik during his voyage to argue with the German-Roman emperor Sigismund that Southern Jutland could not be a fief with an independent duke, because there were no fiefs in Denmark at all. There were provinces and territories, but not fiefs. It was an explanation which the emperor accepted, and he judged that Southern Jutland belonged to Denmark and not under Holstein. The decision ultimately didn't stick. When Erik returned from his pilgrimage, he had to wage long and ultimately fruitless battles against the Holsteins.

Erik's pilgrimage went through Eastern Europe, from Stralsund across Wrocław to Krakow, where he attended the coronation of the Polish Queen. Here he met with Emperor Sigismund, the Byzantine Emperor Manuel II Palaiologos, and the Turkish Sultan Murad who was represented by the despot of Serbia. The Prince Pedro of Portugal was also present. Great negotiations were underway, and the pope was represented by one of his most trusted cardinals, Aeneas Sylvius Piccolomini, the great Renaissance humanist and Latin linguist who later became pope by the name of Pius II. He described in his letters Erik's handsome and manly features which drew women's hearts to him with the longing of love, even the hearts of empresses. During the visit, Erik also naturally participated in the emperor's crusade against the heretic Hussites and became first-hand acquainted with their new tactics, the wagon fortress defended by crossbows and spears, but also by new powder guns. From Krakow, Erik continued to Venice, where he received a magnificent reception and was enamored with a loan of 20,000 ducats and a Venetian galley, which transported him via Dalmatia, where he borrowed more money, to his final destination the Holy Land. Erik traveled incognito as a lay pilgrim and remained unnoticed and safe, in spite of a spy having his portrait painted and sent to the Sultan of Damascus. All in all, the journey has been immensely expensive, and much of it was funded by the princes and cities Erik visited along his pilgrimage. The same approach was taken by several other kings of the Danish Empire during the Middle Ages. Later, other European princes began to undertake the same kind of large diplomatic tours, but apparently the Danish rulers were among the first to use this new political instrument. At its core, it was about connections. Erik of Pomerania and the other Danish kings were taken seriously in European politics and were involved in big decisions, which is why it could be an extremely big advantage for a city or a local prince to be in Erik's good graces and welcome him with pomp and circumstance. The political significance was measurable and visible to all actors involved, and it could be adjusted very quickly. Later King Christian I embarked on a similar diplomatic trip, where he was also received magnificently and got everything paid for him. Among other things, he was entrusted with the task of mediating between the emperor and the mighty Duke of Burgundy. It failed, and Christian's political credibility crumbled instantly. Cities that had previously received him with open arms now closed their gates to him.

Earlier, Erik of Pomerania had married the young Filippa of England, a match that had been personally drafted by Queen Margrethe. The marriage provided many benefits. England had interfered very directly in Icelandic fishing and several times directly attacked and looted Iceland. The marriage halted this, in fact for the benefit of both parties. The Danish empire thus came to bind the Baltic Sea and the North Sea together more tightly than before. Under the rule of Erik of Pomerania, fifty years after the Great Plague of the later Middle Ages, the new European world order was just about established: Eastern Europe supplied grain and timber, and Western Europe meat and cloth. Of course, it is a very simplified picture, and local areas continued to produce for local consumption, but the trend had begun and meant a rapid increase in trade between East and West, which now consisted of large, heavy loads of goods. Just as in the Viking Age, the Danish Empire came to play an important role as a transit country, but now also as a producer—of fish, of grain from especially the Danish islands and Southern Jutland and Holstein, and from Norway and the Baltic possessions of timber and timber products, especially tar. The entire European shipping industry was hastily growing and totally dependent upon large quantities of tar. Because the empire encompassed both coasts of the Sound, it was possible to impose a taxation on all ships in transit. Erik introduced the Customs of the Sound in 1429, which wouldn't be repealed until 1857: during its tenure it became one of the empire's most important sources of revenue. With the revenue from customs, rich accounts books gradually emerged, giving an impression of how voluminous the trade was and who transited the Sound. The earliest preserved accounts of this activity date from 1497, and starting in 1557 there is an unbroken series of Øresund customs accounts. These accounts show that there was also a large immigration of traders from several different countries who settled in Danish coastal cities. Good relations had existed between Scotland and Norway since long ago, which resulted in a treaty in 1266 which ensured merchants from the two countries that they could recover their property if they suffered shipwreck in the other country. This treaty from Perth was renewed several times, including in 1426 by Erik of Pomerania. The aim was clearly to counterbalance English influence in the North Atlantic and establish the Danish Empire as a competitor to the Hanseatic cities, but the treaty also meant that Scots in large groups traded across Denmark to the Baltic and that many settled in Helsingør and Copenhagen. In the next century, large contingents of Scottish soldiers and mercenaries came to play a major role in the wars of the Danish Empire, especially in Sweden.

The Swedish aristocracy had been divided into several conflicting groups, and that schism had paved the way for Queen Margrethe's takeover of power and the rise of the Kalmar Union. Now the schism reappeared, and one of the groups followed Engelbrekt Engelbrektsson and his men from the province of Dalarna in 1434 in open rebellion against the Union ruler. The subsequent unrest led the Swedish Council, during a meeting in Kalmar in 1436 to express their mistrust of Erik of Pomerania, and they were soon followed by the Danish Council of the realm. Erik retreated to his strong fortress on Gotland to ride out the course of events, but in 1439–1441 the councils of the three countries denounced him and terminated their fidelity to him, thereby deposing him as king. This decision was likely to Erik's astonishment. In any case, he remained in Gotland and continued to name himself king, expecting to return to the throne. Not until 1449 did he give up and return to his possessions in Pomerania, where he lived the last decade of his life.

The Councils had a large number of complaints against Erik. One of the first was that he had disappeared to Gotland with the kingdom's treasure and had not kept his territories in order, so that aristocracy and clergy were subjected to attacks by the lay people. Another was that he had not taken up the fight against the Holsteins who attacked Denmark. A third was that he had installed foreign men to the castles, which was against his coronation promises in Kalmar in 1397. The Danish Council of the realm directly mentions the dukes Bugislav, Vartislav and Barnum, and the Counts Hans and Vitslaf. Erik again replied that Bugislav was not a stranger but the son of his uncle, and moreover, the Danish Council had approved him as castle governor when Erik presented him for the position. This explanation was to no avail. Erik's nephew, Christopher of Bavaria, was proposed as king and elected by the three councils in the years 1440–1442. This new royal installation was under close oversight from the councils, who had exhibited that they could replace one king with another: they were now reluctant to relinquish power. The many disputes and objections in connection with Erik of Pomeranian's deposition were expressed in national terms, but truly addressed something else. Engelbrekt's rebellion was portrayed by some contemporaries as a Swedish rebellion against Danish control, but was truly one aristocratic group's settlement dispute with that of another. The Danish council's complaints were expressed as dissatisfaction with foreign fiefholders, but it was truly foreign individuals whom they had previously approved themselves. The core of the situation was that the three councils made a successful attempt to create a form of an aristocratic republic, which could depose and appoint kings as they pleased. The balance between the two Kalmar government principles in 1397—the *regime regale* and the *regime politicum*—was tipped in favor of the regime politicum, in favor of the nobility. Moreover, it was a development which, with more or less success, was attempted in many places in Europe during the same period, and which matched contemporary theories of power and authority within the church. The hierarchically-ruled papal church with top-down command structures competed with the conciliar movement, wherein the huge church meetings served as the center of power. The aristocratic republic was short-lived in the Danish empire when it came to banishing kings, but it was realized. In turn, the councils in the time of Erik of Pomerania gained more and more influence on the king's local courts and thus gained control of part of the king's juridical power (Fig. 5.2).

The Kalmar Union emerged during a period rich with unions, all organized in their own way. Several arose via marriages between the rulers of two countries. This includes the Polish-Lithuanian Union from 1386, but the two countries tried to integrate, among other things, by creating a common aristocracy. In 1413, 43 Polish noble families adopted a similar number of Lithuanian nobles, thus allowing them to use the coat of arms of the Polish families.

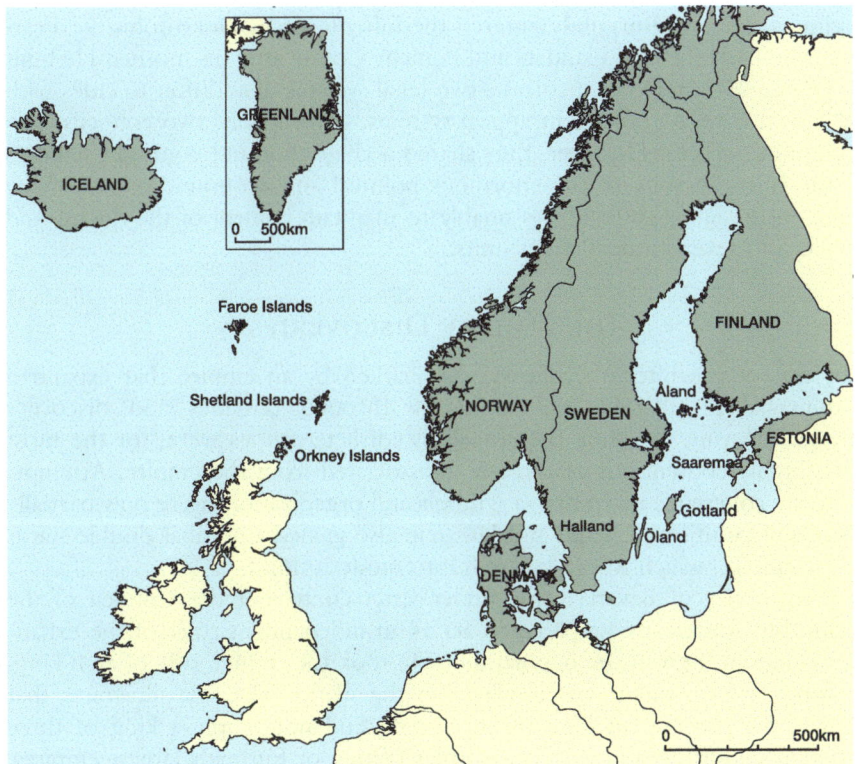

Fig. 5.2 With the establishing of the Kalmar Union in 1397, the Danish empire got a double orientation towards both the Baltic Sea, the North Sea, and the Atlantic. The most important fishing areas and the most important communication lines of Western Europe was controlled by one rule who strove to support trade and expand east–west connection. Øresund became of uttermost strategic and economic importance, and the royal toll imposed on all ships passing through the sund became one of the most important financial sources of the empire for hundreds of years after its establishment in 1429

Aragon, Valencia, and Catalonia were united in a confederation where cooperation and procedures were so well developed that the confederation could continue even without a king. While each of the three countries had a seneschal, a vice-chancellor, and a certain number of representatives in the joint royal council, they also each had their own assembly of estates, council of the realm, and permanent administration of legislation and taxation. When King Martí died in 1410, the three kingdoms continued to work without issue for two years before the nobility decided whom they would nominate as king. During the fifteenth century, this developed into an agreement between the king and the people of the three kingdoms, which differed from place to place according to local custom. Nevertheless, it was a pure expression of a regime politicum. Burgundy entered the inheritance of Duke John the Fearless, who had inherited Flanders and Franche Comte after his mother. He built an empire with mirror structures—two legal systems in addition to cities with their own laws, two different appeal systems, two capitals, two councils, two accounting offices. However, they shared a chancellor and common symbols of the ruler. In spite of the enormous political and economic power of the duke, in the late 1400s he was unable to maintain control of the duchy, and it split into several independent units.

THE TIME OF DISCOVERIES

The rest of the fifteenth century was marked by an empire that expanded commercially, militarily, and politically through crusades and discovery voyages. During this time the crucial Swedish territories were, for the most part, highly contentious or directly disassociated from the empire. Attempts to create coherence by common symbols and organizations were only partially successful. Southern Jutland and Holstein also gained a peculiar double status in the empire, which would last well into modern times.

Christopher of Bavaria came under strict control of the Council of the realm, but was clearly prepared to act as an independent ruler of the expansive kingdom if given the opportunity. He took the strange title of arch king, *archirex*, a term unknown elsewhere in the world. The title illustrates that he was the preeminent king of an empire, and not simply a king of three different countries, and that he, as ruler of one of Europe's largest empires, was immediately under the German emperor himself. In 1445, he married Dorothea of Brandenburg, a traditional but wise choice if he were to assert himself in Northern German politics. That same year, he apparently planned a major expedition into the eastern Baltic territory. He forged an alliance with the Teutonic Order for a joint crusade against the schismatic Russians, and at the same time gave benefits to the bishop of Øsel, thereby marking that there was still a Danish claim to Estonia.

Christopher died suddenly in 1448, perhaps from blood poisoning. He left no sons, but a young widow who had gained considerable property in Norway, Denmark, and Sweden as a wedding gift. An intricate political and economic problem was solved when the councils proposed that Christian from the relatively insignificant Oldenburg become the new king and that he should marry Dorothea. Christian was six generations removed from a Danish king, but the marriage with Dorothea gave him the necessary legitimacy. Initially, the Swedish Council of the realm chose Karl Knutson Bonde as the new king, and the Kalmar Union thus run the risk of breaking into two camps. The following seventy years were characterized by a continuing struggle to bring the two parts of the empire together until the final rupture became irreparable in the 1520s. In the first instance, Christian I, after six years of war, succeeded in defeating Karl Knutson, who had to flee to Danzig in 1457 and seek refuge with the Teutonic Order. Karl soon returned and became a Swedish king 1464–1465 and again from 1467 until his death in 1470. In contemporary Swedish propaganda of the time, these constant wars were portrayed as national revolts, but should rather be understood as internal power struggles between various factions of the Swedish aristocracy.

When Christian became king, he had to confirm in 1448 the agreement from 1326 to the powerful Schleswig–Holstein knighthood that Southern Jutland never would become part of the kingdom of Denmark and would never share the same ruler. This was in direct contrast to Erik of Pomerania's claim that Southern Jutland was a Danish province. The ratification of the 1326 agreement shows how truly weak Christian stood as a new ruler of a large empire, with fragile legitimacy. That changed. In 1460 the situation was quite different, and the Schleswig–Holstein aristocracies chose Christian for Duke of South Jutland and Count of Holstein with the clause that the two principalities should remain united in perpetuity—*up ewig ungedelt,* forever undivided. This strengthened Christian's standing significantly, both financially and politically. His new power bore fruit in 1474, when the German emperor elevated Holstein, Ditmarschen, and Stormarn from county to duchy and inaugurated Christian as duke. However, that did not make the constitutional position of Christian and his successors easier. As Duke of Schleswig, he—and his successors—now had to be elected by the Knights of Schleswig, but approved by the Danish King who was himself. In other words, he was a vassal for himself. At the same time, as Duke of Holstein, he was prince of the Holy Roman Empire and vassal to the emperor. The indivisibility clause gave special frictions within the nineteenth-century nationalism between Danish and German, which was not resolved until the Civil War in 1848.

Christian actively supported trade and tried to balance the various international participants. He gave advantages to Amsterdam in 1460 specifically to weaken the Hanseatic League. At the same time, he sought to strengthen trade in the North Atlantic areas of the kingdom, especially Iceland, and this often occurred in competition with England. From 1469–1473, there was direct but interrupted war between England and an alliance of the Danish Empire, Burgundy and Scotland. The alliance had been sealed with a marriage in 1469 between Christian I's daughter Margrethe and Jacob III of Scotland. To cover the dowry, Christian pledged the Orkney and Shetland Islands to Scotland, but under quite obscure legal conditions. Actually, it was apparently only the royal claim to the royal estates that was given as a mortgage, which in reality excluded the true sovereignty of the islands. However, the mortgages have never been redeemed.

The fall of Constantinople to the Turks in 1453 marked the greatest setback to the European Crusade movement since the loss of Jerusalem in 1187 (Bysted et al. 2012; Jensen 2007). In the coming decades it led to a number of joint European initiatives, in which the Danish Empire participated wholeheartedly. When Christian I was given the news of the fall of Constantinople, he expressed with great conviction that Sultan Mehmed the Conqueror must be the "great beast" described in the Book of Revelation. Christian immediately allowed 6000 nobles from the realms to travel to Constantinople, illustrating how high a priority it was for the countries of the Kalmar Union to participate in the war. We do not know for sure how many nobles actually arrived in Constantinople; Christian later complained that some had been prevented by Swedish rebels. In 1454, the German emperor convened a general European meeting of all important princes to plan a crusade. Christian and Karl Knutsson, however, canceled their attendance because they were still fighting each other. "Scots, Danes, Swedes and Norwegians are living at the extreme edge of the world, and they are not interested in anything outside their own home," Cardinal Aeneas Piccolomoni wrote. That was not quite a fair statement. In 1457, Christian promised the pope that he would lead a crusade through Russia with 200,000 men, which he himself would spearhead. He could guarantee this now that Karl Knutsson had fled from Sweden. Christian's crusade plan was developed in correspondence with others, including his brother-in-law the Duke of Milan, as well as the King of Aragon. In his letters, Christian described the threat posed from the Tatars, Kumans, the people of Erpion and Manbres and Sami, and several other peoples. Some of these have existed, others are totally impossible to recognize.

The pagan attacks on Europe sought to impose on Christians pagan worship and blasphemy, King Christian claimed in his letter. They were located close along the borders of the Kalmar Union and had already penetrated far into Norway; the Norwegians were in danger of converting to the Russian Orthodox faith. Christianity was thus threatened both in the north and south by schismatics and pagans, and so the defense of the Kalmar Union became in itself a defense of Christianity. The Danish Empire, because of its size and its long frontiers to non-Christians, was a stronghold of Christianity against other religions and held a special role in the crusades, Christian concluded. The Crusade efforts were not successful in 1457, but later plans for reattempts were made again and again. By 1471, the emperor called for an assembly in Regensburg, where the threat of the Turks was one of the main topics. Christian was represented by his envoys, especially the prince of Brandenburg, who presented Christian's detailed plans. He suggested an attack on three fronts. The emperor and the German princes were to attack the Turks in the Balkans, and the pope and the Italian cities were to sail across the Adriatic and attack from the coast. Then Christian himself would lead the third army, consisting of contingents from all the countries of the Danish Empire as well as allies, both England, Scotland, Brandenburg, and the great cities along the Baltic Sea. Christian was to go directly to Jerusalem and liberate the Holy City, while the Sultan was distracted by the emperor and the pope. Christian strengthened his proposal by citing two contemporary prophecies which confirmed that his plan would succeed. The first originated from St. Birgitta, who had forecast that the Holy Sepulcher would come into Christian hands through a Christian king named Christopher, a name that Christian also bore, he pointed out. The plan was taken completely seriously on the German imperial diet, which in itself is evidence that the plan was actually feasible. By the total effort of the German Empire and the Danish Empire, it would be possible to recapture Jerusalem, according to the best military strategists of the day. It was decided that the army should set out on April 24, 1472, and the German princes alone were to contribute with 60,000 men. This ultimately did not happen for many reasons: the pope died, the German princes did not show up. But the core reason was that Christian did not manage to arrive (Fig. 5.3).

Christian had promised to conquer Jerusalem in 1471, which clearly had a connection to Karl Knutson's death in 1470. The greatest threat from Sweden had passed. When the German imperial diet backed Christian's plans, he wrote to the Swedish nobility in September 1471 and commanded them in the name of the pope, the emperor, and all of Christianity to surrender and return to the Kalmar Union. They didn't. On the contrary, large parts of the Swedish nobles rallied behind the rebel Sten Sture the Elder. As a result, Christian decided to settle the case militarily and marched towards Stockholm in October. There he suffered complete defeat on October 10 1471 at the Battle of Brunkeberg, where a bullet also smashed some of Christian's teeth. In the years to come, Christian wrote several times to European princes and to the emperor, pledging that he would lead a crusade when everyone in his realms were unified and obeyed him. That time never came.

Christian embarked on a pilgrimage and diplomatic journey through Europe in January 1474, ending in Rome (Jahnke 2014). Initially, he met with Emperor Frederick III in Rothenburg, where he participated in lengthy negotiations. One of the delicate and precarious topics that were discussed was the Burgundian duke, who had addressed the emperor the previous year and requested to be appointed king of Burgundy, king of the Romans, and to act as the emperor's deputy. The request could not simply be outright rejected due to Burgundy's military strength; over the past three years, the Duke had restructured his entire military organization and now had a large and highly effective standing army. Christian was to mediate between the emperor and duke: as part of the negotiations, Holstein, Stormarn, and Ditmarschen were elevated to duchies, which the emperor granted Christian on February 14. The inhabitants of the duchy were to be free from paying customs duties in Germany, and the rest of the Danish empire was granted other customs privileges. Christian's pilgrimage continued as nearly a triumphant parade. In Innsbruck he was received by the Archduke of Austria and 50 maidens on horseback and three gilded wagons. After he crossed the Alps, Christian was received by 500 knights sent by the Duke of Malpaga. In Milan he was greeted by 400 boys in white robes and bearing flags with the Danish and the Milanese coat of arms. Prince Sforza revealed to Christian his desire to be named king of Milan and sought his help to beseech the emperor. From there the pilgrimage continued to Mantua and Duke Gonzaga, who was married to a sister of Christian's wife, Queen Dorothea. Christian revisited him on his way home, where a tournament was held in his honor with more than a hundred participants and many deaths. A medal was commemorated for the event and a long

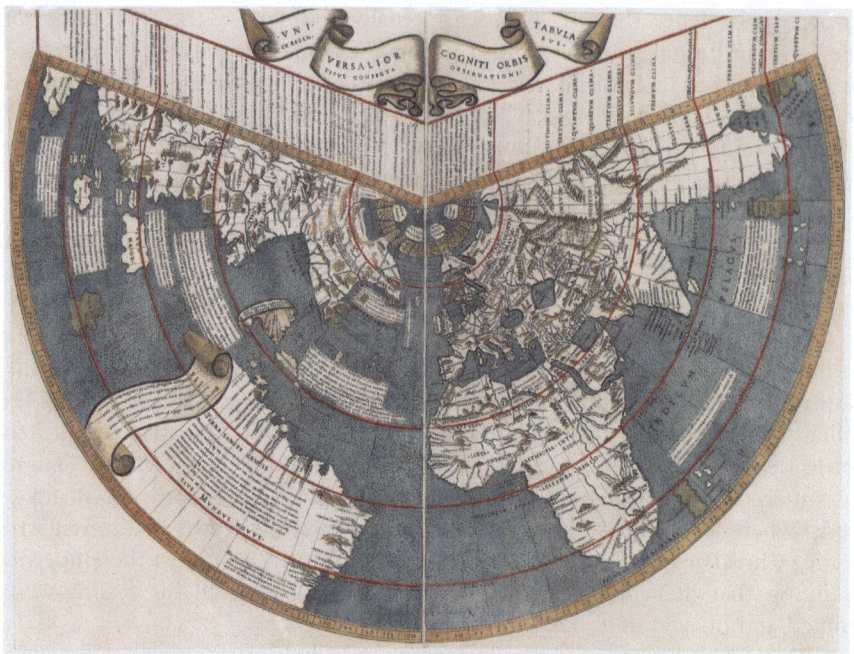

Fig. 5.3 The world map of Johann Ruysch from 1507–07 illustrates how the world suddenly had become much larger around 1500. The Pacific Ocean west of America was yet unknown to Western Europeans, only to be described by Magellan in 1520. Ruysch therefore assumed that the West Indies were close to India and even considered—as Columbus had done—whether the island of Spagnola (Hispaniola) was the Spangu (Japan) described by Marco Polo in the 1270s. America is placed at south on the map and designated as "The Land of the Cross" or "The New World," inhabited by cannibals and women dressed only in birds' feathers, but flowing with gold and pearls. Towards the North Pole is the frozen sea from where ships only seldom return. To the far north in Asia is the Mongolian capital Karakorum and the land of the ten lost tribes of Israel, and immediately to the south of this is *Gruentlant,* the westernmost promontory of Asia and very near to Scandinavia. West of Greenland is the great desert and the mythical peoples of Gog and Magog. With his interest in geography and the New World, King Christian II could certainly see the advantage of approaching Jerusalem from Greenland instead of through the Mediterranean. https://en.wikipedia.org/wiki/Johannes_Ruysch#/media/File:Ruysch_map.jpg (Creative commons: Public Domain)

poem was written in tribute to Christian, which emphasized that he had been elected ruler and had not inherited his kingdom. This was certainly intended as a praise to Christian's personal qualities, but it was also a discreet way of expressing support for the idea of aristocratic republics. Christian attended a meeting in Rome with the College of Cardinals and a grand service with the pope. Christian's stately figure resulted in admiration from the crowd, but also comments on his lack of knowledge of the Italian and Latin languages. "Beautiful animal, a shame it can't speak," the pope noted. In Rome, Christian was honored with the Golden Rose, the pope's most distinguished distinction and usually a crusade order—in every way Christian received the most magnificent reception imaginable. Christian's gifts to the pope consisted mostly in a few barrels of herring from Iceland, and perhaps most importantly in a deliberate and sensational humility, where he knelt much longer in front of the pope than expected, and where he chose in processions to go after the cardinals and not before, as was otherwise justified by his rank. The political message had been well prepared and clear to contemporaries, namely that the ruler of the Kalmar Union did not have to give gifts to anyone, but in turn voluntarily submitted to the church. The coming period also included a number of important privileges, such as the papal permission, which led to the establishment of the University of Copenhagen in 1479. Christian thus continued the tradition of the great, spectacular and religious European journey instituted by his predecessors, and demonstrated that it was still a unique feature of the rulers of the Danish Empire, and not common among other European princes.

After returning home, Christian went to Burgundy to negotiate with the duke, as agreed with the German emperor. The negotiations apparently went well, but with a backdrop of pressure. Christian was spied upon by imperial envoys and subjected to two assaults and an attempted assassination. In the end, however, the negotiations fell apart, which in their contemporary time was explained astrologically with the unfavorability of the stars. A war between Burgundy and the emperor ensued.

In practice, Christian took several important steps towards the establishment of a state church with the king as its head, helped by way of his special ecclesiastical counselor, Marcellus, who previously acted as the traveling papal tax collector but had been appointed bishop of Bergen. At the same time, Christian maintained a very good relationship with the pope both due to his crusade commitment and to his well-developed ability to play the great political role of the time as an extravagant, princely consumer while maintaining an image as a humble son of the holy church, faithfully holding the pope's stirrup. In his reign of the Danish Empire, Christian continued the combination of local and central government. The three councils continued with the usual responsibilities, adding the Schleswig–Holstein knighthood, which came to serve as a fourth council. The knighthood operated more independently in relation to Christian than the Danish and Norwegian councils. At the same time, the joint chancellery and high-ranking officials continued to function at the very top, and closest to the king.

In 1459, Christian instituted a new knightly order, the Order of the Elephant, which received its own chapel in Roskilde Cathedral, the Chapel of the Three Kings, completed in 1464. It was decorated with murals showing the Danish Saint Canute and the Norwegian Saint Olav; the Swedish Saint Erik was not relevant at this time, as Karl Knutsson had just returned as King of Sweden. The Order of the Elephant was also at that time an exceptional favor bestowed upon foreign princes, as well as the most distinguished noblemen of the Christian kingdoms. In this way, it was clearly intended as a common order for the entire Kalmar Union and an attempt to reward those loyal to the king.

During the fifteenth century, a fleet for the Union was systematically constructed, both for military and commercial purposes. The ports in Copenhagen and Bergen were expanded, and shipyards were established in several places, for example in Lolland. Now the ships, like the castles, became a place of work for the rulers and a means for them to travel around the many lands of the empire. In this respect it is significant that Queen Margrethe died on a ship in Flensburg Fjord when she had just taken the city of Flensburg. Erik of Pomerania issued several of his letters on board, especially from his favorite ship *The Great Ark*. When he was banished, he traveled to Gotland with his entire fleet, but by both recapture, purchases, and new construction, his successors quickly succeeded in creating a new fleet.

In Europe, the fifteenth century was the period of the great explorers. This led, among other things, to a collaboration between Portugal and the Danish Empire to find a route to India (Jensen 2007). The Portuguese Prince Henry the Navigator had written to Christopher of Bavaria about the project, and a Danish nobleman Vallarte arrived in Portugal in 1448 and participated with the Portuguese Order of Christ in a long expedition south of Africa to Cape Verde, where he lived the rest of his life in captivity of the local tribal chief, who turned out not to be Christian, as the expedition had expected. In 1461, King Afonso V of Portugal wrote to Christian I and warmly recommended Christian's herald Lolland. Heralds could function almost as ambassadors and were often named after provinces or landscapes (i.e. Lolland). Lolland had participated in the Portuguese crusades and voyages of discovery to North Africa, and Afonso was so impressed by his bravery that the king knighted him when he returned to Portugal. These connections between Denmark and Portugal were later expanded. Around 1471, when Christian presented his grand crusade plan to the imperial diet in Regensburg, an expedition to the north embarked, led by well-known captains Didrik Pining of Denmark, Hans Pothorst of Iceland, and João Vaz Corte-Real and Alvaro Martins Homem from Portugal. They reached Greenland, where they erected a large memorial on one of the more recognizable mountains. From there, they proceeded to America and reached Newfoundland, which was known among Portuguese fishermen as "terra do bachalau," the land of the stock fish. The goal was to find the northwest passage to India. This was reattempted later. In 1519, Christian II equipped a new expedition under the leadership of the notorious pirate and admiral Søren Norby: prior to this, he had wrought papal bulls that authorized the raid as a true crusade. The goal was to win Greenland back from the pagans, which would only be the beginning. At the time of Christian II it was believed that Greenland was the outermost peninsula of the great Asian continent, and if one could lead a crusade there, one would be able to confront the Muslims with a two-front war. At the same time, Christian's army would land in the Far East near where the legendary Christian priest-king Prester John was supposed to live in a giant kingdom ready to support Christian Western Europe in the fight against Islam. During the fifteenth century, it was said that Prester John was descended from Holger the Dane, hero to Charlemagne, and thus King Christian's distant ancestor. The Danish empire was so large that it included not only huge areas of the north with diverse peoples, but also a bridgehead to Asia. However, the Great Crusade to Greenland and Asia never commenced, because Christian II became preoccupied with problems in Sweden.

Bloodbath and Reformation

The last medieval period became a transformative time, where kings shifted from relying on the nobility to rely on commercial bourgeoisie, and where the universal Catholic Church was replaced by a local, royal Lutheran church. It was also at this time that Sweden conclusively separated from the empire (Helle 2003).

When King John was elected in 1481, he had to sign very tough charters of liberty in Denmark and Norway, which not only sought to limit his power but also institutionalized a form of nobility rule. He had to promise not to rule through the empire's public officials in the lands where he wasn't personally present. In distant territories, day-to-day governing was to be managed by a group of four people appointed by the local council. The councils were in turn consulted on appointments of fiefholders and other important economic and political decisions. At the same time it was made quite clear from the councils that the charters should function as a contract between the people and the king, and that they, as the people, could oust the king if they found it necessary. When John finally signed and assumed the throne, the king's power was near the lowest it had ever been throughout the Middle Ages. In Sweden the negotiations broke down completely, the party supporting the regent Sten Sture was too strong and John was not elected king in that territory.

Both John and his little brother Frederik were elected dukes in Schleswig and Holstein and were to share the lands, but at the same time keep them unified forever, as their father had promised in 1460. This meant that they divided the two duchies into a number of smaller sections, and both of them retained land in each duchy. At the same time, the knighthoods and councils of each territory were to recognize both John and Frederik as rulers, and a joint assembly was established to oversee the future of Schleswig and Holstein. These measures occurred in 1490, when Frederik had come of age, and he now proposed to divide Denmark proper in the same manner. John, however, did not agree to this and in 1494 got a resolution from the Council of the Realm that Denmark was an electoral kingdom and therefore could not be divided.

Both the Baltic and the North Sea were plagued by pirates: The Hanseatic cities accused King John of looking the other way, perhaps even supporting some of the piracy in secret. It's not far from the truth. The captains Pining and Pothorst, who had led the expedition in Greenland in 1471, plundered far and wide from Norway to Gibraltar. But John would also have been completely aware that they also attacked English ships, thus restricting England's fishing in the North Atlantic. Christian I had also appointed Pining governor in Iceland. In the safety of the Visby fortress in Gotland, Ivar Axelssson Thott plundered indiscriminately and almost succeeded in creating a small independent principality, but in 1487 was expelled by King John with Pinning's help. Gradually, the royal use of pirates was increasingly replaced by power that was vested in trade and fleets—a shift that was enabled by John's support, for example by his founding of the shipyard in Nakskov in 1510.

The relationship with Sweden was complicated. John had not been elected king, and Sten Sture the Elder served as regent of the Swedish kingdom, but without a royal head of state. At the same time, Queen Dorothea had for years brought proceedings against Sten Sture and tried to get the pope to excommunicate him because he had taken possession of the land estate in Sweden that Dorothea was gifted with at her wedding to Christian I. In 1485 John received support from Pope Innocent VIII against Sten Sture: the pope wanted John to lead a crusade against the schismatic Russians. The pope stated that anyone who tried to stop John in his efforts would be excommunicated, and at the same time addressed John as king of Sweden. An important ideological ally was won, but also a fickle ally. In 1493, John negotiated with the Grand Prince Ivan the Great of Moscow, and they agreed to form an alliance against Sten Sture. Sture then, as a countermove, went in league with the Teutonic Order and, perhaps with their help, received a papal bull which authorized Sture's war against John as a real crusade. It didn't help, though. The Russians attacked Finland in 1495–96, and John was able to enter Sweden the next summer, defeating Sten Sture in a major battle at Rotebro near Stockholm in 1497. John could then be acclaimed Swedish king. The victory was due to the large number of soldiers and noblemen, but especially the Black Guard of Saxon mercenaries, who were expensive but equally effective against noble equestrian armies and peasant revolts. Modern warfare had really come to Scandinavia. However, John's dominion over Sweden was short-lived. In 1501 a rebellion erupted, which, despite great efforts from John, was not suppressed. At the same time, Swedish noblemen made contact with Norway, where Akershus and Tønsberg were conquered by local nobles. Sten Sture conquered Stockholm Castle in 1502 and imprisoned Queen Christine for a year and a half. The outrage spread. It was brutally suppressed in Norway, but John ultimately had to give up Sweden. In the following years he continued to try to win Sweden with both war and diplomacy, but in vain.

In 1503 Sten Sture died, and in 1504 the Swedish Council elected Svante Nilsson as regent of the realm. The title is interesting and distinctive precisely for an empire that was composed of several entities with varying degrees of independence. In Sweden during this period, the title went back to Engelbrekt Engelbrecktsson, who was appointed by the Swedish Council as commander of the realm *(rigshøvedsmand)*, which first of all meant as the head of the military. Karl Knutson was first commander, then regent, and then king. At his deathbed, he conferred the defense of Sweden to his sister's son Sten Sture the Elder, whose choice was then confirmed by the members of the council, appointing him as the new regent. The idea of this transfer of power was that the council was able to play the regent's authority against that of the king's and swing from supporting one to supporting the other. The council would continue this approach throughout this period. The Swedish Council of the realm thus gained greater power and came closer to establishing an actual noble republic than it would have done by electing another king instead of the king of the union.

At the same time, with these almost incessant wars in Sweden, in the year 1500 John tried to conquer Dithmarschen with noblemen from Denmark, Schleswig, and Holstein and particularly with the help of the Black Guard, a force totalling up to 10,000 men. It did not succeed and the campaign drowned in mud. The people of Dithmarschen opened the levees, and it rained heavily, making it impossible to use cannons. The armored warriors were weighted down and could not move, but the Dithmarschens swung over the trenches on long spears that had support beams, and almost all of John's army was cut down. The flag of Dannebrog, which had fallen from the sky almost three hundred years earlier, was conquered and hanged in the Meldorfer Church.

John had halted the rebellion in Norway by installing his son Christian there as viceroy in 1506 (Bisgaard 2019). Christian resorted to a policy that he was to follow later, namely to support the new merchant citizenry rather than the nobility. In Norway he quickly gained a poor reputation as a suppressor of both peasants and nobles alike, while he gave far-reaching privileges to Dutch and Norwegian traders. Christian settled in Bergen and had a close relationship with the merchants, most notably the Dutch merchant Sigbrit Willom's daughter Dyveke, whom he installed as a permanent mistress. When he succeeded John in 1513, he also had to sign a charter that limited his power but it was nowhere near as stringent as that of his father's. He promised not to install non-aristocrats in the fiefdoms of Denmark, but that did not become a point in the Norwegian charter, perhaps because there were simply far fewer members of the Norwegian aristocracy than in the Danish. The Swedish Council had almost recognized John as King just the year before, but had again fractured into conflicting factions. In 1514 Christian II married Elisabeth of Austria, sister of Charles V, heir to Austria, Burgundy, the Netherlands, the Spanish countries, Italy and much more. It is probably the most politically significant marriage any Danish king has ever sealed. The marriage may be an indicator of the Kalmar Union's international strength at the time. However, it was unfortunate that Christian continued to openly live with his mistress Dyveke, which led to angry diplomatic envoys from the Habsburgs. This resolved, when Dyveke died suddenly in 1517, perhaps as a poison victim of murder. Christian II's connection to the Habsburgs was a critical step towards an alliance with Poland-Lithuania, and in 1516 an alliance was forged between the Danish Empire and Russia.

Christian deliberately chose a new policy, inspired by international developments. He wanted to transform the empire into a princely state in line with the Netherlands, with a strong prince with bourgeois advisers and a solid economy. The role of the nobility was diminished and any thought of a noble republic would be prevented. State development at the time followed that path. Ideologically, Christian's program was described by the contemporary Italian philosopher Machiavelli in his thoughts on the Prince; state-wise there were several examples to follow in Western Europe; and militarily the role of the nobility was vanishing or at least undergoing rapid change. Christian surrounded himself with non-aristocratic advisors such as big-trade merchants, mayors, and Sigbrit, who stayed by the king's side for the rest of his life, even after Dyvke's death, and quickly gained an excellent relationship with Elisabeth. He sought to strengthen the economic role of cities with privileges and modern Dutch city laws, with a royally appointed mayor. At the same time, Christian sought to create a trading company to secure the lucrative Baltic Sea trade. This was to be done in collaboration with the Netherlands and was to be financed through the acquisition of shares. Christian's policy led to fierce protests from the nobility, but to no avail. Important fiefs were not occupied with nobles, and in Norway the Council was effectively stripped of power, among other things by the fact that no new members had been appointed since 1515. A very harsh taxation on Norway also led to rebellion, which was suppressed. In 1521 Christian tried to better integrate Denmark and Norway by introducing a common law for both kingdoms, but by then it was too late.

In Sweden, Regent Sten Sture the Younger came into conflict with Archbishop Gustav Trolle over a castle, and this led to the imprisonment and ill-treatment of the Archbishop. He was severely beaten on the head with an iron war-hammer, according to his later complaints. Christian II tried to help Gustav Trolle militarily in 1517, but lost. In the years to come, Christian prepared himself, among other things, by borrowing large sums of money all around, and in 1520 he could invade Sweden again—both because he wanted to claim the throne and because he wanted to execute the papal sanction on Sten Sture to punish him for the mistreatment of the Archbishop. In the ensuing battles, Sten Sture was wounded and died, and Christian conquered Stockholm and made peace and finally he could be crowned king of Sweden. This occurred on November 4, 1520. Four days later the gates of the castle were shut: Gustav Trolle read a letter of indictment against the assembled Swedish noblemen who were condemned as overt heretics. About 100 people were executed by decapitation and as heretics denied a Christian burial; they were burned instead. This resulted in an immediate revolt led by Gustav Vasa, who was elected regent in the same year, and declared king in 1522. The remnants of the Swedish Council bowed, realizing that it was a time with need for a strong kings. And the Danish kings had to realize that they could no longer hope to be recognized as rulers in Sweden. Christian II's successors abandoned the claim. The revolt spread from Sweden to Denmark. Christian turned everyone against him. Lübeck supported Duke Frederik of Gothenburg in Schleswig and Holstein, and soon gained support from the Jutland nobility. In 1523 he let himself be hailed as King at the assembly of Northern Jutland in Viborg, and Christian was forced to retire (Fig. 5.4).

During this period of the Kalmar Union's history, from its founding in 1397 to the massacre in Stockholm in 1520, Sweden was intermittently a part of the union during 1397–1448, 1457–63, 1497–1501, and 1520–21. The Oldenburg state system was founded so that Denmark, Norway, and Schleswig–Holstein had the same person as ruler or king, who in each country would rule via a council with representatives from the nobility and the bishops.

Fig. 5.4 King Christian II.s siege of Stockholm with many details, giving an impression of the art or warfare of the time. The large warships are equipped with canons, and the city is bombarded constantly from the ships and from Christian's camp on land. The picture comprises events from several days. To the left is depicted the conclusion of peace, sealed with communion administered by archbishops and several bishops. To the right is the main event of the following day, when Christian was hailed as king. In the frieze below are depicted first the crowning festivities with tournaments and immediately afterwards the Stockholm Bloodbath. Heads of Swedish nobles and of two bishops are cut of on the main square in Stockholm and collected in big barrels, seven monks were drowned. The illustration was made in the 1520s on the request of Gustav Vasa, after he had expelled Christian and declared himself king. It is an early example of the new propaganda in the public sphere that the technique of printing enabled, and it has probably been spread in several copies. They are all lost, and the picture is known today only from this copy, a copper engraving from 1676. http://www5.kb.dk/images/billed/2010/okt/billeder/object395449/da/ (Royal Library, Copenhagen: Public Domain)

At the same time, the prince's legitimacy in the three countries was justified differently. Norway and Schleswig–Holstein were hereditary lineages, while Denmark was an electoral kingdom and thus through charters gave greater power to the nobility. During the fifteenth century, the ideology of the council spread to all three countries in the form of attempts to create noble republics, but at the end of the period the power of the prince was nevertheless strengthened in relation to the aristocracy.

References

Bisgaard, Lars. 2019. *Christian: En biografi.* Copenhagen: Gads Forlag.
Boniface IX, letter. 1401. https://diplomatarium.dk/dokument/14010329005. Accessed 6 Aug 2021.
Bysted, Ane, et al. 2012. *Jerusalem in the North: Denmark and the Baltic Crusades, 1100–1522.* Turnhout: Brepols.
Christiansen, Eric. 1997. *The Northern Crusades: The Baltic and the Catholic Frontier 1100–1525.* London: Penguin [1 ed. 1980].
Etting, Vivian. 2004. *Queen Margrete (1353–1412) and the Founding of the Nordic Union.* Leiden: Brill.
Hedemann, Markus. 2018. *Danmark, Slesvig og Holsten 1404–1448—konflikt og konsekvens.* Aabenraa: Historisk Samfund for Sønderjylland.
Helle, Knut (ed.). 2003. *Cambridge History of Scandinavia,* vol. 1: *Prehistory to 1520.* Cambridge: University Press.
Imsen, Steinar. 2007. The Union of Calmar: Northern Great Power or Northern German Outpost? In *Politics and Reformations: Communities, Polities, Nations, and Empires,* ed. Christopher Ocker, 471–90. Leiden: Brill.
Jahnke, Carsten. 2014. Two Journeys and One University: King Christian I and Queen Dorothea's Journeys to Rome and the Foundation of the University of Copenhagen. In *Denmark and Europe in the Middle Ages, c. 1000–1525: Essays in Honour of Professor Michael H. Gelting,* ed. Kerstin Hundahl, Lars Kjær, and Niels Lund, 139–153. Ashgate: Farnham.
Jensen, Janus Møller. 2007. *Denmark and the Crusades. 1400–1650.* Leiden: Brill.
Kubon, Sebastian. 2016. *Die Außenpolitik des Deutschen Ordens unter Hochmeister Konrad von Jungingen (1393–1407).* Göttingen: Vandenhoeck & Ruprecht.
The Danish Medieval Laws. The laws of Scania, Zealand and Jutland. 2016. Ed. Ditlev Tamm and Helle Vogt. London: Brepols.
Urban, William. 2003. *The Teutonic Knights: A Military History.* London: Greenhill Books.

CHAPTER 6

The Princely State: The Decline of Baltic Power 1536–1720

STATE TYPE: CONGLOMERATE STATE

Although state power underwent significant changes during this period, it is still reasonable to say that the state type remained under the same label of a conglomerate state. A conglomerate is defined as a whole composed of disparate parts, and a conglomerate state consists of different territories held together by the prince and the ruling royal family—by a few other factors. Each territory, or rather the elite within each territory, has its individual relations with the prince: its own laws, privileges, administrative, and judicial systems. The prince cannot or will not attempt to implement legislative, administrative, or judicial alignment of his various territories. This type of composite state—or as it was also called a princely or dynastic state—was the norm of the time (Bonney 1991; Elliott 1992; Gustafsson 1994). For example, starting in 1603 Britain became a personal union including England, Wales, Scotland, and Ireland, where only the king's person and the royal family held these territories together as a state. Likewise, the scattered Habsburg territories shared one thing in common: the Habsburg monarchy, whether through the title of king, archduke, duke, or count.

The Danish Empire can also be described as a loosely composed state with very little integration and harmonization among the various territories that were part of the state. This conglomerate state is called the Oldenburg state (by the name of the royal family, which originally came from the duchy of Oldenburg in present-day Germany), which just underlines that the various territories had little else in common than the prince (who in some of the territories was king, and duke in others) and the prince's family.

The Kingdom of Denmark, which included Scania, Halland, and Blekinge, extended to the small river Kongeå, which marked the border with the Duchy of Schleswig. Denmark was characterized by a strong nobility who, through the noble council, ruled in cooperation with the king. The Council of the Realm chose the king, who had to accede to a charter, which established the king's rights and duties, as well as the nobility's. The majority of the population were peasants and most peasant farmers were located either on the estate of the nobility or on the king's estate (royal estate). But the Kingdom of Denmark was also very dissimilar internally. As a result, the Kingdom did not have a common law code, but was rather divided into areas of law where Jutlandian Law, Scanian Law, and Sealandian Law respectively applied.

In the Kingdom of Norway, the conditions differed from the Danish in several ways. Norway had a country-wide law code. The nobility was neither strong in number nor politically-economically powerful, the peasantry was far more independent, and if the peasants were farmers, they were usually under less land ownership than in Denmark, as Norway's variant geography did not foster opportunities to create and operate large estates. On the other hand, the geographical conditions enabled other business opportunities than those known in Denmark: forestry, mining, and fishing played a greater role in the economy. Norway's constitutional status was altered in 1536: in the so-called Norwegian Article in the charter of King Christian III in 1536, it was stated that if the king could get possession of Norway, it would fall under the crown of Denmark, and no longer an independent kingdom. Norway would become "a limb of Denmark's realm and forever under Denmark's crown." This is often interpreted as a change in Norway's status from a separate kingdom to an integrated province in Denmark on par with Sealand and Jutland. But that isn't necessarily the case. Territories (such as Sealand, Jutland, etc.) were not provinces in the modern sense, but their own regions of law. Thus, Norway was not aligned to Danish conditions, because Danish conditions were not uniform. The crown of Denmark meant, in contemporary language, the authority exercised jointly by the King and the Council of the Realm. From the Norwegian point of view, it is claimed that the cause in this shift was due to the king's desire for more power and the Danish nobility's desire to gain fiefdoms. But the reason was rather linked to the precarious foreign policy situation in 1536. Though Christian II was imprisoned, his relatives, including Holy Roman Emperor Charles V, still posed a threat to Christian III, whose rule they did not recognize. And in 1531 when Christian II attempted a comeback, it occurred in Norway. Sweden was also interested in Norway. As a result, there was a risk that powerful groups in Norway could independently establish contact with Denmark's enemies. All this would be prevented by subordinating Norway's crown to Denmark. Moreover, as Norway unlike Denmark was a hereditary kingdom, other members of the dynasty that were not acceptable were seen from a Danish point of view. The Norwegian Article was aiming at preventing this. After 1536, Norway's legal status was that it was no longer a kingdom *in its own right*, but still remained a separate kingdom (Ladewig Petersen 1973). In 1537, Christian III sent a naval fleet to Norway, but by then Norway's real leader—Archbishop Olav—had already given up and fled abroad. Any other resistance soon collapsed. Christian III thus succeeded in gaining control of Norway far easier than anyone had dared hope for when the charter was concluded in 1536. The Norwegian Article of the charter was not published in Norway. This indicates that the aim of the article was the uncertain situation in relation to abroad. There is no indication that Norway was degraded to a Danish province. The kings were still titled as kings of Denmark and Norway. Norway's status as a traditionally hereditary state stood in contrast to Denmark—an electoral kingdom—but was maintained and gained importance during the first part of the seventeenth century, when the Danish royal power sought to strengthen itself by also trying to introduce hereditary kingdoms. However, Norway now came under increased Danish control. This is reflected by the fact that the fiefs in Norway were now almost exclusively given to nobles from Denmark.

The Faroe Islands, Iceland, and Greenland also belonged to Norway. Although there had been no contact between Greenland and Norway (and Denmark) since the fifteenth century, the king nevertheless continued to claim supremacy over the country, which was even expressed in the Royal Coat of Arms.

The duchies of Schleswig and Holstein were in personal union with the kingdoms of Denmark and Norway, but since the Ribe agreement in 1460 the two duchies were also a real union. This did not rule out that Holstein was also a member of the Holy Roman Empire of German. The duchies were socially characterized by agriculture with large noble estates and even more tenant farmers than in the Kingdom of Denmark. The local nobility organized in the Aristocratic Corporation (in German: Ritterschaft)—had a large influence in the duchies.

A legal and constitutional change of far-reaching political and fateful significance that affected the duchies took place shortly after the Reformation: inheritances of the duchies in 1544 between Frederick I's three sons: Christian III, John, and Adolphus. The reason for the split was that the younger princely sons needed a means of permanent support, a widespread problem at the time. In the Kingdom, the Council of the Realm did not agree to such a division as it feared it could be the beginning of territorial dissolution. And as Norway was a hereditary kingdom, such a division was here precluded in advance (Fig. 6.1).

Thus, in the conglomerate state, there were large differences between the various state entities, as well as within each territory. But the regime seems not to have found an issue with this, let alone display any desire to unify and harmonize conditions. Only at one point did the government actively intervene and seek to create uniform conditions: in the political and religious spheres of the Lutheran Reformation. In the duchies, especially in Schleswig, the Reformation movement had grown in strength as early as the 1520s, through the support and promotion by Frederick I, and especially his son, the

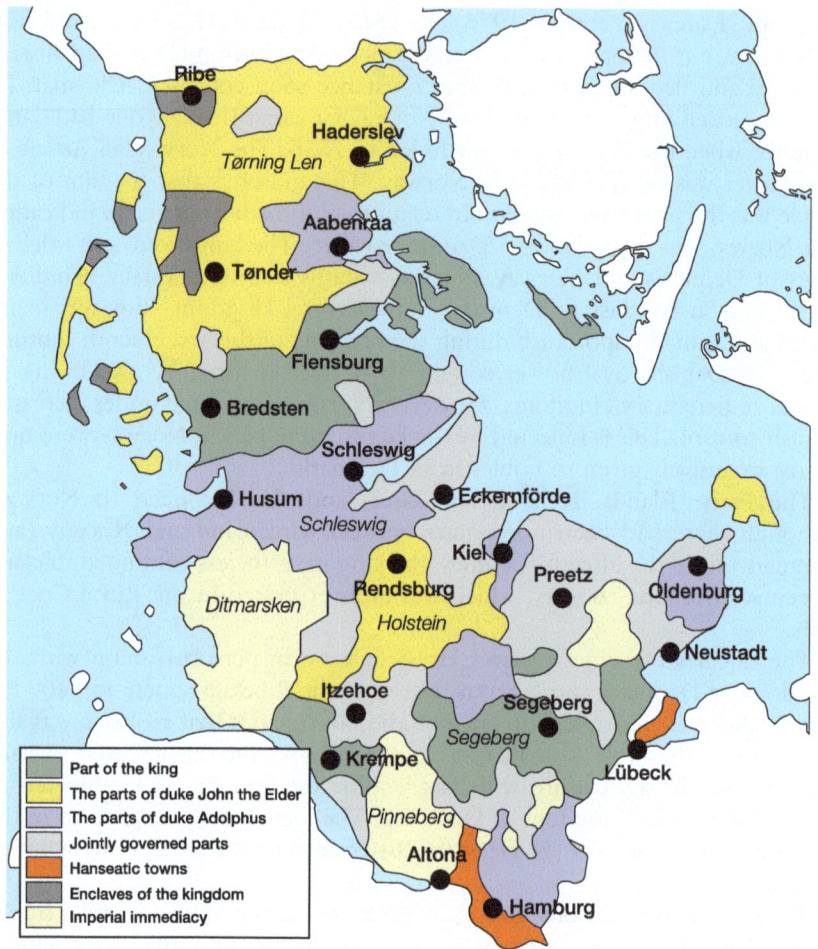

Fig. 6.1 Map of the partition of the duchies in 1544 between Christian III and his brothers John the Elder and Adolphus. What was divided was the ducal authority and the right to revenue from the peasant population. Schleswig and Holstein remained two and only two duchies, the ducal authority was, however, shared between several dukes. The specific territories of each of the dukes remained being in a vassal relationship to the king of Denmark as for Schleswig and to the German emperor as for Holstein. Yet, when later sub-partitions took place, the local nobility managed to force through that the new dukes would not have any governmental authority in their districts but merely be landlords. Several later territorial partitions between the sons of the dukes took place and both the Augustenburg and the Glücksburg lines descend from these ducal sidelines. Unlike the other dukes, Adolphus managed to secure his territories against partition through inheritance and the Gottorp family descends from him. Certain areas were ruled jointly by all the governing dukes. Parts of Holstein belonged to the Hanseatic League or to the bishopric of Lübeck and were thus outside the control of the Danish Empire. The royal enclaves were legally and administratively parts of the kingdom of Denmark even if they were placed in Schleswig geographically

later Christian III. The Reformation Movement was supported by several local priests as well as members of the nobility and the town's citizens. The movement spread to the kingdom in the 1520s. In some parts it was met with great enthusiasm among the priests and other sections of the population (Viborg, Copenhagen, Malmø), but other parts were untouched (Ribe) by the movement. After Christian's victory in the Count's Feud in 1536, the Reformation was officially completed. The organization of the old church was purged, the bishops imprisoned, monasteries and church property were expropriated by the Crown, but the clergy in the ministry remained, now as Lutheran clergymen. In 1537, the church ordinance was issued, which was the legal basis for the new Evangelical-Lutheran State Church.

Thus, both in the duchies and in the Kingdom of Denmark, the Reformation was carried out with a top-down approach, but it was done with considerable assistance from large sections of the clergy and the lay population. The introduction of the Reformation in other parts of the empire was a different case. The Danish church ordinance of 1537 was extended to Norway that year, which had come under Danish control. The Catholic priests remained in their positions, while new bishops and eventually also new Lutheran clergymen—virtually all Danish-born—joined.

In the Faroe Islands, the Lagting—the parliament—recognized Christian III in 1535, and when the bishop objected to the new church ordinance, he was dismissed and replaced by a Lutheran. In 1557 the Faroe Islands ceased to be a separate diocese and were placed under the Diocese of Bjørgvin in Norway. It was far more elaborate and dramatic when the Lutheran Reformation was introduced in Iceland. In an attempt to bring ecclesiastical lands to the crown, one of the king's prominent officials was assassinated in 1538. In 1541, an armed expedition was sent to Iceland, which imprisoned one of the two Icelandic Catholic bishops and enabled the Reformation to gradually actualize. But in 1549, the second Catholic bishop succeeded in reintroducing Catholicism by a coup, imprisoning his Lutheran colleague and banishing a prominent representative of the king. In 1551, therefore, a significant military expedition was sent from Denmark to Iceland, but when it arrived, everything was in chaos. The Catholic bishop had clashed with the local Icelandic grandee, who had seized and executed him. Order was now restored and the reformation introduced—even in Iceland (Fig. 6.2).

A comparison of how the Reformation was introduced in the various parts of the empire suggests that increased control over the periphery was being enforced by the central power. The reformation strengthened the king's power in three ways: first, the king was now the head of the church, and no power outside the king's kingdoms and lands could interfere in ecclesiastical affairs. Second, the royal power acquired ownership of the church's extensive lands, thereby strengthening the crown financially. Third, the priests now became state employees and served as state power representatives and local spokesmen.

The Reformation and the religious uniformity it entailed were the exception in the conglomerate state. There were no other spheres in which state power unfolded similar resource-consuming efforts to harmonize conditions in the widely heterogenous state entities. It was considered a condition of being a loyal subject that one adhered to the Lutheran faith.

◀Fig. 6.2 The Icelandic bishop Guðbrandur Thorlaksson (1542–1627) translating the Bible into Icelandic. The early modern Danish empire was very heterogenous—constitutionally, legally, administratively, economically, socially, linguistically, and culturally and the government did not seek to enforce uniformity. Only in one respect, however, was uniformity being actively enforced: religion. Every inhabitant had to belong to the Evangelical-Lutheran state church of which the king was the head. It was considered a necessary condition for the integrity of the state and the loyalty of the subjects that all the inhabitants of state were belonging to the same confession and therefore no other confessions were being tolerated. Especially in Iceland, there had been serious problems in implementing the Lutheran reformation, thus two attempts at reintroducing Catholicism here had taken place. Guðbrandur who served as bishop of Holar for 56 years and it was during this exceptionally long term of office that Lutheranism was being consolidated in Iceland. As this confession was emphasizing God's own words and consequently the importance of the vernacular and of the literacy of all believers, he edited and Icelandic version of the Bible in 1584 where he had translated several parts himself and moreover, he edited a hymn book and was the author of several devotional books. This all contributed to preserve Icelandic both as a spoken and written language, even if Iceland was being governed from Denmark for more than 550 years (Wikicommons). https://commons.wikimedia.org/wiki/File:Portrait_of_Gu%C3%B0brandur_%C3%9Eorl%C3%A1ksson.jpg

STATE FORM: FROM DOMAIN STATE TO TAX STATE

"Conglomerate state" is a comprehensive term for the structure of the state during the period 1536–1720: disparate, loosely composed, and largely only held together by a common head of state. But the fact that the structure of the state was the same does not mean that the scale, scope, and organization of the state were the same throughout the period. On the contrary, significant changes took place in these respects, which had a profound social significance in the various internal parts of the state and partly in the relationship between the central power and the individual territories. One could say that the conglomerate state evolved from being a domain state to a tax or military state. The development of military technology meant that the noble defense organization, the cavalry, was no longer sufficient. The justification for the nobility's freedom from tax and other privileges was precisely its military obligations. Therefore, many were now wondering why the nobility continued to have privileges if its contribution to the state's defense had now become militarily obsolete (Jespersen 1983, 2000; Ladewig Petersen 1975).

In short, it can be said that these developments led to an increased interest in extracting resources (manpower, taxes, products). However, it took place in different ways and with various intensities. The central parts of the empire appear to have carried the heaviest burdens. In Iceland, there was little notice of increased taxation and military discharges. The Kingdom of Denmark and the duchies, on the other hand, experienced a particularly sharp increase in the tax burden, just as these parts of the state had to lay the ground for more hostile occupations during the 1600s (cf. later). These developments thus reinforced the gaps between the central and peripheral parts of the empire. When the central parts carried most of the increased burdens, it was due to the fact that these parts were easier to control, and therefore they could be burdened more heavily. If a rebellion were to erupt here, it would be easier to strike down and not have as good a chance of spreading—as was the case in the more distant parts of the empire. Furthermore, the transport costs of increased resource extraction from the peripheral areas and the risk of loss along the way could easily exceed revenues.

Active Commercial Policy

As mentioned, the transition from domain state to tax and military state meant a rapidly growing tax burden in most places in the empire. And this development was also felt throughout the empire—but undeniably in different ways and to varying degrees—by the active state commercial policy that was implemented. This policy was to encourage the state to trade and engage in commercial production, partly to promote domestic production and save on imports from abroad, and partly to seek to boost exports and prevent imports. And if imports were not to be avoided, then it should be conducted under the auspices of the Danish state, and without foreign intermediaries, so that merchants from the Danish kingdoms were the ones who gained profit. The purpose of the active commercial policy was in the narrow sense to provide the state with more revenue, but in a broader sense to promote the formation of an enterprising and wealthy commercial bourgeoisie which could in turn lead to general prosperity and credit opportunities in the community. The Netherlands was an example of this policy in action.

This type of policy is called mercantilism, but there was no thought out and consistent economic theory. The term mercantilism was not used at the time, as it was invented by later economists and historians (Bregnsbo 2009). It meant that there was an increased interest in mapping, exploiting, and developing production and natural resources from the various areas of the empire. Norway was of great importance in this regard, in particular mining operations (silver, copper, iron) and metal processing. In Iceland, in 1568, the king took over the operation of the sulfur mines (sulfur was important for the production of gunpowder), but by this time these mines were depleting. The initiative led to a general increase of interest in Icelandic trade in Copenhagen. In 1602, the merchants in Copenhagen, Helsingør, and Malmø were granted monopoly on all trade in Iceland in order to keep out competitors from Hamburg, England, and Scotland. This trade monopoly, which existed until 1776, and which applied only to the merchants in Copenhagen from 1619, contributed to the emergence of a wealthy merchant environment in the Capital. Monopoly was the solution of the time in mercantilist policy: it secured trade for Danish subjects at the expense of foreign competitors. The monopoly was justified to Iceland by the desire to ensure stability and security of the supply network. The reality could be viewed differently. Although there were fixed prices for the prices, they were not always compliant. The Icelanders had to appreciate the goods supplied by the monopoly merchants, they did not have the opportunity to buy them at lower prices and/or better quality elsewhere. All exports of goods produced in Iceland had to go through the monopoly trade at prices often below the prices of the international market. In addition, all communication between Iceland and the outside world had to occur via the monopoly company's ships.

Trade in Finmarken, a large territory in northern Norway that was very thinly populated and mostly inhabited by the Sami, was monopolized, originally by a joint effort of Bergen and Trondheim, then solely by the Bergens starting in 1681, and finally by various trading companies after 1712.

As part of the active commercial policy, factories were set up, partly under state management, and partly by private individuals with considerable government support and protection against competition. Such developments took place especially in Copenhagen, and the production was mostly for military purposes, such as weapons and ammunition, the naval dockyard, and the manufacture of clothing for soldiers. The commercial policy also supported whaling in the North Atlantic (sometimes even state-run whaling) as well as the construction of new cities in the Kingdom of Denmark, Norway, and the duchies. Thus Christianshavn was founded in 1618 (incorporated into Copenhagen in 1674). When Oslo was ravaged by fire in 1624, Christian IV ordered inhabitants to rebuild the city at the Akershus fortress, and the new city was named after the king: Christiania. In an attempt to increase competition with the rich trading town of Hamburg, and ensure that a large part of the trading revenue there instead went through the Danish state, the city of Glückstadt by the Elbe was founded in 1616. While it commercially did not gain great importance, Glückstadt instead became a fortress.

The establishment of the Danish East India Trading Company in 1616 was another result of the mercantilist commercial policy. It aimed to establish direct trade in Indian products (cotton, spices) between merchants within the empire and India, so that the profits would not go to third party foreign merchants: a clear expression of mercantilist economic policy. The company was organized as a joint-stock company. The royal family bought shares and sought to pressure the nobility to do likewise. The citizens of Denmark, Norway, and the duchies also invested money in the enterprise. When it was organized as a private limited company rather than a public one, it was able to gain private investors in the field, but the company received royal support in the form of tariff relief, which the king also provided to ships and sailors.

In November 1618, the so-called "Indian Fleet" of five ships (two belonged to the company, the other three were warships) under the command of Admiral Ove Gjedde left Denmark and arrived in May 1620 after 535 days' journey to Ceylon (Sri Lanka). While the Rajah (the local prince) was extremely skeptical, they ended up entering into a friendship, trade, and defense treaty. When it came to fruition, the rajah refused to fulfill the agreement, and the project lost momentum. The expedition had better luck on the east coast of India. There, they managed to gain the small fishing village Tharangambadi (soon to be transformed into Tranquebar) which was under the control of the Nayak of Tanjore, who was interested in Danish commercial activities to counterbalance the activities of other European countries. The Nayak was provided with European military hardware in return for the village. In addition, a permit was granted to trade, to establish a fortress called Fort Dansborg, and the right to collect taxes and duties. In this way Tranquebar was acquired, and this colony was to remain as part of the Danish empire for more than 200 years, until 1845. Before the expedition resumed its course, Fort Dansborg was built. Part of the ships and crew remained, while the rest of the ships were loaded with Indian goods. In March 1622, the expedition reached Copenhagen again after more than 40 months of absence. A strong trade relationship with India had now been established, although at times the frequency of travel was greater than others. While Tranquebar was provisionally not a formal part of the Danish kingdom as it belonged to the private limited Danish East India Company, the company itself had considerable royal privileges and other forms of support from the crown.

Other continents were also the subject of the active commercial policy aimed at securing direct trade relations outside of foreign intermediaries. Several attempts to gain a commercial foothold on the Gold Coast of Africa to acquire goods such as gold, ivory, palm oil, and enslaved people failed. Only in 1659 did a trading company, based in Glückstadt, gradually gain a foothold on the Gold Coast and build forts (fortified trading stations). These were established after permission was granted and tribute payments were made to a local African King, but for a long time the company had to fight against Dutch and Swedish competitors, with whom King of Denmark also at war back in Europe. However, the Glückstadt Company was unable to make it function, and in 1672 therefore transferred the possessions to the King, who in 1674 transferred them to a newly founded West Indies-Guinean Company. However, for many years this new company led a rather languishing existence and was unable to make gainful use of its monopoly.

Areas in the West Indies were also acquired. Trade relations with this part of the world had already been established in Christian IV, but an expedition was not sent until 1672, issued by the West Indies-Guinea Company, staking a claim to the Caribbean island St. Thomas. The island, whose main asset was a natural harbor, was intended as a support point for the company's merchant ships, and previous attempts to take possession of the island had been unsuccessful. The company also claimed the nearby small island of St. John, but not termed a "possession" until 1718. The Danish claims in the West Indies were completed in 1733 when the island of St. Croix was bought from France.

Politics in the Vicinity of the Baltic Sea, the North Sea and Northern Germany; the Empire's International Position

However, at the beginning of the period, the kingdoms and lands of the Danish king constituted a dominant and significant power in Northern Europe. It claimed supremacy over both the Baltic Sea and the North Sea as well as sought to assert its power over areas of northern Germany. Most significant was the supremacy of the Baltic Sea, as it enabled the Danish king to collect highly lucrative customs revenue from trade traveling through the Danish straits, first and foremost the Sound. This made the king a personally extremely wealthy man in the European context. At the same time, the king's control of the Danish belts and straits meant that the empire had the opportunity, in wartime, to impose a barrier to all shipping traffic to and from the Baltic Sea.

On April 17, 1599, a naval squadron departed from Copenhagen, sailing along the coast of Norway to the island of Kildin on the Kola Peninsula. The squadron was led by General Captain Christian Frederiksen, another term for Christian IV himself. This was an indication that the state leadership considered it necessary to assert sovereignty over not only Northern Norway, but also across the North Sea from the coast of Norway to Iceland (and Greenland). In Northern Norway, the borders were unclear and nebulous. Both the Danish-Norwegian, Russian, and Swedish sides claimed the right to tax the Sami population. In the years after 1600, a marked increase in fiscal and mercantile activity in this regard was developed by Sweden with the Sami, increasing the competition. This Swedish business was a major factor in the deteriorating Swedish-Danish relationship that led to the Kalmar War (see below). A lasting result of the peace in Knäred in 1613 was that the border line between Sweden and Norway was established, and Sweden was compelled to recognize the Danish-Norwegian right to tax the coastal Sami in Northern Norway and otherwise abandon its activities. In the case of the North Sea, the Oldenburg monarchy claimed it to be a closed holding for the monarchy in question. Some international shipping to the port of Arkhangelsk in Russia was a thorn in the side for state leadership, as it meant that trade to and from Russia went around the Baltic and thus avoided customs in the Sound. Therefore, the Oldenburg state demanded tariffs on shipping in the North Sea, but with the exception of England, other powers were unable to agree to it, as it was difficult to implement these sovereign demands due to the extent and remoteness of the area.

In northern Germany, the Danish Empire sought to assert its interests. Northern Germany was divided into several principalities, in addition to the free cities which were under direct control of the emperor and were independent of the local princes. In the historiography of such small and medium-sized principalities as well as the free cities, the image of Denmark presented is often one that is very far from the well-known image of Denmark as a peace-loving and conflict-free small country. Instead, one gains a picture of raw power politics, where might made right. Compared to the small German principalities, the Danish empire was a great power, and often behaving as such. The city of Hamburg was a free imperial city, but since it was originally founded on Holstein land, the King of Denmark, in his capacity as Duke of Holstein, demanded that the city recognize him as lord. This usually occurred, but only after long negotiations, and without Hamburg coming under Danish-Holsteinian authority. Hamburg was, due to its status as a lucrative commercial city it was, highly sought after (Bregnsbo 2010).

Another interest in Northern Germany was the so-called secularized princely dioceses. Prior to the Reformation, most bishops had also been lords of separate principalities in the German Empire. After the Reformation, the Catholic bishops were deposed in the Protestant territories, but their principalities could not immediately be overtaken by the local, secular prince. These secularized princely dioceses could not be given to a Protestant bishop, who was subordinate to the local prince and his state church. Instead, royal sons were appointed princely bishops in such situations. This meant that they were administrators over these principalities, but held no ecclesiastical functions. Often it was the younger princely sons who were instated as prince-bishops, in that way they were able to gain a permanent source of income, resolving a similar issue to that which had caused the division of the duchies of Schleswig and Holstein in 1544.

In the time of Christian IV, via a mixture of negotiation, bribery, and use of power, the younger sons of the king succeeded in being elected Archbishop of Bremen and Bishop of Verden (Frederik, later Frederik III) and bishop of Schwerin (Ulrik). It brought some areas close to Holstein under the king's control, as much as possible. The dioceses did not become Danish, they were not hereditary, and the position of the bishop in relation to the local cathedral chapters that elected the bishops was often so weak that he was in fact unable to act as an agent of the interests of the Danish empire. Furthermore, acquiring them was costly, and as a condition of having a son placed there, Christian IV had to provide comprehensive security policy guarantees. However, the King of Denmark and Norway had good opportunities to exert influence in Northern Germany in his capacity as Duke of Holstein and thereby a member of the German Empire. It also enabled him, as king, German prince, and Lutheran, to act as a type of unofficial Protestant leadership.

During the 1600s, the Danish monarchy acquired small holdings in India, Africa, and the West Indies. Contrary to the Baltic Sea, the North Sea, and Northern Germany, these remote territories did not follow in any way the doctrine of having supremacy over the local seas, which would also have been unrealistic.

By virtue of extensive land and sea territories and far-reaching spheres of influence, the Danish state was a dominant power in Northern Europe, and a medium-sized European power which definitely was not without importance in international politics. This can be illustrated by the following three examples.

1. Around 1536, the Danish monarchy was considered a kind of "rogue state" in international European politics, as its king was not recognized, but was rather considered an usurper since the rightful king, Christian II, had been deposed and later imprisoned. Christian II was a brother-in-law to the German emperor Charles V who, by virtue of the family connection, was obliged to seek reinstating his brother-in-law as king. Charles, as a Catholic, was also in strong opposition to Christian III. In 1544, Charles V decided, however, to set dynastic-familial relations and religious priorities aside and instead signed the Speyer Treaty, whereby he acknowledged Christian III's rule. Christian III, in turn, promised to refrain from continuing to encourage Protestant faith in Germany, which was a win for Charles.

   Danish historians in the twentieth century confused today's small state of Denmark with the Danish empire of the day. They therefore regarded Christian III's long-standing conflict with the emperor as reckless and foolish and similarly, that the conclusion of the Treaty of Speyer in 1544 was an expression that the king was fortunate enough to come to terms before his foreign policy had catastrophic consequences. Thus, in 1932, the social-liberal and highly anti-militarist and pacifist historian Erik Arup wrote that the Speyer Treaty "was a dictation from a powerful world ruler to an utterly inferior opponent; but it was a peace offering, and it was certainly wise that Denmark seized the outstretched olive branch" (Arup 1932, 497–500). This is a severe underestimation or perhaps even an overlook of how geographically extensive, and how militarily and economically resourceful the Danish kingdom and territories were. Although the Danish empire was not as large as Emperor Charles V, Christian III was by no means a "completely inferior opponent."

2. In 1612, the Protestant Union, an alliance of Protestant princes in Germany, seriously considered naming Christian IV a candidate for the German imperial crown.

3. After 1639, due to war and economic crisis, the East India Company was no longer able to equip ships for Tranquebar for the next 29 years. In fact, there were serious attempts in favor of selling the colony. It was not until 1668 that a new expedition was launched. When it arrived in 1669, it found that the Danish flag was still waving over the Dansborg fortress in Tranquebar, and that there was still a Danish garrison. This episode sounds almost too fantastical to be true. The explanation for why

no other powers, neither Indian nor European, had seized Tranquebar was that it belonged to the King of Denmark. And the King of Denmark was considered a mighty man, even in international, European politics: he controlled all traffic to and from the Baltic, just as he charged the Sound customs. And besides, local Indian power holders were having an interest in being able to play off the various European powers off against each other and the Danish colony was of interest in this connection. Therefore, no one had dared to acquire his colony for the past 29 years (Feldbæk 1991).

The Empire's policies in the northern European region, such as Sweden, Norway, the Baltic region, and northern Germany, were closely linked to the international situation in Europe and the position of the empire in relation to it. This, in turn, took place within the context of the military revolution and its consequences, as described earlier in this chapter. In Europe, the period was also marked by war and change. Ecclesiastical divisions and religious wars in the sixteenth century. A significant breaking point was the Thirty Years War, 1618–48. It began as a rebellion in Bohemia against the Habsburg emperor, but spread to the German Empire. As the imperial Catholic forces began to become too victorious and threatened the international balance of power, other powers began to become troubled. Not primarily for religious reasons, but because they feared imperial domination. In turn, other powers intervened. First Christian IV with disastrous results. Next, Sweden's King Gustavus Adolphus, for whom things went much better, and after his death, France intervened. During this war, the political decision-makers lost control of the military apparatus, which operated on its own as a war-keeping force. With the Westphalian Peace Treaty in 1648, the war ended, the military came under political control, and an international power balancing system was created to intervene if any European threatened to become too strong and gain hegemony. For the rest of the period, France is thus seen on several occasions to have threatened supremacy, which is why a coalition of other powers intervened to restore equilibrium. By and large, it can be said that after 1648 international European politics were largely about deciding for or against France. The naval powers of Britain and the Netherlands became increasingly dominant on the seas: as they could no longer feed themselves, but rather depended on grain imports from the Baltic Sea, their interests in this region naturally became so much stronger, and it was something which the local powers, including Denmark, came to feel to a great extent. Their interests were not least due to the fact that a number of products of maritime importance (wood, tar, metals, hemp for ropes) were produced within this region. At the beginning of the eighteenth century, Russia, which had hitherto been barred from the Baltic Sea, gained access, and as a result soon developed considerable naval power.

These were—very briefly and simply put—the basic conditions under which the foreign and military policy of the Danish empire operated. The Empire's main problem was an almost permanent conflict and rivalry with Sweden. During the 184 years between the period 1536–1720, Denmark was at war for 34 years, i.e. entering conflict roughly every 5th or 6th years as an average. Even though it was not solely with Sweden that the empire was at war (but it was the case in 29 of the war years), the empire's other international entanglements were continuously rooted in the antagonisms with Sweden.

When it comes to the empire's foreign and security policy, the core focus was on unconditional dominion over the Baltic Sea. It was by virtue of this dominion that the king of Denmark could claim the profitable revenue from the Sound custom. This also applied to the policies towards Northern Germany and Northern Norway. The acquisition of colonies in Asia, Africa, and the Caribbean was, in relation to this, of marginal and peripheral importance.

In what follows, we shall seek to find trends and context in the many wars that the empire involved itself in, and the consequences they induced. Below are some of the main trends (Fig. 6.3):

- The Danish empire gradually lost its position as the dominant power in the Baltic Sea.
- The Danish empire was reduced and weakened by several occupations and significant territorial cessions.
- Sweden became a European superpower during the seventeenth century, but lost its status in 1720.
- The Baltic Sea area became internationalized and local powers no longer ruled over the area.
- Gottorp became a serious security policy issue for the empire.
- Absolute power was introduced in Denmark in 1660.

THE EMPIRE'S FOREIGN POLICY UNTIL THE DISASTER OF 1658

In the effort to maintain dominion, Sweden was the main and most serious opponent. After the dissolution of the Kalmar Union, neither Christian III's nor the Swedish king Gustavus Vasa's government was internationally recognized, and until the Treaty of Speyer, the two powers were therefore forced to cooperate despite mutual mistrust and rivalry.

In connection with the dissolution of the State of the Teutonic Order in the late 1550s, Frederick II claimed Estonia, but was not in favor of a Danish conquest initiative on the eastern Baltic coast. However, he managed to acquire the island of Øsel (today, Saaremaa) off the coast of Estonia, which was handed over as a secular diocese to Frederik II's younger brother, Magnus.

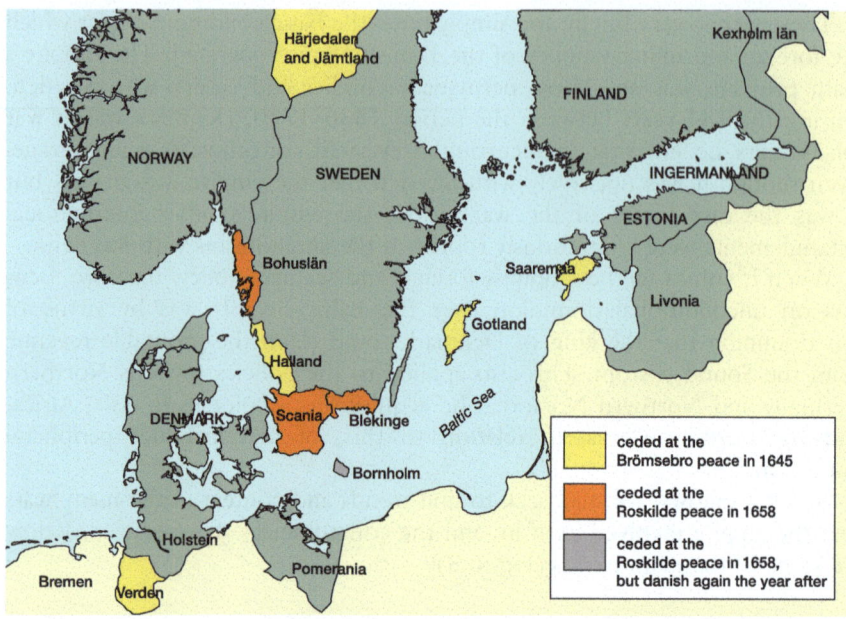

Fig. 6.3 Map of the Baltic area during the seventeenth century where the supremacy of the Danish empire and its status as a regional great power in Northern Europe gradually got lost, especially after the Peace of Roskilde in 1658. Sweden, on the other hand, built a strong empire both through conquests from Denmark and by subjecting large areas at the eastern coast of the Baltic (approximately corresponding to the area of the present-day Baltic states Estonia, Latvia and Lithuania) and in Northern Germany. Sweden thus became a European great power—for a while. The Baltic area was of great international importance, particularly for the sea powers Britain and the Netherlands. These countries did not grow enough grain for their own needs but had to import grain from the Baltic area. Furthermore, a number of strategically important products such as timber, iron and tar was produced here. Consequently, the conditions of the Baltic area became a matter of vital importance for the Western European states and could not be left to the whims of the local powers, Sweden and Denmark

The idea was that as the king's younger brother, he should receive a permanent source of income, that is, the same issue we saw in connection to the division of the duchies in 1544 and the policy of Christian IV in northern Germany. Magnus, however, sought to expand his power and take possession of the Estonian mainland. This policy did not have the support of his brother, Frederik II. An island like Øsel was defendable, but attempts to acquire and retain possession on the mainland could easily push the Danish empire into unmanageable and undesirable military engagements with the Order State, Poland, and Russia. Magnus' activity in the area caused unrest. Several cities turned to the King of Sweden, fearing both Danish and Russian expansion, and found that Sweden was the best power to provide protection. Estonia was of importance to Sweden as it could be used by other powers as a springboard for an attack on Finland, which was at the time part of Sweden. Tensions between the Danish Empire and Sweden grew. The King of Denmark added the Swedish three crowns to his coat of arms, while Sweden replied by adding the three Danish lions and the Norwegian lion to his own coat of arms. Both these heraldic provocations and the engagements in remote Estonia may not seem sufficient to lead to an outbreak of war let alone a prolonged conflict. However, government coat of arms were not just symbols, but political declarations both internally and externally, and as such they were taken seriously. The engagement in Estonia centered on dominion of the Baltic Sea: Denmark's claim to supremacy precluded that it had to respond if any threatening action was made towards the Baltic Sea—and as an extension the Danish king's authority. This resulted in the Nordic Seven Years War from 1563 to 1570, an internal Danish-Swedish conflict. Foreign powers were impacted by this war, as it occurred in the Baltic regions, where England and Netherlands had strong trade and maritime interests. Denmark would occasionally blockade entry to the Sound in an attempt to cut Sweden's lines of supply. Denmark and Sweden tore each other apart both militarily and financially. The war showed that Denmark continued to dominate the Baltic Sea, but on the other hand was not strong enough to subdue Sweden and restore the Kalmar Union. Both parties gave up their conquests at the Peace of Stettin in 1570. Sweden relinquished Estonia to the German emperor, who in turn handed over Øsel and possessions on the Estonian mainland to the King of Denmark. Furthermore, it was decided that future issues between Denmark and Sweden should be decided in a committee, equally composed of members of the Danish and Swedish councils of the realm resp. If one of the kings refused to accept a decision made in this committee, the councils would be released from their oath to him.

In the following decades, Estonia and Livonia were subject to conflict between the Danish Empire, Sweden, Poland, and Russia, and the Danish Empire managed to expand its possessions here. These mainland possessions were, however, militarily difficult to defend, and after heavy deliberation, Frederick II abandoned them and in 1585 sold Kurland to King Stephen Báthory of Poland. However, the island of Øsel remained part of the Danish empire and was ruled by a Danish governor.

Sweden, in turn, expanded on the eastern Baltic coast to great concern in Denmark. Sweden also expanded elsewhere. In 1607, the king of Sweden, Charles IX, assumed the title of "king over the Lapps (i.e. Samis) in Nordland," which indicated that he regarded himself as the rightful ruler of this part of the Danish empire. The young King Christian IV had long warned against Charles' ambition, and in 1601 and 1603–1604, he suggested war with Sweden to his unwilling Council of the Realm. It was not because the council did not share the king's view of Sweden as a threat, but it was against direct war. This was linked to the Peace of Stettin of 1570, which gave the Danish and Swedish Councils a great influence on the settlement of disputes between the two kingdoms. Of course, this would only last as long as there was no state of war. In the event of war, all cooperation between Danish and Swedish councils would cease, and war would deprive the nobility of its great influence on foreign policy. In 1611, however, things escalated to war. The Council disagreed with this decision, but since the council had no authority in the duchy of Holstein, Christian IV had already threatened to declare the war in his capacity as Duke of Holstein. The Kalmar War lasted until 1613. It was the last time Denmark made an attempt to conquer Sweden and restore the Kalmar Union. However, without success: after a lucky start the Danish offensive was halted. An attempt to lead an attack from Norway by creating an army of drafted Norwegian peasants failed. They lacked the necessary military equipment, and the drafted peasants proved undisciplined and recalcitrant. Similar to the Nordic Seven Years War, trade blockades on the Sound were also launched, which again was a major nuisance for the naval powers of England and the Netherlands, who did not intervene militarily, but instead offered mediation. At the peace in Knäred in 1613, Denmark and Sweden returned their conquests. However, Sweden would only regain the fortress of Elfsborg near present-day Gothenburg once it had paid a million rixdollars to Denmark within the period of six years. Elfsborg was of geostrategic importance as it was located on a strip of land between the Norwegian and Danish border that gave Sweden access to the sea of Kattegat. The Knäred peace treaty resolved the disputes in Northern Norway. The Kalmar War had demonstrated that Denmark remained the dominant, yet not hegemonic power in the Baltic Sea.

The next conflict in which the Danish Empire participated was the Emperor War (Kejserkrigen) of 1625–1629. While this war was with the German emperor, Denmark's rivalry with Sweden nevertheless played an important role. The war was a phase of the Thirty Years War (1618–1648). The German imperial power and its Catholic allied members of the German Empire were militarily victorious and had upset the balance of power not only within the German Empire, but also in the rest of Europe. This alarmed the Protestant princes in Germany. The German Empire was divided into circles, including among other things defense. As Duke of Holstein, Christian was a member of the Lower Saxon Circle, whose members were all Protestants. In 1625, Christian IV succeeded by a staggering majority in being elected Circuit Colonel, i.e. the circuit's chief of defense. He became a member of the circle in his capacity as Duke of Holstein and not as the king of Denmark-Norway. Of course, it also played a role that he was a member of the circle who had extremely large resources at hand, as king of Denmark and Norway.

Powers outside the German Empire, the Netherlands, England, and France were also anxious about the imperial developments and the distortion of the balance of power it entailed. However, none of them were able to intervene militarily at that moment: the Netherlands was involved in a war with Spain, England was more or less paralyzed by the conflict between the king and parliament, and France was also affected by internal strife. In addition, while Catholic France was alarmed at the advance of the imperial armies, it could not directly support the emperor's opponents because of the strong Protestant rhetoric they were utilizing. Instead, the European powers were in search of a prince willing to lead an anti-imperial coalition and restore the balance of power. There were two options, namely Christian IV and Sweden's King Gustavus Adolphus. Neither king wanted the other to be named leader of such a coalition. Although the great powers nominated Christian IV, the fact that they had the opportunity to appoint Gustavus Adolphus instead limited Christian's ability to impose excessive conditions. The Council of the Realm opposed the king going to war. Instead, Christian IV went to war as Duke of Holstein, as the council could not dispute his actions under that title. The kingdom of Denmark itself was not technically belligerent.

The war led to the defeat of Christian IV's forces in 1626 at the Battle of Lutter am Barenberge at Wolfenbüttel in Germany. The following year his army was pushed over, and Holstein, Schleswig, and Jutland occupied, ravaged, and plundered by imperial troops. As the navy of the empire was having the upper hand, the imperial forces could not reach the islands. The Allies' subsidies and troop resupply shipments did not arrive on time or to the agreed extent, and Christian IV was abandoned by most of his allies in the Lower Saxon Circle as the war began to wane. Peace talks with representatives of the emperor commenced, but they stalled initially because the imperial demands were considered unacceptable. In this situation, Christian began negotiations with Gustavus Adolphus in 1629 on a Danish-Swedish alliance. No agreement came out of it, and it is doubtful whether Christian IV's initiative was seriously intended at all. The purpose of the Danish-Swedish royal summit was quite different: to send a signal to the emperor with the ongoing negotiations. When the emperor heard the rumor that the two kings had met and discussed an alliance, he immediately relaxed his demands on Christian IV (Jespersen 1982). Thus Christian IV achieved his ulterior goal in the meeting with the Swedish king. At the peace in Lübeck between Christian IV and the emperor, the Danish empire did not lose land, but Christian had to commit to abandoning his politics in Northern Germany and promise not to interfere in future affairs of the German Empire beyond what lay within his capacity as Duke of Holstein.

The dominion of the Baltic continued to exist, but Christian IV had suffered a loss of prestige, his kingdoms were suffering economically, and Jutland and the duchies were ruined. The Emperor War was the beginning of the end of the greatness of the Danish empire. Christian IV has historically received a lot of criticism for his politics. But part of the criticism comes from the fact that historians have mistakenly confused Christian's kingdoms and lands with the current small state named Denmark, and thus a number of conditions in the king's policy of war seemed illogical and reckless. However, when taken into account that Christian IV was the ruler of a much larger empire, the picture becomes different in several respects, explored below.

The fact that Christian IV went to war as Duke of Holstein when the Danish Council of the Realm refused to support the initiative has been seen as a dirty trick on the part of the king. It probably was too. Prior to the Kalmar War, he had also threatened to declare war on the same basis. However, it was more than that. As Duke of Holstein, Christian IV was a German prince, a member of the German Empire, represented in the German Diet and thus had legitimate interests to pursue in Germany. In Germany he was "only" Duke of Holstein, but unlike other dukes, as also a king he had very large resources at hand and was thus a German ruler of extraordinary influence. He was thus not just a "military fill-in" as he has been otherwise written off as. In his capacity as a German prince, Christian IV looked at international politics with a lens that did not quite coincide with those of his Danish Council of the Realm. Historians have often described the Council as the voice of reason, moderation, and advocate of peace, but unfortunately unable to control the warlike king. In reality, the council's position was rather dictated by the fact that in peace time, it would have a profound influence on politics, whereas war would give the king increased powers and thus weaken the Council's position. As a result, the council acted as a curb on defense spending and thus helped to weaken Christian IV militarily. Even while the war was still raging, the Council of the Realm, which in its time had warned in vain against the war, criticized the politics of the war. And the rest of Christian IV's time was marked by growing conflict and mistrust between king and council (Lockhart 1996).

The war ended disastrously, but this had not been foreseen when Christian IV entered the conflict. The imperial commanders certainly did not consider Christian as a military lightweight. The cause was that Imperial Commander Albrecht von Wallenstein succeeded in raising his own, new army as a military contractor. He funded the army by letting it occupy lands it then taxed/plundered for itself. Thereby another imperial army could be established in record time, crucially changing the strategic situation. However, Christian IV could not have foreseen this when he decided to join the war.

The year after the Peace of Lübeck in 1629, Sweden entered the Thirty Years' War in Germany, winning formidable victories and becoming a European great power. Christian IV, on the other hand, was obliged by the treaty to conduct a neutrality policy while at the same time safeguarding his own interests. While Sweden was on the offensive in 1633, the emperor acknowledged Christian's good will and therefore bestowed on him the right to levy customs on shipping on the Elbe for a four-year period. When Sweden was distressed following the defeat at Nördlingen in 1634, Christian IV used the relationship to regain the territories of Bremen and Verden, which were otherwise lost until the peace in 1629. His son Frederik III was reinstated as administrator (secularized prince-bishop) there in 1635 and 1636.

As a neutral power, considerable defense preparedness also had to be maintained and taxes were established to finance this. The mutual distrust between the King and the Council of the Realm led the latter to often oppose new taxes for defense measures that the former found necessary. Therefore, the king had to make use of his personal source of income, the Sound customs. There were drastic increases in customs duties, the largest being a 19-fold increase in customs on saltpeter (potassium nitrate), introduced in 1638. The saltpeter, which was an important strategic material because it is used for gunpowder, was destined for the Netherlands. The naval powers of the Netherlands and England had been annoyed by Danish dominance and blockades on the Baltic Sea for years, and the experience in 1638 convinced them that Denmark's position as the guardian of access to the Baltic Sea had to be addressed. Politically, Christian IV's customs policy was unwise, but it emerged from a desperate need for funding, which was exacerbated by the fact that the Council of the Realm was opposing increased defense for defense purposes.

Sweden's success in Germany was a source of unease for the Danish king, and since it was not possible to enter the war himself, he offered his services as a mediator to the belligerent parties. These endeavors by King Christian have traditionally been dismissed as an attempt to disempower Sweden diplomatically, to achieve at the negotiating table what he could not achieve on the battlefield. Of course, King Christian's motives were not purely idealistic, and of course, he was having the interests of his own state in mind in his mediating activities. Yet, his genuine desires to restore peace have probably been underrated. In 1641, peace negotiations were established under Danish leadership. At the same time, however, Christian IV kept other foreign policy options open, including the possibility of an alliance with the emperor facing Sweden. This was not least why Sweden, in the so-called Torstensson War after the Swedish supreme commander invaded and occupied the duchies, Jutland, and Scania in December 1643 without a formal declaration of war. The Swedish intentions behind this assault were this duplicity from King Christian as a dishonest mediator as they saw it, at least they strongly emphasized this alleged duplicity in order to justify having attacked without any prior declaration of war. But an important Swedish motive was also to make the king discontinue his mediating activities fearing that the Swedish gains of the war might thereby be reduced, Yet, even if the situation for the Danish state was disastrous, it was not completely hopeless, partly since Denmark succeeded in pushing Swedish forces out of Scania, and partly since Denmark was still having naval dominion. The disaster truly occurred when a number of Danish naval squadrons in October 1644 attempted to prevent a Swedish fleet from entering the Sound. As a result, 17 Danish warships set out to battle as many as 44 Swedish ships, clashing at the Battle of Fehmarn on October 13, 1644. It ended in total Danish defeat. The historian Steffen Heiberg considers the defeat at Fehmarn a landmark event: it meant that "Denmark was no longer a power capable of securing its territorial integrity with its own forces, and has not been the case since" (Heiberg 1988, 420).

At the Second Treaty of Brömsebro (the "Peace of Brömsebro") on August 13, 1645, the Danish empire had to surrender considerable lands and grant concessions in customs of the Sound to Sweden and the Netherlands. The latter had not directly participated in the war with Denmark, but was strongly hostile because of Danish tariff increases and trade blockades, and welcomed the weakening of Denmark that the peace entailed. Denmark lost its claim of dominion in the Baltic. After the conflict in 1643, Christian IV gave up all mediation activities in the Thirty Years War, and as a result, was not a co-signer of the Westphalian Peace in 1648.

Christian IV died in 1648, two and a half years after the Peace of Brömsebro. He was succeeded by his son Frederik III, who, until the Torstensson war, had been the administrator of the territories of Bremen and Verden. The king's power in Denmark was not hereditary, it was the council that elected a new king. Admittedly, the council usually appointed the son of the deceased king. This likened much to the hereditary monarchy of Norway, since if Denmark's council elected someone other than the deceased king's son, the empire would split apart. Nevertheless, Frederik was in a weak negotiating position and had to accede to a charter which significantly reduced the king's powers compared to Christian IV's rule. The Council's distrust and previous monarchic experiences clearly had a prevailing impact.

During the rule of Christian IV, the Council of the Realm opposed activist foreign policy and ambitions of war. However, in 1657 it was in fact the Council together with representatives of the other estates of the realm that directly supported the declaration of war against Sweden which would become the catastrophic Charles Gustavus Wars. At an assembly of estates in Odense in February 1657, all representatives voted for increased taxes to be used for a military buildup, and thus the decision for war was indirectly confirmed, although the declaration of war was not formally issued until June 1st. The context to these decisions was that Sweden had built a Baltic Sea empire with large territorial areas on the eastern part of the Baltic Sea coast, and furthermore had acquired the former Danish-controlled areas, Bremen and Verden in northern Germany. There was no doubt that Sweden would sooner or later attack Denmark. In 1656–1657, however, the international situation seemed favorable for the Danish Empire to strike first. A Swedish army led by King Charles X Gustavus was stuck in a campaign in Poland. Yet, after receiving the declaration of war, Charles Gustavus used the opportunity as a heaven-sent pretext to disengage from Poland and instead march towards Denmark. As in 1643, the duchies and Jutland were occupied, but the transition to the islands was not possible as Denmark retained dominion at sea. But the situation was radically changed by the fact that it was ice winter and the Belts froze to ice. This allowed Charles Gustavus's army to make an audacious, but fatally successful move: to march across the ice to Funen, Langeland, Falster, Lolland, and on to Sealand. Given the circumstances, the Danish leadership was forced to make peace by accepting the terms that were offered—and they were extremely unfavorable. At the peace in Roskilde on February 26, 1658, the Kingdom of Denmark had to cede Scania, Halland, and Blekinge—a third of its territory. This meant that the Sound, the entrance to the Baltic Sea, was no longer solely Danish waters, the dominion of the Baltic Sea was now finally lost. Copenhagen, which used to be in the middle of the kingdom, now became a frontline town. Norway was cut in the middle as the Diocese of Trondheim had to be ceded too. In addition, large parts of the king's territory had been ravaged and plundered. The naval powers of the Netherlands and Britain, who had long felt their trade and maritime interests bothered by the Danish presence in the Sound, welcomed the fact that a single force could no longer dominate access to the Baltic Sea.

Yet, this applied whether this power was called Denmark or Sweden, as it explains why the naval powers intervened in favor of Denmark when half a year later Charles Gustavus decided to exploit the Danish weakening to conquer the entire Danish empire. Most of Denmark was occupied, but Copenhagen bravely and resolutely resisted when under siege. However, in Norway, the Norwegian forces succeeded in capturing the diocese of Trondheim and Bohuslen. In December, a group of inhabitants of the Baltic island Bornholm succeeded in overpowering the Swedish commander Printzenskiöld and taking possession of the Hammershus fortress, thereby freeing the island of Swedish forces. A delegation was sent to Copenhagen to offer inheritance and ownership of the island to Frederik III. Bornholm thus liberated itself and returned to Denmark, but on other terms than before the war, namely as the Danish king's inheritance, while the rest of the kingdom was based on an electoral system. Even as far away as the Gold Coast of Africa, there was a Danish-Swedish front in this war. However, the conflict here was fought without coordination with or directive from the respective state leaders, and in reality it did not have a significant impact on the outcome of the overall war. The Netherlands sent a rescue fleet to the beleaguered Copenhagen. Dutch forces assisted in denying a Swedish attempt to storm the city on the night between February 10 and 11, 1659, and subsequently expelled Swedish troops from the islands. At the same time, the duchies and Jutland were occupied by Polish-Brandenburg-Imperial auxiliary forces, who displaced the Swedish troops, but otherwise plundered the area as the King of Denmark could not afford to pay them, so they supported themselves.

On the diplomatic front, France, along with Britain and the Netherlands, intervened and ensured peace in Copenhagen in 1660. The legal foundations were the Peace of Roskilde, and while some adjustments were made for the Danish empire (the Diocese of Trondheim and Bornholm), the cessation of Scania, Halland, and Blekinge was upheld. The course that led to the Peace in Copenhagen in 1660 showed that the Baltic Sea area had become internationalized. Danish-Swedish conflicts were no longer local disputes, but matters in which major European powers had vital interests. The Sound's central importance in the international economy was compared by historian Knud J.V. Jespersen to today's current significance of the Strait of Hormuz for the world's oil supply. Today, if a power is able to block the Strait of Hormuz, it will be able to enact a stranglehold on the economy of the Western world, and therefore it is of vital importance that no single power be able to do so (Jespersen 1994).

Royal Absolutism

The Danish empire was mutilated, looted, and humiliated. In the wake of the war epidemics wiped out large sections of the population. Beyond this was the state's desperate financial need. To solve this, a meeting among the estates of the realm was convened in Copenhagen in the autumn of 1660, and it was this meeting that led to the introduction of not only a hereditary monarchy but also of royal absolutism and the abolition of the Council of the Realm. In 1665, the Royal Law that was such a contradiction in a term as an absolutist constitution which furthermore stated the order of succession to the hereditary throne was issued.

The introduction of royal absolutism in 1660 was a purely internal Danish (royal) affair, which was only later applied to other parts of the empire, without negotiations or bloodshed, but as a *fait accompli*. Norway had no influence on the change in the constitution, and the government overthrow in Copenhagen was announced in Norway in November 1660. In August 1661 an assembly of the Norwegian estates was held in Christiania. Here, a ceremony of acclaim, in reality, the Norwegian estate representatives were hereby compelled to also sign an act on absolute government similar to the Danish one. In other words, absolutism was introduced on the same occasion. There is no information on whether there were any protests; on the contrary: according to the official report, the Norwegian estate representatives welcomed the introduction of absolute power with "the greatest joy and pleasure." In reality, the absolute power act of sovereignty—as well as the Norwegian reaction of "joy and pleasure"—was drafted well in advance in Copenhagen. In Iceland, absolute power was approved by a court meeting in July 1662. Here, however, there was some fear, as the document stated that the Icelanders should renounce existing laws and privileges. Here, too, there was no serious resistance, partly since the Icelanders were generally unarmed and subject to the domination of the trade monopoly. It was also partly due to the fact that many within the Icelandic government saw a self-interest in supporting the king. The document was signed at the Faroe Islands in August 1662 without further ado (Tønnesen 2013, 31–75, 81–87). While Norway, Iceland, and the Faroe Islands were not central aspects of this new structure of absolute power, the change demonstrated the distribution of power and resources within the empire. In the duchies, however, the situation was far more complex. Firstly, since Holstein was a member of the German Empire, the Duke of Holstein was subordinate to the German emperor, so for that reason alone absolutism could not be introduced here. Secondly, the nobility of the duchies was having a strong position organized in the Aristocratic Corporation and those of them who owned landed estates in Holstein would thus have the possibility to appeal decisions of the duke to law-courts within the German Empire. Certainly, the assemblies of the estate of the duchies ceased to meet after 1675, yet, the Aristocratic Corporation continued to exist and subsequent regents had to show it serious consideration, if not formally, then certainly in practice.

The introduction of absolutism meant that the Danish Council of the Realm was abolished and that the nobility's exclusive right to the high positions of civil and military administration in the Kingdom of Denmark dissolved. In principle, these positions were now open to all: noble or bourgeois locals, foreigners, and people from other parts of the empire. The monarchy also sought to create a new social order by an orderly ranking, and neither foreigners nor people from other parts of the empire were in principle barred from being included if they met the conditions. The introduction of absolutism thus, in a sense, signaled a small step towards harmonizing the relations among the various parts of the empire, but under the dominion of the Kingdom of Denmark.

The Gottorp Problem

Another security policy problem for the Danish empire grew out of the many wars of the seventeenth century, namely the issue of Gottorp. The Gottorps were descendants of Duke Adolphus, who by the succession of the duchies in 1544 had gained the area near the town of Schleswig where Gottorp Castle was situated. During Christian IV's rule, the relationship with the Duke of Gottorp had been strained for several reasons. First, King Christian was zealous to procure secularized princely dioceses for his sons in northern Germany, but in the Gottorp Duke's view, had not shown to the Gottorps the considerations they felt were expected from their royal lord. During the Emperor War, like the rest of the duchies, the Gottorp areas had been occupied and looted without the assistance from the vassal lord, Christian IV. For this reason, the Duke of Gottorp had begun negotiations with the imperial army commanders and also achieved certain reliefs. These conditions greatly contributed to a mood of mistrust between the king and the duke after the war. At the next occupation, the Torstensson War, the Duke of Gottorp chose to declare himself neutral. This was a clear breach of the duke's oath, but by the Second Treaty of Brömsebro in 1645 Christian IV had to commit himself not to hold the Duke of Gottorp accountable. In doing so, the Danish empire had a hostile, Swedish-backed duke within its territories. In the next war of 1657, the Duke of Gottorp not only declared himself neutral, but entered into a direct alliance with Sweden. And at the peace in Roskilde, the duke was highly rewarded sense. He was released from his vassal oath to the King of Denmark and was thus now a sovereign duke, and was now only a vassal in Holstein, to the German emperor. King Frederick III of Denmark had named himself Duke of Schleswig via a vassalship. Not to be left inferior to the Duke of Gottorp, Frederik III now declared himself sovereign duke in Schleswig. In other words, he declared himself to be independent of the King of Denmark, that is, of himself. That may seem a bit of a repetitive formality, but prestige was of great concern in international politics. Both domestically and internationally, it was important for Frederick III to signal that the Duke of Gottorp was not his superior. From now on, the Gottorp areas became almost an independent state, but the constitutional status of the duchies, which had hitherto been jointly ruled by the two dukes, was not changed. However, the fact that the jointly governed territories were ruled by two arch enemies inevitably gave rise to an endless series of prestige and competence struggles. The union between the Kingdom of Denmark and the duchies continued to exist.

The territories of the Gottorp Duke were small and spread throughout Schleswig and Holstein. Militarily, the Danish Empire could put the Gottorp areas in their place. But the problem was that the issue could not be decided militarily. The Gottorp dukes were allies with Sweden, Sweden was Gottorp's protector, and Gottorp was a Swedish satellite state. This meant that a Danish military action against Gottorp would also mean war with Sweden. And a Danish-Swedish war was not just—as stated above—an internal Nordic conflict, but a conflict in which not least Britain and the Netherlands, the main naval powers, and France had vital interests. Any unilateral Danish action against the Duke of Gottorp would therefore immediately have serious international consequences for the entire Danish Empire. In the late 1660s, however, there was a short-term reconciliation between the Danish Empire and Gottorp. The reason was that the ruling princely lineage in the North German counties Oldenburg and Delmenhorst, which were original homelands for both the Danish royal family and the Gottorp duke family, died out in 1667. Here both Frederik III and the Duke of Gottorp had common interests, such as preventing the Duke of Plön, a descendant of Frederik II's brother John the Younger (John II), from inheriting the two counties. However, in 1670, the newly appointed king, Christian V, pressured the Duke of Gottorp to renounce his inheritance claim to these two counties, which came under the control of the Danish Empire. This cased the Duke of Gottorp to be further driven into the arms of Sweden.

Revenge Attempts Against Sweden Within the Framework of Great Politics

By the Westphalian Peace in 1648, which brought an end to the Thirty Years' War, a European power balancing system had been created. This system did not preclude or prevent new wars, but it meant that if one power sought to gain hegemony, coalitions of other powers would rise against that power to secure the balance of power. In the second half of the seventeenth century, France sought hegemony in Europe, and through a variety of wars other powers sought to counter this. It can be described that in those years foreign policy of a European state lay in relation to France, either as an ally or an enemy. The two most important foreign policy goals of the Danish Empire—the re-acquisition of the provinces east of the Sound and a solution to the Gottorp problem—were not immediately resolved during these international trends. Thus, when the Danish empire sought to recapture the Scanian territories and solve the Gottorp problem, it had to happen within a major political framework. The Scanian War 1675–1679 was not just an isolated

Danish-Swedish conflict, but the culmination of a European Great War in which Sweden was allied with France and the Danish Empire with France's enemies. Hostilities between Sweden and Denmark thus became one front among many in this European conflict. The Gottorp Duke's territories were occupied, and Danish troops landed in Scania, but the Danish army suffered defeat in the Battle of Lund in 1676. However, it managed to conquer some of Sweden's provinces in northern Germany. In Norway, the king's half-brother, the dynamic Ulrik Frederik Gyldenløve (the war is called in Norway for the Gyldenløve War), was entrusted with leadership of the defenses, and on the Swedish-Norwegian front the empire started to notice progress. But, as mentioned, the war was embroiled in an international conflict between France and its opponents, so when these other conflicts concluded in peace in 1679, neither party had any interest in continuing the Danish-Swedish war. This is why France simply made peace at the palace of Fontainebleau south of Paris on Sweden's behalf without the inclusion of the Swedish government. Denmark was also faced with a French dictation: the conquered territories, which were still under Danish control in 1679 (Bohuslen) as well as the Swedish possessions in Germany (Wismar, Bremen and Verden) had to be returned to Sweden, and the Duke of Gottorp would regain the authorities he had held before the outbreak of the war. Thus, the pre-war state was restored without any of the original causes of war having found any satisfactory solution for the empire.

In the following years, the empire aligned itself with France as an ally. This certainly provided security policy benefits, even if France did not have as much interest in the Baltic region as the maritime powers of Britain and the Netherlands. It also had no direct interest in a reconquest of the Scanian territories, let alone actively supporting such a conquest. Nor was a settlement with Gottorp in the direct interest of France. Yet, in the shelter of the alliance with Europe's most powerful entity, Christian V quietly allowed the occupation and incorporation of the Schleswig-parts of Gottorp into royal possessions. However, when he sought to subjugate Hamburg in 1686, strong international protests emerged, as such a move would disrupt the balance of power in Northern Germany. France's position in Europe was weakening at the time, so Christian V was forced to bow to international pressure and reinstate the Duke of Gottorp at the Altona settlement in 1689. A new Danish occupation in 1698 ended in the same result. And yet another occupation in 1700 led to a similar end state—but only after a short war with Sweden.

Like the Scanian War, the Great Nordic War of 1709–1720 must also be seen as a Danish-Swedish front in a larger European war. During this war, a last but unsuccessful Danish attempt to recapture the Scanian territories was made. The Duke of Gottorp, on the other hand, was expelled. On the front in Northern Germany, the empire's luck was mixed, but not without victories. Thus, several of Sweden's territories in Northern Germany were conquered and a civilian Danish administration was inaugurated here. Clearly, the state leadership was intending at incorporating these territories permanently. In the context of the empire, the war is also remarkable because Norway became a main front in its final phase. In the spring of 1716, southern Norway was invaded by numerically superior Swedish forces, and for a while occupied Christiania, but not the nearby fortress of Akershus. Norway had now become the scene in the war. Reinforcements had to be added from Denmark, such as the fleet, which was instrumental in the fight against the Swedish forces. The transfer of military resources between the two kingdoms was something new, in previous wars both battles had been fought, but on fronts that were independent of each other. Although the military situation in Norway during both the Torstensson War of 1643–1645 and during the Gyldenløve War in 1675–1679 had been far more favorable than in the Kingdom of Denmark and the duchies, it was nevertheless the situations of the latter two that was ultimately decisive for the conflict at that time. Now Norway became the decisive front. In the autumn of 1718, a Swedish offensive was launched in several places in Norway, and a siege of the Fredriksten border fortress was initiated. During an inspection of the trenches there on 12 December, the Swedish King Charles XII was hit by a gun shot and died. It is still debated whether the shot came from the Norwegian side or whether he was killed by friendly fire (Andersen 2021, vol. 2, 453–462; Liljegren 2008). After that, Sweden's offensive power depleted. The Frederiksborg Peace in 1720, like previous peace treaties, was a great power dictate. Denmark had to vacate and return all conquered territories, and in return Britain and France guaranteed the Danish king's right to the Gottorp parts of Schleswig (but not Holstein). The Scanian territories were not regained, but Sweden's time as a great power was over. Neither Sweden nor Denmark was now the supreme powers in the Baltic. Now it was the naval forces, especially Britain, who held the most sway, and as a result of the war, Russia had also become a leading force in the Baltic Sea.

During the short 200 years from 1536 to 1720, the Danish empire experienced a considerable weakening and serious land divisions. From being a medium-sized European power, enjoying supremacy over Sweden, the dominant power in the Baltic Sea and Northern Germany as well as in the North Sea, Denmark's positions in the Baltic Sea region and in Northern Germany were overtaken by Sweden. Moreover, the more vital interests of Britain and the Netherlands in the trade and shipping in the Baltic Sea meant that the conditions became internationalized, and both the Danish Empire and Sweden had to submit to the dictates of super powers. This is also seen in the Danish empire's failure to recapture the Scanian territories or its numerous futile attempts to solve the Gottorp problem, although this was otherwise Denmark's primary security priority. The prolonged conflict that the empire engaged with Sweden led to extensive efforts to strengthen the Danish empire inward and outward through the introduction of the tax and military state, of an active and multifaceted business policy and of royal absolutism in 1660. But all in all, both the empire and Sweden (despite conquests from Denmark and Norway) were in the long term weakened by their continuous rivalry. Perhaps the efforts to maintain the position of power that the Danish Empire still had in 1536 were simply too great a burden: the empire was thinly spread geographically, had relatively small resources, and a small population. Perhaps this was an inevitable situation, because the trade and shipping on the Baltic Sea were so vital to the larger naval forces. At the very least, by 1720 both the Danish Empire and Sweden had been transformed into actors (albeit not puppets) in an international system in which Britain and Russia set the bar.

References

Andersen, Dan H. 2021. *Store Nordiske Krig*, vol. 1–2. Copenhagen: Politikens Forlag.
Arup, Erik. 1932. *Danmarks Historie*, vol. 2. Copenhagen: Hagerup.
Bonney, Richard. 1991. *The European Dynastic States, 1494–1660*. Oxford: Oxford University Press.
Bregnsbo, Michael. 2009. Merkantilisme. In *Økonomisk teori – i historisk belysning*, ed. Preben Etwil and Søren Kolstrup. Copenhagen: Knuths Forlag.
Bregnsbo, Michael. 2010. Das dänische Imperium aus norddeutscher Sicht – Streifzüge durch die Historiographie der norddeutschen Territorien in der Frühen Neuzeit. In *Regna firmat pietas. Staat und Staatlichkeit im Ostseeraum. Festgabe zum 60. Geburtstag von Jens E. Olesen*, ed. Martin Krieger & Joachim Krüger, 209–222. Greifswald: Ernst-Moritz-Arndt Universität Greifswald.
Elliott, J.H. 1992. A Europe of Composite States. *Past and Present* 137: 48–71.
Feldbæk, Ole. 1991. No Ship for Tranquebar for Twentynine Years. Or: The Art of Survival of a Mid-Seventeenth Century European Settlement in India. In *Emporia, Commodities and Entreprerneurs in Asian Maritime Trade, c. 1400–1750*, ed. Roderich Ptak and Dietmar Rothermund, 29–36. Heidelberg: Südasien-Institut der Universität Heidelberg.
Gustafsson, Harald. 1994. Conglomerates and Unitary States. Integration Processes in Early Modern Denmark-Norway and Sweden. In *Föderationsmodelle und Unionstrukturen in der frühen Neuzeit vom 15. Bis 18. Jahrhundert, Wiener Beiträge zur Geschichte der Neuzeit*, ed. Thomas Fröschl, vol. 21, 45–62. Wien & München: Verlag für Geschichte und Politik/R. Oldenbourg Verlag.
Heiberg, Steffen. 1988. *Christian 4. Monarken, mennesket og myten*. Copenhagen: Gyldendal.
Jespersen, Knud J.V. 1982. Kongemødet i Ulfsbäck præstegård februar 1629. En dansk diplomatisk triumf på tragisk baggrund. *Historie*, New Series 14: 420–439.
Jespersen, Knud J.V. 1983. Social Change and Military Revolution in Early Modern Europe: Some Danish Evidence. *Historical Journal* 26: 1–13.
Jespersen, Knud J.V. 1994. Rivalry Without Victory. Denmark, Sweden and the Struggle for the Baltic, 1500–1720. In *In Quest of Trade and Security. The Baltic in Power Politics 1500–1900*, ed. Göran Rystad, Klars-R. Böhme, and Wilhelm M. Carlgren, vol. 1, 137–176. Lund: Lund University Press.
Jespersen, Leon, ed. 2000. *A Revolution from Above? The Power State of 16th and 17th Century Scandinavia*. Odense: Odense University Press.
Ladewig Petersen, Erling. 1973. Norgesparagraffen i Christian III's håndfæstning 1536. Studier over det 16. århundredes fortolkning. *Historisk Tidsskrift* (Denmark), 393–463.

Ladewig Petersen, Erling. 1975. From Domain State to Tax State. Synthesis and Interpretation. *Scandinavian Economic History Review*, 23: 116–148.
Liljegren, Bengt. 2008. *Krigarkungen. En biografi över Karl XII*. Lund: Historiska Media.
Lockhart, Paul Douglas. 1996. *Denmark in the Thirty Years' War, 1618–1648: King Christian IV and the Decline of the Oldenburg State*. Selinsgrove: Susquehanna University Press.
Tønnesen, Allan, ed. 2013. *Magtens besegling. Enevoldsarveregeringsakterne af 1661 og 1662 underskrevet og beseglet af stænderne i Danmark, Norge, Island og Færøerne*. Odense: Heraldisk Selskab/Syddansk Universitetsforlag.

CHAPTER 7

From the Conglomerate State to the Unitary State 1720–1814

The conglomerate state and unitary state are both concepts that did not emerge until much later in history. The empire was never fully a conglomerate state nor fully a unitary state. But in certain periods there were perhaps more elements of one type of state present than the other. In the period of 1720–1814 for example, more features can be identified that are associated with a unitary state, while features that belonged to a conglomerate state disappeared. In 1814 the Danish empire had more features of a unitary state compared with in 1720. The concepts of conglomerate state and unitary state are of course human-constructed ideas, but such constructions can be useful when making comparisons (Gustafsson 1994).

A unitary state may well be a nation-state if there is a majority language and culture within its territory. Of course, this was not the Danish Empire in the period from 1720 to 1814, but this does not exclude the existence of national identities and perhaps even national schisms.

Of course, even before 1720 one can point to features that would lead to the formation of a unitary state. The introduction of absolutism in 1660 was a step in that direction (see Chapter 6). An important attribute in this respect was when Danish Law Code was implemented in 1683. It was a general collection of laws that replaced the older Danish regional laws (Jutland Law, Sealand Law and others) and made the inner Kingdom of Denmark a common area of unified law. The Kingdom of Norway had been a common area of unified law since the thirteenth century. The whole Danish empire was still not under a unified law, but the number of different legal codes was reduced (Fig. 7.1).

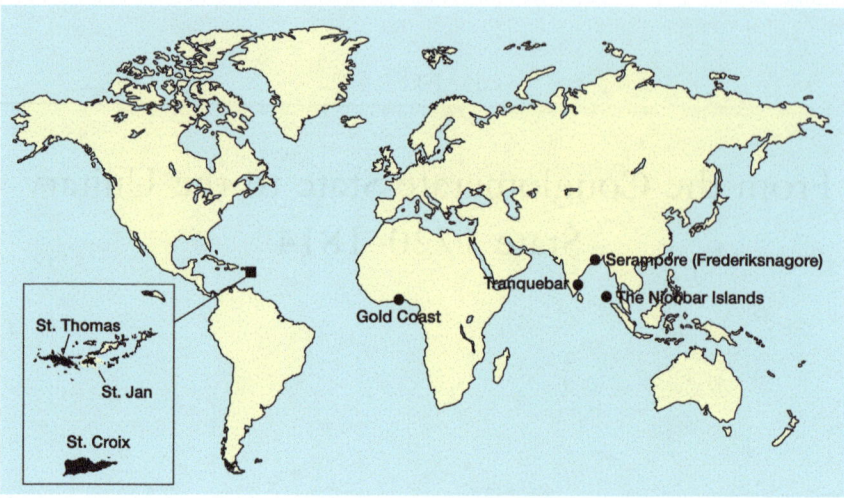

Fig. 7.1 Even if they were all diminutive in international comparison, the Danish Empire nonetheless had tropical colonies both in India, Africa and the Caribbean Sea. The colony Tranquebar in India was acquired from the local Indian ruler in 1620 in order to import first and foremost textiles and spices, Serampore (in Danish called Frederiksnagore) was acquired in 1755. No longer being profitable, both were sold to Britain in 1845. The Nicobar Islands in the Indian Ocean were acquired in 1756, yet due to the inhospitable nature and the danger of malaria there, they were practically inhabitable and never got any importance for the Danish Empire. In fact, the Danes soon gave up and left them. Yet, Denmark did not officially give up her sovereignty of them till 1868, when they were donated to Britain gratuitously. The colony at the African Coast (the Gold Coast) was acquired in 1658 and its main purpose was exportation of enslaved Africans across the Atlantic even if importation of palm oil and ivory was also playing a role. In 1792 the Danish government issued a ban on Transatlantic slave exportation (coming into effect in 1803), but the colony remained under Danish rule till 1850 where it was sold to Britain. The uninhabited Caribbean islands of St. Thomas and St. Jan (St. John) were acquired in 1665, whereas the island of St. Croix was bought from France in 1733. They, especially the latter mentioned, had an important role in production and exportation of sugar and rum. Yet, during the nineteenth century, the soil had been exhausted and was no longer fertile and the islands became a financial liability for Denmark. Consequently, after two previous, vain attempts the islands were sold to the US in 1917 and are today known as the US Virgin Islands. This purchase was the last time in history when one state sold a territory to another

A king like Frederik IV sought absolute power and as much as possible wanted to decide all important matters personally and not leave them to advisers and officials. His son, Christian VI, endeavored to do the same, but did not succeed, partly due to inability and partly since the administration had grown and the volume of cases had become overwhelming. After Christian VI's death in 1746, his son Frederik V succeeded to the throne. He was unable to rule personally, as he was addicted to drinking and sexual violence. The absolutist state thus had a king who failed to exercise his absolute power. One would think that this would mean a serious management crisis, but this was not the case. Thanks to the men in the state's administration, the king was not needed as the supreme decision-maker. Frederik V entrusted boundless confidence in his Lord Chamberlain A.G. Moltke, and this also resulted in a trusting relationship with the ministers of the King's Council. Thus, the Danish empire continued to function steadily by virtue of loyal prince servants. After the death of Frederik V in 1766, the empire got a king, Christian VII, who was also unable to exercise his absolute power. Unlike his father Frederik V, Christian VII was not even able to play the role of absolutist king externally, but—although it was not recognized immediately—was mentally ill and unable to make decisions. This was not in itself a problem, Frederik V. had not effectively wielded his power, and nevertheless the state had functioned anyway. But while Frederik V's royal advisers had been sure that the king would only sign the papers that they laid for him, Christian VII was prone to influence. Therefore, a number of replacements took place at the top of the state leadership in the years following his accession to the throne. The path to power of Johann Friedrich Struensee, the German adventurer, physician, courtier, and lover of the queen was due to his ability in securing power over the feeble king. Struensee's successor and another courtier, Ove Høegh-Guldberg, did the same in 1772. In 1784, Guldberg was overthrown in a coup initiated by Christian VII's son and heir, Crown Prince Frederik (VI). The Crown Prince also secured his father's signature, namely on a document which stipulated that in future a royal order should only be valid if it was co-signed by the Crown Prince. Although the sick Christian VII still had to sign all orders, it was actually Crown Prince Frederik (VI) who was the de facto king. It was therefore no great change, as he also became the de jure king at the death of Christian VII in 1808. The decades after the coup in 1784 were a fruitful period of reform in the kingdom. The state leadership included men like Foreign Minister A.P. Bernstorff and the head of the financial administration, Christian Ditlev Reventlow. Reforms were particularly implemented in the field of agriculture. The most famous reforms include the Ordinance of June 8, 1787, on the legal status of tenant farmers which secured against arbitrariness on the part of the landowners, as well as the Ordinance of June 20, 1788, which ordered the abolition of the adscription, which allowed landowners to prohibit young peasants from leaving their native estates. Likewise, many villages were enclosured, so that each farmer was able to gather all his land in one place, and many tenant farmers bought their farmsteads and became their own masters.

The fact that the king, to an increasingly lesser degree, personally exercised absolute power was not just an expression of the fact that two kings (Frederik V and Christian VII) were unable to govern personally. It reflected the growth of the administrative apparatus, the number of items to be addressed growing in volume and becoming so extensive and so complex that no singular individual could have an overview of and insight into them all. In addition, the number of fields that the state administration addressed expanded, just as the state administration became more activist by virtue of the expansion of the unitary state. As a result, the loyalty of the state officials thus came to lie much more with the state than with the monarch personally.

This period is called The Long Peace; it is aiming at the fact that the Danish empire managed to stay out of the many European wars of the period, not least the Austrian War of Succession of 1740–1748, the Seven Years' War in 1756–1763, the American War of Independence (which was also a war between Britain and European powers) in 1775–1783, and the wars of 1792 in the wake of the French Revolution. In Danish history, the second half of the eighteenth century is called "the flourishing trade period." Ships under the neutral Dannebrog (Danish flag) could carry goods to the warring countries without fear of being captured by enemy warships and as a result Copenhagen became the center of import and export of products to the warring countries. Copenhagen was thus not just the capital of the agricultural country of Denmark, nor just the capital of the Danish empire, but also a European city of great economic importance (Bregnsbo 2008).

Why? The political leadership of the Danish empire did not pursue a fundamentally different or more idealistic or peaceful foreign policy than other governments. However, as stated in the previous chapter, the Baltic Sea area had become part of an international system and not just a Danish-Swedish area of interest. This meant that wars between the Danish Empire and Sweden, let alone the conquest of land, were not tolerated by the great powers. Denmark and Sweden thus had no larger incentive to wage war. Furthermore, until the late eighteenth century the Danish state was a significant naval power and thus able to maintain its neutrality.

The Gottorp Problem

In 1721, King Frederik IV, pursuant to the Frederiksborg Peace of 1720, implemented an incorporation of the former Gottorp parts of Schleswig. The official announcement stated that the king had decided to "unite this part [the Gottorp parts] with his own and incorporate it." At the ensuing succession, representatives swore allegiance to the new lord. Here they had to sign a declaration in which His Majesty announced that he had decided to "unite the hitherto princely [Gottorp] part of the Duchy of Schleswig with his own and again to incorporate it forever in the crown as an old piece torn away by unfavorable times." The question for posterity is: what was incorporated into what? Were the Gottorp parts of Schleswig incorporated into the parts of Schleswig which were belonging to the king of Denmark? Or was the whole of Schleswig incorporated into the Kingdom of Denmark? Was the Danish absolutism extended to also apply in Schleswig? And did that mean that the Order of Succession to the throne that was applying in the kingdoms of Denmark and Norway also came into force there? (Henningsen 2008, 336). These matters became significant more than 100 years later (see Chapter 8). Although the incorporation can be seen as an effort to integrate Schleswig and thus a step towards the unitary state, the incorporation was not followed up by attempts to harmonize Schleswig's distinctive legal and administrative structures.

The incorporation of the Gottorp parts of Schleswig was not recognized by Russia. The Duke of Gottorp himself, who continued to rule over the Gottorp areas of Holstein, did not recognize it either. The Gottorp question thus posed an unresolved security problem for the Danish empire, and it was exacerbated when the reigning Gottorp Duke Charles Peter Ulrik, who was the grandson of the Russian Tsar Peter the Great, was appointed Russian heir to the throne in 1742. Furthermore, the following year his uncle, Adolphus Frederick, who was the former head of the regency government for the Gottorp parts of Holstein, was also elected Swedish successor to the throne. The problem became acute when Charles Peter Ulrik in 1762 became Russian tsar under the name Peter III. He was determined to use his Russian resources to regain the Gottorp parts of Schleswig. Russia was involved in the Seven Years' War when he ascended the throne and was facing a crushing blow in Prussia. But Peter III chose instead to make peace and start a war against the Danish empire. The empire stood alone and isolated. Nonetheless, the state leadership chose to enter the war with Russia. At first glance, this decision may sound completely foolish. However it is worth remembering that it was the Danish empire, not the current small state called Denmark, that chose to make war. Admittedly, the military and economic resources of the Danish Empire were far inferior to that of Russia's, but the decision for war was not entirely pointless. Militarily, the Danish Empire had a fleet that was far larger than the Russian, so a Russian army, which admittedly due to the war against Prussia was in northern Germany, had to march, rather than sail, the whole way. The wars of the seventeenth century had revealed that the duchies and Jutland were easy for an enemy to invade. Taking lessons learned from these experiences, the Danish military leadership chose to move into the Duchy of Mecklenburg, next to Holstein, to take the first blow there. Some might ask what the Duchy of Mecklenburg said to this Danish imposition. The answer is that vis-à-vis the small states in northern Germany, the Danish empire was a regional great power and behaved 1762 as such. It was also perceived that the Danish empire had occupied Hamburg to extort a large loan from the city. The free royal city of Lübeck rejected a request that Danish troops could be billeted in some villages that belonged to Lübeck's territory, but the billeting was imposed anyway. A request to Lübeck that Danish forces be allowed to enter the city of Travemünde was only presented after Danish forces had already occupied Travemünde. In addition to regiments from the Kingdom of Denmark and the Duchies, a large part of the crew in the fleet were Norwegian conscripts. In a quite unusual move, land troops from Norway had been transferred to Mecklenburg.

The expected confrontation with Russia never materialized. The tsar was overthrown in a coup, led by his wife, who was subsequently proclaimed reigning tsarina under the name Catherine II. She was interested in an alliance with the Danish Empire against Sweden, and held out a solution to the Gottorp problem. Again, one must remember that it was not the present Denmark, but the Danish empire that Catherine II wanted as an ally. Despite the land cessions in the seventeenth century, the empire remained a medium-sized European power with significant military resources. And Denmark's geostrategic location meant that in the event of war, Sweden would have to fight on several fronts: to the east (Russia) and to the west (the Danish empire). Therefore, a Russian-Danish alliance was likely meant to encourage Sweden to restrain itself.

The solution to the Gottorp problem was to exchange the Gottorp parts of Holstein with the counties of Oldenburg and Delmenhorst, which had been a part of the Danish empire since 1667. A preliminary treaty was concluded in 1765, but the de facto change was not completed until 1773. Delmenhorst and parts of Oldenburg had between 1711 and 1731 been pledged to the Elector of Hanover (who was also named King of Great Britain as George I in 1714). Otherwise, the counties' affiliation with the Danish Empire had merely meant that the central authorities in Copenhagen had been inserted as an additional administrative and judicial body in comparison with the situation before 1667. The Danish Empire had not left any decisive mark. Among other things, this was due to the fact that the post of the king's chief official in Oldenburg-Delmenhorst was often filled with persons who had fallen into disfavor at the court in Copenhagen. Therefore, these individuals had rarely been in a strong position to implement effective reforms. The Exchange Treaty also meant that the Danish Empire had to give the Gottorps financial compensation and relinquish all influence in future elections of archbishops of Lübeck, in favor of the Gottorps.

Norway

With the territorial exchange in 1773, a long-standing security policy problem was finally satisfactorily solved for the Danish empire. By then, however, another security issue had begun to emerge: Norway. Sweden was increasingly interested in conquering Norway, which had already been demonstrated by the final phase of the Great Nordic War. After the end of the war, however, absolutism was abolished in Sweden in favor of a weak royal power with a strong parliament in four estates (nobility, clergy, citizens and peasants) as the de facto vector of power. This form of government meant that the decision-making process prior to armaments and a declaration of war would take a very long time and would have to be discussed by a large circle of people. Therefore, it would hardly be possible to keep such an ambition secret let alone to launch a surprise attack. After 1720, the threat from Sweden was thus not imminent. In 1772, however, Sweden's new king, Gustavus III, led a coup that greatly strengthened the monarchy. And Gustavus III aimed to acquire Norway. The integrity of the Danish empire was once again threatened. Thanks to the alliance with Russia, however, Norway was provisionally secured, but this alliance also meant strong dependence on Russia, which was not always in Danish interest.

Until the cessation of Norway in 1814, foreign policy was governed by the desire to protect the empire's interest in Norway from Sweden. The internal policy pursued by the government in Copenhagen in relation to Norway was also carefully dictated by this. The eighteenth century was a period of growth and prosperity for Norway: the population grew, and Norwegian industries such as forestry, logging, mining, fishing, and shipping benefited from increasing international demand. Especially in the second half of the eighteenth century. The first part of the century, on the other hand, was marked by war and economic crisis. In an attempt to mitigate the worst effects of the crisis, the government in Copenhagen in 1730 introduced a monopoly on Norwegian iron in the Danish market. And as a similar support measure for agriculture in Denmark and the duchies, an exclusive right to grain from these areas was introduced in 1735 in southern Norway. The iron monopoly existed until 1797, and the grain monopoly lasted until 1788.

In continuation of these policies, questions were raised regarding the burden-sharing between Norway and the other parts of the empire. An inventory from around the year 1800 shows the following about the various elements of the empire's share of population and of state revenue (Table 7.1).

At first glance, it appears that the duchies' share of state finances corresponded to their share of the population, that the Kingdom of Denmark provided a disproportionate share, while Norway was heavily favored, and that the population faced low taxes. Furthermore, it can be argued that since a large part of Norway's government revenue came from customs duties on timber exports, it was rather the foreign buyers and not the Norwegian taxpayers who paid this money. Incidentally, the Norwegians seem to be far more difficult to tax than the inhabitants of the rest of the empire. In 1762, an extra tax was levied on inhabitants of Denmark, Norway and the duchies. The purpose was to improve the empire's finances after the looming war against Russia in 1762, and as something new and unique, the same level of tax was levied in all parts of the empire. The tax was a poll tax, i.e. that all taxpayers, regardless of income and wealth, should pay the same amount. If someone was too poor to pay, the parish's other taxpayers similarly had to pay more. In the duchies it was fairly possible to complete the payment, in the kingdom of Denmark it succeeded after certain initial difficulties until it was abolished in 1812—after

Table 7.1 Population and state revenue around 1800

	Denmark	Norway	The Duchies
Share of population (%)	38	36	25
Share of state revenue (%)	56–59	15–16	25

Feldbæk (1998, 239)

50 years. In Norway, on the other hand, things went completely wrong. The rural population here exercised its old right to send delegations to the king in Copenhagen to petition for exemption from the tax. Thereby, certain concessions were achieved. But this did not satisfy the population. In 1765, there was a riot and almost open revolt in Bergen, and it ended with the government in 1772 completely abolishing the extra tax for Norway.

However, it is too hasty to conclude that Norway was favored. The grain monopoly in question meant that the population had less money to pay tax with because it had to pay higher prices or grain or at least indirectly had to support grain producers in the other parts of the state. If the Norwegians were generally poorer, then their tax burden weighed relatively more (Gustafsson 1999, 2001; Rian 2000). However, it seems that in the second half of the eighteenth century Norway was characterized by growth and prosperity. And by then there were other public burdens than taxes. Young men of the peasantry in Norway were conscripted, which must also be taken into account in considering the burden-sharing between the various parts of the empire. In the Kingdom of Denmark and the Duchies, the main force of the army had consisted of recruits and often foreigners, but this changed during the eighteenth century. At the end of the century, the armies here also came to consist mainly of conscripted young men from the peasantry, so conscription became a very significant burden—also in Denmark and in the duchies. There was then a tendency for harmonization between the various parts of the empire, entirely in the spirit of the unitary state. But disadvantages faced by Norway can be identified in other fields. Norway, unlike Denmark and from 1788 the duchies, had no bank. This meant that Norwegian credits had to go via Copenhagen, which many Norwegians considered a disregard for Norway and a favor for Copenhagen. Norwegian export products and markets also differed from those of Denmark and the duchies. Norwegian exports were oriented towards England, and consequently Norwegian businesses became strongly British oriented, not just in business terms.

Britain had a different type of government than the Danish Empire, namely with an elected parliament as the central body of power. This did not prevent British visitors to Norway from being struck by the degree of freedom that prevailed there. The women's rights activist Mary Wollstonecraft wrote in 1795, "Though the king of Denmark is an absolute monarch, yet the Norwegians appear to enjoy all the blessings of freedom." She continued, the "Norwegians appear to me to be the most free community I have ever observed" (Wollstonecraft 1796/1987, letter seven, 101f.).

This relative freedom does not change the fact that in broad groups in Norway there was a feeling of common Norwegian identity and compassion, and a perception of being disadvantaged within the empire. There were complaints about economic exploitation, and the grain monopoly was highlighted as a particular example. Another frequently raised demand was the desire for a Norwegian university. This demand was raised at regular intervals since the 1770s, but until 1811 it was kindly but firmly rejected by the regime in Copenhagen. The existence of an overall Norwegian sense of identity is indisputable, but the question is whether it also had attributes of nationalism and whether the goal was Norwegian independence. Nationalism means that there was a requirement for one Norwegian language and one Norwegian culture and a desire for Norwegian independence as a state. Language does not seem to have played any role. There was no Norwegian written language, they wrote in Danish and likely spoke with a local Norwegian accent. It may not have been Norwegian independence that stoked the growth of Norwegian identity. Rather, it was the desire for better consideration of Norway and Norwegian business, financial and cultural interests within the empire. Norway lay the foundation for several peasant uprisings in the eighteenth century, such as the one mentioned above against the extra tax in 1762, the Lofthus uprising in the 1780s, and the Hauge movement, a combined religious revival and social uprising in the first decade of the nineteenth century. Common among these movements was that at no time was criticism voiced against the king in Copenhagen nor against the union with Denmark. Instead, the movements targeted citizens and officials in Norwegian market towns even if this might have been ulterior motives.

However, the government in Copenhagen rejected Norwegian requests for an independent bank and university, just as it would not entertain the proposal of central administrative bodies that had exclusively Norwegian affairs as their field of responsibility. These rejections seem all the more strange since the duchies had such institutions. For example, there was a university in Kiel, and in 1788 the duchies received a bank. Norwegian judicial, religious, and educational affairs were administered through the Danish Chancellery in Copenhagen, which, as the name suggests, was also responsible for the corresponding affairs in the Kingdom of Denmark. Schleswig and Holstein's judicial, religious, and educational affairs, on the other hand, were managed through a special institution for the duchies, called the German Chancellery in Copenhagen. The duchies had their own governor. Norway only had a governor for parts of the period. Until 1797, Norway had a joint Norwegian high court from which sentences could be appealed to the Supreme Court in Copenhagen. It was then replaced by four diocesan courts, one in each of the four diocesan towns, and each with the right of appeal to the Supreme Court. The duchies continued to have a single court. Separate, nationwide Norwegian bodies did not exist in the military, financial, and customs administration either. With the customs reform of 1797, the Kingdoms of Denmark and Norway were made into one single customs territory, while the duchies were given a different customs regime. Unlike the duchies, Norway was thus exclusively a geographical unit and did not exist in an administrative sense within the empire. The only special Norwegian administrative body in Copenhagen was a mining board, which existed between 1773 and 1791. De jure the body was a general imperial mining directorate, but since Norway was virtually the only place in the empire where there were mines, it actually became an informal special Norwegian body.

Why would the government in Copenhagen not meet the wishes for special Norwegian institutions, especially since the duchies already had such administrative representation? And why did the government seek to counteract the need for administrative and judicial bodies for Norway? The answer lies in the Swedish threat to Norway. It was important to integrate Norway as closely into the Kingdom of Denmark as possible. The government in Copenhagen feared that special Norwegian institutions could nurture Norwegian separatism, and that was exactly what the empire wanted to avoid. If Norway had the ability to form its own administrative unit and institutions, then the kingdom could conceivably be relatively easy to transfer to Sweden. This would be more difficult if Norway was closely integrated into and dependent on Denmark.

The North Atlantic

On the Faroe Islands, no major changes took place during this period. Until 1708, this archipelago had been leased to a Danish noble family, Gabel, after which the Rentekammeret (the economic administration of the kingdoms) in Copenhagen itself took over the administration and maintained a monopoly on all trade. Contrary to many people's beliefs, the main occupation was sheep farming and not fishing. As mentioned, the Faroe Islands had become a member of the Danish empire via Norway and as a result it was Norwegian Code from 1687 and not the Danish Code of 1683 that applied. In 1620, the islands were transferred ecclesiastically from the Diocese of Bergen in Norway to the Diocese of Sealand. During the eighteenth century, the connection to the Kingdom of Denmark rather than with Norway became stronger, and in 1776 they were placed under the Sealand governor. Thereby they were both in ecclesiastical and secular terms part of the Kingdom of Denmark. The Lagting (the Faroese Parliament) had long ago lost its significance as a political arena, but it still existed as a distinctive Faroese court. In 1816, this and the office of the Faroese Lawman were abolished in favor of a more "streamlined" judicial system similar to the systems that existed in the rest of the empire. The unitary state had also certainly emerged in the Faroe Islands.

While the eighteenth century in Denmark and Norway was considered a period of peace, progress and prosperity as reflected in expressions such as "the flourishing trade period" in Danish history and "the golden age" in Norwegian history, Iceland's eighteenth century became a dark time. All land in Iceland was owned either by the crown, the church, or an elite mainly consisting of civil servants leasing it to the peasants: in other words, an agricultural system that did not differ much from that known in the Kingdom of Denmark. The country was characterized by social and occupational stagnation, which the trade monopoly that Iceland was subject to greatly contributed. When Bishop Ludvig Harboe 1741–1745 resided on the island, attributes of the unitary state were increasingly introduced. His work led i.e. efforts to increase the population's literacy, but also with increased social control, i.e. restrictions on people's right to move. But by the middle of the eighteenth century, factories were set up by Icelandic initiative, but with financial and other support from the royal power in Copenhagen, to promote Iceland's economic and social development. These were mainly wool processing factories. However, there were many initial difficulties: deliveries did not occur, deficits necessitated large subsidies from Copenhagen, until the factories were for a time transferred to a private trading company headquartered in Copenhagen, before taken over by the state. Nevertheless, this initiative was of great importance for the modernization of Icelandic society. A factory was built near Reykjavik, and around this a settlement grew, which in 1786, when it had approx. 300 inhabitants, received a municipal charter. Iceland had thus gained its first city. The central government in Copenhagen intervened again in the early 1770s and sought to secure the social and legal rights of the peasant population vis-à-vis Iceland's elite landowners. It was also a result of these efforts that in 1774 the state took over the monopoly of trade from a private company. 12 years later in 1786, the monopoly was abolished, trade was now free, but admittedly only to the king's subjects. But between 1774 and 1786 something terrible also happened in Iceland. In 1783, the island was hit by a volcanic eruption that has been characterized as "one of the largest volcanic eruptions in recent millennia of Earth's history." (Thorsteinsson 1985, 190). Large areas were flooded by lava, toxic ash rained down over most of the island and the sky was covered with volcanic mists. All this, together with violent earthquakes, destroyed the vegetation and thus Iceland's agriculture in the following years. It is estimated that approx. 20% of the population died as a result of these natural disasters, and a smallpox epidemic in 1785 deepened the crisis. All the previous decades' attempts to commercially develop Iceland were now in ruins. It was in that context that the trade monopoly was abolished. The following decades saw the sale of land to tenant farmers, an action that was also done in the Kingdom of Denmark. This, too, can be seen as an attempt to bring the social and occupational structures within the Danish empire closer together, although there were undeniably large differences and the basic conditions were highly disparate. The old Althing (unicameral legislature in Iceland) was moved from the historic Tingvellir to Reykjavik in 1798, and in the year 1800 the Althing was abolished in favor of a national court and judicially trained judges. Thereby, a century-old institution had been erased. Both the move and the abolition two years later were justified with practicalities. Reykjavik was considered easier to reach than Tingvellir, and the replacement with a national court can be seen as an expression of bureaucratization and another attempt to streamline the systems throughout the different parts of the empire. Iceland in the eighteenth century came to witness first-hand the intrusive unitary state, but compared to other parts of the empire there were hardly other places where the opportunity for growth of the unitary state was greater.

Although there had been no contact with Greenland for a long time, the king had always claimed supremacy over this distant island in his capacity as king of Norway. But it was not until the 1720s that the connection with Greenland was restored. This happened on the initiative of the northern Norwegian priest Hans Egede, who in 1721 together with a group of merchants and shipowners in Bergen, Norway founded the Bergen Greenlandic Company, called the Bergen Company. The goal was twofold: religious mission and commercial trade. Originally, the group sought to engage not with the indigenous Greenlandic population, but rather descendants of the old Scandinavian settlers that were assumed to exist. It was also not without significance that Dutch whalers developed greater and greater activity in the waters off of West Greenland and occasionally went ashore and both plundered and traded with the local population. The king saw this as an opportunity to seek to assert his supremacy. In the summer of 1721, Hans Egede arrived in Greenland with the company's ship. There were no Scandinavian descendants, so instead the missionary efforts were directed at the indigenous Inuit population.

The Bergen Company had to give up in 1726. For the next 50 years, several attempts were made to organize trade and shipping to and from Greenland. In 1729, the starting point for trade was moved from Bergen, Norway's largest trading city, to Copenhagen. This was probably due to the fact that Copenhagen was the empire's largest trading city and royal residence, rather than that it was the capital of the Kingdom of Denmark. On the other hand, it cannot be denied that Copenhagen was the heart of the Kingdom of Denmark. In Greenland, Danish law, rather than Norwegian law as one may have expected, began to apply.

After 1726, the trade was handed over to various merchants and semi-public trading companies, but none of these would, in the long run, bring success. In 1776, trade and shipping to and from Greenland were therefore placed in the hands of The Royal Greenlandic Trade and Fishing state enterprise (KGH). Unlike its predecessors, this lasted a long time: KGH maintained a trading monopoly until 1950, and the company still exists as a privatized company under the name Royal Greenland. Although it had a trade and production monopoly, and thus a great influence on the indigenous population in general, there was no question of total dominance. The KGH had no authority over the mission company, which could sometimes lead to conflicts of interest. The missionaries wanted to gather the Greenlanders in settlements as much as possible so that it would be easier to teach them and preach to them. KGH, on the other hand, wanted the population to be dispersed, as this was estimated to ensure the greatest possible supply of Greenlandic export goods.

Schleswig and Holstein

The duchies' situation is already touched upon in our discussion of the Gottorp question, which for a large part of the eighteenth century was the dominant security problem, but which found a satisfactory solution in 1773. In the duchies there were also other dukes who were descendants of John the Younger (John II). Unlike the Gottorps, these dukes did not have political powers and therefore did not pose immediate security concerns to the empire. Nevertheless, the leadership of the state sought to grant the king full sovereignty over these duchies and to rectify the division that started in 1544. On the whole, the king sought to integrate the duchies into the empire, and it was likely viewed as a type of compensation for the lost Scanian territories and the resulting economic, military loss of prestige to the empire. Parts of the Duke of Plön's possessions were acquired by the king in 1722 and 1729, such as Nordborg and parts of Ærø. When the last Duke of Plön Duke died in 1761 without a male heir, his remaining possessions were placed under royal control in Holstein. In 1749 the possessions of the Duke of Glücksburg at Ærø were acquired, whereby the whole island came under royal control in Schleswig. When the Duke of Glücksburg died in 1779 without heirs, the remaining Glücksburg territories also fell to the king. Later, however, a new Duke of Glücksburg was established, although this was only titular. A descendant of a grandson of John the Younger, Duke Wilhelm of Holstein-Beck, married Louise in 1810—a niece of Christian VII—who was also the sister of Frederik VI's queen Marie Sophie Frederikke. Due to his close connection to the Danish royal family, Wilhelm was given the title Duke of Glücksburg in 1825. His son Christian became Danish king in 1863 as Christian IX, so it is from that Duke of Glücksburg that the present Danish royal family descends.

Another area that was not under the full sovereignty of the Danish king was the German county of Rantzau in Holstein. An imperial count was a member of the German Empire who was directly under the control of the German emperor and thus was independent of the local prince in the area of which he lived. But in 1721, the incumbent Count was assassinated, and the killer claimed it was the Count's brother who was behind it. The brother was therefore arrested, and after he had been sentenced to life in prison in 1726, Frederik IV took the opportunity to seize the territories of the county. As a local prince, he had no real authority over the county, even though it was within his duchy, and so Emperor Charles VI also staged a strong protest. But nothing more was done, as the German imperial power at this time was not strong enough to actively intervene, just as greater political priorities ensured the avoidance of a direct confrontation on this relatively distant and subordinate issue.

The duchies continued to have their own distinctive administrative and legal structures. The nobility of the duchies, organized in the Aristocratic Corporation, stood strong. At the Exchange of Territories of 1773, the duchies had been in a position to ensure that its privileges would be respected under Danish rule. For example, the so-called "biennium" was established, which stated that anyone wishing to be employed as officials in the duchies must have studied at least two years at Kiel University. Officially, the government in Copenhagen claimed that absolutism also applied in the duchies. Therefore, it officially rejected any form of negotiation with the Aristocratic Corporation. In practice, however, it took far-reaching considerations into account and tacitly acknowledged its "executive committee," Die fortwährende Deputation, as a negotiating partner. The duchies were far more urbanized and economically developed than the Kingdoms of Denmark and Norway: cities such as Flensburg and Altona had industrial enterprises and far-reaching trade and shipping connections to the West Indies, just as Flensburg had significant trade relations with Norway.

The conditions of the rural population were diverse. In certain places such as Ditmarschen and the marshlands at the western coast the peasants were owning their own farms and thus not without similarities with their peers in Norway. In Schleswig the peasants were usually tenant farmers of the landowning elite according to the same pattern found in the Kingdom of Denmark, whereas in Holstein and other places in Schleswig a serfdom existed following the Eastern European pattern. That is, the peasants were under the control of a landowner and were bound to the land. The landlord could even sell them with the land, and so it was a system that was far more extreme than what was found in the kingdom.

There was also a need for agrarian reforms in the duchies, similar to those that had been implemented in the late 1780s–early 1790s in the Kingdom of Denmark, such as, securing the legal position of the tenant farmers vis-à-vis the landowners. In the kingdom, absolutism prevailed, which meant that reforms could be carried out without any of the parties needing to consult and consent. In the duchies on the other hand, the regime had to take into account the Aristocratic Corporation and its privileges. Therefore, it was not until 1804 that a decree could be issued abolishing serfdom starting on January 1, 1805.

These national contradictions were not noticed much in the eighteenth century. When tensions began to arise between the kingdom and the duchies around 1800, it was curiously due to causes other than national contradictions. In 1796, an inspection trip was led throughout the duchies by a member of the Council of the Realm and head of the economic department of the central administration, Count Christian Ditlev Reventlow, known as a strong political proponent of peasant-friendly reform. He noted the need for reforms, including the harmonization of existing social, legal and administrative structures. In the duchies this could not be done immediately, as the Aristocratic Corporation here had to be consulted. In 1802, the government in Copenhagen nonetheless imposed a new tax on the aristocratic elite without having obtained its consent beforehand (Bjørn 1994).

The Aristocratic Corporation did not necessarily refuse to pay the tax, but the elite was offended that they had not been consulted beforehand and viewed it as an assault. A prominent member of the state leadership, Cay Reventlow, head of the German Chancellery and relative of Christian Ditlev, resigned in protest. It was clear that a rift emerged within the ruling elite: a rift between the state leadership in Copenhagen and the Aristocratic Corporation. But it was also clear that it was not national contradictions that caused the break. The Aristocratic Corporation, moreover, represented only a part of the duchies' estate. Many landowners were not a part of the Corporation elite.

Several of these landowners were therefore in opposition to the Corporation and were consequently not as dismissive of the idea of a unitary state that could intervene and harmonize the conditions in the duchies.

In 1806, the German Empire was dissolved as a result of the Napoleonic Wars. Thereby Holstein, where the Danish king had been in vassal relations as duke with the German emperor, became politically orphaned. In that situation, the government in Copenhagen chose to incorporate Holstein. So that this duchy should then "be connected with the monarchy subordinated with the whole of our scepter, as an in any respect complelety unseparated part of this." While this statement likely was not the sole creator of the unitary state, it did secure Holstein's affiliation to the Danish empire under the new and turbulent international political conditions." However, it was also followed by measures that can almost exclusively be seen as an attempt to create a unitary state, and even as an attempt at Danish nationalization. In 1807, it was decided that all future laws for the duchies would be announced in both German and Danish, just as officials were expected to know Danish. Theologians, educated at the University of Copenhagen, were to have access to posts as clergymen in Schleswig, and in 1811 a professorship in Danish was established at Kiel University. By these measures, some of the seeds that would later lead to the conflict based in nationalism in the nineteenth century were sown (Bregnsbo 2014).

THE COLONIES IN THE TROPICS

During the period covered in this chapter, the colonies of Asia, Africa, and the Caribbean saw immense economic prosperity in the Danish Empire, but after this time, their heyday was a thing of the past. Originally, these colonies were formally administered by private monopoly companies, which had received significant state aid and privileges. However, during this period, the state itself took administrative control of the colonies and increased trade competition, rather than the original monopolization. This had several reasons. One reason included the hope of increasing private capital; another included the need to pull together. A reason for letting these colonies formally seen been the property of a private company was the fact that it enabled the Danish state leadership in Copenhagen to dissociate itself from it if necessary. If the companies got into conflict with other European powers, it could be argued that the Danish party of the conflict was a private company and not the king of Denmark. Thereby, the conflict might be limited and contained without leading to war. When the state itself took over the administration of the colonies, it was out of the desire to ensure free and fair competition rather than monopolization. If the former monopolies had continued to own ports and other facilities, it would have been to the detriment of competitors.

Throughout the period, both the colonies of Asia and Africa were under the control of the king, although they were formally administered by private enterprises. The islands in the West Indies, on the other hand, were legally the property of a private company and were not a part of the king's kingdoms and countries until 1754. Until then, some may argue that the three West Indies islands should not be included in this account at all, as they did not formally belong to the Danish empire. The islands' histories should still be considered, as it can also be argued that their status as the property of a private company was more de jure than de facto, since the company in question had a royal charter, received significant government subsidies and other benefits, the royal family owned shares, and that it at the insistence of the government that the company did not give up its presence in the West Indies. A significant difference between the West Indies and the other colonies was that these islands had been largely uninhabited when they came under the control of the company. In both India and Africa on the other hand, the Danish presence depended on the acceptance of local indigenous princes.

In 1729 the Danish East India Company was liquidated. However, the presence and trade relations with Tranquebar were too important to give up, and Tranquebar was therefore transferred to the Danish Asiatic Company, founded in 1732. It gained a 40-year monopoly on trade with both India and China and was provided with significant administrative and economic favors. Christian VI himself owned shares in the company, but declared publicly that he would not interfere in the company's dispositions, a decision that was meant to reassure the other investors. It was especially textiles that were exported from India, but also rice, spices, potassium nitrates (saltpeter), and bamboo. The company expanded its activities when in 1755 it acquired the site Serampore (as it was renamed Frederiksnagore) in Bengal north of Calcutta, close to the border with present-day Bangladesh. This place was bought from a local Indian prince. On the whole, it is characteristic that the presence in India occurred on the terms with the local rulers and taking into account the presence of other European powers. In 1756, the Nicobar archipelago was also acquired in the waters between India and present-day Thailand. However, these islands proved uninhabitable due to malaria and therefore never gained significance for the empire. In addition, the company hosted a number of small trading posts (lodges). Serampore became very important for trade, indeed it almost displaced Tranquebar as the main trading hub, especially during the years of war when the Danish empire remained neutral.

In the Danish West Indies, the island of St. Croix was bought from France in 1733. With this the Danish possessions in the West Indies had reached their full extent. After the acquisition, St. Croix was divided into uniform plots of land offered for sale. The company had imagined that settlers from the Danish empire would settle here, but it piqued so much interest that access was eventually extended to other Europeans, and many Dutch and British settled there. Thus, it was only in a limited sense a permanent Danish society abroad. Conflicts of interest gradually arose between the company and the local planters and traders. The dispute was resolved in 1754 when the state took over the administration of the islands from the company, and thus the three islands formally became part of the Danish empire.

The territories on the Gold Coast of Africa were administered by the same company, the Danish West India Company (also known as the Danish West India–Guinea Company), which was also responsible for the three West Indies islands. This lead to conflicts of interest in the atrocious history of the slave trade: the company was both a slave buyer and a slave supplier. In Africa, the company was dependent on local African kings and traders and on trading companies from other European powers. After St. Croix had been bought and as plantation owners had settled here, demand for enslaved people as labor on the plantations grew, and this resulted in increased activity on the Gold Coast. In 1747, the company succeeded in obtaining significant capital from a group of Copenhagen investors. However, they demanded that the company again monopolize the export of enslaved people to the Danish West Indies, which caused strong dissatisfaction among the plantation owners. In 1755 the Danish state liquidated the company and took over the administration of the colony in Africa itself. In the coming decades, however, the administration of the Danish establishments, as they were called, was again left to trading companies. During the American Revolutionary War of 1778–1783, the Danes succeeded in expanding their territory in Africa by conquests against the warring state of Holland. In 1792, the state again took over the Danish colonies, but by then the situation had undeniably changed: a ban on the slave trade had been issued. During the 1780s, public opinion around Europe, based on Enlightenment and human rights, became increasingly critical of the practice of slavery. The Danish government feared that the two major slave trade nations, Britain and France, would reach an agreement on a ban on the slave trade. In that case, these countries would not accept that others continued slave trade. Instead, the Danish government chose to ban the slave trade itself. This happened in 1792. However, it only meant a ban on exports of slaves from Africa and on imports into the Caribbean; in other forms, slavery at the West Indian islands was allowed to continue. And it was not until 1803 that the ban would take effect. The expected Anglo-French pressure did not materialize, however, since Britain and France went to war in 1793, just as the House of Lords in Britain rejected a bill to abolish the slave trade (Gøbel 2016). At the beginning of the nineteenth century, the question remained on what the Danish empire would do with the African colonial establishments in the future, when the export of enslaved people had ceased. Attempts were made to trade in other products, e.g. palm oil. Attempts were also made at establishing the growing of sugar canes in Africa so that transportation of enslaved people across the Atlantic could be avoided, even if the sugar plantations in Africa were supposed to have enslaved manpower too. However, this proved logistically difficult, and nothing came of it.

Danish, Nordic, or German Identity?

It appears that distinctive Norwegian and German (Holstein) identities can be traced during this period. Furthermore, an unmistakable Danish identity arose in the second half of the eighteenth century. The government in Copenhagen at the time of Frederik V was, as before, dominated by many foreign-born who had entered the service of the Danish king. The majority of the members of the King's Council as well as the heads of the administration and at the court were born outside the Danish king's kingdoms and countries, especially in Germany. Often they did not speak Danish at all. This internationally oriented aristocratic elite, which formed the leadership of the state, pursued an ambitious and cosmopolitan cultural policy. This included convening foreign-born cultural personalities to hold illustrious positions in Denmark (i.e. the educator Basedow and the poet Klopstock). Furthermore, it awarded civilian and military posts as well as business privileges to foreign-born protégés. This international orientation had been the case for a long time, but it was increasingly perceived by the growing middle class, especially in Copenhagen, as an omission and oversight of local talent. The middle class was growing, and as it became more involved in foreign trade, it gained increased weight in society during the flourishing trade period, particularly in opposition to the great aristocratic landowners. After the middle of the eighteenth century, the middle class began to cultivate the Danish language, culture, and history as a protest against the internationally oriented aristocratic state leadership. The German-born Struensee, who in his short reign from 1770 to 1772 introduced radical reforms, which, however, had been ill-prepared and revealed his lack of knowledge of Danish conditions and traditions, just as his relationship with Queen Caroline Mathilde had aroused public indignation. His actions further fueled the development of nationalism. Unlike Struensee, his successors, Frederik V's Dowager Queen Juliana Maria, her son, the king's half-brother, Prince Frederick and her closely connected statesman, Ove Høegh-Guldberg, understood that they had to appeal to public opinion and to win the favor of the frustrated urban middle class.

Immediately after coming to power, they made Danish the administrative language for Denmark and Norway rather than German, and the following year Danish was made the command language in the army and in 1775 Danish was made a formal subject in the grammar schools. The crown jewel of their efforts was the Naturalization Act of 1776, which stated that only those who were born within the Danish king's kingdoms and countries, i.e. the empire, could in the future hold public offices. This law seems to have been met with spontaneous enthusiasm in Copenhagen and other cities across the country. How should this Danish identity be interpreted? The question is whether the Danish-German national antagonisms that tore apart the entire Danish state in the nineteenth century can be traced as far back as the eighteenth century. Perhaps in the eighteenth century it was first and foremost a matter of contradictions between an aristocratic and internationally oriented upper class and a more domestically oriented bourgeoisie (middle class), whose importance in social and economic was growing. Germans made up approximately a fifth of the capital's population, a representation of the fact that Copenhagen was the center of the entire empire and not just the kingdom of Denmark. Yet, the Naturalization Act was not aimed against these people since it was applying to everyone in the empire and was aimed at foreign-born, in practice Germans, but—significantly—not at German-speaking Danish citizens from the duchies or Copenhagen. In 1790, however, a heated debate unfolded: the so-called "German feud." The German-speaking fellow citizens and their alleged dominant position were conceptualized as a threat. The feud, however, ceased again, presumably because other problems on the political agenda took precedence, such as agricultural reforms. These national identities ultimately led to the dissolution of the empire, but the question is whether secession from the empire was an idea that originated in the eighteenth century or, whether the dispute at that point solely concerned the distribution of rights, duties, burdens, and privileges between the various nationalities within a perennial empire. There was not necessarily anyone at the time who thought nor desired that these schisms would eventually lead to dissolution, although in hindsight it may certainly seem the case. The development towards an identification with those whose nationality, language, culture, and country one shares, rather than identification by status and as a subject in a particular territory under a particular prince, and where the language was secondary, was an expression of the unitary state. Here, as in the conglomerate state, the empire was not held together by the subjects' duty of obedience to their prince, but by the loyalty of the citizens to their fatherland, state, and nationality (Feldbæk 1992).

THE EMPIRE AND THE NAPOLEONIC WARS

The Napoleonic Wars, or rather the Revolutionary and Napoleonic Wars denote a period in European history between 1792 and 1815, which was marked by an almost permanent state of war between France on one side and Britain on the other with various coalitions. The wars began as a struggle against the French Revolution and all its goals, but they later turned into a general European showdown, especially after Napoleon became French head of state (first consul) in 1799 and in 1804 crowned himself emperor. In the first years of the conflict, the Danish empire remained neutral and knew how to use the war situation to transport goods for the warring powers under the neutral Dannebrog, just as had been the case during the previous wars in the second half of the eighteenth century. Although the Danish Empire had officially adhered to the principles of neutrality, that its ships could sail for anyone with anything, the state leadership had in practice adapted to the shifting international power balance. When Great Britain, the undisputed ruler of the world's oceans, was militarily distressed, Denmark was able to take advantage of the situation. When Great Britain took over again, Denmark had to adapt. However, seen in the eyes of posterity, there were situations during these wars, where Danish exploitation of neutrality seemed risky and hazardous. Even during the Revolutionary and Napoleonic Wars, there were large-scale attempts to organize the transport of colonial goods for Britain's enemies, France and the Netherlands. Several of the men in the upper echelons of the Danish Empire's management were personally involved in these projects and pushed for these ships to be escorted by Danish naval vessels, which should actively resist British attempts of inspection and detention.

When such a Danish convoy in 1800 met a British naval squadron in the English Channel, it resulted in battle. The Danish warships had to surrender, but apparently at the political level there was an opportunity for other neutral states, Russia, Sweden, and Prussia to put collective pressure on Great Britain to accept neutral shipping. But the international situation changed. Russia and France, the continent's two major powers, entered into an alliance against Britain. They agreed on a continental blockade, an exclusion of British ships from all the continent's ports and wanted to force the remaining neutral powers, including the Danish Empire, to follow suit. The Britain was dependent on imports, not least of grain from the Baltic Sea region. Therefore, the British decided to send a fleet to the Sound to force access to the Baltic Sea. The Danish Empire, as an ally of Russia which was the guarantor of the empire's territorial integrity, had to attempt to prevent this British fleet from entering the Baltic Sea. The Danish government knew in advance that it did not have the naval capacity to stop a British naval fleet, but in the face of its obligations to Russia, the Danish empire had to fight. The state leadership was aware that if it did not fight, then Russia would let Sweden invade Norway and Prussia would invade the duchies and Jutland. For the sake of the empire's continued existence, there was nothing to do but enter a battle that was already lost before its inception. And so the Battle of Copenhagen commenced against the British on 2 April 1801. However, with the news of the Russian Tsar Paul's death, Denmark was able to withdraw from its alliance of neutrality without resulting in a mutilation of the empire (Feldbæk 2002).

The empire was not as fortunate in 1807 as it had been in 1801. France had gained control of almost the entire European continent, but Britain ruled the world's oceans. Neither of the two main opponents could beat each other militarily. Therefore, France resorted to economic warfare. It declared, as in 1801 with Russia, that all ports on the European continent should be closed to British ships, and that France and Russia would jointly force the few remaining neutral countries to join this continental blockade and enter the war on the French side; else, France would declare war. In other words, it was a French ultimatum. Around the same time, the Danish government also received a British ultimatum: join an alliance with Britain or face war. The Danish Empire was instructed to either place its fleet under British command or hand over the fleet to Britain for the duration of the war. The British ultimatum was rejected, and in August British forces landed on Sealand and encircled Copenhagen. Denmark did not expect this. Until then, the state leadership had expected that the empire could be involved in the war via the duchies, so therefore the main army and Crown Prince Regent Frederik (VI) stayed in Holstein. Copenhagen was ordered to hold its ground, but after a three-night terror bombardment of the civilian population in early September 1807, desperate citizens pressured the city's military leadership to acquiesce the British main demand: the surrender of the navy. With the loss of its navy, the Danish empire lost most of its military power, and saw no other possibilities than allying with France. As such, the empire had to declare war on Sweden and join the continental blockade. In Norway, fighting occurred in 1808, but a planned Danish invasion of Scania never materialized. This was no attempt to regain the Scania countries: the planned campaign had only aimed to open a new front and thereby ease the pressure on Norway. In 1809, peace was reached with Sweden without any border changes.

Sweden suffered some defeat on other fronts, and Russia conquered all of Finland. However, this was not something that the foreign policy leadership in Copenhagen gloated about, because it meant that the value of the Danish empire as a Russian alliance partner was diminished, and that the Swedish interest in conquering Norway would grow even more. Presumably, Russia would support such a Swedish desire for territorial compensation for the loss of Finland. Frederik VI therefore returned to the alliance with Napoleon, and the Danish empire was, so to speak, dragged along in his downfall. As Napoleon's star dimmed after a disastrous campaign against Russia in 1812, there was no shortage of offers for the Danish king to break with Napoleon and enter the war on the Allied side.

Both from perspectives in his own time and historians of posterity, Frederik VI had to face a lot of criticism for his foreign policy and his alleged misplaced loyalty to Napoleon, which made him cling onto the alliance, even after it was clear that Napoleon's fate was sealed. But Frederik VI had one specific goal throughout the war: to keep Norway within the empire. And only Napoleon could offer support towards this goal. Frederik VI was not dismissive of Allied attempts to join with the Danish empire, as long as the Allies could guarantee him Norway. But the Allies badly needed the Swedish military forces for the final showdown with Napoleon, and Sweden's price was already determined to be Norway. Therefore, in Frederik VI's view, there were no other options. Still, the fact that he renewed the alliance with France as late as July 1813 would seem to indicate that Frederick VI was stubborn, lacked the sense of realism, and stayed naïvely loyal to Napoleon. And it may very well be so. The motives behind was, it seems, that King Frederick was expecting the war to end with a general peace congress where Napoleonic France would also be represented. In order to get French support at the expected congress to maintain Norway for the Danish empire, he stuck to Napoleon. The abdication of Napoleon was something that King Frederick had not seen coming. When Napoleon suffered a decisive defeat in the autumn of 1813, the duchies and Jutland were vulnerable to an invasion of Russian and Swedish forces. In that situation, there was nothing to do but negotiate peace. On 14 January 1814, therefore, peace was made in Kiel, where the

Swedish army commander and Crown Prince, Charles XIV John, had established his headquarters. Here Frederik VI had to cede Norway to the king of Sweden and in return received the island of Rügen and Swedish Pomerania as compensation (Bregnsbo 2014). The Empire's main foreign policy goal since 1772 had failed. The Danish negotiator, Edmond Bourke, ensured that Greenland, Iceland, and the Faroe Islands were not included in the terms of the peace treaty. A popular myth postulates that Bourke was smart and took advantage of his Swedish counterpart's lack of historical knowledge that these three North Atlantic areas had originally been Norwegian dependencies. It's possible. But the reason the North Atlantic islands were not also ceded was that Sweden simply did not demand to receive them (Feldbæk 1990). The Swedish draft treaty, which was presented to the Danish negotiator, stated that Sweden demanded the Kingdom of Norway, defined as "the dioceses listed here: Kristiansand, Bergen, Akershus, and Trondheim as well as the northern areas and Finnmark to the border of the Russian Empire" (Alin 1889, annexes 12–15). Greenland and the Faroe Islands belonged to the diocese of Sealand, and Iceland constituted an independent diocese. The North Atlantic islands were thus not on Sweden's wish list; it was only a clarification of this that Bourke successfully negotiated into the text. At the Peace Congress in Vienna 1814–1815, which marked the end of the Napoleonic Wars, Denmark exchanged Rügen and Swedish Pomerania for the small duchy of Lauenburg, which bordered Holstein. These territories were the size of Lolland, so as a replacement for Norway it was only symbolic.

The Napoleonic Wars thus ended in disaster for the empire. How could it get this far? Since the middle of the seventeenth century, the Danish Empire had largely been at the mercy of the whims of the great powers, and the great powers had largely dictated the conditions in the Baltic Sea area (i.e. in 1659, 1679, 1700 and 1720). The Danish empire was no longer able to guarantee its own security. This was also the case in the eighteenth century, and probably even more so since Britain had become the ruler of the world's oceans. During the long peace in the eighteenth century, the empire had only experienced this by adapting to Britain in its international trade under the neutral Dannebrog. During the Napoleonic Wars, it became clear that the Danish Empire could not defend itself nor its sovereignty, and that during the eighteenth century it had only been able to survive and be allowed to survive because other powers accepted it or had an interest in its continuance. Finally, during the Napoleonic Wars, the Danish empire was almost dissolved.

After the loss of the Danish fleet in 1807, British warships controlled Danish waters and the entrance to the Baltic Sea. The connection between Jutland and the islands was disrupted, but not completely severed. In the final stages of the war, the duchies were forced to succumb to an enemy occupation.

During the war of 1801, British troops occupied the colonies of India and the Caribbean, but had lifted the occupation when the war had come to an end. In connection with the outbreak of war in 1807, they were re-occupied. There was no military resistance from the Danish side, which would have been hopeless. The occupations proceeded peacefully, and the British authorities respected property rights. At St. Croix the planters were mandated to export to the British market. The establishments in Africa were not occupied, but even here the connections to the Danish empire were interrupted between 1807 and 1814.

1807 also meant the interruption of traffic between Denmark, Norway as well as the North Atlantic islands. This was catastrophic, as these communities could not feed themselves and were dependent on imports. Here the King of Great Britain, for humanitarian reasons, and probably also because the islands lay outside the central fronts of the Napoleonic Wars, took the islands under his protection. Merchant ships between the islands and Denmark–Norway were allowed to sail despite the state of war, on the condition that they called at a British port on both the outbound and inbound voyages. A drama unfolded in Iceland in 1809, when a Danish-born assistant to a British merchant, Jørgen Jürgensen, was proclaimed "Iceland's Commander-in-Chief," declared a cessation of all Danish authorities, and announced that the otherwise disbanded Alting would convene. After six weeks, a British warship arrived in Iceland, and when the commander regarded Jürgensen's efforts Bonapartism, that is, what the British were fighting against in the ongoing war, the Brits put an end to Jürgensen's activity.

Norway was deeply affected by the empire's involvement in the Napoleonic Wars. The supplies of grain from Denmark and the duchies were hampered by British seizures of grain ships, and in Norway there was real hunger and distress during the war years, which Norwegian historiography has called the "years of distress" (Worm-Müller 1918). Until now, the government in Copenhagen had been dismissive of the idea of special Norwegian institutions, but due to the lack of connections to Copenhagen, a temporary government commission was established in Norway. By February 1809, the situation in Norway had become so desperate that the Government Commission was forced to send the following ultimatum-like situation report to Frederik VI: "If Your Majesty's wisdom does not save Norway by the use of extraordinary means before the end of April, the army will no longer be able to be kept together due to lack of food. The kingdom is then devoid of defense and exposed to invasion by the enemy; the earth is unsown, famine with all its inevitable consequences ensues; the famine, which in the common people produces despair and rage, drives the people to anarchy and bloody means. The kingdom will then sink into nameless misery and be lost" (*Meddelelser* 1890, 150). The Government Commission begged for a peace treaty with Britain, but Frederik VI refused. In return, he eased the trade blockade and allowed some shipping and trade between Norway and Britain despite the prevailing state of war, which stabilized the supply situation. In 1811, the king finally had to acquiesce to the long-standing Norwegian desire for a university. This opened in Christiania in 1813, in the very last hour of the Danish-Norwegian union.

In 1812, Napoleon demanded stricter enforcement of the continental blockade against Britain, and Norwegian ports had to be closed again against any shipping with Britain. At the same time, a failed harvest added damage. Frederik VI continued to hold on to his alliance with Napoleon, partly because Napoleon was the only one who could secure Norway for the Danish empire, and partly because a break with Napoleon would lead to a French occupation of the duchies and Jutland. These were Norway's main sources of grain, and a hostile occupation of these areas would mean a total disruption of grain supplies to Norway.

But the critical supply situation in Norway led many Norwegians to begin to doubt the extent to which their welfare and security could be guaranteed by Copenhagen. As previously mentioned, large parts of the Norwegian business community had strong export interests with England and were therefore already British oriented. The war with Great Britain had to be experienced by many Norwegian business people as if the foreign policy pursued in Copenhagen was to the direct detriment of their economic interests, and to Norway in general. Ironically, it seems that in Frederik VI's pursuit of his core foreign policy goal to preserve Norway for the empire, leading circles in Norway gradually felt that Copenhagen could no longer guarantee their safety and welfare. These circles therefore began to be open to other solutions, including other possible state affiliations.

Conclusion

1720–1814 was a period in which the efforts towards a unitary state led to the expansion and streamlining of state power both locally in Copenhagen and in other parts of the empire. In particular, the last decades of the eighteenth century were characterized by internal reforms and a tendency to seek harmonizing conditions in the various parts of the empire. It now became more than the king's person who held the empire together. A significant part of the period was characterized by the absence of war and the possibility as a neutral power to exploit the conditions of war in international trade. Economically, things went well and the colonies in the tropic got their heyday. One consequence was also that the middle class, the bourgeoisie, gained more weight in society and began to identify as Danish, Norwegian, and German respectively, although not quite yet in the modern, national sense. However, "the long peace" helped to obscure the fact that the Danish empire only existed because other powers accepted and allowed it due to their (temporary) interest in it. The Napoleonic Wars mercilessly exposed that the empire had become so weak internationally that it could neither defend its territory nor hold its sovereignty together by its own power. The competition between the states had increased, and the tension between large and small states had grown. Previously, supremacy at sea had been the key to the cohesion of the Danish empire, but now Britain had gained that role as early as the eighteenth century. That the empire managed to stay united for as long as was the case should, in fact, amaze posterity.

References

Alin, Oscar. 1889. *Den svensk-norska unionen. Uppsatser och aktstycken*, vol. 1. Stockholm: Norstedt.
Bjørn, Claus (ed.). 1994. *Reise Bemerkungen Sr. Excellenz des Herrn Geheime Staats Ministers und Kammerpræsidenten Grafen v. Reventlow auf seine Reise durch die Herzogthümer im Jahre 1796*. Odense: Odense Universitetsforlag.
Bregnsbo, Michael. 2008. Copenhagen—The Capital of an Empire. In *Danish Town During Absolutism: Urbanisation and Urban Life 1660–1848. Danish Urban Studies*, ed. Søren Bitsch Christensen and Jørgen Mikkelsen, vol. 4, 133–152.
Bregnsbo, Michael. 2014. The Motives Behind the Foreign Political Decisions of Frederick VI During the Napoleonic Wars. *Scandinavian Journal of History* 39 (3): 335–352.
Feldbæk, Ole. 1990. Denmark and the Treaty of Kiel 1814. *Scandinavian Journal of History* 15: 259–268.
Feldbæk, Ole. 1992. Clash of Cultures in a Conglomerate State: Danes and Germans in 18th Century Denmark. In *Clashes of Cultures: Essays in Honour of Niels Steensgaard*, ed. Jens Chr. V. Johansen, Erling Ladewig Petersen, and Henrik Stevnsborg, 80–93. Odense: Odense University Press.
Feldbæk, Ole. 1998. *Nærhed og adskillelse 1720–1814. Danmark-Norge 1380–1814*, vol. 4.
Feldbæk, Ole. 2002. *The Battle of Copenhagen, 1801: Nelson and the Danes*. London: Pen & Sword Military.
Gøbel, Erik. 2016. *The Danish Slave Trade and Its Abolition*. Boston and Leiden: Brill.
Gustafsson, Harald. 1994. Conglomerates or Unitary States: Integration Processes in Early Modern Denmark–Norway and Sweden. In *Föderationsmodelle und Unionsstrukturen. Über Staatenverbindungen in der frühen Neuzeit vom 15. bis 18. Jahrhundert, Wiener Beiträge zur Geschichte der Neuzeit 21*, ed. Thomas Fröschl. Vienna and Munich.
Gustafsson, Harald. 1999. Reflexioner över Danmark-Norges historia. *Historisk tidskrift* (Norway) 1999: 4.
Gustafsson, Harald. 2001. Identiteter i Danmark-Norge. Reflexioner över Øystein Rians refleksjoner över mina reflexioner. *Historisk tidskrift* (Norway) 2001: 2.
Henningsen, Lars N. 2008. Mønsterregion i det danske monarki 1721–1814. In *Sønderjyllands historie*, vol. 1. Aabenraa: Historisk Samfund for Sønderjylland.
Meddelelser fra Krigsarkiverne. 1890. Published by the General Staff, vol. 4. Copenhagen: Gyldendal.
Rian, Øystein. 2000. Danmark-Norges historie. Refleksjoner Over Harald Gustafssons refleksjoner. *Historisk tidskrift* (Norway) 80: 3, 376–384.
Thorsteinsson, Björn. 1985. *Island*. Copenhagen: Politikens Forlag.
Wollstonecraft, Mary. 1796/1987. *A Short Residence in Sweden, Norway and Denmark*. In *Mary Wollstonecraft and William Godwin. A Short Residence in Sweden and Memoirs of the Author of 'The Rights of Woman'*, ed. Richard Holmes. London: Penguin Books.
Worm-Müller, Jacob S. 1918. *Norge gjennem nødsårene. Den norske regjeringskommission 1807–1810*. Kristiania: Steen.

CHAPTER 8

1814–1864: From United Monarchy to Nation-State

Before the cession of Norway, the Danish state had an area of approximately 380,000 square kilometers; after the cession it shrank to approximately 60,000 square kilometers. The population decreased correspondingly from around 2.5 million to around 1.5 million people. While the ratio between Danish-Norwegian inhabitants and German inhabitants had until then had been 4:1, the ratio between Danish and German now became 2:1. The German population element was now far more prominent within the state.

During this period, the Danish empire appeared to be a united monarchy (*helstat*), i.e. a state consisting of the Kingdom of Denmark and the three duchies of Schleswig, Holstein, and the newly acquired duchy of Lauenburg. Furthermore, the Faroe Islands, Iceland, Greenland, the Danish West Indies, and—at least for some duration—the colonies in India and Africa continued to belong to the Danish king's territories. However, their place on the political agenda and in the general consciousness of the time period is peripheral. Internally, it was the united monarchy of the kingdom and the duchies that was in focus: in particular, it was the national contradictions there that overshadowed issues in other parts of the empire. During this chapter we will seek to answer the question of *how—after centuries of affiliation the relationship between the duchies and the Danish state deteriorated to the point of war and separation in 1864?*

The Danish state consisting of the territories: the kingdom of Denmark and the duchies of Schleswig, Holstein and Lauenburg will in this chapter be called "the united monarchy" (in Danish: *helstaten*) and institutions which were common for all the territories mentioned will be called "monarchy-wide" (e.g. a monarchy-wide parliament) unlike institutions for one of those areas only (Fig. 8.1).

© The Author(s), under exclusive license to Springer Nature Switzerland AG 2022
M. Bregnsbo and K. V. Jensen, *The Rise and Fall of the Danish Empire*,
https://doi.org/10.1007/978-3-030-91441-7_8

Fig. 8.1 The united Danish monarchy (*helstaten*: [literally] the whole state) consisting of the kingdom of Denmark and the three duchies Schleswig, Holstein and Lauenburg. The Ejder river was marking the border to the German Federation and thus Holstein and Lauenburg were members of that. The Kongeå (King's River) from Kolding to Ribe was marking the border between the kingdom of Denmark and the duchy of Schleswig. The population of Schleswig was ethnically mixed. The northern part was mostly Danish minded, the southern part mostly German minded, yet, the German language was advancing northwards. The prevailing political currents within the kingdom of Denmark and the three duchies 1848–1864 were making mutually incompatible political demands: there were those who wished to maintain the united monarchy intact whereas the supporters of the *Ejder policy* wanted to integrate Schleswig closer into the kingdom and separate Holstein and Lauenburg. And the Schleswig-Holsteiners (with a hyphen) were in favor of closer integration of Schleswig and Holstein including admitting Schleswig to become a member of the German Federation

The German Confederation

The German Confederation was established after the Napoleonic Wars to replace the defunct German-Roman Empire. It was an alliance among large and small German states, Prussia, and Austria. Although it was a loose union, it was nevertheless more cohesive and active: the involvement of the new confederation was greater within wider circles of the public in Germany than had been the case under the previous empire. During the Napoleonic Wars, a number of German states had been overrun and occupied by French forces. It had evoked an invigorated German national consciousness with demanded German unification across the various German states.

Holstein, which as mentioned had been included under the Danish crown in 1806, entered according to the agreements at the Congress of Vienna in the German Confederation in 1815, and so did Lauenburg. This meant that the Danish king was not only king of Denmark but also a member prince of the German Confederation in his capacity as Duke of Holstein and Lauenburg. The Duchy of Schleswig did not become a member of the Confederation, just as it had not been a member of the Old German Empire. At the Congress in Vienna, it was also decided that all member princes should establish Estates Generals in their countries. This posed a problem for Frederik VI, for how could he set up an Estates General that had the right to express views on public affairs in two of his duchies, while he also ruled as an absolute ruler in Schleswig and in the kingdom? Meanwhile, the years after the Napoleonic Wars were marked by political reaction, reluctance to anything reminiscent of the French Revolution and its results, such as liberal political forces demanding free constitution, political co-determination, and nationalism. Prussia and Austria in particular were eager to fight against any movement towards political liberalism and freer conditions in the state. The demands for German unification were also at odds with Prussia and Austria's great power ambitions, so in that context, the rising German national consciousness posed a lesser problem for the Danish king. When the Holstein Aristocratic Corporation in 1823 addressed the German Confederation with demands for support in a constitution of estates, which would include the Duchy of Schleswig, they received no such support.

As a member prince of the German Confederation, Frederik VI was also obliged to provide soldiers to the Confederation. If the German Confederation or some of its prominent members became involved in a European war, Frederik VI, as Duke of Holstein and Lauenburg, would also have to supply troops. It must therefore be questioned to what extent the rest of the united monarchy would be able to remain neutral in such a war when the king was directly involved via Holstein and Lauenburg duke. Membership of the German Confederation could thus become a hindrance to Denmark's foreign policy.

Advisory Provincial Estates

Neither were the years after 1814 auspicious for liberal movements in the Kingdom of Denmark. It was connected with the fact that the end of the Napoleonic Wars heralded a severe economic depression, from which the country's main sector, agriculture, was hard hit. In addition to this, the consequences of the monetary breakdown in 1813 took time to overcome. Social reforms were no longer on the political agenda of the regime. After the end of the war, many had hoped that the flourishing pre-war trade and shipping could be resumed in Denmark, but this did not happen due to several reasons. First, foreign powers could now arrange navigation themselves without having to resort to the neutral Dannebrog as a flag of convenience. Second, the economic conditions were generally sluggish, and third, competition in the world market had become fiercer. The colonies in India, Africa, and the West Indies were no longer the gold mines they had once been, and even sugar plantation owners in the Danish West Indies were affected by the crisis. For the time being, however, the government chose to maintain the colonies in the tropics.

It was not until the economic conditions began to change around 1830 that this dormancy was brought to an end. In 1830, another revolution broke out in France, leading to the overthrow of King Charles X, the inauguration of Louis Philippe, as well as liberal constitutional reforms. Other places in Europe were also affected by political furor. The Kingdom of Denmark passed unscathed, but in the duchies, the 37-year-old land bailiff Uwe Jens Lornsen on the island of Sylt in the Wadden Sea, published the pamphlet *Über das Verfassungswerk in Schleswig-Holstein* (About a Constitution for Schleswig-Holstein). In this he demanded a free constitution for Holstein and Schleswig, so that the affiliation of these two duchies to the kingdom in the future would be of looser in the form of a personal union. The king would be obliged to take up residence in the duchies part of the year. The national identities that had crystallized in the second half of the eighteenth century now began to have political consequences. Lornsen's pamphlet attracted a great deal of attention, but the Aristocratic Corporation in Holstein did not sympathize with its liberal tendency. The government in Copenhagen intensely examined the case, and Lornsen was removed from his office and sentenced to prison. After being released in 1833, he went to South America, returned to Europe, and died in Switzerland in 1838. All this still could not prevent the emergence of a new and separatist ideology, Schleswig-Holsteinism, which threatened the integrity of the Danish state, and would ultimately also lead to the splintering of the united Danish monarchy.

Otherwise, the ripples caused by the July Revolution in Paris in 1830 meant that Frederik VI could no longer evade the promise of giving Holstein an estate constitution. And as it would hardly be politically possible to rule as an absolute ruler in the kingdom and Schleswig while simultaneously allowing Holstein and Lauenburg to have estate constitutions. Instead, he chose to also have estate assemblies established in Schleswig and the kingdom. Thus, on May 28, 1831, an ordinance on advisory provincial estates was issued. In this document the main brushstrokes were introduced, and after these had been discussed in a forum of "enlightened" men in the kingdom and "experienced" men in the duchies, a final estate decree was issued on May 15, 1834. The assemblies had only advisory powers. The government promised to present any new legislative or fiscal initiative to the assemblies to discuss and pass recommendations upon. Yet, the government was free to take their advice or not as it pleased. Nonetheless, the establishment of these advisory assemblies of estates meant that a public debate and a political public emerged. The electorate was subdivided into three electoral groups (called estates), namely property-owners in the cities, great landowners, and peasants having a farm above a certain size no matter if they owned it or were leasing it.

With the introduction of advisory estate assemblies, the government took several considerations into account. In order not to draw too much attention to the assemblies, their meeting locations were relegated to quiet provincial towns. The Holstein assembly was thus to meet in Itzehoe rather than the politically engaged academic city of Kiel; the Schleswig group met in the city of Schleswig, not in the duchy's leading business city of Flensburg. The islands' estate assembly was hosted in Roskilde, not in Copenhagen; and Northern Jutland's meetings were housed in Viborg, not in the region's larger and more enterprising cities such as Aalborg or Aarhus. The creation of separate assemblies for Schleswig and Holstein did not agree with the ideology of Schleswig-Holsteinism. But since there were also separate assemblies for the Islands and Northern Jutland (in other words, no joint assembly for the kingdom), the government could claim that the estates' constitution did not mean any differential treatment between the two duchies. Thus, the state leadership had by establishing the assemblies of estates been able to secure the absolutist system as far as possible by splitting the estates and relocating them to small, quiet provincial towns, and thus preventing the estates from becoming a platform for Schleswig-Holstein separatism.

The separation of Schleswig and Holstein in the estate constitution aroused dissatisfaction among the duchies. The government sought to rectify this by establishing a joint appellate court for the two duchies in 1834 as well as merging their provincial administration into one institution (the provincial government) located in Gottorp, tasking this new institution with tasks which had previously been handled by the central administration in Copenhagen.

In the two estates assemblies within the kingdom, the following main political groupings crystallized: Conservatives who aligned with the absolutist system, Liberals who wanted free constitution and societal reforms in the economic field, and a group called the Friends of Peasants. The latter posited that the peasantry was disadvantaged in terms of conscription and tax burdens and therefore called for reforms—they were in some respects close to the Liberals. Incidentally, the estate assemblies were generally critical of alleged extravagance in the state's expenditures and demanded savings and tax cuts. In this connection, the conditions of the Danish colonies in the tropics were also a topic of debate, and demands were made that the state should abandon the colonies as soon as possible, mainly based on a financial benefit argument. However, the representatives of the Flensburg commercial bourgeoisie, who had significant economic interests in the Danish West Indies, spoke out in favor of active Danish policy to assist and promote the colonies in the Schleswig Estates Assembly. Slavery in the West Indies was also discussed. Here there was broad agreement that slavery was reprehensible and should be abolished, but only against compensation to the slave owners, something that the representatives of the assemblies were unwilling to grant from the public purse.

The duchies' estate assemblies, like the royal ones, came to function as political forums where national, political, and social differences collided. In Itzehoe, dissatisfaction was expressed with the fact that Schleswig and Holstein did not have a joint assembly of estates, and concern was raised regarding the economic disadvantage that many Holsteiners perceived in relation to the rest of the united monarchy. Linguistically, Holstein was vast majority German-speaking, but the Duchy of Schleswig was linguistically mixed. In the south, the population was predominantly German, in Central Schleswig, it was mixed though the German language was expanding, and in the north, it was predominantly Danish.

"Denmark Will Not!"

Originally, the liberal wings in the kingdom and the duchies had to a large extent been able to pull together to demand a free constitution and freer conditions in the state and society. However, the Schleswig-Holstein ideology with its demands for a common constitution for Schleswig and Holstein was unacceptable to the liberals north of the Kongeå. This point of contention escalated in the late 1830s. Economic conditions were improving, and within the German Confederation there were voices that called for closer political and economic integration of the member states. Voices were raised that Schleswig should also follow Holstein into closer integration within the German Confederation. From the German side, it was even claimed that the Kingdom of Denmark was basically too small and economically and militarily weak a country to be able to fend for itself and that Denmark should therefore also join the German Confederation as an "admiral state," i.e. a supplier of a merchant marine and a war fleet for the Confederation. This stirred up much commotion both in the kingdom and in Danish circles in Schleswig. Faced with the ideas of the admiral state, many felt that in that case one should let Holstein and Lauenburg be separated from the united monarchy and let them join an enlarged German federation, and in return bind Schleswig closer to the kingdom. But among the German part of the population in Schleswig, there were many who wanted to see Schleswig follow Holstein and become a member of the German Confederation. The Danish liberals therefore became national liberals, and the contacts they had previously cultivated with their liberal allies in Schleswig and Holstein were now severed and replaced by national schisms. National considerations thus came to overshadow common ideological and political values.

At a party in Copenhagen in 1842 on the eleventh anniversary of the ordinance on advisory estates, the National Liberal Ejder Policy was proclaimed. The Ejder river bordered between Schleswig and Holstein, and the policy declared that Schleswig should be linked to the kingdom and not to Holstein, which could be separated by the Danish state to join the German Confederation. The leading figure of the National Liberals, Orla Lehmann, stated this: "Should it become necessary, we will write with the sword on their [the Germans'] backs the bloody proof of that truth: 'Denmark will not!'" (Ploug 1872–1874, 263–267).

The national Danish political efforts in Schleswig were also reflected in publications, libraries, mass meetings, and association formations, such as the first Danish folk high school, which was established in 1844 in Rødding. Similar national political efforts were also made on the German side. The topic of Schleswig's national status was also addressed in the Kingdom's estates, something that German-oriented Schleswigs and Holsteins found was untimely interference in the duchies' internal affairs, and the government in Copenhagen considered it outside the competence of the estates.

Although the Danish-German disputes dominated the political agenda both in the kingdom and in the duchies, this did not mean that the demands for political and social reforms were silenced. However, there was general agreement that such reforms would hardly be possible as long as Frederik VI was alive. After his death in 1839, great expectations were placed on his successor, Christian VIII. As king of Norway, he had accepted the free constitution in 1814 even if he had shortly afterward had to abdicate as a consequence of the Swedish-Norwegian union. Yet, the estate assemblies now hoped to be given legislative and tax approval authority, beyond their current advisory abilities. But Christian VIII reportedly did not find the time appropriate for a free constitution. He had possibly become more conservative over the years, but he also foresaw that freer conditions in constitutional life could lead to the splintering of the united monarchy. His policy during his eight-year reign was marked by attempts to interchange his priorities between the Danish and German issues as well as by the moderate domestic political reforms, i.e. in the municipal areas. In 1840, he fulfilled the desire of the Danish estate assemblies to make Danish the official language of legal practice and authority in Schleswig in those districts where it was already a church and school language. This move aroused joy north of the Kongeå, but dissatisfaction among the Schleswig-Holsteins, who considered the reform to be an attempt to shift Schleswig's identity toward Denmark. In 1842, the king made reshuffles in the State Council so that prominent men from Schleswig and Holstein were admitted. These were not Schleswig-Holsteiners, but aristocratic-conservative supporters of the united monarchy and strong opponents of an Ejder policy.

This was intended as a welcoming gesture towards the duchies, but it instead provoked anger in national circles of the kingdom. The king's attempts to balance and favor neither Danish- nor German-oriented citizens ultimately led to an increase in national issues.

Within the Danish public there were many persons who agreed with the analysis on the German side that the Danish state had after 1814 become too small and too weak to be able to survive as an independent state in the long run. Yet, they did not see the "admiral state" and incorporation in the German Federation as the solution. Instead, they turned to Scandinavism with the desire for closer cooperation between Denmark-Schleswig and Sweden–Norway as a counterweight to the German unification efforts (Glenthøj and Ottosen 2021).

The Faroe Islands and Iceland

The Faroe Islands and Iceland were, as mentioned, only represented in the Islands' estates assembly through royally appointed representatives. Self-awareness and identity in the North Atlantic also began to flourish, evident in the interest of language and culture. Icelandic was an ancient written language and was considered the origin of the Scandinavian languages. Faroese, on the other hand, was perceived as a Danish dialect. It did not exist as an independent written language; the church and teaching language was Danish. During the first half of the nineteenth century, both Danish linguists and self-conscious Faroese became increasingly interested in this, and these efforts culminated with the pastor V.U. Hammershaimb's creation of a doctrine on the Faroese language around 1850 (Debes 2001, 115).

As described in the previous chapter, the Faroe Islands and Iceland had both impacted the centralist and integrative unitary state. In 1821, a provincial governor was appointed to replace the defunct office of "lawman" (i.e. head of the Faroese Lagting), which was abolished in 1816. The Faroese had hosted provincial officials before, but never with residence in the Faroe Islands. From then on, the Faroe Islands became a Danish province, although the economical and geographical conditions were peculiar. Unlike Iceland, all economic relations between the Faroe Islands and the outside world continued to operate through a state trade monopoly. Although it provided predictability and meant security against change, it also calcified the existing economic structure and counteracted growth and dynamism. The monopoly trade had little understanding of the development opportunities for fisheries in the Faroe Islands and maintained agriculture as the mainstay. This primarily meant the sectors of sheep breeding and stocking knitting as the main industry, with stockings as the main export item. From the Icelandic perspective, a desire was raised already in the time of Frederik VI for not only elected representatives but also for a special advisory assembly of estates in Iceland.

This claim was supported by national liberals and the Friends of Peasants, but it wasn't until Christian VIII came to the throne that anything happened.

In 1843 the Althing (the national parliament) was re-established as an advisory assembly consisting of six royally elected and 20 elected members; the latter were elected according to roughly the same rules as the estate representatives in the kingdom. However, the competence of the Althing was limited to purely Icelandic matters. From the Faroese side, petitions were also submitted to the Estates Assembly in Roskilde for the establishment of a similar advisory body for the Faroe Islands, and although this request enjoyed support in broad circles, it was not implemented within the era of absolutism. Nevertheless, many Faroese conditions were addressed in the estate assembly, such as criticism of the monopoly trade, of the allegedly self-willed Danish officials, the desire for school reforms, and securing the Faroese language.

It was certainly the Danish-German national contradictions that dominated the political debate in these years. Nevertheless, the expanding Danish-German disputes had an impact on Icelandic and Faroese conditions. The growing Scandinavian sympathy, in part due to the Danish-German clashes, led to increased interest in the Icelandic language and culture as a root of the Scandinavian languages and consequently an interest and sympathy for Iceland in general. The advance of Germanism in Schleswig and a lack of affirmation of the Danish language led the folklore researcher Svend Grundtvig (son of the hymn poet N.F.S. Grundtvig) to publish the book "Dansken paa Færøerne, Sidestykke til Tysken in Schleswig" (Danishness at the Faroese islands, a parallel to Germanness in Schleswig) in 1845. In this, the government's planned school policy for the Faroe Islands, which left no room for the Faroese language, was sharply criticized: Denmark could not complain about the oppression of the Danish language in Schleswig when the Faroese were not allowed to have their own language (Debes 2001, 112–117).

India and Africa

The connection to the overseas colonies in India and Africa had been restored in 1814 after the interruption during the Napoleonic Wars. Although the good economic conditions from before 1801 did not recur, the government chose for the time being to maintain its presence and wait and see. Frugal members of the estate assemblies kept a good, or rather evil eye, on them. The colonies in India gradually gained a growing British population and a vanishingly small Danish share, which largely consisted of colony officials. Thus, there were no longer close physical ties. Finally, in a treaty in 1845 these colonies were sold to Great Britain, or more precisely: to the British East India Company, which until 1858 administered British India. The price was 1,125,000 rix dollars.

The Danish presence on the Gold Coast in Africa was still characterized by (1) a collaboration, toleration, and opposition with local African states and (2) the fact that Great Britain was the area's dominant European power. The Danish position was further weakened by the fact that after 1814 a significant reduction was made in the number of forts and employees as part of the state's general austerity efforts. The ordinance of 1792 had forbidden the subjects of the Danish king to engage in the slave trade, but it did not prevent African and other middlemen entities from engaging in the slave trade just outside the gates of Danish forts, just as Danish merchants could legally make deliveries to foreign nations' slave ships. Attempts were made by the government to colonize the area by providing state aid for plantation operations (cotton and coffee), but in the long run it was defunct. Not all merchants in the area were interested in being under Danish authority, just as the competition from more capital-rich British merchants was fierce. Additionally, there was neither any will nor ability from the Danes to make the extensive investments that continued presence would demand. Therefore, in 1840, the government made a decision to sell the area to Britain. The British did not seem interested at first, but at the same time let it be known that they would not allow Denmark to sell to any other European power. After several attempts to resume sales negotiations, it succeeded in 1849, and in 1850 the Dannebrog flag was lowered for the last time on the Gold Coast.

Dynastic Problems

From the end of the 1830s, another serious problem was added to the growing ideological and national points of contention within the Danish united monarchy: dynasty politics. It became clear that the male line in the Danish royal house would likely die out with Prince Frederick (VII). The problem was which succession applied in the different parts of the monarchy. In the case of the kingdom and Lauenburg, there was no doubt: the agnate-cognate succession of the Royal Law of 1665 applied, i.e. that the throne could be inherited by male descendants of female members of the royal family. Women were excluded from the line of inheritance, but a son of, e.g. a king's sister could inherit. Whether the same rules applied in Schleswig was more controversial. The provisions of 1721 (see previous chapter) were unclear. The Danish government claimed that the provisions of the Royal Law also applied in Schleswig, but there was no agreement on this internally or externally. In Holstein, on the other hand, the inheritance provisions of the Royal Law did not apply. Here, the Russian tsar could make inheritance claims. The Duke of Augustenborg, whose ducal lineage went back to the division in 1544, maintained that in both Schleswig and Holstein the agnate succession applied: that only male members and their male descendants were entitled to inherit. The duke found that this would mean that it was the Augustenborg family who should inherit the ducal title of both Schleswig and Holstein. The variant succession laws in different parts of the united monarchy could thus be argued to have led to the dissolution of the united monarchy at the death of Frederik VII.

The Dissolution of Absolutism

The royal, absolutist government in Copenhagen realized that a constitutional change was necessary in the face of several contextual conditions: increasing dynastic problems, ideopolitical tensions between supporters of the absolutism and of a free constitution, national tensions between the duchies, the kingdom, and in Schleswig. In the last days of Christian VIII, a decision was made on the abolition of absolutism, but the king died on January 20, 1848, before the constitutional amendment was announced. It therefore fell to the new king, Frederik VII, to abolish the old regime a week later through the so-called January Proclamation of January 28, 1848. The proclamation was announced that the existing estate assemblies were to be supplemented by a united monarchy-wide assembly of estates, which would have decision-making authority. It was an attempt to balance between the different parts of the united monarchy: by letting the monarchy-wide assemblies include both the kingdom and the duchies, the government wanted to ensure that the interests of the duchies were met by letting them have equal numbers of members. In addition, there were a number of royally elected members. It was also an expression of consideration for the duchies that the monarchy-wide assemblies should meet alternately in Copenhagen and Gottorp. The proclamation also outlined the main points of the draft constitution and announced that a number of experienced men would convene to further draft the new constitution.

In Schleswig-Holstein liberal circles, however, the January Proclamation caused dissatisfaction because leading political forces, despite the provisions to secure the duchies against "majority dictatorship," feared that they in the monarchy-wide assemblies would always be in the minority and be outnumbered. However, there were also conservative forces, more specifically within the Aristocratic Corporation, who viewed the proclamation with sympathy because the draft constitution granted the corporation a prominent role. Among the Danish national liberals, there was dissatisfaction with the fact that the duchies would have as many seats as the kingdom, but on the other hand, they could not deny that the January Proclamation meant fulfillment of one of their main political demands: a free constitution to replace absolutism. The proclamation was thus an expression of the "divide and conquer" policy of the absolutist government. It had succeeded in splitting its various opponents so that it would get the upper hand in the coming constitutional discussions. At least that's what it looked like. The absolutist government had taken the initiative to abolish itself without having been exposed to any direct pressure, it had itself been able to determine its exit conditions. But in February 1848 a revolution broke out in Paris, which, among other things, led to the fall of the French kingdom. The revolutionary wave spread to the rest of Europe (except Britain and Russia), and in Berlin, Vienna, Budapest, and other big cities there was bloody conflict before the monarchs had to make liberal concessions. Within the German Confederation, the revolutionary movement was accompanied by demands for a united and more closely integrated Germany. Elections were called and a joint German parliament was elected in Frankfurt to introduce a constitution for the whole of Germany. However, nothing came of this on that occasion. First, the great powers would not tolerate such a shift in the balance of power in Europe. Second, the German great powers Prussia and Austria did not intend to give up their position and enter into a Greater Germany, and furthermore a political reaction occurred later in 1848 and 1849. While this did not sympathize with the liberal spirit of the joint German parliament, the events of 1848 led to a strong and lasting national uplift throughout German territory.

This national elation echoed in the duchies and the Germans in Schleswig. Meetings were held with demands that Schleswig alongside Holstein and Lauenburg should join the new German Federation that seemed to be on the drawing board. In Copenhagen, national liberal circles were concerned about this development, and counter-demands were made to secure Schleswig's position within the Danish empire. The government was also blamed for its passivity on this issue, and a new government was demanded that could ensure that Schleswig did not go alongside with Holstein into the new Germany. On March 21, a large demonstration marched to the king's palace at Christiansborg demanding a free constitution and the safeguarding of Schleswig's continued affiliation to the kingdom of Denmark. Frederik VII granted an audience with the leaders of the demonstration, informing them that the old ministry had been dissolved and that Schleswig's inseparability would be ensured. The next day, a new ministry was formed, a broadly based coalition of the former national liberal opposition and conservative members of the old absolutist government. The king stated on that occasion that from that day forward, he considered himself a constitutional monarch, effectively dissolving the absolute monarchy.

Civil War and Free Constitutions

In Schleswig-Holstein, however, these events were perceived as a coup d'etat, and a provisional government was formed in the name of the "captive duke" (Frederik VII). This wording sought to persuade the conservative Aristocratic Corporation to join the rebellion by claiming that the government was simply acting on behalf of the duke, who was a prisoner of the new rulers in Copenhagen. Government of the duchies was broadly composed of conservative aristocrats, German national liberals, and radical democrats. In most of the rest of Europe, these groups otherwise fought each other, but in both the Danish kingdom and in the duchies, it seems that the national schisms are more or less overshadowed existing political, ideological, and social differences—at least for a time.

In April 1848, the first military clashes occurred between Danish and Schleswig-Holstein troops. Soon after, Schleswig-Holstein received support from Prussia and other members of the German Confederation. This war, which lasted from 1848 to 1850, is called in Danish history the Three Years War. Internally, the political change of system in March 1848 and the outbreak of the Three Years' War resulted in true national potential ("the spirit of '48"). The new government called for elections for a Constitutional Assembly, which met in October 1848 in Copenhagen. In this situation, the question of the right to vote in the Danish parliament (*Rigsdagen*) gave rise to deep disagreements, as the left wing of the assembly stubbornly demanded a unicameral parliament elected by equal and universal male suffrage, a demand that was too far-reaching for the right wing and large parts of the center. It ended with the adoption of a compromise, whereby the Rigsdag was composed of two chambers, the Lower House (*Folketing*) and the Upper House (*Landsting*). Suffrage was equal and universal apart from the following groups: women, servants without their own households, paupers receiving or having received public poor relief, people with a criminal record, foreigners, and people having legally been declared incapable of managing their own affairs. Furthermore, the constitution enshrined a number of rights. The Constitution of the Kingdom of Denmark was adopted by the assembly on May 25, 1849 and signed by King Frederik VII on 5 June. With its provisions on equal and universal suffrage, the Constitution was uniquely and boldly democratic compared with its contemporary norms. This is all the more emphasized by the fact that, as it was adopted, similar Constituent Assemblies in Austria and Prussia were dissolved by military force without succeeding in obtaining a constitution. Of course, it can be debated whether the form of government was now truly democratic or not. The term "democracy" was not being used about the new system in the contemporary political discourse where "democracy" was a term of abuse except within left-wing circles. But ultimately, a new form of government, a free constitutional one, had now been introduced in comparison with absolutism (Nevers 2011, 95–117).

Danish historians have often proudly highlighted how Denmark succeeded in implementing a constitution despite the Three Years' War. However, the fact that the constitution was so liberal as it was not in spite of but rather due to the war. The assembly met and negotiated when the war resumed in the spring of 1849. While the assembly debated, Danish soldiers fought and fell for the homeland. Admittedly, as early as 1848, conscription had been introduced, so that it was no longer only young men from the peasantry who were obligated to become soldiers. It did not change the fact that the majority of the soldiers in the army were of peasantry. Given that context, it was difficult for the founding fathers to tell ordinary people that they and their sons were good enough to fight and die for the fatherland, yet did not deserve the right to vote. Without the Three Years' War, suffrage would hardly have been extended as far as it ultimately was.

During the war, Schleswig-Holstein, also held elections for a constitutional assembly, which resulted in the adoption of a state constitution. However, it was not as democratic as the one in the Danish kingdom. The Three Years' war centered on Schleswig's affiliation, to the kingdom or to Holstein and the associated German Confederation. In Schleswig itself, the population was divided between German and Danish sympathies. The war began as a revolt on the part of Schleswig-Holstein against the government in Copenhagen. These duchies belonged to the same state as the Kingdom of Denmark, namely the Danish united monarchy. Therefore, the Three Years' War was ultimately a civil war within the Danish united monarchy, an internal conflict between Danes and Germans concerning Schleswig's affiliation. It is true that the Civil War was quickly internationalized by the intervention of Prussia and other members of the German Confederation on the Schleswig-Holstein side, just as Sweden–Norway, Russia, and Great Britain intervened. But that does not prevent it from also being a civil war. Until recently, the Danish and Schleswig-Holstein troops had belonged to the same army and state. In Schleswig, family members and neighbors became nationally divided (Bregnsbo 2010). And the deep bitterness on both sides lasted after 1850. One would think that one seemingly obvious solution to the conflict would be to divide Schleswig along national lines, as would happen in 1920. That idea was actually pitched on several occasions. From the Schleswig-Holstein perspective, the idea was put forward immediately before the outbreak of the Civil War in March 1848, but from the Danish perspective it was rejected. And during the civil war, when Denmark was in dire need, the idea of division was raised by the Danes—however, at this time the opposing side had no interest. In general, it did not resonate within any of the political groups in Denmark, let alone among Danes in Schleswig. This was mainly because a division would mean that Dannevirke, with its great national mythological significance, would be located south of the border. Additionally, the resentment against the Schleswig-Holsteins and the Danish perception of their own victory did not promote the idea of division either.

The Three Years' War was not just a civil war: it quickly became internationalized. Prussia and other members of the German Confederation intervened on the Schleswig-Holstein side, as the Schleswig-Holstein case was a high priority for the joint German parliament in Frankfurt. Sweden–Norway predominantly supported Denmark without directly participating in the war. Although Britain wanted to maintain the Danish united monarchy, it also wanted to support Prussia to counterbalance the great powers of Austria and Russia, so the British intervention in favor of Denmark ultimately was not energetic. The Russians, on the other hand, were. As mentioned, the Russian tsar, Nikolai I, had a claim to inherit in Holstein and was therefore not sympathetic to an independent Schleswig-Holstein state. Furthermore, he regarded the Schleswig-Holstein uprising in March 1848 as a revolt against a legitimate monarch and thereby in blatant opposition to the conservative state ideology he espoused. The *tsar* saw the planned German unification as a threat to the balance of power and also disapproved of its liberal tendencies. Prussia was therefore under strong Russian pressure and in May 1848 had to hastily withdraw its troops from Jutland and to stop actively participating in the fight for the Schleswig-Holstein regime. But the tsar's support for Denmark was dictated by a conservative-legitimist view of the state order. The domestic political development in Denmark (such as the liberalizing system change and the June Constitution) and the desires for an Ejder policy did not have his sympathy.

The London Protocol

In the London Protocol of 1851-1852, the great powers determined that the Danish united monarchy should be restored to the form it had had before the outbreak of war, and outlined the conditions for its existence:

Schleswig was not to be incorporated into the kingdom, nor should preparatory steps be taken. Schleswig and Holstein must not be more closely linked than they each were to the kingdom. The Danish parliament (Rigsdag) and the estate assemblies in the duchies would contribute to draft a new joint constitution for the united monarchy. In addition, the dynastic problems were resolved by the great powers acknowledging that Prince Christian of Glücksborg (later Christian IX) and his male descendants were to be heirs to the throne of the united monarchy. In turn, the Duke of Augustenborg received financial compensation for his lost inheritance.

With the London Protocol, none of the parties in the war achieved what they originally wanted and had fought for. Admittedly, Denmark had separated Schleswig and Holstein administratively and prevented Schleswig from joining the German Confederation, just as Danish and German became equal languages in Schleswig. But in return, the Ejder policy had to be abandoned. It was only a small and not unconditionally positive consolation that the issue of succession had been resolved. The Schleswig-Holsteins not only witnessed the German unification efforts crumble but also had to come to terms with the dissolution of the Schleswig-Holstein state, and that these duchies would again belong within the Danish united monarchy, the very state they had rebelled against. The participants in the Civil War were thus forced to live together in the united monarchy that none of them really wanted. In the economic field, closer integration occurred, as the kingdom and the duchies now became a customs and currency union. Politically, on the other hand, it failed to integrate the united monarchy ... and it would end in disaster in 1864.

Two Conflicting and Incompatible Principles

Before we take a closer look at the ill fate of the united monarchy, it is time to ask what it really was that led to the armed conflict within the Danish state immediately after the absolutist regime in 1848 had resigned and a new, constitutional government was announced. It is too simplistic to say that it was only due to conflict between the concepts of absolutism against constitutional governance (some have even called it a democracy) or about Danish-German national schisms. These factors were certainly included, but the question remains: how? It was not about the form of government or nationalism per se, but about the way decisions are made and legitimized. Under the absolutist regime, the existing state structure had been justified by "*historical legitimism*," i.e. by reference to existing, legitimate rights such as the right of succession of the prince or dynasty, as well as historical documents such as the Agreement in Ribe 1460, the Royal Law of 1665 and the hereditary acclamation of 1721. Opposite this principle stood the *principle of popular sovereignty*, i.e. that the power comes from the people, and that it is the people who are entitled to decide, regardless of historical precedence. These two conflicting principles were thus divergent from one another.

In the Schleswig question, the problem was exacerbated by the existence of two nationalities, both of whom insisted on exercising popular sovereignty over Schleswig. The absolutist regime had held on to the historical legitimacy, Schleswig's constitutional position was determined by legal precedence, which trumped the sentiments of the people who lived there. Under the principle of popular sovereignty, on the other hand, it was the wishes of the people of Schleswig that carried the most weight, and since the population was nationally divided, it was a problem. It was compounded by the transition from absolutism to constitutional state because it fundamentally changed the way decisions are made and legitimized. In the constitutional state first, the political decisions were made by a majority of votes in competent and elected assemblies, which included public debate, where public opinion in general could be voiced. The elected representatives were elected based on policies in which they, as elected representatives, promised to promote, even though according to the Constitution they were bound solely by their personal convictions and not by any directions from the electorate. However, they could hardly hope for reelection without being receptive to public opinion, which heavily influenced their decision-making when they voted for or against a policy. It is true that even after 1849 it was still the king who sovereignly appointed ministers, and that foreign policy was to a large extent a government matter that was not discussed in the Rigsdag. But the Rigsdag had legislative and appropriating authority, which also concerned foreign policy directly, such as determining defense spending and use.

In contrast, the absolutist government had not relied on a majority of votes to make decisions. This does not mean that the absolutist regime had been unaffected by public opinion. It had actually been largely the case since the eighteenth century, and since 1834 its legislation had been discussed in the elected new estate assemblies. Although the absolutist regime could also be subjected to public pressure, which it usually sought to conform to, it was ultimately the king who made the final decision. He could make decisions according to what he estimated would benefit the united monarchy as a whole, not just the kingdom or the duchy of Schleswig or the two duchies of Schleswig and Holstein. For these reasons among many others, it had been possible to restrain the growing antagonisms between Danish and German identity during the last decades of the eighteenth century so that the integrity of the united monarchy had not been seriously threatened. This had also been demonstrated when in 1834 not only Schleswig and Holstein but also the Islands and Jutland had separate estate assemblies. Such a thing could hardly have been achieved through a majority decision among the voters in the territories concerned. The absolutist kings were not dependent on national special interests. Therefore, it had not been a problem that more peoples lived within the territories of the Danish king, or that there were twice as many Danes as Germans, because it was not by a majority of votes that the decisions were made. It was different in the constitutional state, where the German sections of the population feared that their numerical inferiority to the Danes would mean that they would always be in the minority and outnumbered.

Popular Sovereignty in Other Parts of the Empire

Originally, the new Danish government in 1848 had imagined that Iceland, as part of the Danish state, should be represented in the Rigsdag alongside with Danish representatives. Iceland was also represented in the Constituent Assembly. However, both the Icelandic representatives there and the parliamentary representatives back home in Iceland opposed this and wanted Denmark and Iceland to be considered as two independent nations in relation to the king. From the Icelandic perspective, the problem was that in a Danish parliament they would constitute a small minority in relation to the Danish representatives so that Iceland would be governed by a Danish majority and not by the Icelanders themselves. It was thus an attitude similar to that put forward by the Schleswig-Holsteins. The Constitution of the Kingdom of Denmark was therefore not extended to apply in Iceland. However, in Iceland there was a growing national and social stir at the twilight of absolutism, and in the years that followed large public meetings were hosted. An election was held in 1850 for an Icelandic national assembly to decide on a proposal from the Danish government on Iceland's future constitutional status in the united monarchy. However, when the assembly, in the opinion of the royal governor, exceeded its competence by not simply taking a position on the proposal but began discussing Iceland's position in general, he had the assembly dissolved. Thereafter, Iceland's position in the empire remained unresolved: absolutism continued to function here, the Althing continued to function as an advisory body.

Unlike Iceland, the Faroe Islands were represented in the Danish parliament. In the first election to the Rigsdag, the Faroese voters marked their dissatisfaction with the self-interested Danish-born officials who ruled them, by rejecting the established Danish-born officials and instead choosing native Faroese. As a result of the special conditions, the Faroe Islands gained some autonomy in 1852 with a restored local parliament, and in 1856 the trade monopoly was abolished. Even though the Faroe Islands operated under the Danish constitution and the Danish parliament, the new form of government nevertheless helped to awaken the desire for independence and national and political awareness.

In the Danish West Indies, social upheavals primarily came to dominate the social landscape in 1848. This notably includes governor-general Peter von Scholten's proclamation on the emancipation of the Black slave population in early July 1848. The liberal movements in Denmark and elsewhere in Europe had helped create anticipation and momentum for freedom of the black population of the Caribbean. The sentiment on the islands among the Black communities had been extremely tense and was on the verge of an open revolt: Scholten's proclamation was issued to prevent violent escalation. Von Scholten left the islands shortly after and was deposed in Denmark as governor-general, but was later acquitted by the Supreme Court. The abolition of slavery was preserved.

Denmark's Minister of Finance, Wilhelm Sponneck, who was also responsible for the islands, initially agreed that the islands should be represented in the Rigsdag. However, he later abandoned the idea. Giving the Black population the right to vote, let alone voting eligibility was fully out of the question. Beyond this, the majority of the white population on the islands was of foreign origin, and many could not speak Danish at all. In the light of the important role that the principle of nationality played elsewhere in the empire, representation of the islands in the Rigsdag was not considered desirable. Instead, in 1852, a colonial law was enacted that granted the islands some autonomy. A colonial council was to be consulted in all matters concerning island affairs. To have the right to vote for the council, a fortune of at least 500 West Indian dollars was required or at least 5 West Indian dollars in taxes were paid annually. With these stipulations, 95% of the population of the islands was excluded from political life. In 1863 the Colonial Act was renewed. Although the overall legislative competence remained with the Rigsdag in Copenhagen, the colonial councils' opportunity for participation in legislation for local affairs was increased, just as it was formulated as a goal that the islands came to rest more financially on their own.

Greenland was largely unaffected by the changing political winds of 1848, no one so much as thought of letting this distant colony be represented in the Rigsdag. After long deliberations, however, in the years 1862–1863, the local "principalships," which were local councils led by the local officials with appointed "Greenlandic self-reliant and independent men" were introduced as members. The councils managed local social affairs and had some judicial authority. However, rather than viewing the principalships as a fruit of the spirit of 1848, they should be seen as a legacy of the reform efforts of the late absolutist regime, which also manifested itself in the kingdom with increased involvement of sections of the population in local administration.

Constitutional Problems

After this brief digression to other parts of the empire, we return to the problems in the Danish-Schleswig-Holstein-Lauenburg united monarchy. The aforementioned London Protocols of 1851–1852 were a *diktat* that the united monarchy should be restored and that a united monarchy-wide constitution should be created. The great powers even demanded that this should have a conservative character and also demanded that Danish national-liberal politicians resign from the government and be replaced by prominent conservative Holstein nobles.

This enforced united monarchy policy was released by the government in the January Announcement of January 28, 1852. It stated that the government would maintain the estate assemblies in the duchies, but that they would be given legislative powers and that a common constitution for the whole, united monarchy should be introduced. The common affairs of the united monarchy, such as foreign, defense, and fiscal policy, were to be removed from the Constitution and the Rigsdag and, instead being dealt with at the monarchy-wide state level. The government was to be called the Privy Council (Gehejmestatsrådet), and here the king—and not the head of government—would chair the meetings. Three ministers were to deal with internal Danish affairs, four ministers were to be ministers of the united monarchy and only partly responsible to the Danish parliament, while the minister of Schleswig and the minister of Holstein solely answered to the king. The January Announcement not only meant an abandonment of Ejder policy but was also a step backwards towards authoritarianism. It placed limitations on the June Constitution, and it was questionable whether it could gather a majority in the Danish parliament. The government highlighted the need to fulfill the international agreements that guaranteed the continued existence of the united monarchy, calling it "the European necessity." The National Liberals were embittered by the abandonment of the Ejder policy. The Friends of Peasants party was divided, of whom many were not moved by the nationalist tones, while others were willing to vote for a united monarchy constitution if they obtained the guarantee that the June Constitution—apart from the restrictions imposed by European necessity—was allowed to pass unharmed in internal Danish affairs. A new government, led by A.S. Ørsted, a former prominent official in the absolutist administration, however, went further and sought to restrict the June Constitution's provisions on liberties to an extent that exceeded the needs dictated by "the European necessity," whereby the Friends of Peasants retracted their support.

Ørsted's next step was to seek a united monarchy-wide constitution implemented by charter, i.e. carried out unilaterally by the government without consulting the Rigsdag. Such a constitution (the July Ordinance), which almost reintroduced absolutism, was issued in 1854. Both the constitution and the way in which it was implemented provoked an outcry. In a subsequent parliamentary election, the government's supporters suffered a scorching defeat, but according to the rules of the time, it was the king who appointed a government and this did not need to have a majority in the Rigsdag. This meant that the government did not automatically resign. However, it ultimately occurred shortly thereafter, because influential people in Frederik VII's court pulled strings and convinced the king to dismiss the ministry of Ørsted.

The new government became a coalition government of conservative supporters of the united monarchy and moderate national liberals: it would seek to change the constitution of the Ørsted government in a more liberal direction, and this would happen with the participation of the Rigsdag. It succeeded in adopting a new united monarchy-wide constitution in October 1855. The constitution was in principle a kind of a federal constitution (but that term was not used at the time), where the Council of the Realm (*Rigsrådet*) was the federal parliament, and the Danish parliament and the estate assemblies in the duchies were reduced to state parliaments. It succeeded in passing this constitution in the Rigsdag, but without much enthusiasm. The National Liberals were dissatisfied that Schleswig was not more closely linked to the kingdom. Admittedly, the Friends of Peasants found the constitution more liberal than the original one, although they did not like that there would be members elected by the king. In particular, the provisions on certain minimum tax payment and annual income as a condition of suffrage were a thorn in their side as this meant that the entire lower middle class was excluded from political life on monarchy-level. Not even in the duchies did the constitution bring joy. Here it was protested that the estates of the duchies had not been consulted for discussion prior to the constitution, as was originally agreed. The concern was correct in that respect: the government had assumed that it would hardly be possible to reach agreement on anything if these estates had also been consulted. The negative attitude of the Schleswig-Holsteins meant that the constitution never really worked. From the Holstein side, complaints were made to the German Confederation, and protests were even made to the great powers of Prussia and Austria.

One must bear in mind that the various parts of the united monarchy had fought a civil war a few years before. From the Danish perspective, no attempt was made to institute a reconciliation. After Danish rule had been re-established in Schleswig in 1851, officials who had supported the Schleswig-Holsteins were purged and dismissed. Granted, the government had to have loyal officials, but it pushed too hard and prevented reconciliation. The maintenance of censorship and a ban on associations in Schleswig also did not help to break down the mutual resentment. Worst, however, were the so-called Language Ordinances (*Sprogrekripterne*) from 1851, according to which the language of instruction in the linguistically diverse Middle Schleswig was to be Danish, while the church language was to be alternately Danish and German. It was carried enacted without regard to local conditions and was portrayed by its opponents as abuse and damaged Denmark's external reputation.

In 1858, the German Confederation declared the 1855 Constitution invalid for the Member States of Holstein and Lauenburg and also demanded to be informed of the constitutional plans that the united monarchy government would put in place. Likewise, the Confederation threatened with war. The Danish government responded by suspending the monarchy-wide constitution as far as Holstein and Lauenburg were concerned, and when this step did not satisfy the German Confederation either, it had the constitution repealed in November 1858 for Holstein and Lauenburg. These duchies were now once again ruled absolutely with estate assemblies with advisory authority. However, this action did not engender satisfaction in the duchies, because Schleswig had thereby been given a different status than Holstein in violation of international agreements.

Ejder Politics

Gradually, the perception began to spread in Denmark that coexistence within the united monarchy between Danes and Germans and between the kingdom and the duchies was hopeless and untenable and that it was necessary to cut through politically: that Schleswig should be linked to Denmark, and that Holstein and Lauenburg should be left to their own devices The sentiment was that no matter what the Danes did, they were walked all over by the Schleswig-Holsteins and the German Confederation. The idea of a resumption of Ejder politics became more widespread. Particularly as the Danish government in 1861 felt an increasing Danish-nationalist pressure of opinion with demands for resolve towards the German-minded and for an active policy in support of Danishness in Schleswig. These national demands also became widespread among the Friends of Peasants and the rural population in general.

The National Liberal government thus embarked on an Ejder policy. As expected, this provoked protests in the German Confederation, but the Danish government continued its course with the support of leading political circles. In November 1863, the so-called November Constitution was adopted affiliating Schleswig closer to the kingdom while separating Holstein and Lauenburg from the state. This constitution was an expression of the political desires of the National Liberals. It was opposed by Danish conservative supporters of the united monarchy arguing that it would be in conflict with the London Agreements from 1851 to 1852. Furthermore, the Friends of the Peasants were against being dissatisfied with the limitations on the suffrage to the upper house. Furthermore, it also elicited resentment in the German Confederation, among the great powers, and Schleswig's estate assembly (even though there were Danish-minded members who were in favor of the policy). The fact was, however, that in order to have the right to vote in this assembly of estates, it was necessary to have such a large fortune that large sections of the middle class were excluded. And it was precisely among the middle class and the lower sections of society in Schleswig that Danish identity had the most supporters so therefore the Danish-minded layers of the population were underrepresented in Schleswig's assembly of estate.

Two days after the adoption of the November Constitution, King Frederick VII unexpectedly passed away without having signed it into law. The new king, Christian IX, refused to sign. He was a staunch supporter of the united monarchy and perceived the November Constitution to be a breach of existing agreements, and he also foresaw that this policy could have catastrophic consequences for Denmark. The pressure on the king, both politically and publicly, was fierce. The fact that the new king was in favor of preserving the united monarchy led many to view him as a covert Holstein. Several of the king's brothers had sided with Schleswig-Holstein and Germany during the Three Years' War; Christian IX had not, but the fact that German had been his first language and spoke Danish with an accent helped to strengthen the suspicion. And the pressure was great. For example, the Copenhagen police commissioner made it clear that he did not see himself able to guarantee peace and order in Copenhagen if the king did not sign the constitution. After a few days, the first Glücksburg monarch succumbed and signed reluctantly.

Why did the government, the Danish-minded majority within the monarchy-wide parliament, and parliament for the kingdom of Denmark pursue a policy that directly challenged the German Confederation? This was due to several factors. First, it was a perception that had to be demonstrated, as the united monarchy policy seemed to be unworkable. Second, the myth that Denmark had won the Three-Year War by its own strength of arms had created a dangerous overestimation of its own military capability. Third, the Danish government believed that Prussia was in an internal political crisis and that Denmark's opportunities were therefore favorable at that time; it erred and underestimated Prussia's new Prime Minister, Prince Otto von Bismarck. Fourth, there were high expectations among the Scandinavian to receive help from Sweden–Norway. Frederik VII and the King of Sweden–Norway Karl XV met and on festive occasions gave toasts about Scandinavian friendship and cooperation, and the Swedish king had promised Swedish-Norwegian support to defend Dannevirke as not just Denmark's territory, but as the southern border of the entire Scandinavia. Sweden's Foreign Minister Ludvig Manderström and Sweden–Norway's envoy to Copenhagen, Henning Hamilton, were supporters of a Scandinavian defense alliance and gave the Danish government and other key Danish decision-makers the impression that Sweden–Norway would enter into an alliance. It turned out, however, that the views of Charles XV and his foreign minister had no support in the Swedish government. While this was simply not conveyed in clear language to the Danish government, gripped by wishful thinking for further Scandinavian cooperation, the Danes likely refused to recognize the situation.

The enthusiasm for the Ejder policy on Danish identity and Scandinavianism that prevailed in national liberal circles caused them to look with deep distrust on Christian IX, who was a proponent of united monarchy and German raised. In 1863, several high-ranking National Liberal ministers told the Swedish envoy that they preferred to let Denmark join a Scandinavian union rather than preserve the united monarchy and have Christian IX as king.

Sweden, however, rejected such flighty and rather obsessive treacherous plans (Glenthøj and Ottosen 2021).

Another reason why the Danish government chose this course of disaster was a hope for support from the great powers, as had happened 1848–1850. However, the situation was different. Russia had supported a policy of maintaining the united monarchy, not the Ejder policy. Since that time, a Russian-Prussian understanding had emerged, and Russia had partially become weakened. During the Crimean War of 1853–1856, Britain proved that its warships could operate in the Baltic Sea regardless of who controlled its entry and therefore found it no longer crucial that Denmark—and not Prussia—should control the important naval port in Kiel.

The Catastrophe of 1864

The German Confederation, Prussia, and Austria demanded the repeal of the November Constitution, and on December 24, 1863, German Confederate troops moved into Holstein, which had been evacuated by Danish forces. Strong anti-Danish demonstrations took place. Duke Christian August II of Augustenburg had waived his inheritance claims under the London Agreements, but his son was proclaimed Duke of Schleswig-Holstein as Frederick VIII. Austria and Prussia in particular were not interested in the creation of an Augustenburg state and quickly took control themselves, driving Frederick and his Schleswig-Holstein separatist supporters astray. On January 16, 1864, Prussia and Austria issued an ultimatum to Denmark demanding the repeal of the November Constitution within 48 hours. The Danish government replied that such a thing was not technically possible, but that they would convene the Monarchy-wide parliament. However, it was too late: on January 31, 1864, Prussian and Austrian forces entered Schleswig. The war commenced.

The morale among the Danish soldiers was good, but it could not outweigh the reality that Denmark was not prepared for an armed conflict. In the period between 1850 and 1863 Danish defenses had been cut. The question of national defense had been addressed by the majority of the Rigsdag and the council from a purely financial point of view and not seen in the context of the united monarchy and foreign policy issues. The government had thus pursued a foreign policy that led to war while also starving the nation's defense. Additionally, foreign policy in the constitutional state was a matter for the government and the king and was not to be dealt with in the elected parliament, which instead focused on tax and appropriation policies. And any increased defense spending would have entailed tax increases, which was detrimental to politicians' chances of reelection, just as it is today.

The army was fortified at the fortress of Dannevirke, which the army command, however, quickly had to admit could not be adequately defended, which is why it withdrew that night between 5 and 6 February. The main army then fortified in Dybbøl, a fortress that had not yet been completed, and which was now subjected to a prolonged bombardment. On April 18, after heavy fighting and steep losses, Dybbøl was taken by storm.

One week after the defeat at Dybbøl, an international conference regarding the war was convened. In addition to Denmark, representatives from Prussia, Austria, the German Confederation, and the great powers of Great Britain, France, and Russia participated, as well as Sweden–Norway. Denmark's position was weak, both due to the recent defeat, as well as the internal divisions among the Danish delegation. In addition, the delegation's instructions were unclear because the government at home in Copenhagen was also split.

A ceasefire was settled on 12 May. Various proposals to preserve the united monarchy in one form or another were discussed, but no agreement could be reached. Britain then offered a proposal to divide Schleswig by the Sli-Dannevirke line. Denmark agreed, but Prussia did not. The German side, in turn, proposed a dividing line from Aabenraa to Tønder and was prepared to agree to an even more southern demarcation that would have been very similar to the present-day Danish-German border, possibly with Flensburg north of the border and Tønder south of it. Denmark refused since no guarantee could be given in advance that Flensburg would join Denmark. Then Prussia proposed a plebiscite, and while Austria had great concerns about the idea, the proposal fell apart when Denmark outright refused. Next, Britain, with French support, put forth a proposal for arbitration where a neutral, benevolent power would draw the line somewhere between the Aabenraa-Tønder line and the Eckernførde-Frederikstad line. While the German powers had strong reservations, it was Denmark who refused, thereby breaking the conference.

The steep Danish position, despite Denmark's dire military situation, was surprising, Especially as everything indicates that Denmark could have achieved a southern border roughly similar to the one obtained in 1920, possibly with Flensburg north of the border and Tønder south of it, In 1864 the time was not ripe to settle such disputes by plebiscite. Public opinion was not prepared to accept any division other than the Sli-Dannevirke line. It also played a role that the king was very preoccupied with the remaining duke of the three duchies and therefore did not support the idea of division. In addition, the Danish delegates deliberately speculated that a breakdown of the conference would lead to the fall of the British Liberal government and to the formation of a new, Tory government, which they believed would be more Danish-friendly. Admittedly, the Liberal government had only a narrow majority in parliament, but the welcome change of government never materialized.

A few days after the failure of the conference, Prussian forces succeeded in capturing the island of Als. After Dybbøl's fall, the main army was now on Funen, so militarily the conquest of Als was not a disaster in itself, but psychologically and symbolically it was a large blow to the Danes. The perception was that Funen and perhaps Sealand were now open to the enemy: the will to fight evaporated, and it now became a priority to seek peace.

Christian IX installed a new ministry consisting of conservative supporters of the united monarchy under the leadership of C.A. Bluhme. The king himself still nurtured hope of being able to retain his ducal titles via a loose personal union between the kingdom and the duchies, even potentially by the kingdom's admission to the German Confederation. The king's stubborn adherence to the idea of a personal union was due to the fact that he had become king solely by virtue of the London Agreements. It would seem a probable idea—and not only to the king himself: if these agreements and the united monarchy collapsed, it could also be argued that the king's right to the Danish throne had lapsed. However, the new government was quite aware that the plans for personal union would not come to fruition.

In the peace negotiations with Prussia and Austria, the Danes now resorted to the idea of dividing Schleswig, but it was too late. At the Peace of Vienna on October 30, 1864, the Danish monarchy ceded Schleswig, Holstein, and Lauenburg to Prussia and Austria. As a replacement for the royal enclaves in Schleswig, Denmark gained Ærø, an area by Ribe and eight parishes south of Kolding. The peace treaty was passed in the Lower House of the parliament of the November Constitution with 75–21 votes, in its upper house with 55–4 and on 12 November received the king's signature.

The peace meant that the united monarchy lost approximately one-fifth of its territorial area (from about 60,000 square kilometers to 39,000) and the population fell from 2.5 million to 1.7 million. However, at the same time, it meant that the Danish empire no longer hosted areas that were members of the German Confederation. The vast majority of the inhabitants of Denmark were Danes, but not all Danes lived in Denmark. From now on, a large group of Danish-oriented Schleswigs lived under foreign rule.

The defeat of 1864 was a traumatic event in Danish history that has had impacts on Danish politics, society, and mentality till today. The policy that led to the war and the Danish attitudes at the peace conference in London have been debated and it is hard to deny that this would seem foolhardy and unintelligible and based on naïve wishful thinking. Yet, recently a possible explanation has been suggested that would it more meaningful and understandable. The Danish national liberal prime minister 1857–1859 and 1860–1863, C.C. Hall, realized that a division of Schleswig along ethnical lines was the only possible solution to the conflict. Yet, he was fully aware that due to Schleswig's importance in Danish national mythology, such a division would be fully unacceptable to a Danish public. But his plan was to let it come to a war where—just as expected—the Danish side would quickly suffer bad luck. However, he also expected that the great powers would soon interfere and hold a peace conference and Hall's expectation was further that the Danish military setbacks would contribute to make the Danish public receptive to the idea of a partition of Schleswig as the lesser evil. And this plan does not seem to have been fully unrealistic. The fact that it did not succeed was due to coincidences, to two unforeseeable events that toppled it. Firstly, the demise of King Frederick VII and the fact that he was succeeded by Christian IX who was a conservative, staunch supporter of the united monarchy. Secondly, that King Christian dismissed Hall's ministry and appointed another one that was not familiar with Hall's scheme (Glenthøj 2014).

From United Monarchy to Nation-State

The underlying reasons for the developments that led to the catastrophe in 1864 can be summarized as the transition from absolute power within the historical legitimacy principle to popular sovereignty, and the pluralism and nationality principle at the system shift in 1848. The population groups within the Danish united monarchy nationally (i.e. as Danish or German), rather than according to political views or material interests, made it impossible to create a common constitution as a framework for a common political culture. However, this was exacerbated by the mutual bitterness on both sides following the Civil War, and by the fact that Germany was in a period of growth and industrialization and therefore the German-minded in the united monarchy seemed far more modern and attractive than the less developed and agricultural country of Denmark. This development was also aggravated by the German Confederation and the great powers of Prussia and Austria, who with various motives supported the case of the Schleswig-Holsteins against Denmark. The Danish language and cultural policy in Schleswig did not strengthen Danish interests internationally either. The Danish government's and the public's wishful thinking about the strength of Denmark's defense and anticipated support from Sweden was even more detrimental even if significant nuances to the Danish policy prior to and during the war have recently been added. The problem was not that both sides were nationalist, but that they were not nationalist enough. If the sovereignty of the people and the principle of nationality had been consistently followed, a division of Schleswig according to the boundaries of language and culture would have been the most logical solution. However, both parties clung to the principle of historical legitimacy. The kingdom claimed its historic right to the entire Duchy of Schleswig as a land of Denmark, with reference to the provisions of 1720. The Schleswig-Holstein perspective relied on the Ribe Agreement of 1460. Although political decision-makers and opinion leaders on both the Danish and Schleswig-Holstein sides claimed that they each adhered to the principles of popular sovereignty and nationality, their behaviors in practice aligned more closely to that of the historical legitimist principle.

References

Bregnsbo, Michael. 2010. Denmark 1848: Political Transition and Civil War. *Revue d'histoire nordique Nordic Historical Review* 10: 113–130.
Debes, Hans Jacob. 2001. *Færingernes Land*. Copenhagen: Multivers.
Glenthøj, Rasmus. 2014. *1864. Sønner af de slagne*. Copenhagen: Gad.

Glenthøj, Rasmus, and Morten Nordhagen Ottosen. 2021. *Union eller undergang. Kampen for et forenet Skandinavien*. Copenhagen: Gads Forlag.
Lornsen, Uwe Jens. 1830. *Über das Verfassungswerk in Schleswigholstein*. Kiel: Königliche Schulbuchdruckerei.
Nevers, Jeppe. 2011. *Fra skældsord til slagord. Demokratibegrebet i dansk politisk historie*. Odense: Syddansk Universitetsforlag.
Ploug, Carl (ed.). 1872–1874. *Orla Lehmann – Efterladte Skrifter*, vol. 4. Copenhagen.

CHAPTER 9

The Empire After 1864

The cession of the duchies in 1864 meant that Denmark now became a nation-state. A nation-state is defined as a state where there is one common culture, one common language, one common history, etc. There were certainly still other nationalities within the Danish empire, namely Icelanders, Faroese, and Greenlanders along with the nationally and ethnically diverse population of the West Indies. However, the relationship cannot be compared at all with the Danish-German united monarchy. When tallied both separately and together the above-mentioned groups represented such a small proportion of the inhabitants of the empire, whereas those that were German-affiliated had made up a third of the inhabitants in the united monarchy. On the other hand, this did not mean that all Danes lived in Denmark. There were around 200,000 Danish-minded southern Jutlanders in Schleswig, who after 1864, became German citizens against their will.

For Prussia, 1864 had been a stepping-stone in a longer process towards a united Germany under Prussian rule. This goal was met in 1870 when Germany became a unified, centralized empire. This put the Danish state in a completely new historical situation. Previously it had been a medium-sized European state, and while Germany had been an empire or later a confederacy, it was relatively decentralized and consisted of many different and both large, medium, and small states. The Danish empire had been larger than many of these German states. Now the balance of power was markedly different: Denmark had in 1814 and even more so in 1864 become a smaller state, while Germany had become the continent's largest power. Denmark's position was thereby extremely vulnerable and threatened. For Denmark, there was nothing to do but pursue a policy of neutrality, but in practice take extensive account

© The Author(s), under exclusive license to Springer Nature
Switzerland AG 2022
M. Bregnsbo and K. V. Jensen, *The Rise and Fall of the Danish Empire*,
https://doi.org/10.1007/978-3-030-91441-7_9

of its overpowering neighbor. During World War I in 1914–1918, Denmark managed to remain neutral by adapting to its great neighbor to the south.

Internally in Denmark, 1864 represented a trauma that had an effect on Danish politics and the general way of thinking for a very long time. Together with Germany's unification in 1870, widespread concern was raised about the extent to which it would ultimately be possible to preserve Denmark as an independent state.

The nation-state of Denmark was the successor to a much larger empire. Copenhagen remained the capital. It was a legacy of the far greater empire that this smaller state should be organized as a highly centralized state with all of its important institutions gathered in the capital rather than following a federal state structure with considerable independent, regional decision-making power. When virtually all nationwide institutions and organizations of importance were also located in Copenhagen after 1849, and that Copenhagen is by far the largest city in Denmark, was a result of Copenhagen's status in the empire transferring to the smaller state of Denmark's capital. It can thus be compared to an overcoat that is several sizes large. The historian Steen Bo Frandsen has written on these conditions: "The construction of a national economy placed Northern Jutland in the role of supplier of raw materials and of people for Copenhagen's expansion. Denmark was designed entirely on the capital's premises and Copenhagen became, if possible, even more than ever the Danish state ... Everything of importance was located in Copenhagen. Industrialization strengthened the city's dominance" (Frandsen 1996, 566).

A new constitution was adopted in 1866. It abolished the parliament of the November Constitution, but to the great disappointment of the Friends of Peasants, the June Constitution of 1849 was not reintroduced in its entirety. The Folketing (the lower house) would continue to be elected by equal and universal suffrage for men, but the Landstinget (the upper house) would have a number of members, elected by the king, and the most taxed voters each got an extra vote in the elections to the upper house. This led to a long-standing constitutional battle between the Folketing, where the Liberal Party (*Venstre*, the successor to The Friends of Peasants-party) had a majority, and a Landsting with a right-wing majority. The aim of the Liberal Party was to have the 1849 constitution reintroduced and demanded parliamentarism, i.e. that if a government does not have the support of a majority in the Folketing then it should resign. However, the Conservatives and King Christian IX insisted that it was the king's sovereign right to appoint governments without having to take into account any parliamentary majority. During the constitutional struggle in the 1880s, the government took several steps to introduce temporary budget bills that had not been passed by the Rigsdag, and in this way finance the construction of a large fortification in the capital. It was not until 1901 that Christian IX finally succumbed to the prolonged pressure and appointed a government that had the support of the parliamentary majority. Parliamentarism was thereby recognized as a principle. The new Liberal government and later successors then embarked on reforms aimed at democratizing society in many areas, and sought to implement a new constitution that rectified the setback in 1866 and reintroduced equal and universal suffrage that had characterized the constitution of 1849, and even to extend it by allowing women and servants to vote. This was implemented in the Constitution of 1915.

Iceland, the Faroe Islands, and Greenland

Iceland's constitutional position within the Danish empire as well as Iceland's constitutional conditions had been unresolved since 1848. But after 1864, when the empire had shrunk considerably, attention returned. In 1871, a law about Iceland's constitutional position within the Danish state declared that Iceland was "an inseparable part of the Danish kingdom with special national rights." In Iceland, the law aroused dissatisfaction because it had been unilaterally passed by the Danish parliament, where Iceland in accordance with its own request was not represented. Shortly afterward, a draft constitution for Iceland was submitted to the Althing, which had advisory authority. It rejected it, however, and the constitution that Iceland received in 1874 was introduced by the king without the participation of Icelandic representatives in the drafting process, let alone adoption. The constitution gave the Alting legislative authority, as the legislative power lay jointly with the king and the Althing. Although the constitution did not arouse enthusiasm either, it was, after all, a step forward in terms of self-government. At Iceland's millennium celebration in 1874, Iceland was visited by its king for the first time. In the following years, the Althing passed constitutional amendments and other laws, which the Minister of Iceland (i.e. the Danish Minister of Justice) recommended that the King refuse to sign. These conflicts can be seen as a counterpart to the simultaneous struggles in Danish political life for parliamentarism. And when these struggles in 1901 found a solution to the introduction of parliamentarism and the formation of a liberal government, Iceland's conditions could also be reformed. The new Danish government was more sympathetic to Icelandic wishes. In 1903, Iceland thus got a new constitution based on home rule. However, this constitution did not bring undivided joy either. The Liberal government had insisted that the Icelandic minister had to present the Icelandic issues that required the king's signature in connection with the meetings of the Council of State: in other words, when the rest of the government was present. From the Icelandic side, it was perceived as a lack of equality. In 1908, a new bill on the constitutional connection between Iceland and Denmark was drafted. This proposal was accepted by the Danish side, and it gave Iceland far more autonomy and further loosened ties with Denmark. Still, it was rejected in Iceland, since the proposal did not provide for the possibility of terminating the union nor did it emphasize Iceland's sovereignty.

It was not until the end of World War I that negotiations resumed. This occurred in the context of the Danish government wanting the Danish-minded population in Scheswig who lived under German rule to have the opportunity to rejoin Denmark. In that situation, it was unsustainable if Denmark itself had a people within the kingdom that did not enjoy a corresponding right to self-determination. Following an Icelandic initiative, it was therefore decided to set up a committee with representatives of the Althing and the Rigsdag, which reached a proposal for a Danish-Icelandic Law of Federation (*Forbundsloven*). With this law, the state connection between Denmark and Iceland had acquired the character of a federal state and a personal union under the common king and a common foreign service. The constitution was voted on in a referendum in Iceland, where approximately 91% of those present voted in favor, but the turnout was low. In Denmark, it was adopted by the Liberal Party, the Social Liberal Party, and the Social Democrats against the votes of the Conservatives. The Conservatives had also refused to take part in the preliminary negotiations with Iceland. The party's opposition was justified on the grounds that the law was allegedly a surrender of sovereignty in violation of the constitution, just as the party found that Denmark and Iceland's status of two sovereign states was an impossible, constitutional construction and that Iceland was favored at Denmark's expense. But the law was implemented. However, it was perceived differently in Denmark and Iceland. Danish political decision-makers believed that the Danish-Icelandic question had thereby found a lasting, sustainable and satisfactory solution. In Iceland, many emphasized the option of repealing the law and truly saw it as the first step towards full independence.

The Faroe Islands, contrary to Iceland, were represented in the Rigsdag, but the political and ideological contradictions in mainland Denmark felt for a long time irrelevant to the Faroese. From ancient times, there had been resentment against the officials (who were usually Danish) and their supposedly self-interested and self-willed administration, but the schisms were political-social rather than concerning nationalism. As political-social issues emerged, so did groups that resembled the Conservatives and the Liberals in Denmark. 1901, the year of introduction of parliamentarism and the appointment of a Liberal government in Denmark, was also the year of the election of a Faroese Liberal to the Rigsdag. The opportunities for trusting and fruitful cooperation between Denmark and the Faroe Islands thus seemed favorable. In 1906, the Danish government presented an offer of increased autonomy, for example in financial affairs, to the Faroe Islands. But in the parliamentary election, the forces that were against this offer of self-governance won. Their opposition was primarily due to fears that the islands would not be able to be self-sufficient economically. Nevertheless, there was now a recalibration of political life in the Faroe Islands, so that they went from being characterized by right-left schism as in Denmark, to now being grouped according to attitudes regarding the relationship with Denmark. A democratization of the composition of the parliament took place in 1916 and 1923, when the voting rights of the royally appointed members in the parliament completely lapsed, the parliament was also guaranteed the right to be consulted by the Danish government in all bills concerning matters of importance to the Faroe Islands.

Although Tranquebar and Serampore were sold in 1845, the colonial experience in Asia was not quite over. The Nicobar archipelago was not included in the sale. However, due to malaria, these islands were uninhabitable, and a last Danish colonization attempt was abandoned in 1848. Thereafter, there was no Danish connection with these islands. The islands were subsequently used as bases for pirates: therefore the British envoy approached the Danish government in 1868 with a request that it, as the holder of sovereignty, would intervene against the pirates and restore law and order, or alternatively hand over the sovereignty to Great Britain. The Danish government astonished the British envoy by not demanding any payment at all for such a transfer. After 1864, Denmark was not willing to risk anything.

The economic relations between Greenland and the outside world continued to be maintained through a state monopoly, namely the Royal Greenland Trading Department. At times, the Danish public voiced both principled and concrete criticism of the monopoly system. Each time it was decided to maintain it on the grounds that the Greenlandic population was not yet ready to sustain competition and the exposure to the rest of the world that a monopoly breach would entail. America, on several occasions in the second half of the nineteenth century and in the twentieth century, offered proposals to buy Greenland, but such proposals were flatly rejected by the Danes. However, Denmark held a completely different position when considering the sale of the West Indies. What caused these different attitudes? Greenland was an old Nordic country whose Nordic connections could be traced back to the Viking Age, even though the Scandinavian population disappeared sometime in the late Middle Ages. The West Indies had been uninhabited and originally bought by a formally private Danish trading company, and the islands did not have long, Nordic, historical traditions. Similar to the relationship with other parts of the empire, the accession of a Liberal government in Denmark in 1901 meant a new will and interest in implementing reforms in Greenland. The result was a law in 1908 concerning Greenland's administration. One of the most important guiding principles of the law was that the monopoly of trade would be maintained, but a separation of trade and administration was sought for balancing purposes, just as it granted the indigenous population co-influence. The old board of principalship was replaced by municipal councils, which were predominantly populated by Greenlanders. Greenland was divided into two regional councils, which were elected by the municipal councils and thus also predominantly composed of Greenlanders, but led by a Danish-born governor. However, the separation of trade and administration soon proved ill-advised in practice, so a merger was carried out again in 1912. Greenland remained without representation in the Rigsdag, and without any nationwide assembly that could speak on behalf of the entire population.

The West Indies were not included in the liquidation of the tropical colonies in the 1840s due to several factors. The colonies of Asia and Africa had been trading colonies where the importance of trade was long past. Apart from a few merchants, the majority of the Danish population there consisted of deployed civilian, military, and clerical officials. They were naturally pulled home when Denmark abandoned these colonies. In the West Indies, on the other hand, there was a significant contingent of planters and former enslaved people of African origin among the population, just as there continued to be business opportunities. However, the islands' profitability declined. The sugar fields were depleted and brought less yield. After sugar beet became widespread in Europe during the 1870s, the islands really began to become a deficit business. However, the islands would temporarily become an integral part of Danish domestic policy above all other parts of the empire (Fig. 9.1).

Slavery had been abolished in 1848 but replaced by labor regulations. According to these, in an employment relationship one was bound to stay for at least one year, the plantation workers had to reside on the plantation, and a ceiling was placed on wages. Black farm workers who did not have work could be sentenced to seek work, and if they couldn't, they could be sentenced to imprisonment or forced labor under conditions that bore great resemblance to slavery. In 1878, years of accumulated discontent snowballed in a violent uprising among the black farm workers on St. Croix, which led to looting, burning, and loss of lives. Back in Denmark, this uprising gained domestic political significance. The government wanted to grant a reconstruction loan, but the Liberal opposition in the Folketing opposed this, partly due to general resentment against right-wing government, and partly due to little sympathy for the West Indies. The government used the parliamentary majority's rejection to hold elections in January 1879 and subsequently had the loan granted without consulting the Folketing.

The uprising on St. Croix had demonstrated a need for comprehensive reforms on the islands, but this was made more difficult by the fact that the islands were constantly in deficit since the late 1870s and that there was no mood in the Rigsdag for major public investment there. At the same time as the islands became increasingly dependent on subsidies from the Danish treasury, they became more economically oriented towards the United States, which became their largest trading partner. It therefore became an obvious thought that the future of the islands lay with the United States In connection with the peace negotiations after the war in 1864, Denmark had considered to cede Iceland to Prussia in exchange for the Danish-minded parts of Schleswig but had quickly perished this thought itself. Iceland was a Nordic country and the language was the original language of the Scandinavian peoples, therefore, this idea was out of the question. Yet, the idea of using the West Indian Islands as an object of exchange with Prussia was the subject of more intense consideration. Prussia was not interested or may have realized that the United States would probably never had allowed such German presence in its hemisphere. Still, the thought also re-emerged on later occasions. This greatly disturbed the United States, who was interested in the islands. In 1867, Denmark and the United States reached an agreement on the sale of St. Thomas and St. John (but not St. Croix) for $ 7.5 million. There was clear support for the sale in the Danish government, parliament, and public opinion, but due to parity

Fig. 9.1 Two black women in front of a hut at St. Croix, one of the three tiny Danish islands in the Caribbean. Production of cane sugar had been the most important trade here and it had been carried out by enslaved black people. Slavery had been abolished in 1848 only to be replaced by laws against vagrancy that had forced redundant black people to take up employment on conditions that were very close to slavery. Only after a violent rebellion among the black labouring population in 1878 had these laws been lifted. Yet, as the soil was getting gradually exhausted during the nineteenth century, sugar production did no longer pay, the more so as production of beet sugar rising back in the Danish mother country. This all lead to great poverty among the black working-class population. Several attempts at introducing other kind of trades in the Danish West Indies had not been successful and it was clear that the investments needed to promote the islands financially were much larger than Denmark able still less willing to make. The idea of selling the islands to the US began to materialize and it happened in 1917 after a referendum. This was only in Denmark, the population on the islands itself was not asked, least of all the black segment. Still, we know of black voices being in favour of selling the islands to the US arguing that they being English-speakers were having much more in common with the Americans than with the Danes and furthermore that the US was having a large black population. https://commons.wikimedia.org/wiki/File:Two_women_in_front_of_a_house_at_St._Croix_(9468858855).jpg The National Museum of Denmark: Public Domain

of votes in the US Senate, nothing came of the agreement. In the 1890s, interest in sales to the United States grew on both the Danish and American sides. The Danish Conservative prime minister, H. Hørring, in his capacity as finance minister (and thereby politically responsible for the islands) used unofficial channels when he hired private agents leading up to the island sale in the United States. However, this attempt fell apart when it was revealed in the American press. However, official negotiations began between the United States and Denmark, and at the end of 1901, an agreement was reached on a sales treaty whereby the islands were to be sold for $ 5 million. In 1902, the treaty was ratified by the United States, but rejected by the Danish Parliament. When the sales negotiations had begun, the incumbent Conservative government had supported the sale. But in 1902, the Conservatives had changed their minds and had the treaty rejected in the Landsting, where, unlike in the Folketing, they were still having the majority. Why this change of attitude? Because a new government had come in office in the meantime. A Liberal government had been formed and the Conservatives had emerged as opposition. It is difficult to ignore the fact that the party's change of attitude was tactically determined and was intended to tease the new government. Opponents of the sale used nationalist arguments and argued that the sale would mean an irreversible stain on Denmark's national honor, just as it was pointed out that the islands had great opportunities for business development.

Attempts were made to reform the islands after the rejection of the sales treaty in 1902, and it was clear that there was a need for social, legal, economic, health, and educational improvements. However, there was no will for the large public investment needed for such efforts. The reform efforts would be piecemeal. By the Colonial Act of 1906, the income limit for obtaining the right to vote in the colonial councils was lowered, but the large majority of the population was still excluded. Opponents of the sale in 1902 had included more than a few prominent businessmen who claimed that the islands had good business development opportunities. This more or less obliged these business circles to invest and engage in the development of the islands. Other forms of agriculture apart from sugar cane cultivation were introduced, such as cotton, tropical fruits, tobacco, and cocoa. These types of production were not profitable, so horse and cattle breeding was introduced. Efforts were also made to improve the condition of ship traffic, and there were great expectations for the possibilities of St. Thomas' harbor, when the Panama Canal, which connected the Atlantic and Pacific Oceans, opened in 1914.

The outbreak of World War I in 1914 made it difficult for Denmark to connect with the islands. Denmark managed to remain neutral in the war, but the country's position was precarious, and the islands could be placed in danger with a continued policy of neutrality, especially after growing tensions between Germany and the United States (who had not yet entered the war). It is conceivable that the United States could simply have taken the islands. Or in the event of a German invasion of Denmark, the islands would come under German control, a nightmare for American political decision-makers. The Danish authorities' control of the islands was also hampered by extensive strikes among the Black population on the islands. After 1902, the idea of selling the islands to the United States was not off the table, and when relations between Germany and the United States deteriorated in 1915, the United States took the initiative to contact the Danish government. On August 4, 1916, an agreement was reached wherein the islands were sold for $ 25 million. Denmark also demanded that the United States recognize Denmark's sovereignty over all of Greenland. The US Secretary of State opposed such recognition, but President Wilson was so preoccupied with acquiring the islands that he agreed to the concession. Seen in light of the later relationship between Denmark, Greenland, and the United States, this was an irony of history.

The sale was supported by the incumbent Social Liberal Party center-left government, including its supporting party the Social Democrats and by the Liberal opposition party Venstre, whereas the Conservatives were opposed. However, there was still a solid majority in support of the sale, so the exchange should seem relatively uncomplicated. But that was not the case. As in 1879 and 1902, domestic policy was involved. The Liberal opposition party Venstre argued that since the island sale had not been up for debate during the recent election campaign, the sitting parliament did not have a mandate from the voters to make a decision on this issue. Therefore, new elections had to be held, which the Liberal Party also wanted for other reasons. The government instead suggested a referendum to avoid elections. However, it seemed like the proposal would likely be rejected in the Landsting, where the Liberals and the Conservatives held a majority. In that situation, King Christian X, who was concerned about a government crisis and an election in the middle of the war, intervened and formed a coalition government, in which the Liberals, Conservatives, and Social Democrats each got a minister in the Social Liberal Party government. At the same time, an investigative commission was set up by members of parliament to assess the sales treaty, and after this was finalized, a referendum was to be held. The referendum was held on December 14, 1916. It was remarkable for several reasons. It was the first nationwide referendum in Danish history. It was also the first time that people voted according to the rules in the 1915 constitution, i.e. the first time that women and servants had the opportunity to vote in a nationwide election.

The debate prior to the vote was fierce. Opponents brought in nationalist arguments and warned against that "the Danish nation of indolence and fear of temporary inconvenience and expense will refuse to accept the task. Such a step will not only in itself testify about serious weakness in the Danish nation, but also in a fateful way show the way to secession of the Danish Empire in other parts of the country, which by language or race may differ from the real population of Denmark." The supporters leveraged economic and security policy arguments, and hailed the sale opponents as—quote—"the most recent friends of Negroes" and as people who had "gone off the rails, moved away from the normal." While it was clear that the Social Liberal Party and the Social Democrats supported the sale and that the Conservatives were clearly against, whereas the attitude of the Liberal Party was not quite clear. Its parliamentary leaders supported the sale, but the party's elected representatives and its press were divided. The general resentment against the Social Liberal center-left government also played a role. Due to the wartime scarcity of goods, the government had intervened in the society's economy to an unprecedented extent, with rationing, maximum prices for grain, and other interventions in agriculture, industry, and trade. Many traders, industrialists, and many farmers (the core supporters of the Liberal Party) were therefore furious with the government and chose to snub it using the referendum. In the West Indies, no referendum was held. However, the daily newspaper Politiken arranged an unofficial referendum on St. Croix, who showed 4727 votes for sale and only 7 against. The colonial councils, which could certainly not be said to be representative of the population of the islands, unanimously recommended selling. The result of the vote was an overwhelming sales majority, 283,670 in favor, 158,157 against. However, turnout was low, presumably because the theme did not have a broad interest in the electorate. On March 31, 1917, the Dannebrog flag was hoisted on the islands for the last time. Almost 250 years of Danish rule was past. Denmark made a good deal: they got a significantly higher price for the islands than in 1902, and they also obtained the recognition of Denmark's sovereignty over Greenland. Six days after the exchange, the United States declared war on Germany (Bregnsbo 2017, 166–177).

Southern Jutland/Northern Schleswig

When the West Indies were sold in 1917, the Danish empire shrank down to its smallest size ever. Incidentally, the transfer to the United States in 1917 was the last time a colony was sold by one power to another. This was due to the development of the principle of nationality, also called the peoples' right to self-determination and its application in international politics. That January, United States President Woodrow Wilson presented his Fourteen Points, which outlined principles of peace-making and of international cooperation following the war. A key element was the principle of self-determination. It was, moreover, the same Woodrow Wilson who in 1916 had bought the three West Indies islands from Denmark and on the same occasion had agreed to recognize Denmark's sovereignty over all of Greenland.

During 1918, Germany declared itself ready to negotiate peace on the basis of the Fourteen Points. When Germany recognized the peoples' right to self-determination, Denmark saw an opportunity for the Danish-minded areas in Schleswig (which would from then on usually be spoken about as Southern Jutland) to be reunited with Denmark. As Denmark did not participate in World War I, it was consequently not entitled to representation at the peace conference. Therefore, the solution was that representatives of the Southern

Jutlanders made a request for reunification to the Danish government, which elevated the issue to allied diplomats. The South Jutland issue was raised at the Peace Conference in Versailles, France. In 1918, there was general agreement in the Danish Parliament among the parties to maintain the people's right to self-determination and only acquire those parts of Schleswig where a plebiscite indicated that the majority of the population wanted to belong to Denmark (Fig. 9.2).

The re-acquisition of the lost parts of the country must—one would think—be a matter would have raised above party strife and the usual ideopolitical lines, but this was not the case. Danish domestic policy handled the matter in a way that can be compared with the feud over the sale of the West Indies a few years prior. Schleswig was divided into three zones for plebiscite. The Social Liberal party government and its Social Democratic supporting party and the majority of the Liberals prioritized the principle of self-determination and wanted a joint, united vote in the first zone, a separate votation in each municipality in the second zone and no vote at all in the third zone. The Conservatives were against this and wanted all of the territory of Schleswig, including Dannevirke. The Liberal Party was officially in favor of the plebiscite, yet parts of it agreed with the Conservative. The parliamentary leaders of the Liberal Party acknowledged that the principle of self-determination was the only viable option. However, they had no qualms leveraging the dissatisfaction of the opposing forces to bother and even attempt to overthrow the government. This succeeded. The Dannevirke people held on to Denmark's historic right to the whole of Schleswig, regardless of what the people living there thought. The movement's supporters were able to lobby at the Versailles Peace Conference to the great inconvenience of the official Danish delegation. The more moderate conservatives in the Flensburg movement, while they claimed to support self-determination, found that a large and important commercial city like Flensburg, where a Danish majority was not present, should still join Denmark. And finally, both the Danes and the people of Flensburg made the argument that Schleswig had been subjected to more than 50 years of forced Germanization, but that they had only had the opportunity to freely develop their Danish identity for a year: therefore, a plebiscite as early as 1920 was far too early.

The change of boundaries in 1920 is commonly termed reunification (*Genforeningen*) to emphasize that the land conquered in 1864 was now returned. What happened constitutionally was from a constitutional point of view, zone 1 (the only zone with a Danish majority) was incorporated into the Kingdom of Denmark. But this was no reunification as Schleswig had never before been part of the Kingdom of Denmark, but had functioned as a duchy with distinctive structures, and whose duke had been identical with and stood in fidelity to the King of Denmark.

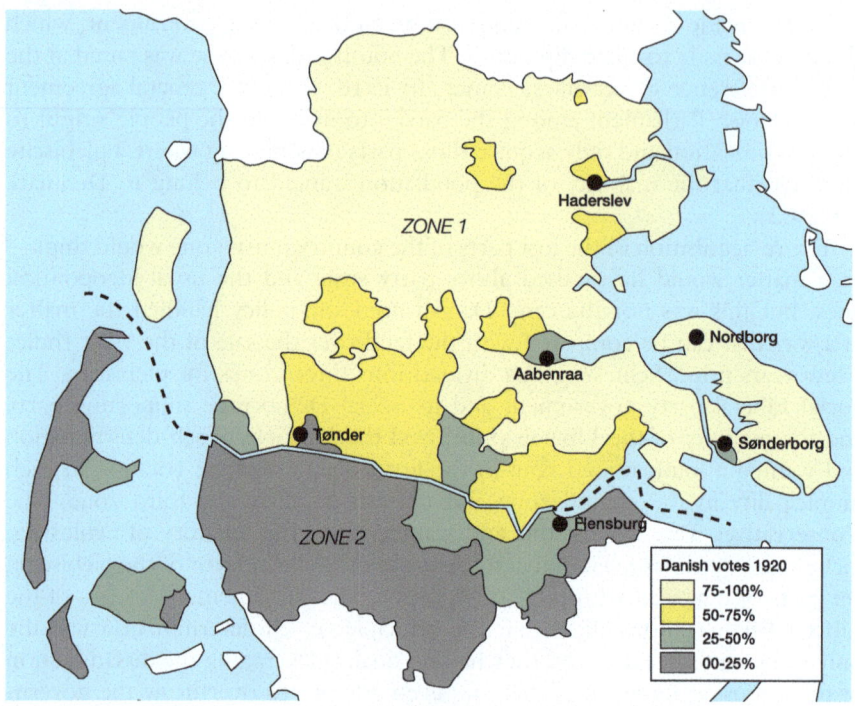

Fig. 9.2 The plebiscite in 1920. Schleswig was divided into three zones. Zone 1 was Northern Schleswig, also known as Southern Jutland, Zone 2 was Middle Schleswig. In Zone 3 (the area south of Zone 2) no plebiscite was held. The division into zones was undertaken on the basis of inquiries of the national dispositions of the population in Schleswig made by the Copenhagen grammar school teacher and Schleswig expert H.V. Clausen back in the 1890s. In Zone 1, the electorate voted *en bloc* and that meant that no adjustments of the border within this zone would afterwards be possible. Consequently, even if certain towns and rural parishes within this zone had a German majority, it was out of the question to move the border northwards up so that they could be part of Germany. In Zone 2, however, each city and rural parish voted separately. Thus, if there had been a Danish majority in any of these, border adjustments would have been possible. The division into separate zones was a political decision. So was the fact that Zone 1 voted *en bloc*, whereas each town and rural parish voted separately within Zone 2. The reason was probably that in case each town and parish within Zone 1 had voted separately, cities such as Aabenraa and Sønderborg would have become German enclaves within Denmark. If the plebiscite had not been organized with either *en bloc* or separate voting in the cities and rural parishes within Zone 1 and 2 resp., the boundary line would have been different

The Interwar Years and Mass Democracy

The period starting with the introduction of universal suffrage by the Constitution of 1915, especially after the reunification in 1920, marks the age of mass democracy. In the period between 1920 and 1940, democracy was secured and expanded in Denmark, and the contours of the social welfare state were drawn. Notably, this occurred despite severe times of crisis and totalitarian undercurrents to the right and left in large parts of Europe.

Internally, there were tensions between different parts of the empire. The fishing in the waters off the Faroe Islands was overcrowded, and therefore Faroese fishermen wanted to be able to fish in the waters off Greenland, as well as build ports in Greenland that could support Faroese fishermen. From the Greenlandic perspective, such a Faroese competition was detrimental. This resulted in conflicting interests between two parties in the Danish empire, and this placed the Danish government in a dilemma. It had to strike a difficult balance by granting the Faroese certain ports and fishing rights in Greenlandic waters (although this actually violated KGH's monopoly), while at the same time labeling these permits as temporary in an attempt to blunt the bitterness this caused in Greenland (Fig. 9.3).

The principle of the people's right to self-determination also had an influence on the Danish government in Greenland. In connection with the Greenland Government's Act of 1925, the report on the bill stated: "The main purpose is the Greenlanders' development towards independence, which is to say such maturity in moral and economic terms that they are enabled to live in free contact with the rest of the world when the country's current state of isolation ceases sometime in the future. However, the Committee believes that the situation in Greenland is still of such a nature that such a reform cannot yet be implemented, but it is instead a goal whose achievement depends on the development of many different factors" (Betænkning 1920, 15, 33). In other words, there was still no majority for giving up the monopoly yet. Despite this, the local government was expanded by the 1925 Act, which introduced district councils that functioned between the regional councils and the municipal councils. The newly established district councils had a ceiling on how many Danes could participate, so that native Greenlanders would always make up the majority. It was thus a cautious type of political training wheels in Greenland's pursuit of greater self-government. However, there was no mood for larger investments in Greenland on the part of the state.

During the interwar period, the Faroe Islands developed support for increased self-government—even independence—but there was far from agreement among Faroese elected representatives. In 1937, Danish and Faroese became equal as a language of instruction. This linguistic development occurred relatively late, as the Faroese elected politicians had till then not reached an agreement among themselves.

Fig. 9.3 The eastern and north eastern parts of Greenland were in reality not colonized and the Danish presence in those areas was minimal. Yet, Norwegian sealers, hunters, fishermen and whalers had increasingly begun to make use of the fishing and hunting possibilities here and claimed that Denmark's sovereignty of Greenland did not apply for this non-colonized part of the great island. With reference to the Peace Treaty of Kiel 1814 they were claiming that Denmark had no right at all to Greenland since this was an old Norwegian dependency. The Norwegians were seen as competitors and did consequently not enjoy much sympathy among the Inuit population. Denmark and Norway both stood firm on their respective claims but in 1924 they reached a temporary agreement without solving the apple of discord. Denmark began to establish settlements in Eastern Greenland in order to demonstrate her sovereignty of this territory. In 1931, however, Norwegian activists occupied parts of Eastern Greenland, hoisted the Norwegian flag and proclaimed the areas occupied Norwegian territory. This took place at private, Norwegian initiative, yet, the Norwegian government was facing a strong pressure from public opinion and found itself compelled to give in support the activists. The Danish government brought the case before the International Law-Court in the Hague whereupon Norwegian activists occupied further parts of Eastern Greenland. Yet, on April 5, 1933 the court upheld the Danish contention and the conflict then ebbed away (Ishavsmuseet, Aarvak, Norway)

THE EMPIRE AND WORLD WAR II

World War II brought the occupation of Denmark on April 9, 1940. The government quickly had to call off all fighting and instead accept an offer from Germany that the Danish state and society would be allowed to continue to function uninfringed. Formally seen, Denmark thereby remained an independent state, no Nazi government was ever installed, even if in practice the Danish government had to adapt and make many painful and humiliating concessions to the demands of the German occupational power. Yet, this policy of cooperation saved Denmark from becoming Nazified. However, a resistance movement against the Germans and the Danish government cooperating with them appeared and due to the activities and pressure from this movement, the Danish government was forced to discontinue the policy of cooperation with the Germans on August 29, 1943. From then on, Denmark had no acting government. This book concentrates on the effects that the occupation and the war had on the empire and—in particular—the relationship between the various parts of the empire (Giltner 1998; Nissen 1983).

The Allied peace with Germany after World War I via the Treaty of Versailles was felt by many Germans (and not only within the Nazi party) as an unjust and dictated peace that should be revised. After Hitler came to power in 1933, increasingly aggressive demands were made for a revision of the Treaty of Versailles, and Denmark feared that demands would also be made for a revision of the Danish-German border from 1920. After the occupation in 1940, this fear did not diminish, but the demand was never made. Why not? The answer lies with the Kiel Canal. This canal crosses Holstein, which connects the North Sea and the Baltic Sea and is of great importance to shipping, was opened in 1895 under the name Kaiser-Wilhelm-Kanal, later referred to as the North Baltic-Sea Canal. This allowed shipping traffic in and out of the Baltic Sea to bypass the Danish straits, and it had great economic and military-strategic significance for Germany. If the canal had been located in the area that Germany, according to the Treaty of Versailles, was to cede to Denmark, the cession of the area and thus the canal would have entailed a very serious economic and strategic weakening of Germany. But luckily the canal was not in the area that was ceded to Denmark. Therefore, Germany had no vital interests in reclaiming this territory. Apparently, the German-oriented Nazi leaders in Southern Jutland made strong demands for reincorporation. However, if Germany had pursued this in 1940, it would have poisoned the cooperation policy with the Danish government and the delivery of Danish agricultural goods that it secured Germany. After August 29, 1943, Germany was so militarily distressed that there was no bandwidth to address the practical and administrative issues associated with a reintegration.

April 9, 1940, demonstrated two things: first that Denmark could not defend itself, and second that the Danish empire only hung together because other powers did not oppose it directly. As during the wars with Great Britain in 1801 and 1807–1814, the German occupation of Denmark in 1940 meant that relations with the North Atlantic parts of the empire were severed. But unlike the Napoleonic Wars, these North Atlantic islands were not peripheral to the war in World War II. On the contrary, the Atlantic was vital to

Allied warfare, and it was across this sea that the transportation of goods, munitions and troops from America to Britain and later also goods and munitions to the Soviet Union relied. The Faroe Islands and Iceland were occupied by British forces on April 10 and May 10, 1940, respectively. Both the Lagting and the Althing protested but were actually relieved that it was the British who had come first, rather than the Nazis. In 1941, before the United States joined the war, American forces, by agreement with Britain, took over the occupation of Iceland. Various parts of the empire were now within the spheres of control of different powers: Denmark within Germany, the North Atlantic islands within the Allies. Greenland's relations with Denmark were also severed on April 9, 1940. But such a situation was foreseen in the Government Act of 1925, and according to this, the two governors present in Greenland would act on behalf of the Danish government.

Greenland was not occupied in 1940 but had to align itself with the United States as it was the only country from which it could import important goods and which could guarantee its security. Apparently, the two governors played a significant role in Greenlandic politics and community life during the war years, but their right to act on behalf of the state did not remain unchallenged. The point was that the United States, which did not join the war until December 1941, had strong strategic interests in Greenland. The Danish envoy in Washington, Henrik Kauffmann, considered his government at home in Copenhagen to be unfree and refused to follow home orders. Instead, on the anniversary of the occupation, on April 9, 1941, to the great regret of the Danish government, he entered into a defense treaty with the United States, which gave the United States the right to establish bases in Greenland. Kauffmann had no authority to establish such a treaty, but the US government could use him to give the event a flavor of legitimacy. The great interest of the United States was due to the fact that the Germans were also strongly interested in Greenland to set up weather warning stations and to be able to use Greenland as a base from which to control and fight the Allied shipping across the Atlantic. Scattered German patrols were sent to East Greenland. During the war, regular battles were fought there between the German forces and members of the Greenlandic Sled Patrol with the support of American forces.

The presence of foreign forces generally led to an economic recovery in the North Atlantic islands. The occupying power demanded labor services and goods locally, which resulted in increased employment and turnover. The occupations also opened up opportunities for goods export for the Allies. The financially good times and the experience of being able to stand on their own two feet and be independent of Denmark provided a basis for great self-confidence in Greenland. In 1944, Iceland seceded completely from the union with Denmark and became an independent republic. According to the Law of Federation of 1918, the Danish-Icelandic union could be renegotiated in 1940 and possibly terminated in 1943. The conditions of World War II rendered the possibility of negotiations in 1940 impossible. The British and later the American occupying forces were not enthusiastic about the Icelandic unilateral declaration of independence. This was based on their long-term considerations of future relations with Denmark, including Greenland—after the war, as well as short-term considerations about the propaganda effect that an Icelandic secession would give the German occupying power in Denmark. In 1942, however, the Americans overcame their concerns. In 1944, a referendum was held in Iceland on independence, and as many as 97.86% of the electorate participated, of which 97.36% voted in support of independence and only 0.51% opposed. At a ceremony in Thingvellir on June 17, 1944, the republic was proclaimed and the Althing elected a president. The following telegram was received from King Christian X: "Regretting that the separation between me and the Icelandic people has been carried out under the prevailing conditions, I would like to express my best wishes for the future of the Icelandic nation and the hope of strengthening the bonds that binds Iceland to the other Nordic countries" (Thorsteinsson 1985, 264ff.). From the Danish perspective, there was great bitterness both during and long after Iceland's secession. It was not because Danish political decision-makers wanted to deprive Iceland of independence, but they found it untimely that Iceland had implemented a unilateral secession and did not wait until after the war, where the separation would have occurred via treaty and negotiation. At this point, it was clear that Germany would lose the war. But it remained unclear whether Denmark would be considered an ally and who would be Denmark's liberators: whether it would be the Western Allies or the Soviet Union. Ultimately, it was most advisable for Iceland to declare independence while there was still time, in order to be able to influence its own fate after the war.

In the Faroe Islands, the economic conditions and political situation of the war years also brought a marked strengthening of calls for independence or at least increased autonomy in relation to Denmark. The British occupation authorities were not enthusiastic to say the least, as Britain was interested in a good relationship with Denmark after the war. Although those who wanted full independence from Denmark never received more than 50% of the seats in the Lagting, it was clear that following the war the relationship between the Faroe Islands and Denmark would change, and be characterized by more autonomy. In the case of Greenland, there was no doubt that colonial rule in its previous form could not continue after the war (Fig. 9.4).

Fig. 9.4 Because of Denmark's immediate surrender to the Germans in 1940 and the subsequent policy of cooperation by the Danish government, Denmark got off relatively cheaply in comparison with other countries involved in WW2. Thus, Danish cities were being spared from devastating, aerial bombardments. Yet, at the end of the war, the isle of Bornholm was—due to its geographical position deeply in the Baltic—within the Soviet area of military operations. The rest of Denmark was liberated on May 4, 1945 as the German occupation forces surrendered to the Western Allies. But as the German commander at Bornholm refused to surrender to the Soviets, the towns of Rønne (the illustration) and Neksø suffered Soviet bombardments. After 11 months' occupation, the Soviets withdrew from Bornholm in 1946, officially because Denmark would now be able to take care of the defense of Bornholm herself. In reality, however, it was a Soviet political gesture having to do with the fact that the Soviet Union was then demanding that British and American forces should be withdrawn from a lot of centers around the world. Even if Denmark in connection with the Soviet withdrawal did not commit herself to any restrictions on her sovereignty over the island, nonetheless, during the Cold War the Soviet Union set up claims about this, and various Danish governments themselves voluntarily imposed restrictions on the Danish military presence at the island. Yet, this should not overshadow the fact that Bornholm was great strategical importance for NATO. Its geographical position deeply into the Baltic made it a valuable listening and observation post for the West in relation to the Eastern Bloc (Bornholms Museum. *Photo* Svend Parksø)

REFERENCES

Betænkning afgivet af det i December Maaned 1920 nedsatte Udvalg til Drøftelse af de grønlandske Anliggender. Copenhagen 1921.

Bregnsbo, Michael. 2017. Kapitel 5. Småstat med kolonier. In *Danmark. En kolonimagt*, ed. Mikkel Venborg Pedersen. Copenhagen: Gad.

Frandsen, Steen Bo. 1996. *Opdagelsen af Jylland. Den regionale dimension i Danmarkshistorien 1814–64*. Aarhus: Aarhus Universitetsforlag.

Giltner, Philip. 1998. *"In The Friendliest Manner": German-Danish Economic Cooperation During the Nazi Occupation of 1940–1945*. New York: Peter Lang Inc.

Nissen, Henrik S., ed. 1983. *Scandinavia during the Second World War*. Minneapolis: University of Minnesota Press.

Thorsteinsson, Björn. 1985. *Island*. Copenhagen: Politikens Forlag.

CHAPTER 10

The Empire During the Cold War, International Integration, and the Welfare State

The end of World War II and the confrontation with the crimes of Nazism meant, as was the case after the First World War, a strong focus on the right of self-determination, now largely combined with the demand for universal human rights. But at the same time, the world situation was dominated by the Cold War: a political, ideological, and economic conflict between the capitalist Western world—led by the United States—and the communist world (the Eastern Bloc), led by the Soviet Union. This conflict impacted all politics and all countries. In 1949 Denmark joined the Western defense alliance by signing the Atlantic Pact and joining the defense organization of NATO. Western defense cooperation was also necessary, as Western Europe was too weak militarily and in terms of resources, and needed US support. It also meant that no state could stand alone, be self-sufficient and pursue an economic policy independent of the others. The result of this was therefore increased trade, economic, and eventually also political integration among the states. The European Economic Community, founded in 1957, is an example in this regard. Domestically, the period after 1945 in Denmark was characterized by the gradual formation of a welfare state, defined as a state that ensures economic and material security for all citizens through tax redistribution, government subsidies, and services, as well as the pursuit of an economic policy to ensure full employment and maximum economic growth to fund such a policy. Both the Cold War, the growing European integration, and the building of the welfare state had an impact on the empire. However, the empire also certainly had an impact on the Cold War, European integration, and the welfare state. Often, the three phenomena are so intertwined that it is

© The Author(s), under exclusive license to Springer Nature Switzerland AG 2022
M. Bregnsbo and K. V. Jensen, *The Rise and Fall of the Danish Empire*, https://doi.org/10.1007/978-3-030-91441-7_10

not possible, let alone meaningful, to treat them as separate from the Danish empire.

Southern Schleswig

As a result of the collapse of Germany in 1945 and the Soviet advance on the Eastern Front, thousands of German refugees from eastern Germany arrived in Schleswig–Holstein. In 1945 and 1946, more than a million people came to Schleswig–Holstein, which in 1939 had a population of 1.6 million. In addition to the enormous administrative, accommodation, and supply problems that such a migration entailed, it also led to a relatively low proportion of Danish-minded inhabitants. Therefore, the Danish minority demanded that Schleswig and Holstein be administratively separated. There were also those who thought further and believed that after Germany's total collapse, the time had come for a revision of the border that went further south than the one achieved in 1920. In May 1945, the Liberation Cabinet of Denmark had in its platform declared that the boundary was fixed. But there were many who viewed the matter differently. Among the people north of the border, the Danish minority in Schleswig, as well as among the German-minded "native" Schleswigers, there was dissatisfaction with the large refugee migration. Finally, members of the Danish minority received food parcels from Denmark in war-desecrated and starving Germany: a clear material advantage. This made some German Schleswigers opt for Denmark and they were consequently scornfully being referred to by their German countrymen as "Speckdänen" (pork Danes). However, the official Danish position was always that the border was fixed. Opponents of a border revision were not convinced of the sincerity and durability of the many newly converted Danes. They also considered potential future political developments: when Germany had regained its power, Denmark could risk having a large German minority within her borders.

In Danish public opinion, both north and south of the border, there was a strong demand for border revision: the positions and the intensity were reminiscent of the storms of opinion in 1916 and in 1920. It did not help that the Liberal Party's prime minister from the end of 1945, Knud Kristensen, declared that he naturally agreed with the government's and the Rigsdag's position on the border issue, but also publicly made it clear that he as a private person was a supporter of a border revision. This comedy was finally brought to an end when a parliamentary majority in 1947 adopted a vote of no confidence against Knud Kristensen. It is highly questionable to what extent the Allies would have been able to agree to a changed demarcation. Britain was in charge of the Allied occupation of Schleswig–Holstein, and Britain was at that time exhausted and ruined by the war: it sought to limit its obligations and commitments as much as possible. The prospect of having to be a guaranteeing power for a changed Danish-German border was not attractive. In the heat of the arguments, other proposals were considered, such as the relocation of all Danish-minded people south of the border to the north and all German-minded people north of the border to the south. However, this phenomenon—which would nowadays be termed an ethnic cleansing—was ultimately not implemented.

Soon the Danish-German antagonisms on the international agenda were overshadowed by the growing East–West confrontation in the Cold War. The issues south of the border persisted, and it did not get any better when the Christian Democratic Union of Germany (CDU) government in 1951 replaced the Social Democrats in Schleswig–Holstein. While the Social Democratic government had recognized the Danish minority and its rights, the CDU government demanded that the Danish-minded Schleswigers made a declaration of loyalty to the state and in other ways actively clashed with the minority. This conflict, like so many others, had to be subordinated to the priority of the Cold War. Prior to the accession of the German Federal Republic to NATO in 1955, H.C. Hansen—Denmark's Minister of Foreign Affairs (and moreover prime minister the following year), at the NATO Council meeting in 1954 expressed to the German Chancellor Adenauer that it would be easier for public opinion in Denmark to accept Germany's accession to NATO if the conditions of the Danish minority were secured. Adenauer understood the point and twisted the arms of his CDU colleagues in Schleswig–Holstein, so that a solution for the minorities on both sides of the border could be found. A definite treaty was undesirable for Denmark, because it would give each state authority to interfere in the other's internal affairs, and it was considered by Danish decision-makers to be a disadvantage for the smaller of the states. Instead, a lengthy negotiation process was agreed upon, with each state issuing a declaration on minority rights within its borders. These Copenhagen-Bonn Declarations of 1955 had been carefully coordinated during the negotiations and were therefore identical. In the declarations, each country announced that it would respect the rights of minorities, including the right to its own schools and other cultural institutions, and that each state should provide financial support to the minority within its borders. The German threshold of 5% for the elections to the state parliament (*Landtag*) in Kiel was eased for the Danish minority. In doing so, a centuries-old national minority problem that had repeatedly given rise to bloodshed had finally found a sustainable solution. This Danish-German minority system has now stood the test of time for almost 70 years. It is sometimes highlighted as an exemplary example of peaceful coexistence between different ethnic nationalities and used as a role model for other situations. However, it can hardly be exported and broadly applied to all ethnic conflicts across the world. The 1955 solution only emerged after more than 150 years of bitter conflict, and only after both countries had suffered decisive defeats, Denmark in 1864, Germany in 1945. Both parties gained and learned from those experiences before they agreed on such an arrangement (Thaler 2009).

The Faroe Islands

Denmark regained sovereignty over the Faroe Islands in 1945, but it was now clear that the Faroese position as a county with extended autonomy as prior to 1940, could not be restored. Negotiations therefore commenced between representatives of the Liberal government, which took office at the end of 1945, and representatives of the Faroese parliament. The representatives of the Danish government were not all equally flexible in the negotiations, which was not facilitated by the fact that the Faroese representatives disagreed with each other. In 1946, the government made an offer of moderate home rule. However, the proposal was hot air: too far-reaching for the political forces on the islands that wanted the connection to Denmark preserved, and not extensive enough for those who desired independence. Nevertheless, this proposal was put to a referendum on the islands, where it was possible to vote yes or no to the following two issues: "1. Do you want the Danish government's proposal to take effect? 2. Do you want the Faroe Islands detached from Denmark?" The result of the vote was woolly: 47.2% voted for proposal 1, and 48.7% for proposal 2. However, the turnout was as low as approximately 33%. Thus, there was a microscopic majority in favor of secession, but well over half of the eligible population had not voted at all. The date of the vote was September 14, 1946, and this date is still an anniversary for Faroese separatists.

The Lagting declared the Faroe Islands independent, which the Danish government considered an illegal act and dissolved the parliament, holding new elections. Here, the parties that supported continued cohesion with Denmark won a clear majority. New negotiations with Denmark were initiated, and they led to the law on Faroese home rule in 1948. Here, the Faroe Islands gained status as a "self-governing nation in the Danish realm." The Lagting was given legislative authority, and the power between the national authorities and the Faroese authorities was arranged according to the principle that the Faroese were given full authority to decide in the matters they themselves fully financed. The affairs that Denmark helped to finance were to be managed jointly with Denmark. The Faroese could at any time select several matters they would manage themselves by independently financing the issue. Faroese were still to carry Danish passports, but their Faroese affiliation would be stated. The Faroe Islands gained their own flag and Faroese was made the main language. The Lagting was given the right to be heard in all legislative matters concerning the Faroe Islands in the Rigsdag. Beyond this, no law passed by the Rigsdag would be valid in the Faroe Islands, unless the Lagting had sanctioned it, summarized in the phrase: "this law does not apply to the Faroe Islands." Foreign and defense policy was to remain common with Denmark, and the Faroe Islands continued to be represented in the Rigsdag (Debes 2001, 44–53) (Fig. 10.1).

Fig. 10.1 A bitter conflict took place in the town of Klaksvik at the Faroe Islands in 1955. The apple of discord was the hospital doctor Olaf Halvorsen who had been a Nazi and after the end of the war had had an official disapproval imposed on him by the Danish Medical Association. Furthermore, he had been sentenced to pay the costs, around 600 Danish kroners. As he refused to pay, he had been expelled from the Medical Association and consequently he was not allowed to work as a general practitioner which was a condition for having the position at the hospital in Klaksvik. Yet, many inhabitants in Klaksvik wanted to keep him. This led to a conflict that included refusal to pay taxes, loss of liberty and other kinds of harassments of public servants, strikes, bomb explosions, sabotage and mining and blockade of the harbor of Klaksvik. But it also included mediation from the Danish government and sending of Danish police officers to Klaksvik. The conflict was abundantly being utilized by Faroese separatists, yet, fundamentally seen it was a conflict between the home rule government in the Faroese capital of Thorshavn and the inhabitants of Klaksvik, moreover, internal social tensions within Klaksvik contributed to increase the disagreements. The Danish government did not intervene till late and only at the express request of the Faroese home rule government. https://commons.wikimedia.org/wiki/file:patruljerende_politi_i_klaksvig.jpg (Danish Police Museum: photo Svend Aage Larsen)

Greenland

After the liberation in 1945, Danish sovereignty was re-established. Danish decision-makers reckoned that the arrangement with Greenland from before the war could continue with certain moderate reforms. However, the Danish sovereignty over Greenland was half-truth, because the Americans still had bases there according to the Kauffmann Treaty of 1941. The treaty could only be terminated until both parties found that "the current dangers to the American continent have ceased." According to the Americans' interpretation, these dangers were not past, in fact they were as great as ever due to the impending East–West conflict. Consequently, the Americans did not intend to withdraw from Greenland. This meant that Denmark's position in the Cold War when joining NATO in 1949 was as well as pre-established. The United States was preoccupied with expanding its Greenland bases, not least the Thule base to the north, because the Soviet Union was now the main opponent, and the shortest distance between the United States and the Soviet Union's major population centers was via the North Pole. This was far more important to the Americans than the size of Denmark's own defense. It is clear that the accession to NATO in 1949 launched an extensive Danish rearmament, and many Danes felt that the sums involved were enormous. However, when compared to other countries, the Danish defense spending was relatively low. For example, in 1960 Denmark spent 2.7% of its gross domestic product on defense, while the United States spent 8.8%, Great Britain 6.4%, France 6.3%, the Netherlands 3.8%, and Belgium 3.4%. Among the NATO countries, The only countries that spent less than Denmark were small Luxembourg (0.9%) and Iceland, who did not have its own defense at all (Sivard 1996, 45; World Armament 1975, 122). At the same time, in NATO contexts, Denmark often took a critical stance on other countries, especially the confrontational Cold War policy of the US. During the 1980s, a left-wing majority of the Danish parliament forced the Conservative-Liberal government to carry out the so-called "footnote policy" which made Denmark stand out within the NATO alliance distancing itself from central NATO defense policy doctrines. Denmark was able to keep its defense budget at a low level in international comparison, take a critical and reserved stance, while simultaneously obtaining NATO's guarantee and protection, because Denmark gave the United States full military authority in Greenland. However, this was not publicly discussed in Denmark. The United States' complete control also included the right to host nuclear weapons in Greenland, although Denmark's official foreign policy was otherwise not to allow nuclear weapons on Danish territory (*Grønland under den Kolde Krig* 1997) (Fig. 10.2).

This so-called "Greenlandic card" was Denmark's most important contribution to the Western alliance. The Americans had probably considered the idea of buying Greenland, but it was more advantageous for Denmark to keep Greenland and thereby have a valuable political asset in the relations with the United States. However, this necessitated that Denmark seriously assert its sovereignty over the world's largest island. In addition, colonial powers were viewed with skepticism by the newly formed UN, and Denmark suddenly had to see itself in the company of states with which one would not like to be compared. This, but especially the US bases, led to a decision to change Greenland's status from a colony to an equal part of Denmark and to initiate extensive investments and modernizations, including lifting the trade monopoly and raising the Greenlandic standard of living. These efforts began with the Social Democratic Prime Minister Hans Hedtoft's visit to Greenland in 1948, where representatives of the two Greenlandic regional councils had

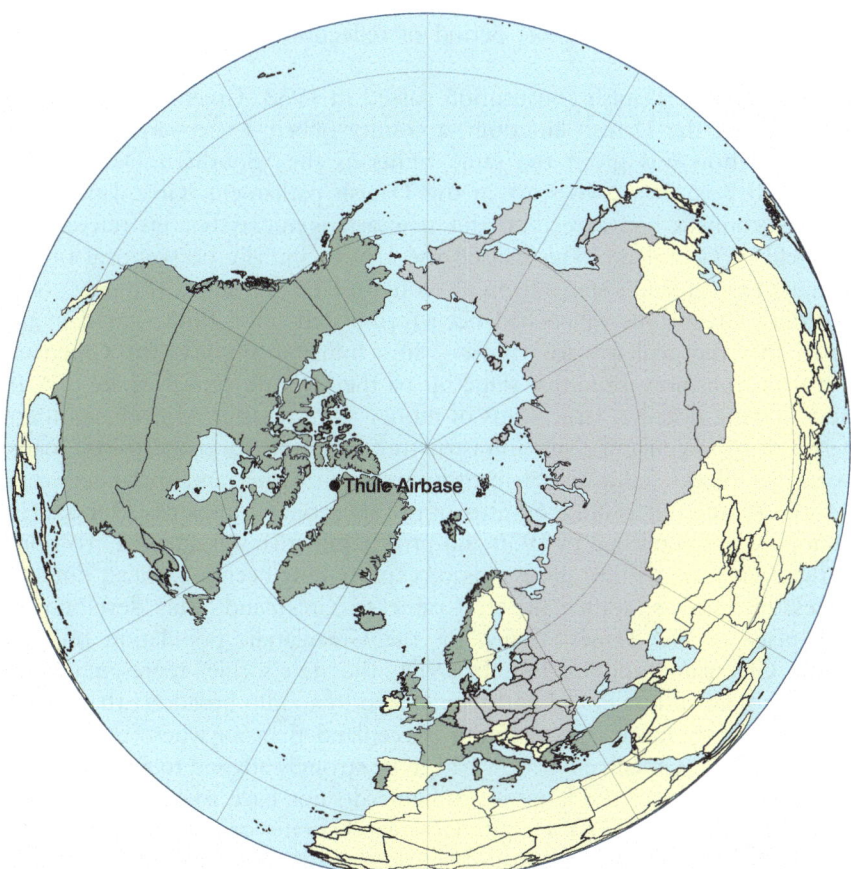

Fig. 10.2 Map showing Greenland's central position during the Cold War. The fastest way between the population centers in the US and the Soviet Union was via the North Pole and Greenland was, thus, the outermost outpost of the West towards the East. This explains the great interest of the US to have airbases here. In the rest of Denmark, Greenland had (and has) hardly any pronounced place in the everyday political and national consciousness, yet, during the Cold War, it was Greenland's belonging to the Danish state that was decisive for Denmark's orientation to the Western Alliance and it was also one of the reasons why Denmark managed to get relatively cheaply off the membership of NATO. Thus, it was first and foremost the Danish empire and not Denmark proper that was a member of the Western defense alliance. In recent years, the melting of the ice at the North Pole as a consequence of increased global heating has enabled new ship lanes and made a number of natural resources (minerals, oil) in Greenland and in the waters off Greenland accessible and possible to exploit. This has opened up for a number of economic opportunities in the Arctic, not only for Greenland, but also for great powers such as the US, Russia and China. Furthermore, the new economic opportunities at land and at sea may also lead to social and environmental problems, just as the increased interest in the area of the great powers is beginning to make the Arctic an area of strategical tensions

the opportunity—after a short period of reflection—to agree on a plan for these goals.

With the new Danish constitution passed in 1953, Greenland became an equal part of the Danish kingdom, a county (albeit a very large one), and the population was given the same rights as the "Southern Danes," and Greenland was given two seats in the Danish parliament. Greenland's two national councils had agreed to this new arrangement, but no referendum was held in Greenland. This caused the UN to initially be skeptical of this change in Greenland's status from a colony to a Danish state. The new policy regarding Greenland, which had been formulated since 1948, stated in the report that the goal was to—quote—"in a humane way lead the Greenlanders from the more primitive stage up to the level we ourselves are at." In the following decades, large sums of money were transferred from Southern Denmark to Greenland. New infrastructure was built (ports, airports, roads, apartment blocks, educational institutions, health care, and social services), factories sprang up, as did a number of private service companies after KGH's monopoly was abolished in 1950 and private initiative was allowed. To bring all these changes to life, thousands of experts (engineers, teachers, doctors, nurses, technicians, craftsmen, etc.) came to Greenland. This development took place on the Danes' terms, for the Greenlandic population but not by the Greenlandic population. In 1954, the state's chief representative in Greenland, Governor Poul Lundsteen, stated in a radio broadcast that "there were apparently more lazy people in Greenland than anywhere else on the planet, and that Greenlanders now had to be strongly advised to get motivated and work so that all the large investments do not have to be meaningless" (Hammerich 1977, 227f.). Despite Greenland's status as an equal part of the Danish kingdom and the full Danish citizenship of Greenlanders according to the 1953 Constitution, the attitude towards Greenlanders among the expert elite sent from Denmark was often characterized by a sense of superiority and condescension.

This development policy in Greenland can be seen as an extreme version of the building of a welfare society in Denmark today. But precisely because the Greenlanders started at a different stage, the transition was far more difficult. Self-employed hunters were relocated from small settlements to newly built cities, where they got jobs as wage workers in industry. It goes without saying that such an abrupt transition to a life as a city dweller and wage worker with a completely new and unfamiliar form of work organization and discipline might give rise to adjustment problems. These came in the form of alcoholism, broken families, violence, crime, unstable labor, and excess mortality. In the face of this, one should not romanticize the conditions in Greenland prior to 1948, which were characterized by great poverty and mortality. For example, the number of deaths per 1000 inhabitants in Greenland in 1950 was 25.5, the corresponding figure in Denmark was 9.2. Ten years later, Greenland had decreased to 7.9, while Denmark was 9.5. In 1950, tuberculosis was the cause of 32.2% of the deaths in Greenland, while Denmark at 1.5%. Ten years later, the figures for Greenland and Denmark were 4.6 and 0.4, respectively. Child mortality in Greenland, which around 1950 was 15 (measured by the number of deaths under 1 year per 100 live births) was more than twice as high as in Denmark. This number was by 1960 reduced to 6.8 compared to 2.2 in Denmark (Statistisk Årbog 1950–1963).

The reason for urbanization was that the seal population had decreased, so that it was no longer possible to support oneself as a hunter in a remote settlement. Instead, they had to focus on cod, and later, shrimp fishing, which required far more centralization and cooperation, partly in the form of large trawlers and processing industries. Therefore, people necessarily had to move together in cities rather than live scattered in settlements. This does not erase the fact that actions were taken against the Greenlanders as new citizens, which have since been recognized as abuse and the abhorrent result of colonial rule. When the United States was to expand the Thule base in 1953, local hunters were forcibly relocated at short notice. Officially, the Danish government said that the move had taken place voluntarily and that the fishing and hunting grounds that had been designated as a replacement were as good as the old ones. It would take over 40 years before Denmark officially acknowledged that there had been a forced relocation and deterioration of living conditions. As part of the efforts to raise Greenlanders "up to Denmark's level," a number of Greenlandic children were forcibly removed in the 1950s and sent to foster families in Denmark. This has also since been recognized as assault.

One factor that deeply provoked a backlash from Greenland was the so-called birthplace criterion. This meant that all publicly employed Danish-born experts who worked in Greenland received higher salaries and a number of benefits such as housing and free trips home to Denmark, while Greenland-born experts with exactly the same qualifications were paid much less. This was highly regarded as discrimination. The reason that was given was that the number of Greenland-born experts was very low, and if they received as high a salary as their Danish-born colleagues, it would create enormous wage differences within the Greenlandic population. It was also argued that large allowances and benefits for experts from Denmark were necessary to be able to attract qualified people. Nevertheless, the birthplace criterion was a strong contributor to the formation of a Greenlandic political awareness with demands if not for secession, then at least for significantly more Greenlandic participation and development on Greenland's—and not just on Denmark's—terms.

In particular, the consideration of Denmark's accession to the European Community (EC) helped to promote the demand for home rule in Greenland. From the beginning, the Faroe Islands had opposed the EC, and pursuant to the Home Rule Act, the Faroe Islands did not join. Greenland, on the other hand, was formally a Danish county. In the referendum on the EC in 1972, 71% of the voters in Greenland voted "no," but when these votes were counted together with the votes cast in Southern Denmark, there was still a majority supporting the accession and Greenland joined the EC. The aversion to the EC in Greenland was mainly due to fears of competition from other EC countries in the fishing waters. Shortly after the EC vote, a Greenlandic home rule arrangement was therefore initiated by Greenland. One such agreement was established in 1978 and came into force in 1979. The arrangement was very similar to the Faroese: Greenland got its own parliament (Landsting) with legislative power, and its own government. Similar to the Faroe Islands, the Greenlanders could choose which areas they themselves wanted to administer fully and completely, as long as they were able to independently settle all expenses for the issue in question.

A point of contest had been the rights to the valuable minerals in the Greenland subsoil. Here the parties had to settle for a compromise, after which the Greenlanders were given a "fundamental" right to the country's wealth, but not full ownership. On the other hand, the Greenlandic parliament was given the right to veto all decisions regarding the utilization of the subsoil. In the Danish parliament, the Home Rule Act was passed by a large majority: only the outer wings were against. This included the extreme left because the law had been drafted by a joint Danish-Greenlandic commission and not by the Greenlanders alone, and the right-wing populist "Progress Party," because it was opposed to different conditions for citizens in the same state. In 1982, the Home Rule Government held a referendum on the EC in Greenland, where 52% supported resignation, and 46% opposed. On January 1, 1985, Greenland withdrew from the EC (Jensen 2017, 320–371).

The Empire in the Twenty-First Century

Despite the home rule agreements, both the Faroe Islands and Greenland are permanently represented in the Danish Parliament with two seats each. Although the Faroese and Greenlandic members of parliament generally seek to avoid interfering in Southern Danish affairs, a vote is a vote—and can be crucial, even if one refrains from making use of it. There have been many situations where the North Atlantic mandates were decisive for which side should form the government, just as these have sometimes made the difference when important internal Danish matters had to be decided. As both the Faroe Islands and Greenland have been given home rule and thus legislative power, lawyers have determined that the term unitary state no longer applies to the Danish kingdom. According to the Danish constitution, the union of Denmark, Greenland, and the Faroe Islands is called "the unity of the realm" (in Danish: *rigsenheden*). Yet, colloquially, also in politics, the term *community of the realm* (in Danish: *rigsfællesskabet*) is being used. "Unity" is suggesting authority, heirarchisation and subordination whereas "community" is signaling values like voluntariness, solidarity, and equality. "Rigsfællesskab" literally means "community of the realm" but might also be translated as Commonwealth (Harhoff 1993).

Greenland and the Faroe Islands are still a part of the Danish Empire, because they came under the control of the Danish crown together with

Norway and remained there, even after Norway ceded in 1814. Why have Greenland and the Faroe Islands not followed in Iceland's footsteps and seceded from Denmark? There can be several reasons for this. Optimists will say that the Commonwealth functions as a fully satisfactory framework so that they have no reason to secede. More sober observers will point out that these areas may not be financially independent enough to function without the large subsidies from Denmark. There may also be other reasons. In the Faroe Islands, the attitude of the political parties on secession from Denmark does not follow the political, ideological, and social lines of division that otherwise separate the parties. The two parties with the strongest stance on independence are the People's Party on the right and the Republican Party on the left. Supporters of the existing affiliation with Denmark include the Union Party, which is close to the Danish liberal party Venstre, in addition to the Social Democrats and the center party Self-Government. According to the Home Rule Act, an incumbent government must be a majority government. The Faroe Islands must therefore be governed by coalition governments. The People's Party and the Union Party can probably agree on the economic and social policies, but disagree on the relationship with Denmark. Here, the People's Party is closer to the Republicans and the Union Party is closer to the Social Democrats. This means that supporters of continued cohesion as well as supporters of secession find it difficult to agree on much else domestically, because these dividing lines do not follow a traditional right-left scale. Yet, in principle, all parties have agreed to work for greater Faroese independence.

Similar trends are prevalent in Greenland where home rule in 2009 was extended to autonomy government. Greenland has copious natural resources, especially minerals—and in extraordinarily high concentrations. The ownership for these (Danish or Greenlandic only) is a contested question. Adherents of Greenlandic independence from Denmark have argued that by means of these natural resources, it will be possible to finance full Greenlandic independence. But voices have also been raised that such a utilization of the mineral resources will necessitate large investments in technology and infrastructure with possible, serious environmental consequences. And moreover, such an economic development would entail immigration of foreign experts and manpower with strong, demographic consequences for the composition of the population in Greenland. A further problem in this massive but sparsely populated country is that sovereignty will also have to be decided in the case of independence. And someone has to do it. Whether the Greenlanders themselves have the will and resources for this is not currently certain, as it would require the establishment of some form of defense force. Then another power must maintain sovereignty, since such a geostrategic area will not go unnoticed. If not Denmark, then who will be responsible for such enforcement of sovereignty? The United States, which already has a massive military presence, is an obvious option. The question is whether Greenland prefers dominance by the US (and whether such a choice would increase Greenland's chance for independence) over the dominance of Denmark. Or—alternatively—whether the current system, which really means Danish dominance in the civilian field and American dominance in the military, remains the option that provides the greatest scope for the possibility of independent Greenlandic politics.

The Danish empire at the beginning of the twenty-first century now finds itself in a world that is becoming increasingly internationalized and globalized. Denmark is experiencing growing international political, economic, and military cooperation. This is taking the form of increased European integration under the auspices of the EU. Military and security policy cooperation is expanding in NATO. Other international involvement takes the form of development aid and active membership of the UN. In both NATO and the UN, Denmark has actively contributed militarily. During the Cold War, active involvement was limited to the deployment of UN forces to international hotspots, and the possibilities for this were further limited by the logic of the Cold War. However, after the fall of the Berlin Wall in 1989, Denmark has become much more actively involved internationally, under the auspices of the UN and NATO in the Balkans in the 1990s, in Afghanistan from 2001 till 2021, and as an ally with the United States against Iraq in 2003. Although Denmark has now tried to act as an occupying power, the goal of such occupations is neither colonization, nor the introduction of Danish legal conditions among the local population, let alone the incorporation of these areas under the Danish crown or in the Commonwealth. In other words, these activities fall outside the definition of empire expansion and can't really call it the formation of an empire. Or … is it perhaps empire formation—in the sense of establishing command authority over an area—of a new kind?

Within the empire itself, the Commonwealth, it can be stated that the Faroe Islands and Greenland operate outside the EU, while Denmark becomes more deeply integrated. But this is not so different from the past, where different parts of the empire could have different constitutional status; some could be members of the German Empire, while others not; some had a duke as head of state, others a king, etc.

In both the Faroe Islands and Greenland, constantly stronger voices are emerging to demand more, if not full independence, for more extensive autonomy. Supporters of (greater) independence claim that the financial subsidies from Denmark lead to dependence. They argue that in the long run, such a situation is neither healthy, sustainable, nor worthy of a nation. The desire to exit the commonwealth ("rigsfællesskab") is not necessarily an expression of hatred against Denmark or perception of Danish colonial mentality. On the contrary, there are several who emphasize that a precondition for full equality and mutual respect between the Danish, Faroese, and Greenlandic nations is precisely that the latter two achieve economic dependence and emerge from Denmark's political guardianship. Some may find that such national attitudes of independence are in direct opposition to the prevailing internationalization and globalization. This does not necessarily have to be the case. Neither in the Faroe Islands nor in Greenland is it imagined that increased autonomy should occur in isolation from and independent of the rest of the world.

These connections to the rest of the world just don't necessarily need to go via Denmark.

Yet, this is not something for Denmark, Greenland, and the Faroese Islands alone to decide. The Arctic is becoming an increasingly tense part of the world. Due to global heating, ice is melting at the North Pole to an extent that enables transport of goods by ship along sea lanes that due to the ice have not till now been navigable. Furthermore, the melting of the ice will enable access to natural resources (e.g. oil, minerals). All this make the Arctic a most contested area not only by the local Arctic powers (the US, Canada, Russia, Norway, and Denmark) but a rising political and economic power as China has strong shipping and commercial interests in the Arctic. All this is placing Greenland in an important, strategic situation which is posing challenges both for Greenland and Denmark. Due to Greenland's geographic position close to the United States, the US government will hardly ever accept Russian or Chinese political, infrastructural, and economic presence and influence in Greenland while the strategic interest of the United States in Greenland is growing correspondingly. This is the background behind the surprising offer from President Trump in the summer of 2019 that the United States should simply buy Greenland from Denmark. Both the Danish government and the Greenlandic autonomy government immediately and concurrently declined. Nonetheless, the increased US strategic interests mean that the United States would hardly ever accept Russian or Chinese shipping, commercial, or industrial activities here still less an independent Greenland entering into business and infrastructure relations with Russia or China so that an independent Greenland would be dominated by the US. Even if Trump's offer was turned down, the increased tensions and strategical interests in the Arctic will necessitate that Denmark should spend more military and civilian resources to claim and maintain its sovereignty of Greenland. On the other hand, this might also give some political advantages for Denmark: if Denmark did not have Arctic territories, it would only be a tiny country of which the rest of the world would hardly take much notice. However, being an Arctic power, Denmark is a fellow player in international politics and thereby able to obtain political influence to an extent that a Denmark without Arctic territories would never have. Seen from a great powerpoint of view, it may contribute to easen tension in the Arctic that Greenland is under the sovereignty of a small European state instead of, e.g. the US. Seen in that perspective, one can still meaningfully speak about a Danish empire. Yet, one never knows for how long: the increased international interest in Greenland and the North Atlantic in general has led to increased national and political self-confidence in relation to Denmark in the Greenlandic public. The autonomy government that took office after the Greenlandic election in 2021 is a token of that. And at international conferences and summits dealing with subjects of relevance for the North Atlantic, representatives of the Greenlandic and Faroese autonomy governments are now taking actively part alongside members of the Danish government. So the traditional order, hierarchy, and structure within the Danish empire indeed seem to be changing radically and only time will show to what.

References

Debes, Hans Jacob. 2001. *Føringernes land*. Copenhagen: Multivers.
Grønland under den Kolde Krig, vols. 1–2. 1997. Copenhagen: Dansk Udenrigspolitisk Institut.
Hammerich, Paul. 1977. *Velfærd på afbetaling. Andet bind af en danmarkskrønike 1945–72*. Copenhagen: Gyldendal.
Harhoff, Frederik. 1993. *Rigsfællesskabet*. Aarhus: Forlaget Klim.
Jensen, Einar Lund. 2017. Kapitel 7: Nyordning og modernisering 1950–79. In *Grønland. Den arktiske koloni*, ed. Hans Christian Gulløv. Copenhagen: Gad.
Sivard, Ruth Leger, ed. 1996. *World Military and Social Expenditures*. Washington: World Priorities.
Statistisk Årbog. 1950–1963. Various Years. Copenhagen: Danmarks Statistisk.
Thaler, Peter. 2009. *Of Mind and Matter: The Duality of National Identity in the German-Danish Borderlands*. West Lafayette: Purdue University Press.
World Armament and Disarmament. SIPRI Yearbook 1975. London and Stockholm: Stockholm International Peace Research Institute.

CHAPTER 11

The Danish Empire Through the Ages

Expansion of the Empire

The history of the Danish empire falls roughly into two phases. Until the middle of the seventeenth century it grew, and thereafter it got smaller and smaller. There are of course multiple nuances within this generalization, but it is nevertheless possible to point out some main themes in the development of the empire.

The Danish empire has had a tumultuous fate with great variances in the extent to which its territories reached. The earliest phase can only be speculated from archeological finds, but it seems that there have been extensive connections throughout Europe to the Danish empire in the first centuries after the birth of Christ. A crucial prerequisite for understanding the uniqueness of the Danish empire is its close connection to the sea and the fact that since the early Middle Ages, the empire has usually had an extremely powerful fleet in the context of the international theater. In other words, the Danish empire has been a thalassocracy, a sea kingdom.

In the early Middle Ages, the Danish Empire was centered around the North Sea and included territories in present-day Denmark, England, the southern part of Norway and Scania. This empire split in the middle of the 1000 s, and from around 1100 attention turned to the east, and the empire expanded along the southern Baltic coast. The exact extent of its territories was mercurial, but largely the empire consisted of present-day Denmark, Scania, Germany—north of the Elbe from Ditmarschen to the present North Pole, and then Estonia. In the early fourteenth century, the conflict between two royal houses meant that the Holstein lineage held most of the empire as collateral without a king or with a puppet king. The empire disintegrated to

© The Author(s), under exclusive license to Springer Nature Switzerland AG 2022
M. Bregnsbo and K. V. Jensen, *The Rise and Fall of the Danish Empire*, https://doi.org/10.1007/978-3-030-91441-7_11

some extent, but institutions and historic legal claims on land were sustainable enough to survive despite the dissolution of a central power. Valdemar IV Atterdag from 1340 and 20 years onward would unite the former empire and expand it to include Gotland. The Empire was still centered on the Baltic Sea, but by a successful marriage and inheritance, Denmark, Norway, and Sweden with all their adjacent countries were united within a Union in 1397 at a meeting in Kalmar. The empire swiftly became one of Europe's greatest powers, both in its size and military might. The rulers of the empire became important and accepted actors on the European political scene, while the extent of the empire also became much broader than before. It included the Baltic Sea all the way to the fortress of Viborg, from the bottom of the Gulf of Finland at the Russian border, and all of Sweden and Norway to the northern Arctic Ocean behind the land of the Lapps. It included not only Norway but also the North Atlantic possessions with the Faroe Islands, Iceland, Greenland, and the little-known Vinland. Vinland can be considered the outermost tip of Asia, which the empire could reach westward, instead of the other European powers who had to go east along the cumbersome and dangerous caravan routes through the Middle East. This also included the duchies of Schleswig and Holstein.

The original Kalmar Union lasted—with great difficulty—until the beginning of the sixteenth century and was then divided, after which Sweden with Finland formed their own empire and, in the future, actively engaged both in the German lands on the other side of the Baltic Sea, as well as also militarily against Denmark. However, the Danish Empire was still a middle-sized power with a considerable fleet and was long considered a serious threat by the many smaller principalities and free royal cities in northern Germany. At the same time, the ruler assumed an unusual double role as king of Denmark and Norway, while simultaneously acting as Duke of Holstein and thus a German prince. This resulted in several political maneuvers within the empire and at the same time a close connection to and influence on German politics. The northern possessions of the empire provided large revenues from fishing, and the duchies were rich, grain-producing territories. With the acquisition of colonies in Africa and the Caribbean, Flensburg came to play an important role in a triangular trade among Denmark, Africa, and America, where enslaved people were sold in exchange for rum, sold for gunpowder and bullets, hardware. However, there were certain undercurrents. Unlike other empires, Denmark's overseas possessions were quite small and of little economic importance. The main attention of the empire remained on the Baltic Sea and the North Atlantic.

In its wars against Sweden during the seventeenth century, the Danish empire lost Scania, Gotland, and temporarily Bornholm. This limited the empire's eastern orientation. Sweden, Russia, and later Prussia became the important powers in the Baltic Sea, and the Danish empire had to find a balance among these powers. In practice, it managed to maintain the empire almost intact throughout the eighteenth century through a policy of neutrality that ensured quite unusual for 80 years: peace. However, great upheaval came in the nineteenth century. Norway in 1814, Schleswig and Holstein in 1864. Most of the empire's possessions disappeared and became a part of other empires in just two generations. What was left was the kingdom of Denmark, the West Indies, and the North Atlantic islands. However, now it was a small empire whose continued independent existence there was every reason to doubt.

The focus of the empire shifted once more: after 1864, the Danes turned inward. There is an old motto of the Danish Heath Company in charge of bringing the large moorlands in Jutland under cultivation that describes the situation well: what is lost outwards must be gained inwards. This also applies to historians, who have concentrated almost exclusively on the past of present-day Denmark, but rarely looked beyond modern borders. Over time, the empire's many and large territories were no longer included in Danish history. Greenland, the Faroe Islands, Iceland, and even Norway were no longer mentioned. Danish medieval history was written without addressing the Scanian territories. The past was understood as just a prelude to the modern Danish nation-state, and the assumption arose that Denmark had always been a small, poor country—peaceloving but through history often the victim of the aggression of other powers.

The Purpose of the Empire

Throughout history, what has been the purpose of acquiring and maintaining the Danish empire? Here, two main purposes can be distinguished: an economic one and a security one. The economic purpose can have different forms: to carry out regular looting, to ensure good opportunities for trade and economic life in general, thereby achieving the resulting prosperity not only for the treasury but for society as a whole. Examples of the latter regarding empire formation and maintenance include the acquisition of the tropical colonies and the protection and state support of monopoly trading companies, as well as attempts to dismantle structures (such as the landowners' serfdom over the peasants in the duchies) that hindered economic development. Later it was also on economic grounds that the empire sold the tropical colonies. An empire could be used to create an economic synergy effect, so that the various parts of the empire cooperate economically, creating a force multiplying effect. Specifically, this could occur by making the empire a common market, although efforts in that direction were never fully realized within the Danish empire. The mercantilist efforts to encourage trade and production within the empire were an expression of such a mindset: that all parts of the empire should contribute in the areas that they excelled at. The Danish monopoly on grain exports to Norway and the corresponding Norwegian monopoly on iron exports to Denmark in the eighteenth century were simultaneously justified as an expression of solidarity in the division of labor and burden-sharing among the parties within the same state. When trade with the tropical colonies and Iceland was released, it was only for the subjects of the empire. After 1864, the size relationship between Denmark and the other parts of the empire was so overwhelmingly in Denmark's favor that any talk of an equal economic partnership was not feasible. From being sources of economic gain, the North Atlantic islands and the West Indies became deficit businesses that received money from the Danish treasury. The power was, so to speak, reversed. Yet, there may be political advantages for Denmark having Greenland and the Faroese Islands under her sovereignty that might offset these expenses.

Security policy was another frequently used motivation for an empire: in particular the acquisition of territories could be justified by the desire to put oneself in a better strategic position, both for the defense and/or offense against external enemies. The efforts to gain control of areas of northern Germany (the dioceses of Bremen and Verden) in the time of Christian IV were aimed at acquiring strategic areas from which the Jutland Peninsula could be better defended against invasion. Attempts to gain control of the Gottorp parts of the duchies in the seventeenth and eighteenth centuries also had security policy purposes. But security reasons could also be used when a territory of the empire was abandoned. For example, the possessions on the mainland coast of present-day Estonia were abandoned in the second half of the sixteenth century because these were judged to be too difficult to defend and thus a hindrance to the empire's security. Proponents of the sale of the Danish West Indies pointed out the risk that Denmark incurred by becoming involved in World War I if the islands were retained for the empire. On the other hand, Greenland played a crucial role in Denmark's security policy and alliance protection after World War II. During the Cold War, the Americans' unhindered military use of Greenland was a way for Denmark to enjoy special status in NATO. Seen in that perspective, the extensive subsidies from the Danish Treasury to Greenland were likely an ultimate boon for Denmark. And due to the increasing international strategic interests in the Arctic, it is still so.

A third justification for an empire's interest in preservation is its prestige—both externally and internally. Christian IV enjoyed as Duke of Holstein and thus a German prince extraordinary prestige, because he was also simultaneously king of Denmark and Norway and therefore had extraordinary resources at hand. It was this prestige that made Christian IV at one point a serious Protestant bid for the German imperial crown.

In addition, the maintenance of the empire can be justified as a moral duty. The concept of mission played a large role in the colonization of Greenland in the eighteenth century. After 1945, human rights, democracy, and welfare were used as arguments for the massive Danish investments in Greenland. Opponents of the sale of the West Indies also continued to highlight Danish colonial rule as a moral obligation.

The existence and continued maintenance of the empire was originally justified by the principle of historical legitimacy, that is, legal and diplomatic precedence, which ultimately depended on an order created by God. But from the eighteenth century onwards, this kind of argumentation gradually lost its persuasive power. Instead, the principle of popular sovereignty prevailed, as well as a prioritization of human rights. When a Danish empire still exists, because a majority in Greenland and the Faroe Islands wanted to remain as equal partners or see no preferable alternative. Admittedly, when analyzing the Constitution, it can be argued that they cannot immediately resign. However, if a majority in Greenland and the Faroe Islands ultimately decides to leave the Commonwealth, Denmark hardly has any political or morally legitimate right to prevent it. What the Arctic great powers will think and do in this situation one can only guess.

In illuminating the purpose of the empire, one must differentiate between two questions: How was the empire and its purpose portrayed and justified at the time? What do we believe today with our view of history and the hindsight of posterity, was the purpose of the formation and maintenance of the empire? Nowadays, many will probably be inclined to attach greater weight to economic motives than contemporaries of the past did in their own argumentations, although they certainly weren't blind to the economic aspects. Similarly, today one would be reluctant to buy the arguments of moral obligation. Without denying that such a reason could easily have been used to mask ulterior motives, it is likely that morality as an argument actually carried greater confidence at the time.

The various purposes distinguished above are due in part to an artificial boundary, in fact often can't be isolated from each other at all. This may be witnessed in why Frederik VI did everything to avoid giving up Norway prior to 1814. This was partly due to economic reasons: the renunciation of Norway would mean that Norway's population and its business activities would deeply alter the empire's social life. The king's reasons were partly fiscal policy, as relinquishing Norway would deprive the Treasury of significant revenue. They were also partly security policy because with less state revenue, the remaining parts of the empire would have more difficulty in financing an effective defense and protecting its own continued existence. In the same vein, the loss of Norway also made the Danish empire geographically smaller and thus more exposed. And by relinquishing Norway, the Danish empire would also be weakened in terms of prestige. In the case of Norway in 1814—and in numerous other cases—economic, security policy, and prestige purposes were deeply interwoven.

The terms used to describe the empire in its various phases are expressions of the empire's changing purpose and self-perception throughout history. The Oldenburg state (named after the Oldenburg dynasty) was an expression of the fact that the state constituted a conglomeration of different parts that had few factors in common other than being ruled by the same prince. By contrast, to describe the current Danish kingdom the Glücksborg state (after the present Danish dynasty) would seem absurd. The various parts of the kingdom nowadays have far, far more things in common beyond the royal family. A major change in state structure and perception had occurred during the eighteenth century. A union denotes a whole of disparate entities. A distinction can be made here between a personal union, where the personhood of the regent is the only element that holds the non-uniform parts of the empire together, and a real union, where even without a total unification there are still interconnections among the various parts of the empire. These two types of union roughly correspond to the concepts of the conglomerate state and unitary state, respectively. The latter term can also be called united monarchy, but this book reserves that equivalency solely for the period 1814–64, when Danish-German national schisms increasingly tore apart the empire. Today, the status of nation-state signifies that one nationality in the empire is the dominant one and the others are small minorities. As a collective term for all members of such a nation-state with small national minorities, the term *rigsfælleskab* (commonwealth) is usually used today. It signals voluntary cooperation between large and small, yet equal partners, while the term unity of the realm, which is the expression used in the Constitution, sounds more authoritarian.

How Did the Empire Acquire Its Territories?

The following ways in which the Danish empire acquired its territories may be distinguished:

- Military conquest
- Inheritance
- International agreement
- By plebiscite
- Voluntarily surrender to the empire
- Purchase
- Exchange

Since 1520, the expansion of territory through violent military conquest has not played any major role for the Danish empire. It was not due to a lack of will: both during the Scanian War and the Great Nordic War, attempts were made to conquer Scania, Halland, and Blekinge, and Swedish territories in Germany were indeed conquered, yet the empire ultimately had to hand over the acquisition under pressure from the great powers at the conclusion of the war during the peace processes. Nor did the acquisition of the tropical colonies occur with violent conquest: in India and Africa, the Danish presence took place in collaboration with local, indigenous rulers, and the West Indies islands of St. Thomas and St. John were uninhabited when they came under Danish control, and St. Croix was purchased from France. Acquisition of areas by inheritance occurred much more often, so it was by virtue of inheritance rules that Norway and thus also Iceland, Greenland, the Faroe Islands, and the Orkney and Shetland Islands in 1380 joined the Danish Empire. International agreements were another frequent way of acquiring new parts of the empire.

The acquisition of secularized dioceses in northern Germany at the time of Christian IV was based on diplomatic agreements.

Several unilateral Danish military actions against the territories of the Duke of Gottorp failed, but it was ultimately through international agreements that the areas came under Danish control in 1720 and 1773, respectively. As part of such an international agreement, a referendum about the state affiliation could be held. A famous example of this is the plebiscite in Schleswig prior to the "reunification" in 1920; such plebiscites have also been held in Iceland and the Faroe Islands. Some territories voluntarily joined the empire, such as Bornholm in 1658. The previously mentioned acquisitions of the northern German dioceses in the time of Christian IV were also partly voluntary, but also only just partly. On the other hand, it can be said that the current Commonwealth is actually based on the unspoken premise that Greenland and the Faroe Islands have voluntarily chosen to remain in the empire rather than vote to exit. Denmark's (minus Greenland and the Faroe Islands) accession to the EU can also be seen as a similar example of an entity voluntarily giving itself to a larger community with the surrenders of sovereignty that it may entail. This is because the political and economic benefits of joining are estimated to outweigh the disadvantages. Empire elements could also be acquired through purchases such as St. Croix in 1733, just as bribery was part of the acquisition of the northern German dioceses. Territorial exchanges also occurred, such as in 1773 where the counties of Oldenburg-Delmenhorst, which in 1667 joined the empire via inheritance, were exchanged with Russia for the Gottorp parts of Holstein.

How Did Territories Leave the Empire?

The following ways in which territories left the Danish empire may be distinguished:

- Conquest
- International agreement
- Sale
- Plebiscite
- Secession
- Voluntary evacuation by the mother country

While conquest (including forced relinquishment after military defeat) was rare when it came to acquiring parts of the empire, that scenario was far more frequent when territories exited the empire. Scania, Halland, and Blekinge in 1658, Norway in 1814, and the duchies in 1864 are the most striking examples of this. The conclusion of peace after a war is called renunciation by virtue of international agreement, and within this type can be included the return of conquered areas that the empire had to relinquish at the peace negotiations following the Scanian War in 1679 and the Great Nordic War in 1720. Empire parts could be sold, such as Estonia in 1346, and the Orkney and Shetland Islands, which were pledged in 1469, as well as the Danish West Indies in 1917, which was the last time one state sold one territory to another. Characteristic of the areas sold was that they were territories peripheral to the center of the empire and whose historical connection to the empire was often fairly recent, and they were culturally different from the rest of the empire (except the Orkney and Shetland Islands). The sale of Greenland to the USA has been on the table several times, the latest time in 2019, but never materialized. The sale of territories such as Iceland and the Faroe Islands was out of the question, particularly due to their centuries-old historical, linguistic, and cultural connection to the Danish Empire and to Scandinavia in a wider sense. A plebiscite to decide whether the territories should continue to belong to the empire took place in Iceland in 1944 and the Faroe Islands in 1946. The 1916 referendum on the sale of the West Indies, on the other hand, was held only in the home country, not on the three islands themselves. Areas could secede from the empire, significant examples include Sweden's secession from the Kalmar Union in 1523 and Schleswig–Holstein in 1848. Iceland in 1944 could also be included in this category, as Denmark and Iceland were barred from conducting negotiations due to war. Voluntary abandonment of land without external or local internal pressure was a rare occurrence, but did occur, as seen with the Nicobars in 1868.

The Danish empire has generally not been created by predetermined violent conquest. Coincidences have sometimes occurred, such as the union with Norway through inheritance in 1380. Since then, large parts of what was once under the Danish empire have disappeared. This was partly due to conquests because the empire was able to defend itself less and less due to geographic reasons and lack of resources. And partly—and to some extent as a consequence of the foregoing—because the perception of national identity and the right to self-determination as a legitimate basis for state formation and state affiliation gained widespread popularity.

THE DANISH EMPIRE

In conclusion, one can consider which of the three words should be emphasized within the subject of this book: The Danish Empire. Three emphases may be identified, each offering its own context for the history of the empire.

An emphasis may be placed on The Danish Empire, suggesting that the empire has remained the same through the ages. This is both right and wrong, because, again, we have to distinguish between past self-awareness during changing times and our hindsight and understanding long after the occurrence of the events. It is true that the rulers and historians of the empire and other ideologues have viewed it as one unified empire with a history stretching back more than a thousand years. History has always been able to be leveraged to legitimize the current state, and referring to the empire's long traditions has been such an important argument for the rulers of the empire for so long, their sources have been lost to history. All the way back to Harald Bluetooth's Jelling Stone and his move of Gorm the Old from his pagan burial mound to Harald's new church. It was followed by Saxo's writings about a Danish empire that was as old and large as the Roman Empire itself, and which was ruled with a firm but kind hand by King Frode, who was contemporary to Emperor Augustus and did not stand inferior to him in any manner. It has always been important to emphasize the age of the empire, and it is still emphasized as a vital concept today, as seen in Queen Margrethe II's work as an archeologist, and the current Danish passport which carries the Jelling Stone as a symbol.

On the other hand, it is also clear today that the empire has radically changed over time, so it is only possible to talk about one empire if we are talking about a core element, which over time has been associated with many different areas. The earliest empires in the centuries following the birth of Christ we are only able to distinguish the contours of, but they seem to have been oriented towards the Baltic Sea area and Eastern Europe as far south as the Black Sea. In the early Middle Ages, the empire was centered around the North Sea and consisted primarily of England, Norway, and Denmark. The realm was dissolved, and it was subsequently a matter of definition how one perceives that dissolution. It can be argued that the empire was split into two new empires, the western part of which began to orient itself towards Normandy and parts of southern France, and the east towards the Baltic Sea and the Wendish territories of northern Germany. The Kalmar Union was split into two new empires, a Norwegian-Danish-Holstein and a Swedish-Finnish. And so on, likely with an understanding by the people who lived in the empire. No one felt that they were cut off. The people felt that they were creating something new or that they were part of a new empire; it is always the "others" who were left behind.

One can also—and this is what we have done in this book—choose a constant, core point, namely the present territory of the Kingdom of Denmark, and examine its history back through time as part of an empire with varying scope and extent. It is also a true story to tell, for that is how it has been perceived by many of the area's inhabitants through history. But this is only one of the possible narratives that the changeable fate of the empires has authored.

One may also lay emphasis on the second word, the <u>Danish</u> Empire. It is immediately a more dubious case to argue for because it almost bites itself in the tail. We have chosen to deal with the empires over time of which the Danish core countries have been a part. Therefore, it is of course a Danish empire in the sense that a very large part of the empire's population has always spoken Danish, but it lies within the delimitation of the subject. The language has not been important for the empire, which has been able to live well for several hundred years with a parallel Danish and German administration. The language has been important in a cultural sense at the local level and has been used to separate Holsteiners from Schleswig, Danes from Norwegians, Danes from Greenlanders, etc. However, for the empire as such it has always been secondary. This actually also applies to the oldest and most Danish imperial institution of all: the monarchy. In practice, it has several times had to go beyond the empire's own borders to find new kings from, when the reigning king died without heirs, or when he was deposed by force. One of the most Danish kings in the modern conception was Valdemar the Great, but he might as well have become ruler in northern Germany, in Kiev or in England or Sweden. It was ultimately Denmark, which he also had a fully legitimate inheritance claim to, but one cannot really talk about a special Danish continuity within the royal family. It has been broken on several occasions. Since at least the twelfth century, the empire has had a stable, common, Danish symbol in the flag, the Dannebrog. But otherwise, it is characteristic that the empire has existed within a linguistic, ethnic, and legal diversity, whose prevailing existence may often be witnessed in the concluding remarks to many of the Folketing's resolutions, when it states that, "this law does not apply to Greenland and the Faroe Islands."

Finally, one may consider whether emphasis should be placed on the last of the three words, on the Danish Empire. Along the way, we have discussed the many different terms that could have been used to describe the empire at different times, but none of them cover particularly well consistently throughout the two thousand years we have addressed. We have chosen the term empire, originally to force ourselves to think of Danish history as something else and more than just the history of the present-day state named Denmark. We have attempted to look past the typical nation-state perspective, which has otherwise characterized Danish historiography since 1864, because it has omitted all the many territories that have actually belonged to Denmark throughout time. The term empire was ultimately chosen as it is both particular—meaning that one power rules over the whole area—while also flexible so that it may embrace several different cultures. An empire is larger than a nation-state, an empire is a world characterized by diversity, schisms, and fruitful cooperation. Denmark has certainly fit this description throughout history.

CHAPTER 12

The Danish Legacy

MEMORY AND USE OF THE DANISH PAST IN FORMER PARTS OF THE EMPIRE

When working with this book, we realized that Danish history writing after 1864 in general has neglected the areas that formerly had some connection to the Danish empire. But also the memory of the time under Danish rule is still very much alive in the former part of the empire.

To talk about empire will necessarily give associations to conquest, submission, dominance, and not least imperialism and colonialism. There has internationally been a strong criticism in recent years of colonialism and cultural appropriation which has led to also removal of memorials and statues and in general to a sharp condemnation of misdeeds and injustices perpetrated by former colonial rulers. If one wants to use the concept of empire about Denmark, it becomes essential to ask how the "Danish time" is used in public memory in areas formerly under Danish rule. And not least what the Danish time is remembered for.

The different parts of the empire had different political status vis a vis the central government, and it may have influenced present-day memory of the Danish time. Norway was a kingdom in its own right and in personal union with Denmark, but in praxis governed from Copenhagen by a non-Norwegian elite. Holstein was a duchy and part of the German Empire, and the Danish king as Duke of Holstein was subordinate to the German emperor and other central German authorities. Holstein and large parts of Schleswig were linguistically German and thereby a member of a larger German culture. Iceland and the Faroese islands were Norwegian *bilande*, dependencies, but were not called colonies in contrast to the possessions in India, Africa, and

© The Author(s), under exclusive license to Springer Nature Switzerland AG 2022
M. Bregnsbo and K. V. Jensen, *The Rise and Fall of the Danish Empire*, https://doi.org/10.1007/978-3-030-91441-7_12

the West Indies. The difference between *dependencies* and *colonies* is hard to pin down precisely, and may sometimes reflect merely different attitudes rather than an actual difference in practice between the administrators of the empire and those they administered. However, it seems that the association to the dependencies normally are closer and older, and that the cultural and ethnic connections much stronger, while historical, cultural and ethnic relations to the colonies were much weaker. Greenland was originally a dependency to Norway but became later a colony. The historical connection to Scandinavia remained, however, undisputed, even if the "Apostle of Greenland" Hans Egede did not meet any descendants from the old Norse population as he had expected when arriving to Greenland in 1721.

In the Danish public it is a prolific belief that Denmark was a humane imperial or colonial power. Of course, the conditions have differed from time to time and from territory to territory. For example in the West Indian Islands, most of the planters were not Danish at all and there seems no reason to think that they behaved differently in comparison with planters in other colonies. And if one can point out some mitigating circumstances in territories belonging to the Danish empire in comparison with other territories, it is probably due to the weakness and smallness of the Danish empire rather than any special Danish humaneness.

It is often so as for the memory and legacy in a territory having formerly belonged to an empire that in the territory people tend to remember the bad things such as subordination, exploitation, and suppression whereas the colonizing country tends to remember the more positive things such as solidarity, cultural encounters, mutually beneficial inspiration and transnational cooperation. Slavery as practiced in the Danish West Indies and in Guinea can, of course, never be justified still less "romanticized". Yet, as for many other of the territories the truth about the time under the Danish Empire probably often lies somewhere in between.

In the following, we will present some examples of how the Danish time has been referred to and understood in former parts of the Danish empire. What has been used, by whom, and what for?

Postcolonial Criticism on the Virgin Islands

Denmark got a first experience in 1998 of the criticism of colonialism that has since become much stronger and global. It happened in connection with the commemoration of 150 year since the abolition of slavery on present-day US Virgin Islands. A demand was raised that Denmark should officially apologize for slavery in its former colony, and there was a general disappointment that neither Queen Margrethe II nor any minister from the Danish government took part in the commemoration on the islands. The Danish newspaper *Jyllandsposten* quoted (28.6.1998) the chair of the commission for the commemoration for expressing that "... the exploiters and the victors always write history. They don't want any focus on anything unpleasant for themselves." In the debate that followed, Danish historian Uffe Østergaard stated, that "It is extremely stupid not to apologize at this occasion. It costs nothing to give an apology to those who suffered. … especially now when it has become fashion internationally to apologize and admit to have made mistakes" (*Berlingske Tidende* 3.7.1998). The Minister for Foreign affairs, Niels Helveg Petersen, declined however to apologize with the words "I do not find it meaningful that individuals who have not personally been involved in slave trade, should apologize to persons who have not been exposed to it" (*Politiken* 13.7.1998). In spite of a short discussion in parliament, the solution of the Minister was not changed and no apology was given.

The 100-years commemoration in 2017 of the sale of Virgin Islands led to a much sharper and critical tone towards the colonial past, also from the Danish side. Huge research projects on colonialism had gathered source material and published on the Danish rule, and national television showed programs titled "Denmark's Black Conscience". Virgin Islands donated some sculptures of important or symbolic figures in the fight against slavery to Denmark, and in 2018 an artist from Virgin Islands and one from Denmark created a 7-meter high statue of the black woman Mary Thomas who in 1876 led a rebellion on Virgin Islands. The statue was welcomed by many for symbolizing a Danish revision of its past, but also criticized in broad circles for heroizing a convicted criminal and grossly exaggerating the harshness of Danish rule (Nonbo Andersen 2017).

It is difficult to estimate the long-term importance of such episodes, and whether they actually herald a fundamentally new understanding of the Danish past, or whether they will wither away and be classified as simply short-lived political movements. The history as a colonial power in tropic countries has traditionally not had any prominent position on the political agenda in Denmark or on the foreign relations of the country. There are several reasons for this. First of all, the Danish tropical colonies were exclusively trading colonies without any emigration, so very few in the mother country had and family connections of direct relations to the colonies. Many people emigrated from Denmark in the nineteenth century, but primarily to United States and not to any part of the Danish empire. Secondly, the number of those in the tropical colonies who had Danish as their first language, was limited. Those coming from Europe were first of all English speaking, and attempts to create and spread Danish identity were few and fragile. Thirdly, only few Danish speakers remained when Denmark left. The colonies in India and Africa were sold to Great Britain in 1845 and 1850, respectively, the Danish West Indies to United States in 1917, and the Danish times were soon forgotten both in the mother country and in the colonies where new powers were now in command.

Fourthly, the Danish empire had already begun dismantling its tropical, overseas empire at the age that is normally considered the high epoch of imperialism (1870–1914) (e.g. Gollwitzer 1969). Admittedly, the Danish West Indian islands still belonged to Denmark, but created no longer any economic surplus. There had already been discussions about selling the islands, and there were certainly no plans in Denmark for acquiring new colonies in this time of imperialism. The fifth and last reason is that the Danish tropical colonies were actually small both as for size and inhabitants.

The Former Colonies in India and Africa

As for the former colonies in India and Africa the fact that they were very small and sold as early as 1845 and 1850, respectively, and then becoming parts of the British Empire means that the memory of Danish rule here is rather weak. It is, however, not officially forgotten, the more so that buildings from the Danish era can still be seen. Yet, in the former Danish colonies in India, the fact that the areas in question used to be colonies of another European colonial power than Britain is contributing to endowing their present-day inhabitants with a certain, specific, historical identity (Fihl and Venkatachalapathy 2014). The seat of the government and the president of the present-day republic of Ghana in the capital of Accra was till 2013 placed in the former Danish-built fort Christiansborg (today Osu Castle). Yet, voices were raised that it was undignified that those central governmental and political institutions were situated in a building where enslaved African people had used to be awaiting transportation across the Atlantic and in 2013 these governmental and administrative activities moved away and the castle was converted into a museum (Jørgensen 2017).

Greenland

The example from Virgin Islands is perhaps the most heated debate concerning Denmark's past as an empire, but the topic has also surfaced in public debate for other areas. This is the case with Greenland which according to the new constitution of 1953 changed status from being a colony to being a constitutionally fully integrated part of the Danish kingdom. The equality in status was, however, not without limitations in practice. The same year that Greenland ceded to be a colony, a local fishing, and hunting community in Greenland was forcefully moved from Thule to allow the Americans to build Thule Air Base. The Danish government claimed that the movement had been voluntary and that the new location offered fishing and hunting opportunities that were at least as good as the ones around Thule.

What really had happened was only revealed during the 1990s, and the Danish government had to extend an official apology and give compensation to the victims of the forced movement and reduced living conditions. In contrast to the case with Virgin Islands in 1998, some of those who had forcibly been moved and their closest relatives were still alive and had been affected, and they could personally receive compensation from the state.

It was also revealed in the same period, how 22 children from Greenland in 1951 had been forcibly removed from home and sent to Denmark to be educated in Danish and Western civilization so that they could later return to Greenland as a kind of "ambassadors" to civilize their own population. It was an experiment accepted by the government and with the approval of Danish committees of Red Cross and Save the Children, with the best of intentions but with terrible consequences for the children's identity and feeling of belonging. Only much later did the official Denmark react. The Danish prime minister extended an official apology only ion December 8, 2020, to the six of these children that were then still alive and in March 2022 a general, official apology was given.

Moreover, it was also revealed in 1995 how the Danish Prime Minister H.C. Hansen in 1957 secretly had allowed United States to station nuclear weapons on Greenland, directly against the official Danish foreign policy and without informing his government still less parliament. It was a double game against Greenland, but certainly also against the Danish public.

Furthermore, in 1968 an American military plane crashed down on the inland ice. It was loaded with H-bombs which stirred up some commotion in the public. The health dangers was being kept a secret for the clearing up workers (Jensen 2017, 320–371).

As mentioned, partly due to the increasing international, commercial and strategic interests in the Arctic and the increased possibilities of extracting raw materials from the Greenland underground, a growing national, cultural, and political self-consciousness and self-confidence in Greenland can be observed focusing on the treatment of Greenland and the Inuits from Danish side through history. Here, we see an example that the past is very differently remembered in the mother country and in the territory that has been part of the empire. Thus, the Danish public reacted baffledly and uncomprehendingly when Greenland in 2014—with inspiration from South Africa—established a Commission of Reconciliation (Fig. 12.1).

In connection with the international Black Lives Matter-commotion in 2020, on the Greenlandic national day June 21st the prominent statue of Hans Egede in Nuuk was poured over with red paint and "Decolonize" was written upon it. From Greenlandic political side, voices were raised in favor of removing the statue to a museum as it was seen as a symbol of colonialism and suppression. Yet, other Greenlandic voices emphasized Egede as the one who brought Christianity to the Inuits in Greenland. A month later, a referendum within the municipality of Semersooq which Nuuk is part of was arranged. Nine hundred and twenty-four voted in favor of keeping the statue where it was, whereas 600 wanted it removed. However, as the municipality has around 23,000 inhabitants, most people have not considered the matter important at all in spite of the massive press coverage.

Yet, all this said, there are also counter-narratives characterizing Denmark as a relatively humane colonial power that unlike other colonial powers never used forced labor in Greenland or wiped out the native population but let the Inuits keep their own language and culture. In these respects, the fate of

Fig. 12.1 Statue of the Dano-Norwegian missionary to Greenland, Hans Egede in the Greenlandic capital of Nuuk. It is a copy of a statue by August Saabye placed in front of a Copenhagen church and it was paid for by public subscription in 1921 to mark the bicentenary of Egede's arrival in Greenland. In 2020, however, inspired by the Black Lives Matter-movement and the increasing desires that Greenland should have more if not full independence, the statue was drenched with red paint and "Decolonize" was written on the plinth. A Greenlandic member of the Danish parliament demanded that it should be moved to a museum. Yet, there were also Greenlandic voices against this stressing that Egede had introduced Christianity in Greenland. A referendum within the municipality of Somersooq of which Nuuk is a part was held. 921 voted in favour of keeping the statue where it was, 600 wanted to move it. Yet, as Somersooq has around 23,000 inhabitants, the turnout was very low. For now, the statue is remaining where it is, but the tricentenary of Egede in 2021 was a low-key affair. https://commons.wikimedia.org/wiki/File:Egede_nuuk.JPG (*Photo* Svickova)

the Greenlandic Inuits is differing significantly from that of the native population at the American continent. To this, however, could be argued that this was rather due to the weakness and smallness of the Danish empire and to Greenlandic geography and economic conditions following from that.

Recently, a Danish historian has argued that since Greenland has since the tenth century constitutionally and judicially been part of Norway and later Denmark, Greenland has never been a colony but has been a Nordic (Norwegian and later Danish) territory all the time since then. Furthermore, the argument goes, colonialism should be seen as "a permanent and institutionalized exploitative relation," "where arbitrary injustices are being practiced without hesitations" and to be colonialized is "like being subject to a brutal occupation". As these conditions allegedly never existed in Greenland, she was no colony. As for the secretiveness of the Danish government about the US military activities in Greenland and the forced development, these should be seen as effects of American rather than Danish imperialism. And since the Inuits did not immigrate to Greenland till after the Norse settlers had established themselves there, the Inuits should not be considered an indigenous people, so the argument ends (Kjærgaard 2018, 2019). These views have certainly not won general consent or approval but occasioned a heated debate among historians (Rud 2018; Gad 2018; Olesen 2018; Hernæs 2019; Brimnes 2019) and in the public. This discussion is clearly about much more than merely the history of Greenland and how "colony" should be defined.

Norway and Iceland

The past as part of the Danish empire has been of much greater interest in those areas that later became independent states, and it has often been an issue for public debate far outside the circles of professional historians. In Norway, historians and many others have claimed that their country was neglected by Denmark and solely exploited economically. Danish and other historians have argued that the idea of a Norwegian identity separate from the Danish during the seventeenth and eighteenth centuries is anachronistic. It is also a misunderstanding to claim that the main part of tax income from Norway went to Denmark. It actually went to Copenhagen which was the capital of the empire with its central administration and the royal court. It was an exploitation, not of Norway, but of the province in Norway as well as in Denmark to the benefit of the capital. The main part of taxes from Trondheim went to Copenhagen, but so did the taxes from, e.g. Odense, then the second biggest town of the kingdom of Denmark. It also seems that Norway actually was taxed more leniently the Kingdom of Denmark, to avoid disagreements and separatist movements. Norwegian historians on the other hand have argued that there certainly was a specific Norwegian identity already in premodern times, and a feeling of being governed from Denmark. And if taxes were less heavy in Norway than in Denmark, it was simply because Norwegians were relatively poorer, exactly because they had been neglected and exploited by Denmark (Feldbæk 1998; Gustafsson 1999, 2001; Rian 2000; Lunden 1993).

This debate between professional historians was more intensive and more acute than is normally the case in scholarly debates. It was clear that it not only concerned specific historical problems and interpretations, but was part of a contemporary discussion of Norwegian national policy, identity, and social coherence.

In 2014 was commemorated the two hundred years of Norwegian independence from Denmark, and it had been prepared also by common Norwegian-Danish research projects in history. It led to a number of common publications and to a fruitful scholarly dialog which has been influential in changing and modifying former less flexible positions.

Iceland is another independent state which has formerly been part of the Danish empire. An important event for relations between the two countries in the 1960s and 1970s was the discussion of the Icelandic manuscripts with medieval sagas and other historical works. They had been written in Iceland in the high and late Middle Ages and were collected by the Icelandic born professor Arni Magnusson (1663–1730) in the early eighteenth century and donated to Copenhagen University. These manuscripts are of very great importance as Icelandic national heritage, and it was a high prioritized wish of the new independent nation to have the manuscripts transferred to Iceland. It was, however, against the decision stipulated by Arni Magnusson when he donated them to Copenhagen University. The university and many academics therefore argued against handing over them to Iceland, but many in parliament and public were positive towards the idea and argued that it would reflect a progressive, Nordic and anti-imperialistic values. The case was discussed between prime ministers and ministers of foreign affairs which is unusual for matters of culture. Politically, however, it was important because the handing over of the manuscripts was a prerequisite for normalizing the relations between Denmark and this former part of the empire. Debate was heated, and only after a decision in Supreme Court the transference of manuscripts began in 1971. It continued until 1997 because manuscripts were studied and copied in Copenhagen before being sent to Iceland. The entire collection consists of c 3000 manuscripts of which approximately 1400 remained in Copenhagen because they were late copies of important works, or because they were not dealing specifically with Icelandic matters (Davidsdottir 1999). In 2009, the Arni Magnusson's collection was added to UNESCO's *Memory of the World Register.* In 2018, the first manuscript to be transferred in 1971 was part of the main plot in the Icelandic TV crime series *Flateyjargátan,* where a Danish researcher was shot and the Icelandic professor in Nordic philology found the grave of the last pagan priestess in Iceland. It illustrates that the medieval manuscripts are so important and well-known identity marker that they can be used in a TV series without any further explanation. Maybe it also illustrates that it is no longer a heated and contested issue between Denmark and Iceland, if it can be a plot in crime fiction.

The Faroe Islands

The Faroe Islands are still part of the Danish state. Here, complaints—similar to the Greenlandic, Icelandic and Norwegian ones—about former and present Danish financial exploitation, political, and administrative high-handedness and failure of inclusion of the Faroese political public in decisions of concern for the Faroe Islands can sometimes be heard. Voices in favor of full independence are in between being raised, but so are voices in favor of continued belonging to the Danish realm. It has been argued that the Danish Empire has let the Faroese keep their language and culture unlike what has been the case with the Orkney and Shetland Islands that ended up as part of Britain (Kjærgaard 2016 and objections by Sølvará 2016). Yet, no matter the intentions on both sides, the Dano-Faroese relationship cannot help being asymmetrical due to the fact that the Faroe Islands have around 48.000 inhabitants in comparison with 5.6 million inhabitants in Denmark proper.

Schleswig–Holstein

Much national grudge and bitterness existed on both sides being reinforced by World War II and its aftermath. Yet, the agreements of 1955 have gradually contributed to relax tensions and enable conciliation and peaceful coexistence the more so as new generations without any personal recollection of former national antagonisms have grown up. The fact that the German state is officially called Schleswig–Holstein even if the northern parts of Schleswig were transferred to Denmark in 1920 (where they are now known as Southern Jutland) is by no means causing any Dano-German problems still less suspicions of German expansionism or revanchism. Furthermore, the party of the Danish minority in Schleswig–Holstein, the Southern Schleswig Voters' Association (SSW), has for period been represented in the coalition government at state level in Schleswig–Holstein and the party has during the latest local elections had significant gains, even in Holstein where there has never been a Danish minority. The reason for that may be that many German-minded Schleswigers and even some Holsteiners are sympathizing with the liberal Danish educational traditions and furthermore that the party is increasingly staging itself as a regionally based party focusing primarily on regional issues unlike the other, federal-wide parties. The same goes for the party of the German-minded population in Denmark, the Schleswigian party (SP). During the latest local election campaigns, it has increasingly been appealing beyond the German-minded Danish citizens only, presenting itself as regionally based party safeguarding the interests of the whole population in Southern Jutland and characterizing itself as a "bulwark for the Southern Jutish identity". The parties of both minorities in Germany and Denmark resp. are today stressing the fact that Schleswig–Holstein used to be duchies under the king of Denmark as a factor of a special, common history, identity, and cultural heritage of the area transversely to lingual and national dividing lines (Bregnsbo and Jensen 2013).

Vikings

The Viking age with its conquests, plundering, and colonization in present-day England and France only fitted poorly into the narrative about Denmark and Danish values that was formed after 1864. It did fit in much better with the interest for ancient Nordic (in contrast to Germanic) culture. In countries with former Viking presence, there has been a tendency to stress the plundering and devastation of the Viking, while Nordic and Danish history writing since the 1980s focused on trading and peaceful colonization. This picture has become much more nuanced in the decades after 2000, and also violence is now admitted to have been an integrated part of Viking expansion and Viking society. It is perhaps most obvious in Danish museum exhibitions, permanent or temporary. Around 1990, it could be difficult to find a sword in the part of the museum devoted to Vikings, after 2000 slave chains and weapons have become an integrated part of the exhibitions. Vikings have also become a cultural brand within Denmark and claimed to be the explanation of Denmark's success within sea-based logistics, or even that Danes allegedly should be the happiest people in the world. However, Vikings have little importance for modern Denmark's relations to other countries. They lived more than a thousand years ago, and the countries where they expanded and settled are now superpowers compared to present-day Denmark.

The Danish Past—A Positive Memory

Several of the examples till now have not been without criticism of the past as being part of the Danish empire. But there are also examples of a more positive legacy. Estonia was conquered by Danish crusaders in 1219 and sold by the king of Denmark to the Teutonic Order in 1346; the Estonian island of Saaremaa (Ösel) was part of the Danish empire between 1560 and 1645. That was hardly known or at least not noticed in modern Denmark but well remembered in Estonia. It was referred to directly during Estonia's struggle for independency from the Soviet Union around 1990 to stress the country's long historical connections to Denmark and thereby to Western Europe. After the declaration of independence on August 24, 1991, Denmark was the second country to acknowledge Estonia and to establish diplomatic relations. Strong bilateral support from Denmark in the following years strengthened the connections to Estonia. In the twenty-first century, cultural ties have been strong and led to research cooperation and to common publications and exhibitions commemorating the 800 years of the Danish conquest of Tallinn in 1219.

Estonia is the neighbor of mighty Russia and has therefore joined the NATO alliance to safeguard her own security and independence. And as tensions between Russia and the West began to increase during the 2010s, NATO decided in 2016 to send station troops in Estonia, and a large part of those troops are Danish. During the Russian-Ukranian War in 2022 further troops from Denmark and other NATO countries were sent to Estonia.

The three provinces of Scania, Halland, and Blekinge which were ceded to Sweden in 1658 remained Swedish in spite of several Danish attempts to reconquer them. Today this is an accepted fact and of no political importance in Denmark. The three Swedish provinces have, however, often felt to be or at least be treated as peripheral and far away from the Swedish capital of Stockholm while the metropole of Copenhagen is much closer. Sometimes, the Danish past has been referred to when demands for increased regional independency have been ventilated. Historically, it is pointed out, these three landscapes have not been oriented towards north and Stockholm, but towards Copenhagen and further to Western Europe. Often, the brutal and bloody Swedification after 1658 has been mentioned to stress the difference to the rest of Sweden and to construct a specific Scanian identity (e.g. Röndahl 1981).

In 2000, the bridge across the Sound between Denmark and Scania opened. It was intended to connect Copenhagen and Malmö and create a new, dynamic economic center. Trains run several times each hour and make it possible to live in one country and work in the other, and the past as part of the Danish empire has been used very deliberately by politicians to claim the existence of a historical regional identity. But identity is fragile and can change fast. The so-called refuge crisis 2015–2017 and the Covid-19 pandemic in 2020 led to closing of the borders between Denmark and Sweden and renewed passport control. It also led to very critical and sometimes directly xenophobic polemics about the neighbor in media and public debate. Swedish stereotypes about irresponsible Danes and Danish about politically hypercorrect Swedes were immediately mobilized. The historical past is always present, but it can be interpreted and used in very different ways.

Finally, the fact that the memory of the past as a colonial power is rather weak in present-day Denmark may have to do with the following: Today, immigration from countries outside Europe is high on the political agenda in Denmark. But in contrast to what is the case in many other Western European countries, such as Great Britain, France, and the Netherlands, immigrants to Denmark are not coming from former colonies. In Denmark, there is no link between the past as colonial power and the present immigration from outside Europe (Fig. 12.2).

Fig. 12.2 Four Inuits having been abducted from Greenland, painted during a stay in Bergen in Norway in 1654. Afterwards, they were sent to Copenhagen and Gottorp where they became the objects of the inquisitiveness of the two courts and of scientific examinations. Through the seventeenth century, it happened on several occasions that the crew onboard ships in the waters off Greenland kidnapped native Greenlanders for exhibition back home in Denmark. After Hans Egede's colonization of Greenland in 1721, two young Greenlanders were sent to Copenhagen where they among other things demonstrated in rowing kayak as part of a grandiose show. It seems to have been a special feature by the Danish empire that living human beings from its more exotic parts were being publicly exhibited in its center, Copenhagen. As late as early twentieth century, two black children from St. Croix were being shown publicly at a large-scale colonial exhibition in the Copenhagen Tivoli. https://commons.wikimedia.org/wiki/File:Four_West_Greenlanders._Oil_painting_122_x_168_cm._Unknown_Artist._Bergen,_Norway,_1654.jpg (National Museum of Denmark: Public domain)

References

Berlingske Tidende. 1998. July 3.
Bregnsbo, Michael, and Kurt Villads Jensen. 2013. Schleswig as a Contested Place. In *Anne Magnussen, Peter Seeberg, Kirstine Sinclair, and Nils Arne Sørense*, ed. Contested Places, 155–178. Odense: University Press of Southern Denmark Press.
Brimnes, Niels. 2019. Grønland og den kolonihistoriske analyse. *TEMP. Tidsskrift for Historie* 19: 206–212.
Davidsdottir, Sigrun. 1999. *Håndskriftssagens saga*. Odense: Syddansk Universitetsforlag.
Feldbæk, Ole. 1998. *Nærhed og adskillelse 1720–1814. Danmark-Norge 1380–1814*, vol. IV. Oslo: Universitetsforlaget.
Fihl, Esther, and A.R. Venkatachalapathy, eds. 2014. *Beyond Tranquebar: Grappling Across Cultural Borders in South India*. New Delhi: Orient Black Swan.
Gad, Ulrik Pram. 2018. Thorkild Kjærgaards bjørnetjeneste til Rigsfællesskabet. *TEMP. Tidsskrift for Historie* 17: 153–158.
Gollwitzer, Heinz. 1969. *Europe in the Age of Imperialism 1880–1914*. London: Thames and Hudson.
Gustafsson, Harald. 1999. Reflexioner över Danmark-Norges historia. *Historisk tidskrift* (Norway): 4.
Gustafsson, Harald. 2001. Identiteter i Danmark-Norge. Reflexioner över Øystein Rians refleksjoner över mina reflexioner. *Historisk tidskrift* (Norway): 2.
Henningsen, Anne Folke. 2017. Kapitel 11: Koloniernes spor. In *Danmark. En kolonimagt*, ed. Mikkel Venborg Petersen, 400–445. Copenhagen: Gad.
Hernæs, Per Oluf. 2019. Når et ideologisk korstog slører dømmekraften. *TEMP. Tidsskrift for historie* 19: 203–205.
Jensen, Einar Lund. 2017. Kapitel 7: Nyordning og modernisering 1950–79. In *Grønland. Den arktiske koloni*, ed. Hans Christian Gulløv, 320–371. Copenhagen: Gad.
Jørgensen, Anne Mette. 2017. Kapitel 12: Spor i ord og mursten. In *Vestafrika. Forterne på Guldkysten*, ed. Per Oluf Hernæs, 354–367. Copenhagen, Gad.
Jyllandsposten. 1998. June 28.
Kjærgaard, Thorkild. 2016. Svar til Hans Andrias Sølvará. *TEMP. Tidsskrift for Historie* 13: 235–239.
Kjærgaard, Thorkild. 2018. Kolonihistorie uden koloni. Om grønlandsbindet i den nye kolonihistorie. *TEMP. Tidsskrift for Historie* 17: 138–144.
Kjærgaard, Thorkild. 2019. Duplik om grønlandsbindet i den nye danske kolonihistorie. *TEMP. Tidsskrift for Historie* 19: 186–189.
Lunden, Kåre. 1993. *Nasjon eller union? Refleksjonar og røynsler*. Oslo: Samlaget.
Nonbo Andersen, Astrid. 2017. *Ingen undskyldning. Erindringer om Dansk Vestindien og kravet om erstatninger*. Copenhagen: Gyldendal.
Olesen, Simon Mølholm. 2018. En løs kanon på gletsjeren. *TEMP. Tidsskrift for Historie* 17: 159–164.
Politiken. 1998. July 13.
Rian, Øystein. 2000. Danmark-Norges historie. Refleksjoner over Harald Gustafssons refleksjoner. *Historisk tidskrift* (Norway) 80: 3, 376–384.
Röndahl, Uno. 1981. *Skåneland utan förskoning. Om kungahusens og den svenska överklassens folkdråp och kulturskövling i Skåneland. En studie i omnationaliseringens tragik*. Karlshamn: Lagerblad.

Rud, Søren. 2018. Mod bedre vidende. Grønland og politisk-ideologisk historieskrivning. *TEMP. Tidsskrift for Historie* 17: 145–152.

Sølvará, Hans Andrias. 2016. De britiske engle. Rigsfællesskabet – mellem dansk afmagt og britisk storpolitik. *TEMP. Tidsskrift for Historie* 13: 212–234.

General Literature in English

Due to the topic's chronological, thematic, and geographic scope, there is no end to how much specialized literature for good reason could have been included. Therefore, we must settle for a very limited selection. Furthermore, much of the relevant literature is in Danish or other Scandinavian languages only. In general, we have concentrated on English language titles and have referenced Denmark's broad historical works as well as broad representations of the individual territory's history. But otherwise, there are limited references that could be termed as specialized literature such as monographs and articles on the topics within the book's individual chapters.

General Histories of Denmark

Jespersen, Knud J.V. 2017. *A History of Denmark*, 3rd ed. London and New York.
Jones, W. Glyn. 1970. *Denmark*. London.

General Introductions to Parts of the Empire Through Time

Bagge, Sverre. 2014. *Cross and Scepter: The Rise of the Scandinavian Kingdoms from the Vikings to the Reformation*. Princeton.
Berend, Nora. 2007. *Christianization and the Rise of Christian Monarchy: Scandinavia, Central Europe and Rus' c. 900–1200*. Cambridge.
Bregnsbo, Michael, and Kurt Villads Jensen (eds.). 2016. *Schleswig Holstein—Contested Region(s) Through History*. Odense.
Danielsen, Rolf, Ståle Dyrvik, Tore Grønlie, Knut Helle, and Edgar Hovland. 1995. *Norway: A History from the Vikings to Our Own Times*. Oslo.
Denmark and The New North Atlantic. Narratives and Memories in a Former Empire. 2020. Ed. Kirsten Thisted and Ann-Sofie N. Gremaud. Aarhus.
Fihl, Esther, and A.R. Venkatachalapathy (eds.). 2014. *Beyond Tranquebar: Grappling Across Cultural Borders*. New Delhi.
Helle, Knut, E. I. Kouri, Torkel Jansson, and Jens E. Olesen (eds.) 2003–2016. *Cambridge History of Scandinavia*, 1–2. Cambridge.
Karlsson, Gunnar. 2020. *Iceland's 1100 Years: History of a Marginal Society*, 2nd ed. London.

Libæk, Ivar, and Øivind Stenersen. 1999. *History of Norway*. Oslo.
Sawyer, Birgit, and Peter Sawyer. 1993. *Medieval Scandinavia: From Conversion to Reformation, circa 800–1500*. University of Minnesota Press.
Tamm, Marek, Linda Kaljundi, and Carsten Selch Jensen (eds.). 2016. *Crusading and Chronicle Writing on the Medieval Baltic Frontier: A Companion to the Chronicle of Henry of Livonia*. London.

English Language Journals

Scandinavian Economic History Review. Published by The Scandinavian Society for Economic and Social History and Historical Geography.
Scandinavian Journal of History. Published under the Auspices of the Historical Associations of Denmark, Finland, Norway and Sweden.

Chapter 1: Introduction

Bakardjieva Engelbrekt, A., et al. (eds.). 2020. *The European Union and the Return of the Nation State: Interdisciplinary European Studies*. London: Palgrave Macmillan.
Delanty, G. 2021. Return of the Nation-State? De-Europeanisation and the Limits of Neo-Nationalism. *Journal of Contemporary European Research* 17: 102–115.
Fibiger Bang, Peter et al. (eds.). 2020. *The Oxford Worlds History of Empire. Vol 1: The Imperial Experience*. Oxford: University Press.
Gibbons, Edward. 1776–1789. *Decline and Fall of the Roman Empire*, vols. 1–6 and many later editions. London.
Muldoon, James. 1999. *Empire and Order: The Concept of Empire, 800–1800*. Basingstoke.
The Oxford World History of Empire. 2020. Ed. Peter Fibiger Bang, C.A. Bayly, and Walter Scheidel, vols. 1–2. Oxford.
Pagden, Anthony. 2001. *Peoples and Empires: A Short History of European Migration, Exploration, and Conquest from Greece to the Present*. New York.
Wolmersley, David. 2002. *Gibbon and the 'Watchmen of the Holy City': The Historian and His Reputation, 1776–1815*. Oxford.

Chapter 2: The Himlingøje Empire

Fischer, Svante. 2005. *Roman Imperialism and Runic Literacy. The Westernization of Northern Europe (150–800 AD)*. Uppsala.
Jørgensen, Lars. 2009. Pre-Christian Cult at Aristocratic Residences and Settlement Complexes in Southern Scandinavia in the 3rd–10th Centuries AD. In *Glaube, Kult und Herrschaft. Phänomene des Religiösen im 1. Jahrtausend n. Chr. in Mittel- und Nordeuropa. Akten des 59. Internationalen Sachsensymposiums*, ed. U. von Freeden, H. Friesinger, E. Wamers, 329–354. Bonn.
Jørgensen, Lars, Birger Storgaard, and Lone Gebaruer Thomsen (eds.). 2003. *The Spoils of Victory: The North in the Shadow of the Roman Empire*. Copenhagen.
Price, T. Douglas. 2015. *Ancient Scandinavia: An Archaeological History from the First Humans to the Vikings*. Oxford: University Press.
Randsborg, Klavs. 2007. Beyond the Roman Empire: Archaeological Discoveries in Gudme on Funen, Denmark. *Oxford Journal of Archaeology* 9: 355–366.

Sørensen, Palle Østergaard. 2010. The Political and Religious Centre at Gudme on Funen in the Late Roman and Germanic Iron Ages—Settlement and Central Halls. *Siedlungs- Und Küstenforschung Im Südlichen Nordseegebiet* 33: 225–236.
Storgaard, Birger. 2001. Himlingøje—Barbarian Empire or Roman Implantation? In *Military Aspects of the Aristocracy in Barbaricum in the Roman and Early Migration Periods*, ed. Birger Storgaard, 95–111. Copenhagen.

Chapter 3: The Christian Empire of the North Sea

Bjerg, Line, et al. (eds.). 2013. *From Goths to Varangians. Communication and Cultural Exchange Between the Baltic and the Black Sea*. Aarhus: University Press.
Bolton, Timothy. 2009. *The Empire of Cnut the Great: Conquest and the Consolidation of Power in Northern Europe in the Early Eleventh Century*. Leiden.
Brink, Stefan, and Neil Price (eds.). 2008. *The Viking World*. Abingdon.
Crumlin Pedersen, Ole. 2010. *Archaeology and the Sea in Scandinavia and Britain: A Personal Account*. Roskilde.
Pedersen, Anne. 2014. *Dead Warriors in Living Memory: A Study of Weapon and Equestrian Burials in Viking-Age Denmark, AD 800–1000*. Copenhagen.
Price, T. Douglas. 2015. *Ancient Scandinavia. An Archaeological History from the First Humans to the Vikings*. Oxford: University Press.
Randsborg, Klavs. 2008. King's Jelling. Gorm & Thyra's Palace, Harald's Monument & Grave—Svend's Cathedral. *Acta Archaeologica* 79: 1–23.
Sawyer, Peter H. (ed.). 1997. *The Oxford Illustrated History of the Vikings*. Oxford.

Chapter 4: Crusading Empires in the Baltic

Andersen, Per. 2011. *Legal Procedure and Practice in Medieval Denmark*. Leiden.
Bysted, Ane, et al. 2012. *Jerusalem in the North: Denmark and the Baltic Crusades, 1100–1552*. Turnhout.
Fighting for the Faith—The Many Crusades. 2018. Ed. Kurt Villads Jensen, Carsten Selch Jensen, Janus Møller Jensen. Stockholm.
Gustafsson, Harald. 2017. The Forgotten Union. *Scandinavian Journal of History* 42: 560–582.
Hybel, Nils, and Bjørn Poulsen. 2007. *The Danish Resources c. 1000–1550: Growth and Recession*. Leiden.
Jensen, Janus Møller. 2007. *Denmark and the Crusades, 1400–1650*. Leiden.
Jensen, Kurt Villads. 2017. *Crusading at the Edges of Europe: Denmark and Portugal c. 1000–c. 1250*. London: Routledge.
Skyum-Nielsen, Niels. 1981. Estonia Under Danish Rule. In *Danish Medieval History: New Currents*, ed. Niels Skyum-Nielsen and Niels Lud, 112–135. Copenhagen.

Chapter 5: The Union Empire

Etting, Vivian. 2004. *Queen Margrete I, 1353–1412, and the Founding of the Nordic Union*. Brill.
Gustafsson, Harald. 2006. A State That Failed? *Scandinavian Journal of History* 32: 205–220.

Imsen, Steinar. 2007. The Union of Calmar: Northern Great Power or Northern German Outpost? In *Politics and Reformations: Communities, Polities, Nations, and Empires*, ed. Christopher Ocker, 471–490. Leiden.

Imsen, Steiner (ed.). 2014. *Rex Insularum: The King of Norway and His Skattlands as a Political System c. 1260–c. 1450*. Bergen.

Jahnke, Carsten. 2014. Two Journeys and One University: King Christian I and Queen Dorothea's Journeys to Rome and the Foundation of the University of Copenhagen. In *Denmark and Europe in the Middle Ages, c. 1000–1525: Essays in Honour of Professor Michael H. Gelting*, ed. Kerstin Hundahl, Lars Kjær, and Niels Lund, 139–153. Farnhem.

Riis, Thomas. 1988. *Should Auld Acquaintance Be Forgot. Scottish-Danish Relations c 1450–1707*, vols. 1–2. Odense.

CHAPTER 6: THE PRINCELY STATE: THE DECLINE OF A BALTIC POWER, 1536–1720

Frost, Robert I. 2000. *The Northern Wars: War, State and Society in Northeastern Europe, 1558–1721*. London.

Gøbel, Erik. 2002. *A Guide to the Sources for the History of the Danish West Indies (U.S. Virgin Islands), 1671–1917*. Odense.

Gøbel, Erik. 2016. *The Danish Slave Trade and Its Abolition*. Leiden and Boston.

Gunnarsson, Gísli. 1983. *Monopoly Trade and Economic Stagnation: Studies in the Foreign Trade of Iceland 1602–1787*. Lund.

Gustafsson, Harald. 1994. Conglomerates or Unitary States. Integration Processes in Early Modern Denmark-Norway and Sweden. In *Föderationsmodelle und Unionsstrukturen. Über Staatenverbindungen in der frühen Neuzeit vom 15. bis 18. Jahrhundert, Wiener Beiträge zur Geschichte der Neuzeit*, 21, ed. Thomas Fröschl. Vienna and Munich.

Hall, Neville. 1992. *Slave Society in the Danish West Indies*. Jamaica.

Highfield, Arnold R., and George F. Tyson. 1994. *Slavery in the Danish West Indies: A Bibliography*. St. Croix.

Jensen, Niklas Thode, and Gunvor Simonsen. 2016. Introduction: The Historiography of Slavery in the Danish-Norwegian West Indies, c. 1950–2016. *Scandinavian Journal of History* 41 (4–5): 475–494.

Jespersen, Leon (ed.). 2000. *A Revolution from Above? The Power State of the 16th and 17th Century Scandinavia*. Odense.

Justesen, Ole (ed.). 2005. *Danish Sources for the History of Ghana 1657–1754*, vols. 1–2. Copenhagen.

Kirby, David. 1990. *Northern Europe in the Early Modern Period: The Baltic World, 1492–1772*. London and New York.

Lockhart, Paul Douglas. 1996. *Denmark in the Thirty Years' War, 1618–1648: King Christian IV and the Decline of the Oldenburg State*. Selinsgrove.

Lockhart, Paul Douglas. 2007. *Denmark 1513–1660: The Rise and Decline of a Renaissance Monarchy*. Oxford.

Maarbjerg, John P. 1995. *Scandinavia in the European World Economy, ca. 1570–1625*. New York.

Naum, Magdalena, and Jonas Nordin (eds.). 2013. *Scandinavian Colonialism and the Rise of Modernity: Small Time Agents in a Global Arena*. New York.

Olafsson, Jon. 1998. *Memoirs of Jon Olafsson, Icelander and Traveller to India 1622–1625, as Written by Himself 1661 with the Story of Mads Rasmussen, Chaplain on the Perlen, 1623–1626*. Cambridge.
Olafsson, Jon. 2010. *The Life of the Icelander Jón Olafssón, Traveller to India. Volume II: Memoirs of Jon Olafsson: Icelander and Traveller to India 1622-1625, as Written by Himself 1661*. Surrey.
Rystad, Göran, Klaus-R. Böhme, and Wilhelm H. Carlgren (eds.). 1994–1995. *In Quest of Trade and Security: The Baltic in Power Politics, 1500–1990*, I–II. Lund.
Seesko, Per, Louise Nyholm Kallestrup, and Lars Bisgaard (eds.). 2019. *The Dissolution of the Monasteries: The Case of Denmark in a Regional Perspective*. Odense.
Westergaard, Waldemar. 1917. *The Danish West Indies Under Company Rule*. New York.
www.virgin-islands-history.org.

Chapter 7: From the Conglomerate State to the Unitary State 1720–1814

Barton, H. Arnold. 1986. *Scandinavia in the Revolutionary Era, 1760–1815*. Minneapolis.
Feldbæk, Ole. 1969. *India Trade Under Danish Flag 1772–1808: European Enterprise and Anglo-Indian Remittance and Trade*. Lund.
Feldbæk, Ole. 1980. *Denmark and the Armed Neutrality 1800–1801: Small Power Policy in a World War*. Copenhagen.
Feldbæk, Ole. 2002. *The Battle of Copenhagen, 1801: Nelson and the Danes*. London.
Glenthøj, Rasmus, and Morten Nordhagen Ottosen. 2014. *Experiences of War and Nationality in Denmark and Norway, 1807–1815*. London and New York.
Gunnarsson, Gísli. 1983. *Monopoly Trade and Economic Stagnation: Studies in the Foreign Trade of Iceland 1602–1787*. Lund.
Gustafsson, Harald. 1994. *Political Interaction in the Old Regime: Central Power and Local Society in the Eighteenth-Century Nordic States*. Lund.
Gustafsson, Harald. 1994. Conglomerates or Unitary States: Integration Processes in Early Modern Denmark-Norway and Sweden. In Thomas Fröschl (ed.). *Föderationsmodelle und Unionsstrukturen. Über Staatenverbindungen in der frühen Neuzeit vom 15. bis 18. Jahrhundert*, Wiener Beiträge zur Geschichte der Neuzeit 21. Vienna and Munich.
Hernæs, Per. 1995. *Slaves, Danes, and African Coast Society: The Danish Slave Trade from West Africa and Afro-Danish Relations on the Eighteenth-Century Gold Coast*. Trondheim.
Jensen, Niklas Thode, and Gunvor Simonsen. 2016. Introduction: The Historiography of Slavery in the Danish-Norwegian West Indies, c. 1950–2016. *Scandinavian Journal of History* 41 (4–5): 475–494.
Justesen, Ole (ed.). 2005. *Danish Sources for the History of Ghana 1657–1754*, vols. 1–2. Copenhagen.
Kea, R.A. 2012. *A Cultural and Social History of Ghana from the Seventeenth to the Nineteenth Century: The Gold Coast in the Age of Trans-Atlantic Slave Trade*, vols. 1–2. Lewiston.
Kirby, David. 1990. *Northern Europe in the early Modern Period: The Baltic World, 1492–1772*. London and New York.

Rystad, Göran, Klaus-R. Böhme, and Wilhelm H. Carlgren (eds.). 1994–1995. *In Quest of Trade and Security: The Baltic in Power Politics, 1500–1990*, I–I. Lund.
West, John F. 1985. *The History of the Faroe Islands, 1709–1816*. Copenhagen.

Chapter 8: 1814–1864—From Unitary Monarchy to Nation State

Carr, William. 1963. *Schleswig-Holstein, 1815–1848: A Study in National Conflict.* Manchester.
Hermansson, Birgir. 2005. *Understanding Nationalism: Studies in Icelandic Nationalism 1800–2000.* Stockholm.
Jensen, Niklas Thode, and Gunvor Simonsen. 2016. Introduction: The Historiography of Slavery in the Danish-Norwegian West Indies, c. 1950–2016. *Scandinavian Journal of History* 41 (4–5): 475–494.
Petterson, Christina. 2014. *The Missionary, the Cathechist and the Hunter: Foucault, Protestantism and Colonialism.* Leiden.
Rystad, Göran, Klaus-R. Böhme, and Wilhelm H. Carlgren (eds.). 1994–1995. *In Quest of Trade and Security: The Baltic in Power Politics, 1500–1990* I–II. Lund.
Sandiford, Keith A.P. 1975. *Great Britain and the Schleswig-Holstein Question, 1848–1864.* Toronto.

Chapter 9: The Empire After 1864

Giltner, Philip. 1998. *"In The Friendliest Manner": German-Danish Economic Cooperation During the Nazi Occupation of 1940–1945.* New York.
Kaarsted, Tage. 1979. *Denmark and Great Britain, 1914–20.* Odense.
Lidegaard, Bo. 2009. *A Short History of Denmark in the 20th Century.* Copenhagen.
Nissen, Henrik S. (ed.). 1983. *Scandinavia During the Second World War.* Minneapolis.
Petterson, Christina. 2014. *The Missionary, the Cathechist and the Hunter: Foucault, Protestantism and Colonialism.* Leiden.
Rud, Søren. 2017. *Colonialism in Greenland: Tradition, Governance and Legacy.* London and New York, 2017.
Rystad, Göran, Klaus-R. Böhme, and Wilhelm H. Carlgren (eds.). 1994–1995. *In Quest of Trade and Security: The Baltic in Power Politics, 1500–1990* I–II. Lund.
Sølvará, Hans Andrias. 2016. *The Rise of the Faroese Separatism: Danish-Faroese Relations from 1906–1925 and the Radicalization of the NATIONAL And Home Rule Question, Annales Societas Scientiarum Færoensis* Supplementum LXVI. Tórshavn.
Sørensen, Axel Kjær. 2007. *Denmark-Greenland in the Twentieth Century.* Copenhagen.
Thaler, Peter. 2009. *Of Mind and Matter: The Duality of National Identity in the German-Danish Borderlands.* West Lafayette.
West, John F. 1972a. *Faroe: The Emergence of a Nation.* London.

Chapter 10: The Empire During the Cold War, International Integration and the Welfare State

Christiansen, Niels Finn, Niels Edling, Per Haave, and Klaus Petersen (eds.). 2006. *The Nordic Welfare Model: A Historical Reappraisal.* Copenhagen.

Danish Foreign Policy Yearbook, published by the Danish Institute for International Studies (DIIS).
Einhorn, Eric and John Logue. 1989. *Modern Welfare States: Policies in Social Democratic Scandinavia*. New York.
Lidegaard, Bo. 2009. *A Short History of Denmark in the 20th Century*. Copenhagen.
Rud, Søren. 2017. *Colonialism in Greenland. Tradition, Governance and Legacy*. London and New York.
Rystad, Göran, Klaus-R. Böhme, and Wilhelm H. Carlgren (eds.). 1994–1995. *In Quest of Trade and Security: The Baltic in Power Politics, 1500–1990* I-II. Lund.
Sølvará, Hans Andrias. 2016. *The Rise of the Faroese Separatism. Danish-Faroese Relations from 1906–1825 and the Radicalization of the National and Home Rule Question, Annales Societas Scientiarum Færoensis* Supplementum LXVI. Tórshavn.
Sørensen, Axel Kjær. 2007. *Denmark-Greenland in the Twentieth Century*. Copenhagen.

Chapter 12: The Legacy

Fihl, Esther, and A.R. Venkatachalapathy (eds.). 2014. *Beyond Tranquebar: Grappling Across Cultural Borders*. New Delhi.
Hermansson, Birgir. 2005. *Understanding Nationalism: Studies in Icelandic Nationalism 1800–2000*. Stockholm.
Petterson, Christina. 2014. *The Missionary, the Cathechist and the Hunter: Foucault, Protestantism and Colonialism*. Leiden, 2014b.
Rud, Søren. 2017. *Colonialism in Greenland. Tradition, Governance and Legacy*. London and New York.
Thaler, Peter. 2009. *Of Mind and Matter: The Duality of National Identity in the German-Danish Borderlands*. West Lafayette.
Thisted, Kirsten, and Ann-Sofie N. Gremaud (eds.). 2020. *Denmark and the New North Atlantic: Narratives and Memories in a Former Empire*. Aarhus.
West, John F. 1972. *Faroe: The Emergence of a Nation*. London.

Index of Concept

A

Absolutism, 138, 139, 142, 145, 148, 150, 157, 158, 179, 181, 183, 185–187, 189
Administrative reforms, 72, 150, 153, 158
Adscription, 147
Advisory assemblies of estates, 175
Agrarian/agricultural reforms, 158, 163
Agriculture, 17, 117, 147, 151, 155, 174, 178, 206, 208
Althing (Icelandic parliament), 179, 201, 202, 215
American War of Independence (1776–1783), 148
amir malikun, 4
Aristocracy, 92–94, 99, 100, 103, 111, 114
Aristocratic Corporation (*Ritterschaft*), 117, 138, 157, 158, 173, 174, 181, 182
Asiatic Company, Danish, 160
Austrian War of Succession (1740–1748), 148
autokrator, 4, 35
Autonomy, 187, 188, 201, 202, 215, 222, 229–231

B

Bamboo, 160
basileus, 35, 41

Beowulf-epos, 29
Bible, 16, 38, 65, 121
Black Lives Matter, 247, 248
Black population, 207
Bornhøved, Battle at 1227, 69
Bourgeoisie, 109, 163, 168, 176
Bouvines, Battle at 1214, 67
Brunkeberg, Battle at 1471, 105

C

Cabinet responsibility
Catholicism, 119, 121
CDU (German political party), 221
Charles Gustavus Wars (1657–1658 & 1658–1660), 136
Child mortality, 227
Church of Holy Sepulchre, Jerusalem, 36
Civil war, 59, 84, 103, 182, 184, 185, 190, 196
Code of Jutland, 72, 73, 94
Cold War (ca. 1945–1989), 216, 219, 221, 224, 225, 230, 236
Colonial Act of 1906, 206
Colony/colonialism, 2, 3, 6, 61, 124, 127–129, 146, 159–161, 164, 166, 168, 171, 174, 176, 179, 188, 203, 208, 215, 224, 226, 227, 230, 234–236, 238, 243–249, 253, 254
Commemoration, 244, 245
Commercial policy, 122–124

Commonwealth
Community of the Realm, 228
Composite state, 115
Conglomerate state, 8, 115, 117, 120, 121, 145, 163, 238
Conquest, 5, 26, 31, 32, 36, 43, 51, 54, 55, 57, 58, 61–66, 70, 72, 74, 77, 86, 94, 129–132, 141, 142, 148, 161, 194, 238–240, 243, 252
Conscription, 74, 152, 175, 183
Conservative Party, 189, 200, 202, 206–209
Constituent Assembly (1848–1849), 187
Constitution/constitutionalism, 8, 76, 78, 103, 116, 117, 138, 140, 173–177, 181–183, 185–187, 189–193, 196, 200–202, 207, 209, 226, 228, 230, 237, 238, 246
Continental blockade, 164, 165, 168
Copenhagen-Bonn Declarations of 1955, 221
Copper, 18, 56, 122
Coronation, 68, 93, 98, 100
Coronation Charter, 93
Council of the Realm (*Rigsraadet*), 190
Covid-19 pandemic, 8, 253
Crusade, 51–53, 55, 56, 58–60, 62, 63, 65–70, 74–77, 79, 80, 86, 87, 95–98, 102–105, 107, 108, 110
Customs, 44, 64, 72–74, 93, 99, 101, 105, 125, 128, 129, 134, 135, 151, 153, 185
Customs of the Sound, 99, 135

D

Danish Chancellery, 153
Danish Law Code of 1683, 145
Dannebrog, 111, 148, 163, 166, 174, 180, 208, 242
Defense, 17, 65, 104, 111, 121, 124, 132, 134, 135, 141, 167, 186, 189, 192, 193, 196, 214, 216, 219, 222, 224, 225, 229, 236, 237
Democracy, 6, 8, 183, 185, 211, 236
Dependency, 212, 244
Diet, German (*Reichstag*), 104, 105, 134

Dioceses, 35, 47, 78, 126, 139, 166, 236, 239
Distress, Years of (Norway 1807–1814), 167
Domain state, 121, 122
Dynastic state, 115
Dynasty, 13, 15, 21, 22, 26, 38, 42, 116, 180, 186, 237

E

East India Company, Danish, 124, 160
EC, European Community, 227, 228
Ejder policy/politics, 172, 177, 185, 189, 191–193
Emigration, 245
Emperor's War (1625–1629), 132, 133
Enclosure, 27
Enslavement, 124, 146, 161, 204, 205, 234, 246
Estates, 29, 79, 83, 92, 101, 103, 110, 116, 117, 136, 138, 147, 150, 158, 173–179, 181, 185–187, 189–191
Estonians, 68, 71, 74, 130, 131, 252
Exchange Treaty of 1773, 150

F

Falköping, Battle at 1389, 92
Federal Republic of Germany (FRD), 221
Federal state, 200, 202
Federation, Law of (1918), 214
Fiscal-military state, 121, 122, 142
Fishing, 71, 92, 98, 101, 110, 116, 124, 151, 154, 211, 212, 227, 228, 234, 246
Fleet
Flourishing Trade Period (second half of the 18th century), 148, 154, 162
Folketing
Fotevik, battle at 1134, 57
French Revolutionary Wars (1792–1802), 148, 163, 173

G

Gældker, 80, 95
German Chancellery, 153, 158
Gog and Magog, 106

Golden Bull, 66, 69, 82
Grain, 74, 83, 99, 128, 130, 151, 152, 164, 167, 168, 208, 234, 235
Greenland Government Act 1925, 211
Gunpowder, 122, 135, 234
Gyldenløve's War

H
Hansa, 96
Heath Corporation, Danish, 235
Helstat
Historical legitimism, 186
Højre
Home rule, 201, 222, 223, 227–229

I
Immigration, 99, 229, 253
imperator, 4, 7, 35, 41
Independence, 2, 19, 31, 55, 80, 85, 110, 153, 188, 202, 211, 215, 222, 229, 230, 248, 249, 251, 252
Industry/industrialization, 99, 151, 158, 178, 196, 200, 208, 226, 227, 231
Inuits, 156, 212, 247–249, 254
Iron, 18, 27, 56, 73, 112, 122, 130, 151, 235

J
January Announcement (1852), 189
January Protocol (1848), 181
Jelling Rune Stone, 34, 36
July Ordinance (1854), 189
July Revolution (1830), 174
Jutlandian Law Code (*Jyske Lov*), 116

K
Kalmar Union, 3, 8, 91, 93, 95, 96, 99–102, 104, 105, 107, 108, 111, 113, 129, 131, 132, 234, 240, 241
Kalmar War (1611–1613), 125, 132, 134
khawan khan, 4
Konstanz, Church council at, 1414–1418, 97

L
Lagting (Faroese parliament), 119, 154, 178, 214, 215, 222
Landowner, 74, 147, 155, 158, 159, 162, 175, 235
Landsting
Landtag (German parliament), 221
Language, 4, 30, 33, 34, 46, 53, 61, 63, 71, 85, 97, 107, 116, 121, 145, 153, 162, 163, 172, 176–179, 185, 190, 192, 196, 199, 204, 207, 211, 222, 241, 245, 247, 251, 257
Language Ordinances (1850s), 190
Lawman (*lagmand*), Faroese public servant, 154, 178
Legacy, 25, 31, 45, 58, 78, 188, 200, 244, 252
Lething, naval defence system, 37, 74
Liberal/liberalism, 173–178, 181–184, 188–190, 192, 194, 195, 200–204, 206, 207, 209, 222, 229, 251
Liberal Party, 200, 202, 207–209, 220
Literacy, 121, 154
Lithuanians, 74, 79, 80, 87, 97, 100
Lombards, 25
Lutheranism, 109, 119–121, 126

M
Magyars, 35
Manbres, 104
Manuscripts, Icelandic, 250
Marcomanni, 13
Memory, 22, 53, 243, 244, 246, 252, 253
Mercantilism, 122, 123, 125, 235
Merovingians, 25
Middle class, 162, 163, 168, 190, 191
Military state, 121, 122, 142
Mongols, 80
Monopoly, 122–124, 138, 151, 152, 154–156, 159, 160, 178, 179, 187, 203, 211, 224, 226, 235

N
Napoleonic Wars (1803–1815), 70, 159, 163, 164, 166–168, 173, 174, 179, 213

National liberal/national liberalism, 177, 178, 181, 182, 189–192, 195
Nation, nationalism, national identity, 2–4, 6, 11, 25, 65, 70, 84, 85, 103, 153, 159, 162, 173, 186, 193, 202, 207, 215, 230, 240, 250
NATO, 216, 219, 221, 224, 225, 230, 236, 252
Naturalization Act of 1776, 162
Navy, 37, 55, 74, 133, 165
Neutrality, 134, 148, 163, 164, 199, 206, 234
Nobility, 73, 83, 84, 100, 101, 105, 109, 111–114, 116–119, 121, 123, 132, 138, 139, 150, 157
Nordic Seven Years' War (1563–1570), 131, 132
Norwegian Law Code, 154, 156
Nuclear weapons, 224, 247

O

Occupation, German occupation of Denmark (1940–1945), 213, 216
Oldenburg state, 113, 115, 125, 237
Order of Christ, 108
Order of the Elephant, 107

P

Palm oil, 124, 146, 161
Parliamentarism, 200–202
Parliament, Danish, 183, 185, 187, 189, 190, 201, 206, 209, 224, 226, 228, 248
Parliament, Greenlandic, 228
Peasants, 33, 56, 60, 83, 86, 110, 111, 116, 118, 132, 147, 150, 153–155, 158, 175, 235
Pietism, 2
Plantation/planters, 160, 161, 167, 174, 180, 204, 244
Plebiscite, 194, 209, 210, 238–240
Popular sovereignty, 186, 187, 196, 237
Population, 4, 5, 17, 27, 31, 33, 55, 85, 116, 118, 119, 125, 138, 143, 151, 152, 154–156, 158, 163, 165, 171, 172, 176, 179, 184, 186–188, 191, 195, 196, 199, 201, 203–210, 212, 220, 222, 224–227, 229, 230, 237, 241, 244, 247, 248, 251
Preussenreisen, 96
Princely state, 112
Principalities, German, 3, 126
Principalships, 188, 203
Privy Council, 189

R

Radikale Venstre
Rebellion, 34, 40, 55, 85, 99, 100, 110–112, 122, 128, 182, 205, 245
Reconciliation, Commission of, 247
Referendum, 202, 205, 207, 208, 215, 222, 226–228, 239, 240, 247, 248
Reformation, 109, 117, 119–121, 126
regimen politicum, 93
regimen regale, 93
Rentekammeret (the Danish economic administration), 154
Republican People's Party (Faroese political party), 229
Resistance movement, 213
Reunification 1920, 209, 211, 239
Revenue, 5, 41, 74, 82–84, 86, 92, 99, 118, 122, 123, 125, 129, 151, 234, 237
Rice, 160
Rigsdag
Rigsfællesskabet
Rigsraadet
Ritterschaft
Royal Greenland Trading Department (Kongelig Grønlandske Handel, KGH), 156, 203, 211, 226
Royal Law (1665), 138, 180, 186
Runes, 22, 46

S

Saint Peter vassals, 52
Saltpeter, 135, 160
Sami, 92, 104, 123, 125
Sarmatians, 14
Saxons, 30, 31, 44, 59, 60
Scandinavianism, 12, 19, 28, 32–34, 46, 47, 72, 84, 156, 178, 179, 192, 203, 204, 257

INDEX OF CONCEPT   269

Scania market, 69, 86, 92
Scanian Law Code (*Skaanske Lov*), 116
Scanian War (1675–1679), 140, 141, 238, 240
Schleswigian Party (SP, Slesvigsk Parti), 251
Sealandian Law Code (*Sjællandske Lov*), 116
Secession, 163, 207, 215, 222, 227, 229, 239, 240
Secularized bishoprics, 134
Self-determination
Serfdom, 158, 235
Seven Years' War (1756–1763), 148, 149
shahin shah, 4
Ship-settings, 29, 38
Silver, 12–15, 19, 27, 69, 84, 86, 122
Slavery, slaves, 4, 16, 20, 27, 59, 146, 161, 176, 180, 188, 204, 205, 244, 245, 252
Slave trade, 161, 180, 245
Social Democratic Party/Social Democrats, 202, 207, 208, 221, 229
Social Liberal Party, 202, 207–209
Sound Toll
Spices, 123, 146, 160
Spirit of '48 (1848), 183, 188
SSW, Southern Schleswig's Voters' Association, 251
Stamford Bridge, battle at 1066, 45, 47, 56
Stiklestad, battle at 1030, 45
Sugar, 146, 161, 174, 204–206
Sulfur, 122
Supreme Court, 94, 153, 188, 250
Svantevit, pagan idol, 60

T
Tanmarkar but, 34
Taxes, 5, 31, 44, 74, 75, 83, 87, 107, 121, 122, 124, 125, 134, 136, 151–153, 158, 175, 177, 188, 190, 193, 219, 223, 249
Tax state, 121, 122, 142
Tenant farmers, 117, 147, 158

Teutonic Order, 65, 69, 75, 77, 81, 86, 93, 96, 97, 102, 110, 129, 252
Textiles, 146, 160
Thing, 63, 75
Three Years' War (1848–1851), 183, 184, 192
Torstensson War (1643–1645), 135, 136, 142
Trade, 32, 81, 83, 99, 101, 103, 110, 112, 122–125, 131, 132, 135, 137, 138, 142, 143, 154–156, 158–162, 166–168, 174, 178, 179, 187, 203, 205, 208, 219, 224, 234, 235
Trading companies, 123, 156, 161, 235
Trelleborg, 36–38
Tuberculosis, 226

U
Union Party (Faroese political party), 229
Unitary state, 8, 145, 148, 149, 152, 154, 155, 159, 163, 168, 178, 228, 238
United monarchy (1851–1864), 171–173, 176, 180, 181, 184–187, 189–196, 199, 238
University, 152, 153, 167, 250
UN, United Nations, 224, 226, 230

V
Varangians, 46
Venstre
Verdun, Peace at 843, 35
Viking age, 8, 38, 40, 99, 203, 252
Vikings, 32, 252
Volcanic eruption, 155

W
War, 5, 17, 28, 31–33, 41, 42, 45, 48, 51, 53, 57, 59–62, 64, 77, 82, 83, 86, 87, 93, 94, 97, 102, 103, 107, 108, 110, 127–129, 131–138, 140–142, 148–151, 159–161, 163–168, 173, 174, 176, 183–185, 191–193, 195, 204, 208, 213–216, 223, 238, 239
Welfare state, 211, 219

Wends, 4, 45, 53, 59, 64, 68
West Indian-Guinean Trading Company, Danish, 161
Whaling, 123
World War I (1914–1918), 200, 201, 206, 208, 213, 219, 236
World War II (1939–1945), 212–214, 219, 236, 251

Index of People

A

Abel, king of Denmark (1218–52, king 1250), 75, 76, 78, 80
Absalon, archbishop of Lund (c. 1128–1201), 61
Achilles, Greek hero, 12
Adam of Bremen, historian (c. 1070), 45, 47
Adenauer, Konrad, Western German federal chancellor (1876–1967), 221
Ælfgifu of Northampton, queen (d. after 1036), 42, 44, 45
Æthelred, king of Wessex (d. 871), 44
Aggesen, Sven
Albert, bishop of Riga (d. 1229), 68
Albert III, duke of Mecklenburg, king of Sverige (c. 1340–1412), 91, 92
Albrecht, duke of Braunschweig (1236–79), 76–78
Aleksandr Nevsky, prince of Novgorod (1220–63), 75
Alexander III, pope (1105–81), 62
Alfonso VIII, king of Castile (1155–1214, king 1158), 71
Alfonso X the Wise, king of Aragon and Castile (1221–84, king 1252), 73
Alfred den Great, king of Wessex (849–99, king 871), 33
Andersen, Per, vexilologist, 71
Anders Sunesen, archbishop of Lund (1160–1228), 71, 73
András II, king of Hungary (1176–1235, king 1205), 69
Angantyr, king of Denmark (early 8th century), 30
Ansgar, archbishop of Hamburg-Bremen (c. 800–65), 31
Arminius, Germanic war-leader (17 BCE–20 CE), 11
Árni Magnússon
Arup, Erik, Danish historian (1876–1951), 127
Augustus, Roman Emperor (63 BCE–14 CE), 4, 7, 12, 25, 64, 241

B

Baldwin I, king of Jerusalem (1058–1118, king 1100), 53
Basedow, Johann Bernhard, German pedagogue (1723–90), 162
Beatrice, duchess of Upper Lothringia (c. 1020–76), 48
Beckett, Thomas, archbishop of Canterbury (1118–70), 62
Beowulf, mythical hero, 29
Berengaria, queen of Denmark (d. 1221), 68, 75
Bernhard of Clairvaux, Cistercian Abbot (c. 1090–1153), 58
Bernstorff, Andreas Peter, Danish udenrigsminister (1735–97), 147

Birger, king of Sweden (1280–1321, king 1290–1318), 81, 82
Birgitta of Vadstena, Swedish prophetess (1303–73), 91
Bismarck, Otto von, chancellor of the German Empire (1815–98), 192
Björn Ironside, Viking warrior (mid 9th century), 32
Bluhme, Christian Albrecht, Danish Foreign Minister (1794–1866), 195
Bo Grip, Swedish seneschal (d. 1386), 92
Boleslaw Wrymouth, king of Poland (1085/86–1138, king 1102), 55, 56
Boniface VIII, pope (1235–1303, pope 1294), 79
Bourke, Edmond, Danish peace negotiator (1761–1821), 166
Buris Henriksen, Danish prince (d. 1167), 61

C

Caesar, Gajus Julius, Roman General (102–44 BCE), 4
Canute II the Great, king of Denmark and England (995–1035, king 1018), 41, 43, 45–47, 55, 63, 64, 87
Canute IV (Saint Canute), king of Denmark (d. 1086, king 1080), 95
Canute VI, king of Denmark (1162–1202, king 1182), 62–65, 68
Caroline Mathilde, queen of Denmark (1751–75), 162
Catherine II the Great, tsarina of Russia (1729–1796, tsarina 1762), 149
Charlemagne, Frankish king and German-Roman emperor (742–814), 25, 26, 31, 35, 65, 109
Charles Martel, Frankish prince (688–741), 26
Charles Peter Ulrik, duke of Gottorp, 149
Charles V, German-Roman emperor and king of Spain (1500–58), 111, 116, 127
Charles VI, German-Roman emperor (1685–1740), 157
Charles IX, king of Sweden (1550–1611, king 1604), 131
Charles X Gustavus, king of Sweden (1622–60, king 1654), 136, 137
Charles X, king of France (1757–1836, king 1824–30), 174
Charles XII, king of Sweden (1682–1718, king 1697), 142
Charles XIV John, king of Sweden (1763–1844, king 1818), 166
Charles XV, king of Sweden and Norway (1826–72, king 1859), 192
Christian August, duke of Augustenburg (1798–1869), 193
Christian I, king of Denmark, Norway, Sweden (1426–81, king 1448), 98, 102, 103, 108, 110
Christian II, king of Denmark, Norway, Sweden (1481–1559, king 1513), 106, 108, 109, 111–113, 116, 127
Christian III, king of Denmark and Norway (1503–59, king 1536), 116–119, 127, 129
Christian IV, king of Denmark and Norway (1577–1648, king 1588), 7, 52, 123–128, 130–136, 139, 236, 239
Christian V, king of Denmark and Norway (1646–99, king 1670), 140, 141
Christian VI, king of Denmark and Norway (1699–1746, king 1730), 146, 160
Christian VII, king of Denmark and Norway (1749–1808, king 1766), 147, 157
Christian VIII, king of Denmark (1786–1848, king 1839) and king of Norway (1814), 177, 178, 181
Christian IX, king of Denmark (1818–1906, king 1863), 157, 185, 192, 195, 200
Christian X, king of Denmark (1870–1947, king 1912), 207, 215
Christopher, count of Oldenburg (1504–66), 102

INDEX OF PEOPLE 273

Christopher I, king of Denmark (1219–59, king 1252), 80
Christopher II, king of Denmark (1276–1332, king 1320), 82
Christopher III of Bavaria, king of Denmark, Norway, Sweden (1416–48, king 1440), 100, 102, 108
Christopher, mythical king, prophesized by Birgitta, 104
Conrad II, German-Roman emperor (990–1039, king of the Germans 1024, emperor 1027), 44
Conrad III, German king (1093–1152, king 1138), 59
Corte-Real, João Vaz, explorer (d. 1496), 108

D

Dagmar, queen of Denmark (d. 1212), 66, 68
David, Old Testament king, 38, 57
Didrik Pining, explorer (d. after 1487), 108
Dieussart, François, Flemish sculptor (d. 1661), 7
Dominik of Osma, founder of the Order of Dominicans (c. 1170–1221), 71
Dorothea of Brandenburg, queen of Denmark (1430–95), 102
Dyveke, mistress of King Christian II (1490–1517), 111

E

Eadric Streona, Anglosaxon earl (d. 1017), 42
Ebbesen, Niels
Ebbo, Archbishop of Reims (d. 851), 31
Edgar, king of England (943–75), 35
Edward the Confessor, king of England (c. 1003–66, king 1042), 44
Edward the Martyr, king of England (c. 963–78, king 975), 41
Egede, Hans Povelsen, Danish missionary to Greenland (1686–1758), 156, 244, 247, 248, 254

Elisabeth, queen of Denmark (1501–26), 111, 112
Emma, queen of England, and of Denmark (d. 1052), 42, 44
Engelbrekt Engelbrektson, Swedish rebel (d. 1436), 99
Erik Håkonsson, Norwegian earl (d. after 1023), 42
Erik Magnusson, duke (d. 1317), 81, 82
Erik I the Good, king of Denmark (c. 1056–1103, king 1095), 52, 53, 55
Erik II Emune, king of Denmark (d. 1137, king 1134), 57
Erik II Priest Hater, king of Norway (1268–99, king 1280), 82
Erik III Lamb, king of Denmark (d. 1146, king 1137), 59
Erik IV Ploughpenny, king of Denmark (1216–50, king 1241), 66
Erik V Glipping, king of Denmark (1249–86, king 1259), 78, 81, 82
Erik VI Menved, king of Denmark (1274–1319, king 1286), 78, 80–82
Erik VI of Pomerania, king of Denmark, Norway, Sweden (1382–1459, king 1389/96), 83
Erlandsen, Jacob
Eskild, archbishop of Lund (c. 1100–1181), 58, 59

F

Ferdinand, count of Flanders (1188–1233), 68
Filippa, queen of Denmark (1394–1430), 98
Filoktet, Greek hero, 12
Florina of Burgundy, (d. 1097), 52
Frederick I Barbarossa, German-Roman emperor (1122–90, emperor 1155), 59, 65
Frederick I, king of Denmark and Norway (1471–1533, king 1523), 117
Frederick II, German-Roman emperor (1194–1250, emperor 1220), 129–131

Frederick III, German-Roman emperor (1415–1493, emperor 1452), 105
Frederick III, king of Denmark and Norway (1609–70, king 1648), 139
Frederick VI, king of Denmark (1768–1839, king 1808) and of Norway (1808–1814), 165
Frederick VII, king of Denmark (1808–63, king 1848), 195
Frederiksen, Christian, Danish captain-general
Frodi, mythical king, 64

G
George I, 150
Gérard, Gabriel, French linguist (1677–1748), 4
Gerhard II, count of Holstein (1254–1312), 82
Gerhard III, count of Holstein (1292–1340), 83, 84
Gibbon, Edward, British historian (1737–94), 1, 2
Gjedde, Ove, Danish admiral (1594–1660), 123
Gnupa, king of Denmark (c. 900), 34
Godfred, king of Denmark (d. 810), 27, 31–33
Godwin, Earl of Wessex (d. 1053), 44
Gorm the Old, king of Denmark (d. 958), 34
Gottfried of Bouillon, crusader and king of Jerusalem (1060–1100), 52
Grand, Jens, archbishop of Lund
Gregor VII, pope (1020–85, pope 1073), 52
Gregory IX, pope (1143–1241, pope 1227), 71, 72, 75
Grip, Bo
Grundtvig, N.F.S., Danish theologian (1783–1872), 179
Grundtvig, Svend, Danish folklore researcher (1824–83), 179
Gunhild, daughter of King Canute the Great (11th century), 44
Gustav I Vasa, king of Sweden (1496–1560, king 1523), 112, 113

Gustav III, king of Sweden (1746–92, king 1771), 150
Gyldenløve, Ulrik Frederik, Danish civil servant (1638–1704), 141

H
Haakon VI, king of Norway and Sweden (1340–1380, king of Norway 1355, of Sweden 1362–64), 91
Halfdan, Scandinavian warrior (10th century?), 46
Hall, C.C., Danish prime minister (1812–88), 195, 196
Halvorsen, Olaf, doctor (1913–93), 223
Hamilton, Henning, Swedish envoy (1814–86), 192
Hammershaimb, V.U., Faroese priest (1819–1909), 178
Hansen, H.C., Danish Prime minister (1906–1960), 221, 247
Hans, king
Hans Pothorst
Harald I Bluetooth, king of Denmark (d. c. 987), 35, 37, 40
Harald II Godwinson, king of England (1022–1066, king 1066), 44, 45
Harald Klak, king of Denmark (d. 841), 31, 33, 34
Harboe, Ludvig, Bishop (1709–1783), 154
Hedtoft, Hans, Danish Prime Minister (1903–1955), 224
Heiberg, Steffen, Danish historian (born 1945), 135
Hektor, Greek hero, 12
Helmold of Bosau, historian (c. 1120–c. 1180), 59
Henning Podebusk
Henriksen, Buris
Henry, count of Schwerin (1185–1228), 69
Henry Gotskalksen, Slavic prince (d. 1127), 55
Henry I, duke of Mecklenburg (d. 1302), 76
Henry I the Fowler, king of East Francia (d. 936), 34

INDEX OF PEOPLE 275

Henry II, king of England (1133–1189, king 1154), 62
Henry III, German-Roman emperor (1017–56, emperor 1046), 44
Henry the Lion, duke of Sachsen (d. 1195), 61, 62
Henry the Navigator, Portuguese prince (1394–1460), 108
Henry the Young, prince of England (1155–1183), 62
Henry VI, German-Roman emperor (1165–1197, emperor 1191), 62
Hermann
Hitler, Adolf, German dictator (1889–1945), 213
Høegh-Guldberg, Ove, Danish statesman (1731–1808), 147, 162
Holger the Dane, mythical hero, 109
Homem, Alvaro Martins, explorer (d. 1482), 108
Honorius III, pope (1150–1227, pope 1216), 69
Horik I, king of Denmark (d. 854), 32
Hrotgar, mythical king, 29
Hugh, Abbot of Cluny (1024–1109), 48
Hvide, Skjalm
Hvide, Stig Andersen

I

Innocent III, pope (1160–1216, pope 1198), 66, 67, 71
Innocent IV, pope (1195–1254, pope 1143), 76
Innocent VIII, pope (1432–92, pope 1484), 110
Isabella of Austria
Ivan III the Great, Grand Prince of Moscow (1440–1505, Grand Prince 1462), 110
Ivar, king of Dublin (9th century), 32
Ivar the Boneless, legendary Viking leader (9th century), 42

J

Jacob, Danish count (d. c. 1310), 78
Jacob Erlandsen, archbishop of Lund (d. 1274), 76–78

Jacob III, king of Scotland (1452–88, king 1460), 103
Jacob, Old Testament patriarch, 38
Jarimar I, prince of Rügen (d. around 1218), 61, 62
Jarimar II, prince of Rügen (d. 1260), 76
Jens Grand, archbishop of Lund (d. 1327), 79, 81
Jespersen, Knud J.V., Danish historian (born 1942), 137
Johan the Gentle, count of Holstein (d. 1359), 84
John, king of Denmark, Norway, Sweden (1455–1513, king 1481), 109–111
John of Salisbury, English theologian (d. 1180), 65
John the Elder, prince of Denmark (1521–1580), 118
John the Fearless, duke of Burgundy (1371–1419), 102
John the Younger, duke (1545–1622), 140, 157
Jordanes, Langobard historian (6th century), 26
Judah, Old Testament patriarch, 38
Jürgensen, Jørgen, Danish explorer (1780–1841), 167

K

Karl Knutson Bonde, king of Sweden (d. 1470), 102
Kauffmann, Henrik, Danish ambassador (1888–1963), 214
Kazimir, Pomeranian prince (c. 1130–1180), 61
Keld of Viborg, ecclesiastic (d. 1150), 59
Klodevig, Merovingian king (c. 466–511, king 481), 25
Klopstock, Friedrich, German poet (1724–1803), 162
Kristensen, Knud, Danish prime minister (1880–1962), 220

L

Lehmann, Orla, Danish politician (1810–70), 177

INDEX OF PEOPLE

Lornsen, Uwe Jens, territorial bailiff and writer (1793–1838), 174
Louise, Danish Queen (1817–98), 157
Louis IV, German-Roman emperor (d. 1347, emperor 1328), 86
Louis Philippe, king of France (1773–1850, king 1830–48), 174
Louis the Pious, German-Roman emperor (778–840, emperor 813), 31, 33
Lundsteen, Poul, Greenlandic governor (1910–88), 226

M

Machiavelli, Niccolò, Italian political scientist (1469–1527), 112
Magellan, Fernando, Portuguese explorer (1480–1521), 106
Magnus, duke, prince-bishop of Ösel and Kurland (1540–83), 130
Magnus Eriksen, king of Sweden (1316–74, king 1319–1364), 82, 85, 86
Magnus, king of Norway and Denmark (1024–47, king Norway 1035, Denmark 1042), 45, 46
Magnus Nilsson, prince of Denmark (d. 1134), 59
Magnussen, Finn, Icelandic scholar (1781–1847), 40
Magnússon, Árni, Danish-Icelandic historian and administrator (1663–1730), 250
Manderström, Ludvig, Swedish Foreign Minister (1806–73), 192
Manuel II Palaiologos, Byzantine emperor (1350–1425, emperor 1391), 98
Marcellus, papal tax-collector and bishop (d. c 1462), 107
Marco Polo
Margrethe Fredkulla, Swedish princess, queen of Norway and of Denmark (d. 1130), 57
Margrethe Sambiria, queen of Denmark (d. 1282), 77

Margrethe I, queen of Denmark, Norway, Sweden (1353–1412), 91–95, 97–99, 103, 108
Margrethe II, queen of Denmark (f. 1940), 241, 244
Marie Sophie Frederikke, queen of Denmark (married to Frederik VI) (1767–1852), 157
Matthew Paris, English monk (d. 1259), 65
Mehmed II the Conqueror, Ottoman sultan (1432–81), 103
Merete Ulfstand, noblewoman (14th century), 91
Moltke, Adam Gottlob, Danish Lord Chamberlain (1710–92), 147
Morten the Cook, 79
Murad I, Ottoman sultan (1404–51, sultan 1421), 98

N

Napoleon I Bonaparte, French general and emperor (1769–1821), 165, 168
Nicholas I, Russian tsar (1796–1855, tsar 1825), 184
Niels Ebbesen, Danish nobleman (d. 1340), 85
Niels, king of Denmark (d. 1134), 53, 55–57
Niklot, Wendic prince (d. 1160), 60
Norby, Søren, Danish admiral (d. 1530), 108

O

Odoaker, Germanic general, 25
Odysseus, Greek hero, 12
Olav Tryggvason, king of Norway (d. 1000), 41
Oluf II Haakonsen, king of Norway and Denmark (1370–87), 91, 92
Oluf Sweynsson, Danish prince (11th century), 46, 87
Ørsted, Anders Sandøe, Danish politician (1778–1860), 189, 190
Osfred of Scania, (9th century), 31
Østergaard, Uffe, Danish historian (born 1945), 245

INDEX OF PEOPLE 277

Otto I the Great, German-Roman emperor (912–73, emperor 962), 35
Otto IV of Braunschweig, German-Roman emperor (1175–1218, emperor 1209), 67
Ottokar, king of Bohemia (d. 1230), 68

P

Paul, tsar of Russia (1754–1801, tsar 1796), 164
Paulus the Deacon, Langobard historian (8th century), 25
Peder Bodilsen, Danish magnate (d. after 1142), 58
Pedro, prince of Portugal (1392–1449), 98
Peter I, king of Cyprus (1328–69, king 1359), 87
Peter I the Great, tsar of Russia (1672–1725, tsar 1682), 149
Peter III, tsar of Russia, duke of Gottorp (1728–62, tsar 1762), 149
Petersen, Niels Helveg, Danish politician (f. 1939), 245
Philip II August, king of France (1165–1223), 67, 68
Piccolomini, Aeneas Sylvius
Pining, Didrik
Pius II, pope (1405–64), 98
Podebusk, Henning, seneschal (d. 1388), 86, 91
Polo, Marco, Italian explorer (1254–1324), 106
Pothorst, Hans, explorer (c. 1440 – c. 1490), 108, 110
Printzenskiöld, Johan, Swedish commander (c. 1615–58), 137
Putbus

R

Reventlow, Cay Friedrich, Danish head of Chancellery (1753–1834), 158
Reventlow, Christian Ditlev, Danish statesman (1748–1827), 147, 158
Rickard, duke of Normandy (932–996), 42

Robert I, count of Flanders (d. 1093), 48
Rolf Krake, mythical king, 30
Rollo, duke of Normandy (d. c. 933), 34, 45
Ruysch, Johann, cartographer (1460–1533), 106

S

Salza, Hermann von, master of the Teutonic Order (d. 1239), 69
Sancho I, king of Portugal (1154–1211, king 1185), 68
Saxo, Danish historian (around 1200), 31
Sigbrit Willom, merchant and financial adviser (d. 1532), 111
Sigismund, German-Roman emperor (1368–1437), 97, 98
Sigurd Jorsalfar, king of Norway (d. 1130), 56
Skjalm Hvide, Danish magnate (around 1100), 53
Skjold, Danish mythical king, 29
Sponneck, Wilhelm, Danish politician and Civil servant (1815–88), 188
Sten Sture the Older, regent in Sweden (d. 1503), 105, 110, 111
Sten Sture the Younger, regent in Sweden (1493–1520), 112
Stephen Báthory, king of Poland (1533–86, king 1576), 131
Stig Andersen Hvide, Danish magnate (d. 1293), 78
Struensee, Johan Friedrich, German doctor and courtier (1737–72), 147
Sunesen, Anders, archbishop of Lund
Svante Nilsson, regent in Sweden (1460–1512), 110
Sven Aggesen, historian (c. 1185), 63, 65
Svend, 179, 216, 223. *See also* Sweyn
Sweyn, 40–42, 47, 48, 52, 59–61, 63
Sweyn Ælgifuson, Danish prince (d. 1035), 45
Sweyn, bishop of Aarhus (d. 1191), 61
Sweyn I Forkbeard, king of Denmark (d. 1014), 40

278 INDEX OF PEOPLE

Sweyn II Estridsson, king of Denmark (d. 1076, king 1047), 45–48, 52
Sweyn III Grathe, king of Denmark (d. 1157, king 1146), 59
Sweyn the young, Danish prince (d. 1097), 52

T
Tasso, Torquato, Italian poet (1544–95), 52
Theodosios, Byzantine ambassador (mid 9th century), 27
Thietmar, bishop of Merseburg (975–1018), 30
Thomas Beckett
Thomas, Mary, Danish West Indian rebel (c. 1848–1905), 245
Thorkell the Tall, earl in England (d. 1024), 42
Thorlaksson, Guðmundur, Icelandic bishop (1542–1627), 121
Thott, Ivar Axelsson, Danish magnate (1420–87), 94, 110
Thyra, queen of Denmark (10th century), 34, 36, 40
Trolle, Gustav, archbishop of Uppsala (1488–1535), 112
Trump, Donald, US president (born 1946), 231

U
Ubaldus, cardinal (mid 12th century), 58
Ulfila, Gothic bishop (4th century), 16
Urban II, pope (1042–99), 52, 53

V
Valdemar Eriksen, duke of Southern Jutland
Valdemar I the Great, king of Denmark (1131–82, king 1146), 66
Valdemar II the Victorious, king of Denmark (1170–1241, king 1202), 62, 66
Valdemar III Eriksen, king of Denmark (1315–64, king 1326–1330), 84
Valdemar IV Atterdag, king of Denmark (1320–75, king 1340), 234
Valdemar Knudsen, bishop of Schleswig, 66
Vallarte, Danish nobleman (15th century), 108
Vartislav, duke of Pomerania (d. 1135), 55, 100
Varus, Roman general (d. 9 CE), 11, 18
Vegetius, Roman writer (4th century), 37
Vergil, Roman poet (70–19 BCE), 64
Vitus, early Christian martyr (4th century?), 60

W
Wallenstein, Albrecht von, Bohemian general (1583–1634), 134
Weibull, Lauritz, Scanian historian (1873–1960), 34
Widukind of Corvey, German chronicler (10th century), 35
Wilhelm, duke of Holstein-Beck (1785–1831), 157
Wilhelm of Modena, papal legate (d. 1251), 69
William the Bastard
William I the Conqueror, king of England (1028–87, king 1066), 48
Willibrord, English missionary (d. 79), 30
Wilson, Woodrow, US president (1856–1924), 207, 208
Wladyslaw III Laskonogi, prince of Poland (1167–1231), 62
Wollstonecraft, Mary, English writer and feminist (1759–97), 152

Z
Zenghi, sultan of Mosul (d. 1147), 58

Index of Places

A
Aabenraa, 194, 210
Aarhus, 35, 36, 175
Ærø, 48, 157, 195
Afghanistan, 230
Africa, 3, 6, 108, 124, 126, 129, 137, 146, 159–161, 167, 171, 174, 179, 203, 234, 238, 243, 245, 246
Aggersborg, 36
Akershus, 110, 123, 142, 166
Als, 77, 194
Altona, 141, 158
America, 28, 92, 106, 108, 174, 203, 214, 234
Aragon, 73, 101, 104
Arctic, 225, 231, 236, 237, 247
Arkhangelsk, 125
Årslev, 16
Austria, 105, 111, 173, 182–184, 190, 193–196

B
Båhuslen, 81
Balkans, 26, 104, 230
Baltic Sea, 6, 14, 16, 40, 45, 48, 53, 54, 58, 60, 62, 63, 65, 69, 71, 80, 86, 87, 91, 92, 96, 98, 101, 104, 109, 112, 125, 126, 128, 129, 131, 132, 135–137, 142, 143, 148, 164, 166, 193, 213, 234, 241

Bergen, 107, 108, 111, 123, 152, 154, 156, 166, 254
Berlin Wall, 2, 230
Bethlehem, 53
Bjørgvin, 119
Black Sea, 12, 14, 16, 33, 97, 241
Blekinge, 3, 80, 86, 116, 136, 137, 238, 239, 253
Bohuslen, 137, 141
Bornhøved, 69
Bornholm, 14, 48, 72, 74, 76, 137, 216, 234, 239
Brandenburg, 47, 56, 83, 102, 104
Bremen, 79, 134, 136, 141, 236
Brömsebro, Peace of (1645), 135, 136
Bulgaria, 14
Burgundy, 52, 98, 102, 103, 105, 107, 111
Byzantium, Byzantine empire, 25, 26, 32, 42, 53

C
Calcutta
Canterbury, 62
Cape Verde, 108
Caribbean, 124, 129, 146, 159, 161, 166, 188, 205, 234
Catalonia, 101
Ceylon
China, 6, 160, 225, 231
Christiania, 123, 138, 142, 167

Christiansborg (Ghana)
Christianshavn, 123
Cluny, 44, 48, 52
Copenhagen, 7, 13, 76, 86, 99, 107,
    108, 122–125, 136–138, 148,
    150–159, 161, 162, 164, 165, 167,
    168, 174, 175, 177, 181–184, 188,
    192, 194, 200, 214, 243, 248–250,
    253, 254
Copenhagen, Battle of (1801), 164
Cyprus, 52, 55, 87

D
Dalmatia, 98
Damascus, 58, 98
Danelaw, 33, 35
Danevirke, 26, 27, 29–31
Dansborg, 124, 127
Danube River, 12, 14, 16
Delmenhorst, 140, 150
Ditmarschen, 103, 105, 233
Djursland, 79
Doberan, 77
Dobin, 59
Dorestad, 32
Dublin, 32
Duchies, the (Schleswig, Holstein
    and/or Lauenburg), 3, 6, 91, 105,
    117, 123, 126, 152, 171, 172, 186,
    234
Dybbøl, 193, 194

E
East Anglia, 33, 42
Eastern Bloc, 216, 219
Edessa, 58
Ejder (Eider) River, 44, 69, 77, 172,
    177
Ejsbøl, 18
Elbe River, 11, 12, 54, 69, 83
Elfsborg, 132
Elsinore, 99, 122
Ely, 44
England, 2, 3, 6, 11, 17, 21, 22, 28,
    30, 32–34, 36, 40–45, 47, 48,
    54–56, 62, 67, 70, 87, 98, 103,
    104, 110, 115, 122, 125, 131, 132,
    135, 152, 168, 233, 241, 242, 252

Estonia, 3, 54, 65, 68–70, 72, 74, 77,
    79–81, 85, 86, 97, 102, 129–131,
    233, 236, 240, 252
EU, European Union, 8, 230, 239

F
Falköping, 92
Falster, 12, 48, 55, 58, 74, 80, 85, 136
Faroe Islands, 3, 91, 117, 119, 138,
    154, 166, 171, 178, 179, 187, 201,
    202, 211, 214, 215, 222, 223,
    227–230, 234, 235, 237–240, 242,
    250, 251
Fehmarn, 56, 85, 135
Finderup, 78, 82
Finland, 28, 33, 62, 86, 92, 94, 110,
    131, 165, 234
Finnmark, 166
Flensborg/Flensburg, 94, 108, 158,
    175, 176, 194, 209, 234
Fontainebleau, 141
Fotevik, 57
France, 26, 28, 32–35, 45, 52, 62, 67,
    124, 128, 132, 137, 140–142, 146,
    160, 161, 163–165, 174, 194, 209,
    224, 238, 241, 252, 253
Franche Comte, 102
Franks, 26
Frederiksborg, Peace of (1720), 142,
    148
Frederiksnagore
Fredriksten, 142
Frisia, 31, 60, 65, 74, 80
Funen, 12, 14–18, 20, 21, 27, 29, 48,
    65, 69, 74, 76, 84, 136, 194
Fyrkat, 36

G
Galicia, 32
German Confederation, 173, 176, 177,
    181, 182, 184, 185, 190, 191,
    193–196
German Empire, 6, 48, 68, 74, 105,
    126, 128, 132–134, 138, 157, 159,
    173, 230, 243
Germany, 3, 11, 14, 19, 20, 35, 38, 69,
    82, 105, 125–130, 132–136, 139,

141, 142, 149, 162, 173, 182, 192, 196, 199, 200, 206–208, 210, 212–215, 220, 221, 233, 234, 236, 238, 239, 241, 242, 251
Ghana, 246
Gibraltar, 26, 110
Glücksburg, 118, 157, 192
Glückstadt, 7, 123, 124
Gold Coast, 124, 146, 161, 179, 180
Goths, 4, 13, 14, 16
Gotland, 3, 14, 86, 93, 99, 100, 108, 110, 234
Gottorp, 118, 129, 139–142, 148–150, 156, 175, 181, 236, 239, 254
Great Belt, 28
Great Britain, 8, 150, 163, 164, 167, 168, 179, 184, 194, 203, 213, 224, 245, 253
Greenland, 3, 6, 28, 91, 92, 96, 106, 108–110, 117, 125, 155, 156, 166, 171, 188, 201, 203, 207, 208, 211, 212, 214, 215, 223–231, 234–240, 242, 244, 246–249, 254
Gudme, 15, 16, 21, 27, 29
Gulf of Finland, 33, 234

H

Haderslev, 18
Hagenskov, 76
Hague, the, 212
Halland, 3, 48, 78, 80, 85, 86, 116, 136, 137, 238, 239, 253
Hamburg, 3, 66, 96, 122, 123, 126, 141, 149
Hanover, 150
Haraldsted, 57
Hedeby, 27, 28, 31, 34, 36
Helge River, 42
Helsingør, 99, 122
Himlingøje, 11, 13–17, 21
Hispaniola, 106
Hoby, 12, 13
Holar, 121
Holland, 161
Hollingstedt, 26, 60
Holstein, 3, 6, 7, 54, 65, 72, 77, 82, 83, 85, 94, 96–99, 102, 103, 105, 109, 111, 113, 117, 118, 126, 132–134, 138–140, 149, 150, 153, 157–159, 165, 166, 171–177, 180, 182–187, 189–193, 195, 213, 220, 233–235, 239, 243, 251
Holsteiner, 192
Hormuz Strait, 137
Hunehals, 78

I

Iceland, 6, 91, 98, 103, 107, 108, 110, 117, 119, 121–123, 125, 138, 154, 155, 166, 167, 171, 178, 179, 187, 201, 202, 204, 214, 215, 224, 229, 234–236, 238–240, 243, 249, 250
India, 3, 6, 106, 108, 123, 124, 126, 146, 160, 166, 171, 174, 179, 238, 243, 245, 246
Ireland, 28, 32, 115
Islam, 26, 32, 33, 51, 109

J

Japan, 106
Jomsborg, 40, 45
Jutland, 12, 14, 17, 18, 20, 21, 26, 27, 30, 31, 36, 40, 48, 57, 59–61, 63–65, 71–74, 77, 79, 80, 82–86, 94, 97, 99, 102, 103, 113, 116, 133, 135–137, 149, 164–166, 168, 175, 184, 187, 200, 209, 210, 213, 235, 251

K

Kalmar, 56, 99, 100, 234
Kanhave, 26
Karakorum, 106
Kattegat, Sea of, 14, 132
Kiel, 153, 175, 193, 221
Kiel Canal, 213
Kiel, Peace of (1814), 165, 212
Kiev, 56, 60, 242
Klaksvik, 223
Knäred, Peace of (1613), 125, 132
Kola Peninsular, 125
Kolkata, 160
Kongeå River, 116, 172
Konstanz, 97
Krakow, 98

Kristiansand, 166
Kurland, 131

L
Ladoga, Lake, 33
Langeland, 77, 136
Lauenburg, 166, 171–174, 176, 180, 182, 190, 191, 195
Lechfeld, 35
Lejre, 29, 30, 32
Limfjord, 36
Lindisfarne, 32
Lisbon, 32
Lithuania, 14, 112, 130
Livonia, 65, 71, 131
Lohede, 77
Lolland, 12, 18, 48, 60, 74, 80, 84, 95, 108, 136, 166
London, 32, 195
London, Agreements of (1850–1852), 191, 193, 195
London, Protocol of (1850–1852), 185, 189
Lower Saxony, 16
Lübeck, 47, 69, 71, 77, 81, 83, 84, 87, 96, 113, 118, 133, 149, 150
Lund, 56, 71, 75, 79, 86
Lutter am Barenberge, 133
Lyrskov Moore, 45

M
Mainz, 12, 31
Malbork, 96
Malmø/Malmö, 119, 122, 253
Malpaga, 105
Marienburg, 96, 97
Marseilles, 35
Mecklenburg, 54, 76, 87, 93, 149
Mediterranean, 28, 32, 63, 106
Meldorf, 111
Mercia, 33, 42
Milan, 105
Morocco, 32
Mosul, 58

N
Naestved, 58

Nekső, 216
Netherlands, 111, 112, 122, 128, 130–132, 135, 137, 141, 142, 164, 224, 253
Newfoundland, 108
Nicobar archipelago, 160, 203
Nonnebakken, 36
North Atlantic (Sea), 92, 99, 103, 110, 123, 154, 166, 167, 178, 213, 214, 228, 231, 234–236
North-Baltic Sea Canal, 213
North Cape, 3
North Pole, 106, 224, 225, 231, 233
North Sea, 6, 12, 25, 26, 33, 42, 43, 54, 98, 101, 109, 125, 126, 142, 213, 233, 241
Northumbria, 32, 33, 42
Norway, 3, 14, 19, 20, 30, 31, 36, 42, 45, 46, 57, 59, 78, 81, 82, 91–96, 99, 102, 104, 109–114, 116, 117, 119, 122, 123, 125, 126, 128, 132, 136–138, 141, 142, 148–154, 156, 158, 162, 164–168, 171, 177, 212, 229, 233–241, 243, 244, 248, 249, 254
Norway, Article of (1536), 116, 117
Nuuk, 247, 248
Nykøbing Falster, 77

O
Obotrites, 31, 47, 55, 56
Oldenburg, 56, 102, 115, 125, 140, 150
Olives, Mount of, 52
Øresund, 79, 96, 99, 101
Orkney Islands, 93
Øsel (Saaremaa), 3, 129
Oslo, 123
Osu Castle, 246

P
Paris, 26, 32, 84, 141, 174, 181
Peipus, Lake, 65, 75
Perth, 99
Plön, 140, 157
Poitiers, 26
Poland, 14, 16, 40, 55, 56, 130, 131, 136

INDEX OF PLACES 283

Pomerania, 54, 55, 61, 62, 65, 66, 77, 83, 96, 100
Prussia, 6, 7, 92, 96, 97, 149, 164, 173, 182–184, 190, 192–196, 199, 204, 234
Pyrenees, 26

R
Ravning, 21
Regensburg, 12, 104, 108
Reric, 27, 31
Reykjavik, 155
Rhine River, 11
Ribe, 27, 28, 35, 36, 71, 77, 172, 195
Ribe, Agreement of (1460), 117, 186, 196
Riga, 79, 81
Rødding, 177
Roman Empire, 1, 2, 4, 11–13, 16, 17, 19–21, 25, 35, 64, 65, 103, 117, 173, 241
Rome, 2, 20, 25, 26, 35, 44, 48, 64, 66, 70, 73, 77, 79, 105–107
Rønne, 216
Roskilde, 13, 29, 40, 60, 85, 175, 179
Roskilde, Peace of (1658), 130, 136, 137, 139
Rostock, 59, 81–84
Rothenburg, 105
Rouen, 34
Rügen, 3, 53, 55, 57, 60–63, 65, 68, 72, 74, 76–78, 80, 85, 86, 166
Russia, 28, 33, 60, 65, 81, 96, 104, 112, 125, 128, 130, 131, 142, 143, 149–151, 164, 165, 184, 193, 194, 225, 231, 234, 239, 252

S
Saaremaa, 3, 129, 252
Samsø, 26, 48
Saxony, 16
Scandinavia, 19, 26, 28, 30, 32, 33, 43, 62, 106, 110, 192, 240, 244
Scandza, 26
Scania, 3, 26, 31, 36, 42, 48, 56, 57, 65, 72–74, 79, 80, 82, 84–87, 92, 116, 135–137, 141, 165, 233, 234, 239, 253

Schlei Fjord, 26
Schleswig, 3, 6, 35, 47, 48, 55–57, 59, 60, 63, 68, 72, 77, 82, 94, 96, 109, 111, 113, 117, 118, 126, 133, 139, 140, 142, 148, 149, 153, 157–159, 171–177, 179–182, 184–187, 189–191, 194–196, 199, 204, 208–210, 220, 234, 235, 239, 242, 243
Schleswig-Holstein, 103, 107, 113, 114, 174–177, 181–185, 187, 190–193, 196, 220, 221, 240, 251
Scotland, 17, 30, 36, 41, 99, 103, 104, 115, 122
Sealand, 13, 14, 21, 27, 29, 30, 36, 37, 40, 48, 53, 55, 65, 69, 72–74, 77–79, 83, 84, 86, 116, 136, 164, 166, 194
Seine, River, 32
Serampore, 146, 160, 203
Serbia, 98
Shetland Islands, 91, 103, 238, 240, 251
Sicily, 3, 48
Slien (Schlei), 26, 56
Søborg, 66, 79
Somersooq, 248
Sound (Øresund), 99
Southampton, 32
Soviet Union, 214–216, 219, 224, 225, 252
Spagnola, 106
Spain, 11, 32, 35, 132
Spangu, 106
Speyer, Treaty of (1544), 127, 129
Sprogø, 78
Sri Lanka, 123
Stamford Bridge, 45, 47, 56
St. Croix, 124, 146, 160, 161, 167, 204, 205, 208, 238, 239, 254
St. John (St. Jan), 124, 146, 204, 238
St. Thomas, 124, 146, 204, 206, 238
Stettin, Peace of (1570), 131
Stevns, 13, 21, 36
Stiklestad, 45
Stormarn, 96, 103, 105
Stralsund, 83, 86, 98
Sutton Ho, 21, 30
Sweden, 3, 6, 14, 19, 20, 26, 29, 31, 56, 57, 59, 60, 81, 82, 91–95, 99,

102, 104, 105, 109–113, 116, 125, 128–132, 134–137, 139–143, 148, 150, 151, 154, 164–166, 193, 196, 234, 242, 253
Sweden-Norway (1814–1905), 178, 184, 192, 194
Swedish Pomerania, 166

T
Tallinn, 68, 70, 77, 81, 252
Tårnborg, 78
Teutoburg Forest, 11, 18
Teutonic Order, State of, 129
Tharangambadi
The island of Als, 194
Thingvellir, 215
Thorshavn, 223
Thule, 63, 224, 227, 246
Thule Airbase, 246
Thuringia, 14, 16
Tissø, 27–29, 32, 36
Tivoli, 254
Tønder, 194
Tønsberg, 110
Tranquebar, 124, 127, 146, 160, 203
Travemünde, 149
Trier, 28
Trondheim, 45, 123, 137, 166, 249
Tryggevælde, 21

U
Ukraine, 28

Uppsala, 30
USA, 206, 207, 240

V
Vadstena, 95
Valencia, 101
Västergötland, 56, 81
Vejle, 21, 76
Vendsyssel, 36
Venice, 28, 98
Verden, 134, 136, 141, 236
Verdun, 35
Versailles, Peace of (1919), 209
Viborg, 113, 119, 175, 234
Vienna, Congress of (1814–1815), 166, 173
Vinland, 92, 234
Visby, 86, 110

W
Wales, 115
Wessex, 33, 42
West Indies, 3, 6, 106, 124, 126, 158–161, 174, 176, 199, 203–205, 208, 209, 235, 236, 238, 240, 244
Westphalia, Peace of (1648), 128, 136, 140
Winchester, 44
Wismar, 27, 83, 141
Wolgast, 61
Wolin, 40
Wrocław, 98

The manufacturer's authorised representative in the EU is Springer Nature Customer Service Centre GmbH, Europaplatz 3, 69115 Heidelberg, Germany. If you have any concerns regarding our products, please contact ProductSafety@springernature.com

Printed and bound by CPI Group (UK) Ltd, Croydon, CR0 4YY

16/02/2026

02054049-0005